# THE AMERICAN CENTURY

# A History of the United States since 1941

# THE AMERICAN CENTURY

## A History of the United States since 1941

### FIFTH EDITION

**Walter LaFeber**
*Cornell University*

**Richard Polenberg**
*Cornell University*

**Nancy Woloch**
*Barnard College*

Boston, Massachusetts   Burr Ridge, Illinois   Dubuque, Iowa
Madison, Wisconsin  New York, New York  San Francisco, California  St. Louis, Missouri

# McGraw-Hill

*A Division of The McGraw·Hill Companies*

THE AMERICAN CENTURY: A HISTORY OF THE UNITED STATES SINCE 1941

This book is printed on acid-free paper.

1 2 3 4 5 6 7 8 9 0 DOC/DOC 9 0 9 8 7

ISBN 0-07-036014-6

Editorial director: *Jane Vaicunas*
Sponsoring editor: *Lyn Uhl*
Developmental editor: *Monica Freedman*
Marketing manager: *Annie Mitchell*
Senior project manager: *Denise Santor-Mitzit*
Production supervisor: *Heather D. Burbridge*
Designer: *Matthew Baldwin*
Cover designer: *Joe Zeller, Z Graphics*
Senior photo research coordinator: *Keri Johnson*
Compositor: *Shepherd Incorporated*
Typeface: *10/12 Palatino*
Printer: *R. R. Donnelley & Sons Company*

**Library of Congress Cataloging-in-Publication Data**

LaFeber, Walter.
    The American century : a history of the United States since 1941
/ Walter LaFeber, Richard Polenberg, Nancy Woloch. —5th ed.
        p.        cm.
    Includes bibliographical references and index.
    ISBN 0-07-036014-6
    1. United States—History—20th century.   2. United States—
    Foreign relations—20th century.   I. Polenberg, Richard.
II. Woloch, Nancy, (1940).   III. Title.
E741.L25      1998
973.9—dc21                                                97–12374

http://www.mhcollege.com

# ABOUT THE AUTHORS

**Walter LaFeber** is the Marie Underhill Noll Professor of History at Cornell University. His publications include *The New Empire: An Interpretation of American Expansion, 1865–1898* (1963); *The American Age: U.S. Foreign Policy Since 1750,* 2nd edition (1993); *Inevitable Revolutions: The United States and Central America* (1983, 1991); *The Panama Canal: The Crisis in Historical Perspective* (1978, 1989); *America, Russia, and the Cold War,* 8th edition (1966, 1997); and *America in Vietnam: A History with Documents* (1985), also a coauthored work. He is a Stephen Weiss Presidential Teaching Fellow at Cornell.

**Richard Polenberg** is the Goldwin Smith Professor of American History at Cornell University. He is the author of *Reorganizing Roosevelt's Government, 1936–1939* (1966); *War and Society: The United States, 1941–1945* (1972); *One Nation Divisible: Class, Race, and Ethnicity in the United States Since 1938* (1980); *Fighting Faiths: The Abrams Case, the Supreme Court, and Free Speech* (1987); and *The World of Benjamin Cardozo* (1997). He is the editor of *America at War: The Home Front, 1941–1945* (1968) and *Radicalism and Reform in the New Deal* (1972). He is a recipient of the Clark Award for Distinguished Teaching.

**Nancy Woloch** is the author of *Women and the American Experience* (1984, 1994) and *Muller v. Oregon* (1996); co-author of *The Enduring Vision: A History of the American People* (1990, 1993, 1996), and editor of *Early American Women: A Documentary History, 1600–1900* (1992, 1997). She teaches history at Barnard College, Columbia University.

# CONTENTS IN BRIEF

# CONTENTS

# PREFACE

The enthusiastic response to the first four editions of *The American Century* has confirmed the need for a concise but interpretive twentieth-century American history text that offers adequate coverage of the post-1941 period as well as of the years before World War II. We stress economic and urban growth, social and political change, civil rights and liberties, and the growth of the United States into a global superpower. But we also devote special sections to art, architecture, music, dance, theater, poetry, photography, sculpture, sports, computer technology, and recreation because these topics are of interest to students and offer important historical insights. Further, we give equal attention to U.S. foreign and domestic policies and show how the two are interrelated. To help students understand foreign policy, we include brief analyses of developments elsewhere in the world.

In this new edition of *The American Century* we have adopted suggestions made by instructors and students. We have revised the book to take account of recent scholarship. This new material has been incorporated in a way that makes the book more balanced and inclusive. We have added new sections throughout the volume and have written an account of developments in the 1990s. Updated chapter bibliographies provide students with a selective guide to the recent literature and to the books we have found most helpful.

We wish to thank the scholars who read the various versions of this book and were unsparing in their comments: Katherine Aiken, William L. Barney, Richard M. Dalfiume, Charles M. Dollar, Otis L. Graham, James Hijiya, F. Jack Hurley, Kenneth Jones, Richard S. Kirkendall, Thomas Krueger, Fred R. Mabbutt, William Newell, Sara Lee Silberman, George Skau, David Trask, and Allen Yarnell. We are especially grateful to the editorial and production staffs of the McGraw-Hill College Division, particularly Monica Freedman, Lyn Uhl, and Denise Santor-Mitzit, and Laura Lenz, of Shepherd, Inc.

*Walter LaFeber*
*Richard Polenberg*
*Nancy Woloch*

Women welders in New Britain, Connecticut, 1943. *(Library of Congress, Prints & Photographs Division, FSA/OWI Collection.)*

# CHAPTER NINE

# 1941–1947
## War and Peace

This chapter discusses:
- How Americans went to war in 1941
- What it meant when FDR said that "Dr. New Deal" had been replaced by "Dr. Win-the-War"
- The new doctor's treatment of women, African-Americans, the labor movement—and the wealthy
- Why Martha Graham and modern dance exemplified a new America
- How a stunned, largely unknown Harry Truman led triumphant Americans into less-than-triumphant postwar policies

World War II severely strained American political, economic, and social institutions. The Roosevelt administration had to devise a program that would release the nation's full productive energies and yet restrain rampaging inflationary forces. The government also had to impose restrictions on the daily lives of millions of people without alienating those it depended on for political support. To a large extent Roosevelt found satisfactory solutions to these problems. Americans were united against common enemies, ones they regarded as the incarnation of evil, and were therefore willing to make certain sacrifices. The war, by producing a high level of prosperity, ensured that those sacrifices would not be too painful. Then, in April 1945, Harry S. Truman assumed the presidency, and four months later the war ended. The accumulated pressures of four years suddenly exploded, threatening to make a shambles of Truman's domestic program. Putting the pieces back together again proved an arduous task.

## IMAGES OF WAR

In 1942 anthropologist Margaret Mead published *And Keep Your Powder Dry,* a study of the way in which American character and values might shape the future conduct of the war. Americans fought best, Mead observed, when they believed that the other side had wantonly provoked them and left them no alternative to war, and when they thought that the struggle was between antagonists of roughly equal strength. In addition, Americans needed to believe in the justice, indeed selflessness, of their cause. A steady succession of military advances, interrupted only temporarily by setbacks, would bolster these convictions. A protracted series of defeats, on the other hand, would call them into question. "To win this war," she said, "we must feel we are on the side of the Right."

Throughout the war years most people felt precisely that way. The attack on Pearl Harbor, widely viewed as proof of Japanese barbarity, enabled Americans to enter the war with more unity than had seemed possible during the bitter struggle between isolationists and interventionists. Most people believed that the war was being waged for "the right of all men to live in freedom, decency, and security" or, as Vice-President Henry A. Wallace put it, to usher in a "century of the common man" in which people around the world would gain political freedom and economic security. One congressman declared: "It is a war of purification in which the forces of Christian peace and freedom and justice and decency and morality are arrayed against the evil pagan forces of strife, injustice, treachery, immorality, and slavery." This was only an extreme statement of a commonly accepted view. "Never in our history," said one observer, "have issues been so clear."

The government did what it could to stimulate a sense of loyalty and unity by channeling civilian energies into war-related tasks. The Office of

Civilian Defense organized corps of air-raid wardens, fire fighters, auxiliary police, and nurse's aides. The agency maintained that people could, through discipline and self-denial, contribute to an American victory and gave a "V Home Award" as "a badge of honor for those families which have made themselves into a fighting unit on the home front" by conserving food, salvaging vital materials, buying war bonds, and planting victory gardens. Newspaper, magazine, and radio advertisements also attempted to persuade people to get by with less. B. F. Goodrich asked its customers to conserve rubber tires since "Hitler smiles when you waste miles." The government popularized the slogan, "Use it up, wear it out, make it do or do without." The daily use of certain symbols, particularly the ubiquitous "V" for victory, heightened the sense of shared purpose.

So, too, did the image of the enemy that emerged during the war. In the popular mind, Germany, at least since the time of Otto von Bismarck, had acted as an aggressor nation because of the influence of the Prussian military caste. *Life* magazine described those officers: "They despise the world of civilians. They wear monocles to train themselves to control their face muscles. They live and die for war." Adolf Hitler had seized power with an "insane desire to conquer and dominate the whole world" and had pursued a strategy of piecemeal conquest based on "treachery and surprise," with the ultimate goal of conquering the United States. The Japanese were portrayed as a fanatic people, addicted to the practice of emperor worship and unconcerned about the sanctity of human life. Racist stereotypes shaped perceptions of the Japanese. *Time* magazine referred to American soldiers at Iwo Jima as "Rodent Exterminators" and noted: "The ordinary unreasoning Jap is ignorant. Perhaps he is human. Nothing . . . indicates it." Similarly, a float in a patriotic parade "showed a big American eagle leading a flight of bombs down on a herd of yellow rats which were trying to escape in all directions."

If Americans viewed the enemy as power-mad, militaristic, and brutal, they saw themselves as just the reverse. Perhaps nothing illustrated this better than reporter Ernie Pyle's best-selling *Here Is Your War.* Ostensibly an account of U.S. forces in Africa, Pyle's book in reality assured civilians that, despite the rigors of war, their fighting men preserved fundamental American virtues. To Pyle, the army was a democratic one: enlisted men and officers addressed each other by their first names and observed an easy kind of battlefield informality. American soldiers were fierce in combat—"as indestructible as Popeye and as deadly as executioners"—yet they could not resist giving away candy to hungry children, adopting little puppies, or treating captives with consideration. Although the soldiers came from every section of the nation, the cauldron of war had dissolved all religious, ethnic, class, and racial enmities. Americans saw themselves as democratic and humane, polar opposites of the goose-stepping Nazis. Even when Americans retreated, Pyle concluded, they did so in an "unretreatlike" way, and then only because they lacked sufficient men and material to win. The lesson was plain: if factories turned out more tanks, more machine guns, more bullets, and more airplanes, victory would surely follow.

## THE WAR ECONOMY

The economic problems posed by war differed from those associated with the depression. During the 1930s the Roosevelt administration had attempted to limit productive output, create jobs for the unemployed, and encourage a certain amount of inflation. During the 1940s, however, the government did a sudden turnabout. It endeavored to boost industrial and agricultural production, recruit a sufficient number of workers for defense plants, and hold down wages and prices. The administration sought, wherever possible, to obtain voluntary compliance from businessmen, workers, farmers, and consumers by offering them attractive incentives. But on occasion, when these groups refused to cooperate, the administration resorted to compulsion.

To supply the massive needs of the Allied forces, the government not only induced businesses to expand their facilities and convert them to war production, but also developed new sources of critical raw materials and doled those materials out in a systematic fashion. At the heart of this managerial effort was the War Production Board, which Roosevelt created in January 1942 to exercise general control over the economy. Donald Nelson, formerly an executive with Sears, Roebuck and Company, headed the agency. Nelson wanted "to establish a set of rules under which the game could be played the way industry said it had to play it." In this he echoed the sentiments of Secretary of War Henry L. Stimson, who believed that to carry on a war "you have got to let business make money out of the process or business won't work."

The War Production Board devised various procedures to allow businesses to combine patriotism with high profits. The government underwrote much of the cost of plant expansion by permitting industry to amortize those costs over a short five-year period, thereby deflating taxable income while inflating earning capacity. The government also invented the cost-plus-a-fixed-fee contract, which guaranteed the military contractor a profit above his costs and removed almost all element of risk from the acceptance of war orders. Firms that entered into pooling arrangements were granted immunity from the antitrust laws provided they first obtained consent by demonstrating how their activities furthered war needs. These policies proved effective. By mid-1942 major producers had converted from civilian to military lines. Industry produced nearly twice as much in 1942 as in 1939. As many new industrial plants were built in three years of war as in the preceding fifteen years. Corporate profits after taxes climbed from $6.4 billion in 1940 to $10.8 billion in 1944.

In three other ways the government stimulated industrial output. To compensate for the loss of 90 percent of America's crude rubber supply when Japan seized the Dutch East Indies and Malaya, a new synthetic-rubber industry was created. The government spent $700 million to construct fifty-one plants, which were leased to rubber companies and operated on a cost-plus-a-management-charge basis. By 1944 annual production of synthetic rubber exceeded eight hundred thousand tons. To eliminate logjams in production caused by shortages of copper, steel, and aluminum (all widely used in the manufacture of airplanes, tanks, and ships), the War Production Board introduced the Controlled

Scrap salvage in Butte, Montana, 1942. ( *Library of Congress, Prints & Photographs Division, FSA/OWI Collection.)*

Materials Plan. Under it, each agency awarding war contracts, such as the War or the Navy Department, presented its material requirements to the board, which then allotted the agency a fixed quantity of scarce materials for distribution to its prime contractors. To prevent transportation bottlenecks from developing, the government coordinated rail transportation. Unlike the situation in World War I when Washington took over the railroads, a system was devised under which the railroads submitted to central direction, pooled their resources, and streamlined their operations. By voluntarily complying, the railroads avoided nationalization.

The policies adopted in recruiting manpower resembled those applied in mobilizing industry. Again, Roosevelt relied heavily on what he termed "voluntary cooperation." At first the demand for labor was filled from the pool of unemployed workers, augmented by women and teenagers entering the job market. But by the end of 1942, high draft calls and twelve-hour factory shifts had exhausted available reserves. The administration made only a feeble attempt to force workers into war-related jobs, however, and finally had to abandon even that. In January 1943, the War Manpower Commission (WMC) issued a "work or fight" order. It eliminated military deferments for everyone, including fathers with dependent children, who held unessential jobs. But this attempt to substitute occupational for familial responsibility as a criterion for deferment aroused a storm of disapproval in Congress, and in December the order was rescinded.

*[handwritten margin note: mobilized workforce]*

Not until midway through the war did the administration discover a partial solution to the manpower problem. Spurred to action by a dangerously high rate of turnover in aircraft plants and shipyards on the West Coast, the WMC adopted a plan to align production demands with labor supply. Local committees determined how many workers were available; firms in each area could then receive new war contracts only if a sufficient labor supply existed; and a central employment service had to approve new hiring. This plan went into effect in Seattle, Portland, San Francisco, Los Angeles, and San Diego in fall 1943 and rapidly spread to cities across the country. It represented a middle stage between voluntarism and compulsion. Workers could not change jobs at will, but were not forced to accept jobs against their will.

## WOMANPOWER ON THE HOME FRONT

One effective solution to the manpower shortage, as the WMC realized by the end of 1942, was "womanpower." Depletion of the male labor pool, the loss of 16 million workers to the armed services, rapid economic expansion, and heavy investment in war industry—all created unprecedented need and optimal opportunity for women workers. Accordingly, one of the most dramatic changes of the war years was a vast increase in the employment of women. Between 1940 and 1945, some 6 million women joined the labor force; the number of women wage earners increased by over 50 percent; and the proportion of women who worked rose from 27 percent to 37 percent. Before the war ended, more than one-third of civilian workers were women.

Although women's numbers rose in all occupational categories (save domestic service), the surge was greatest in the defense industry, where the employment of women increased by a staggering 460 percent. As the male labor pool dwindled, thousands of women moved into jobs in airplane plants and shipyards, steel mills and ammunition factories. They ran cranes and lathes, repaired aircraft engines, cut sheet metal, mined coal, and made parachutes, gas masks, life rafts, instrument panels, and electrical parts. Employers accepted women workers with reluctance rather than alacrity. As late as the summer of 1942, the War Department urged producers to refrain from a large-scale hiring of women "until all available male labor in the area had first been employed." But by then, few male workers were available. "You're going to hire women," War Secretary Stimson soon told government contractors. By the war's midpoint, "Rosie the Riveter" had transformed the labor force in defense work and other heavy industry. At seven major aircraft plants, the Women's Bureau reported, women's numbers rose from 143 in mid-1941 to 65,000 by the end of 1942. At automobile plants, now converted to war production, one-fourth of workers were women. And in some defense factories, such as Boeing's huge Seattle plant, half the workers were women.

The ramifications of womanpower were far-reaching. Protective laws were discarded "for the duration" and working conditions improved. Women's geographic mobility increased as women flocked to war production zones such as Seattle and Detroit. Occupational mobility increased as well. Women were welcomed into the armed services as WACs (or the Women's Army Corps), WAVEs (or Women's Reserve, U.S. Naval Reserve), and members of the Nursing Corps; one thousand civilian women worked as Army pilots, flying noncombat missions. Other new opportunities opened up. Black women were able to leave domestic work for sales and factory jobs, from which they had previously been excluded; older women were able to get work that had been unavailable in peacetime; women professionals found new routes to advancement; and women took half the new government jobs created by war. Salaries rose across the board, most drastically in war production. For former waitresses and salesclerks, defense work meant a doubling of wages. The age of the female work force rose, as more and more married women took jobs. During the war, three out of four new women workers were wives. For the first time, a majority of the female work force was married.

*Everyone was getting jobs*

The sudden demand for female labor was accompanied by equally sudden changes in public opinion and government propaganda. During the depression, opinion polls had reflected antipathy to the working wife; now business magazines praised women's skill at precision work and repetitive tasks. Reversing the policies of the 1930s, when women were urged to stay home, the Office of War Information (OWI) and the WMC joined forces to lure women into the defense industry. Wartime advertisements put heavy stress on femininity, glamour, patriotism, and personal relationships. Prospective employees learned that war work could save the lives of male relatives. "Her Man is Out There—Nothing Else Matters," read the caption over a picture of an attractive textile worker, now producing uniforms. In a popular song, Rosie the Riveter's main concern was her boyfriend, Charlie, a Marine. "Rosie is protecting Charlie, working overtime on the riveting machine," ran the lyrics. OWI propaganda also attempted to fuse women's new work roles in heavy industry with familiar domestic images. War workers were reminded that the overhead crane was "just like a gigantic clothes wringer" and that making ammunition was as easy as running a vacuum cleaner.

*why didn't we keep alot of the women workers!*

Women seemed to appreciate new options for high pay more than OWI similes. "The major inducement is money," a housewife wrote to OWI. "Women like to be out taking part in the world," wrote another. But wartime propaganda was intended to minimize the war worker's challenge to traditional roles. Defense work, it stressed, represented only a temporary response to an emergency, rather than a permanent transformation. And in general, women seemed to make few permanent gains during the war.

*was not a permanent transition*

They exerted minimal influence over labor policy; the Women's Advisory Committee to the WMC, formed at the end of 1942, had little leverage. Although the National War Labor Board (NWLB) called for equal pay for equal work, women were often classified as (lower-paid) "helper trainees" or "light" workers. As a result, though all salaries rose, the gap between men's and women's earnings increased. Much ambivalence was voiced about the working mother, "a hazard to the security of the child," according to the Children's Bureau. Concern about high rates of female absenteeism eventually spurred

*weren't paid the same as men*

some day care programs, financed by the Lanham Act of 1941. But only a fraction of working mothers were able to take advantage of them; many remained suspicious of government child care. An additional wartime anxiety was the working woman's impact on family stability. The wartime scarcity of men seemed to encourage hasty courtship, early marriage, and a steep surge in the birthrate. Major concerns were increasing divorce rates, juvenile delinquency, illegitimacy, and sexual promiscuity. In war production factories, the government waged special campaigns to curb female "sex delinquency." Most important, new work roles for women *were* only temporary. They were destined to end when the "emergency" did.

In some industries, plans for the demobilization of women workers were under way as early as 1943. At the war's end, the female work force shrank rapidly. Defense plants closed or converted to civilian production; all industries prepared to make room for returning veterans. Between layoffs and purges, as in the auto industry, some 4 million women lost jobs between 1944 and 1946. Many war workers expected and accepted such losses; others resented them. "War jobs have uncovered unsuspected abilities in American women," claimed a defense worker who did not want to "return to the kitchen." The public, however, feared that women would replace men in the labor force. Advice literature urged women to relinquish their wartime independence and help returning men adjust to civilian life. Another fear was that women war workers had lost their femininity. "After three months in this land of challenging females," a returning *Stars and Stripes* correspondent wrote, "I feel that I should go back to France."

The wartime demand for womanpower, in the end, had no lasting impact on the labor force. In 1945, as new opportunities vanished, concerns that arose during the war—equal pay and child care—vanished too. Day care facilities shut down; when a bill for equal pay in private employment was proposed, Congress defeated it. But the war still left economic legacies for women. Economic recovery plus veterans' benefits spurred the rapid growth of the middle class. The expanding postwar economy, like the wartime economy, soon proved receptive to women workers. By the end of the 1940s, women were once again entering the labor force in unprecedented numbers, though now taking more traditional jobs—sales, service, and clerical work. Finally, the war left a legacy of inflation, one that would eventually legitimize the two-income family and the working wife. It was wartime inflation, indeed, that wiped out the depression. But it was also one of Roosevelt's most pressing economic problems.

## FIGHTING INFLATION

Booming industrial production and full employment, combined with a high level of federal spending and a scarcity of consumer goods, created huge inflationary pressures. When someone suggested that "a little inflation would not hurt," the President replied that he was reminded of "a fellow who took a little cocaine and kept coming back for more until he was a drug addict." To curb inflation, the administration utilized several weapons: wage ceilings, price controls, rationing, taxation, and bond drives. Everyone agreed in principle on the need to check inflation, but no one wanted to come out on the losing end. The administration therefore had a choice: either freeze economic conditions as they stood at the outbreak of the war, and thereby perpetuate certain inequalities; or impose controls selectively, and thereby permit some groups to improve their relative position. The second approach, while perhaps less efficient, was politically more popular and was ultimately adopted.

This was well illustrated by the efforts of the NWLB to halt spiraling wages. In July 1942 the NWLB adopted the "Little Steel" formula, which allowed a 15 percent wage increase to cover the rise in living costs since January 1, 1941. The formula, which applied to all workers, helped those who had not yet benefited from boom conditions. Even labor unions that had already obtained the permissible increase found the formula acceptable. The ruling permitted pay increases through overtime, allowed wage hikes that resulted from the upgrading of job classifications, and affected only cases involving labor–management disputes. Where employers were willing to grant increases—as was often the case, given the labor shortage—they were free to do so. In October 1942 the administration attempted to close this loophole by extending the NWLB's jurisdiction over voluntary wage boosts. When even this proved ineffective, Roosevelt issued a "hold the line" order in April 1943. It prevented revision of the Little Steel formula, but still allowed exceptions in extraordinary cases affecting war production and when exceptions were necessary to correct substandard conditions. By the summer of 1943 the government had largely removed wages from the realm of collective bargaining but had still not brought them under ironclad rules.

Regulating the wages workers earned depended, of course, on controlling the prices they had to pay. In April 1942 the Office of Price Administration (OPA) required every merchant to accept as a ceiling the highest price he had charged that March. This general freeze was difficult to enforce and often unfair, for it failed to control the prices of products whose design or packaging had changed, and it penalized dealers who had not already raised their prices. The cost of living continued to creep upward until April 1943, when Roosevelt's hold-the-line order prevented further inflationary rises. Consumer prices advanced by less than 2 percent during the next two years. To a large extent the success of price control hinged on rationing. The OPA took the initiative by introducing ten major rationing programs in 1942, and others followed later. They served different purposes: gasoline was rationed to conserve automobile tires; coffee, to reduce the burden on ocean transport; and canned food, to save tin. The government could not entirely prevent black-market operations—in 1944 one racketeer was found with counterfeit coupons worth 38,000 gallons of gasoline and 437 pairs of shoes—but rationing ensured a reasonably fair distribution of hard-to-get items, and it protected consumers against inflation.

The Roosevelt administration also reduced inflationary pressure by siphoning off excess purchasing power. Wartime taxes imposed heavy duties on the wealthy. The introduction of the withholding system meant that for the first time in U.S. history virtually all wage earners paid federal income taxes and did so out of current earnings. In addition, Roosevelt launched a campaign to sell war bonds, not through the compulsory plan favored by many of his advisors, but instead through voluntary purchases. Secretary of the Treasury Henry Morgenthau believed that such an undertaking would "make the country war-minded." He recruited advertising men (who invented such slogans as "Back the Attack") and Hollywood entertainers (who put personal possessions up for auction) to aid in the drive. The voluntary program had mixed results as an anti-inflation measure. Seven bond drives netted $135 billion, but large investors bought most of the securities, and the sales of low-denomination bonds were disappointing. Even so, 25 million workers signed up for payroll savings plans, and in 1944 bond purchases absorbed more than 7 percent of personal income after taxes.

At various times both labor and business challenged the system of economic regulation and left Roosevelt no choice but to intervene. When Montgomery Ward, a huge mail-order concern, refused to grant privileges to a union certified by the NWLB, the President authorized a takeover of the firm. Its head, Sewell L. Avery, shouting "to hell with the government," refused to leave the premises and had to be carried out bodily. Yet on balance the administration succeeded in winning public approval for its policies. This occurred in part because most Americans enjoyed greater prosperity during World War II than ever before and therefore did not find most regulatory measures oppressive. Equally important was the manner in which the administration proceeded. It introduced a coherent system of controls, but did so in piecemeal fashion and with a heavy emphasis on inducing the consent of those affected. FDR never used a stick when a carrot would do.

## DR. NEW DEAL MEETS DR. WIN-THE-WAR

World War II solved some of the most serious dilemmas facing social reformers. It brought about full employment and a higher standard of living. It strengthened trade unions, whose membership climbed from 10.5 to 14.75 million. It pushed farm income to new heights and reduced tenancy as landless farmers found jobs in factories. The war also exerted a modest leveling influence. Between 1939 and 1944, the share of national income held by the wealthiest 5 percent of the American people declined from 23.7 to 16.8 percent. In 1944 Congress passed the GI Bill of Rights, a wide-ranging reform measure providing veterans with generous education benefits, readjustment allowances during the transition to civilian life, and guarantees of mortgage loans. Finally, the war seemed to demonstrate once and for all the efficacy of Keynesian economics. Few doubted that soaring government expenditures had produced the boom. In 1943 one reformer noted, "The honest-minded liberal will admit that the common man is getting a better break than ever he did under the New Deal."

Despite all this, the war in many respects weakened social reform and led to profound disillusionment on the part of liberals. In part, this disillusionment derived from a mistaken reading of history. Many reformers, looking back on World War I, remembered only that it had aided their cause by permitting national planning and forgot how it had damaged their movement. In 1943 and 1944, however, liberals detected signs of a conservative resurgence everywhere they looked. Not only did Congress jettison New Deal programs and the administration refuse to support new reform measures, but in December 1943 Roosevelt declared that "Dr. New Deal" had outlived his usefulness and should give way to "Dr. Win-the-War." At that point liberal morale hit rock bottom.

The war obliged reformers to grant priority to military objectives. This often required the setting aside of certain social reforms. Liberals either did not protest or did not protest very loudly when the workday was lengthened to boost industrial output, rural electrification curtailed to free copper for the military, and the antitrust law shelved to permit greater business efficiency. States frequently diluted their child-labor laws so that 14- and 15-year-olds could join the work force and work longer hours. From 1940 to 1944 the number of teenage workers jumped from 1.0 to 2.9 million, and more than 1 million teenagers dropped out of school. "Where a social service doesn't help to beat Hitler, it may have to be sacrificed," observed one reformer. "This may sound tough—but we have to be tough."

Just as the war shouldered aside reforms, so it provided an excuse to abolish various New Deal relief agencies. During 1942 and 1943 Congress—usually with the consent of the administration—snuffed out the Civilian Conservation Corps, the Works Progress Administration, and the National Youth Administration. As a result of job openings in national defense, these agencies' clientele had come increasingly to consist of those last to be hired—blacks, women, and the elderly. Although the agencies tried to justify their continued existence by undertaking projects of military value, they could no longer count on strong backing from Roosevelt. Some reformers urged that the Works Progress Administration be preserved in case it was needed after the war. But in December 1942, asserting that a national work relief program was no longer justified, the President gave it an "honorable discharge."

As military costs escalated, so too did the federal deficit. Congress became more unwilling than ever to appropriate funds for domestic programs not directly related to the war, and Roosevelt, recognizing this, became reluctant to request such funds. When several Senate liberals introduced a plan to extend social security coverage, liberalize unemployment insurance benefits, and create a comprehensive health care program, they failed to gain the backing of the administration and stood no chance of winning a legislative majority. Congress not only refused to broaden social security coverage but froze the rate of contributions at 1 percent, thereby postponing a small scheduled increase. The same desire to trim nondefense expenditures led Congress to slash the budget of the Farm Security Administration, an important New Deal agency that had helped marginal farmers purchase land and equipment.

If social welfare schemes stood little chance in wartime, proposals to help those on the lower rungs of the ladder stood even less. Although most Americans enjoyed higher incomes than ever before, not everyone was well off. In 1944 a Senate committee reported that 20 million people "dwell constantly in a borderland between subsistence and privation." Ten million workers—one-fourth of those engaged in manufacturing—received less than 60 cents an hour. Yet the administration opposed granting them an across-the-board wage hike on the grounds that it would increase inflationary pressure. Raising the wages of the lowest paid would send inflationary ripples through the economy, since to preserve wage differentials, adjustments would be made all along the line. The resulting higher prices would eventually rob the worker of any bene-fit. Roosevelt believed that in wartime the government could do no more than ensure that the poor were "not ground down below the margin of existence."

The war weakened liberalism in one final respect: it raised issues that threatened to rupture the New Deal coalition. Roosevelt had built that coalition—consisting of blue-collar workers, Southern white farmers, ethnic and racial minority groups, and portions of the middle class—around eco-nomic concerns. So long as recovery remained the chief goal, those disparate groups had a good deal in common. But the war subjected this alliance to severe strain. Three sources of division were potentially most disruptive: heightened sensitivity to racial discrimination made it harder to retain the loy-alty of both Northern blacks and Southern whites; issues concerning foreign policy and civil liberties affected the political sentiments of ethnic groups; and the need to curb strikes and regulate the work force ran the risk of alienating organized labor.

## CIVIL RIGHTS AND THE SOUTH

If the Democratic party had an Achilles heel, it was the issue of racial justice. During Roosevelt's first two terms the depression had eclipsed racial concerns. New Deal relief programs had proved as attractive to black voters in New York City, Chicago, and Detroit as to white voters in Mississippi, Georgia, and Alabama. But the war spurred blacks to insist more strongly on racial equality. Many believed that the policy of accommodation had backfired during World War I and that a militant posture would be most likely to win concessions from the Roosevelt administration. Claiming that only the end of racial oppression would ensure their backing for the war, black leaders undertook a "Double V" campaign, one that stressed victory in the struggle for equality as well as vic-tory on the battlefield. Yet throughout the war years white Southerners clung tenaciously to the doctrine of segregation. The President, inevitably, was caught in the middle.

The war inspired civil rights groups to develop new forms of protest. In the summer of 1941, A. Philip Randolph of the Brotherhood of Sleeping Car Porters called for a march on Washington to protest against discrimination and "shake up white America." Randolph's movement differed from existing civil rights organizations in important respects: it attempted to mobilize the black masses rather than the middle class, it sought concessions through direct action rather than through court rulings, and it worked for reforms that would benefit urban blacks in the North as much as those in the South. Moreover, Randolph excluded white people from his organization on the grounds that "Negroes are the only people who are the victims of Jim Crow, and it is they who must take the initiative and assume the responsibility to abolish it."

Separatist in structure, the March on Washington Movement was wholly integrationist in objective. It demanded that the President withhold defense contracts from employers who practiced discrimination and abolish segregation in the armed forces and federal agencies. Anxious to have the march canceled, Roosevelt agreed to compromise. On June 25, 1941, he issued Executive Order 8802, which provided that government agencies, job training programs, and defense contractors put an end to discrimination. He also created a Committee on Fair Employment Practices to investigate violations. The executive order, although it did not provide for integration of the armed forces, was nevertheless hailed by civil rights workers, who concluded "we get more when we yell than we do when we plead."

By 1943 Randolph was advocating disciplined acts of civil disobedience, and the newly created Congress on Racial Equality (CORE) took action along those lines. Founded by pacifists, CORE endeavored to apply the same tactics of nonviolent resistance to the cause of racial justice that Gandhi had used in the movement for India's independence. Unlike the March on Washington Movement, CORE was interracial, but it too stressed direct action and concentrated on the economic aspects of racial injustice. In 1943 CORE sit-ins helped eliminate segregation in movie theaters and restaurants in Detroit, Denver, and Chicago. Most civil rights activity during the war, however, was channeled through the National Association for the Advancement of Colored People. Relying on the traditional means of protest—exposure, propaganda, political pressure, and legal action—the NAACP greatly expanded its membership and influence.

Most Southern whites regarded these signs of increased militancy with mounting apprehension. Committed to the preservation of Jim Crow institutions, whites bitterly resented the charge that their racial beliefs resembled those of the Nazis. A former governor of Alabama admitted privately in 1944 that the Germans had "wrecked the theories of the master race with which we were so contented so long," but added that the Germans had not dented his own belief in white superiority. Southerners attempted to explain away any evidence of black dissatisfaction as the product of outside agitation. During the war a tidal wave of rumors swept the South, culminating in the widely held fear that black women would no longer work as domestic servants but were busily forming "Eleanor Clubs" (named after the President's wife), whose goal was "a white woman in every kitchen by 1943." Because Southerners played a pivotal role in the Democratic coalition, they warned the President to pay attention to their views or else "witness the annihilation of the Democratic party in this section."

In April 1944 a Supreme Court decision abolishing the white primary added to this unrest. The white primary, which effectively disfranchised blacks in eight Southern states, had withstood several court challenges. But in 1941 the Supreme Court decided that primaries were an integral part of the election process, and in 1944, in *Smith* v. *Allwright*, it ruled that political parties were agents of the state and could not nullify the right to vote by practicing racial discrimination. In an effort to mollify Southerners, the Chief Justice assigned the majority opinion to Stanley Reed of Kentucky. But this did not prevent Democratic politicians or editorial writers in the Deep South from construing the decision as part of a broad campaign "to ram social equality down the throats of the white people of the South." Actually, while the decision enfranchised a number of educated, middle-class blacks in large cities, other obstacles to black voting—such as literacy tests and poll taxes—remained as high as ever.

The career of the Fair Employment Practices Committee (FEPC) illustrated Roosevelt's difficulties in mediating between the conflicting claims of white Southerners and civil rights activists. The FEPC represented an ambitious federal commitment to racial equality, and it succeeded in opening opportunities for some black workers. Yet the agency was hampered by restrictions. Theoretically the FEPC had jurisdiction over firms holding defense contracts, but it could act only when a worker filed a formal complaint (many workers were unaware of their right to do so), and even then it could not require compliance with its orders but had to rely on moral suasion. The FEPC could, as a last resort, request the cancellation of a defense contract. But war production always took priority over fair employment practices. Nor could the FEPC always count on strong presidential backing. When the railroad unions flouted a directive to grant equal rights to blacks, the case went to Roosevelt, who swept it under the rug by appointing an investigating committee that never reported. Southerners in Congress bitterly denounced the FEPC. It lost half its budget in 1945 and dissolved within a year.

Black workers made sizable economic gains during the war, usually as a result of manpower shortages. As the labor supply dwindled, many of the traditional barriers to black employment fell. Employers began to relax bars to hiring, and unions found it more difficult to maintain restrictive membership policies. Blacks, who accounted for just 3 percent of all war workers in the summer of 1942, made up more than 8 percent three years later. The number of skilled black workers doubled, and even larger gains took place in semiskilled positions. Black people by the hundreds of thousands left the farm for the factory in search of opportunity. The government helped in various ways—by hiring more blacks for federal jobs and employing them in higher classifications, by outlawing wage differentials based on race, and by announcing in November 1943 that it would refuse to certify for collective-bargaining purposes unions that discriminated.

The armed forces offered as much resistance to racial equality as had industry, but once again the pressures of war forced a revision in policy. In 1940 military leaders expressed open disdain for black recruits. Blacks could not enlist in the Marines or Air Corps. They could join the Navy only as messmen.

*finally let them in
but d~~ttt~~
Didnt let A. Am.
Fight.*

They were accepted in the Army but segregated rigidly. The Army maintained that "leadership is not yet imbedded in the negro race," that black soldiers were inferior fighters, and that the military should not serve as a laboratory for social experiments. Only when it became evident that the existing system involved an unacceptable waste of manpower was it modified. The Navy gradually integrated some of its ships, and the Army began the process of desegregating training camps. It also sent black combat units into battle more often, but continued to resist integration in war zones except in extraordinary circumstances. By fall 1944 there were 700,000 blacks in the armed services compared with 97,000 at the outbreak of war.

The wartime upheaval in race relations sometimes helped trigger deadly riots, especially in overcrowded cities and on Army bases. In June 1943 a violent racial clash engulfed Detroit, leaving thirty-four people dead and seven hundred injured. In such cases, civil rights workers and segregationists usually blamed each other for stirring up trouble. Roosevelt, recognizing that he could not satisfy both sides, generally allowed military needs to dictate his civil rights policy. He supported civil rights advances that contributed to the war and opposed those that seemed to interfere with it. The President summed up his own view in December 1943: "I don't think, quite frankly, that we can bring about the millennium at this time."

*← Bullshit*

## CULTURAL PLURALISM AND CIVIL LIBERTIES

Just as the issue of race affected Roosevelt's hold on blacks and Southerners, so issues concerning foreign policy and civil liberties affected his standing with key ethnic groups. The Democrats had always drawn heavy support from Irish Catholics, Germans, Italians, Eastern Europeans, and Jews. New Deal economic programs solidified this support. But in the 1940s the President faced a growing defection by German Americans, who had grown increasingly isolationist; by Italian Americans, who feared that harsh terms would be imposed on their homeland; and by Polish Americans, who feared that Roosevelt would allow Russian control over Eastern Europe after the war. Even more serious, Irish Americans objected to what they regarded as FDR's subservience to Great Britain and excessive collaboration with Russia. Reports to the White House spoke frequently of ethnic group dissatisfaction, of the "anti-Roosevelt sentiment of the Irish Catholics, Italians, and Germans."

To stem this drift away from the Democratic party, the President offered assurances that a vindictive peace would not be sought, praised the loyalty of German and Italian citizens, and took pains to build a good civil liberties record. "We know in our own land," he said in 1944, "how many good men and women of German ancestry have proved loyal, freedom-loving, and peace-loving citizens." During World War I, fearing the danger posed by ethnic Americans, the nation had stressed assimilation and uniformity. But during the 1940s few were concerned about divided allegiances. Positive values were more often attached to pluralism and ethnic diversity.

Tolerance toward persons of foreign descent was exhibited in several ways. The government placed relatively few restraints on enemy aliens: they could not travel without permission, were barred from areas near strategic installations, and could not possess arms, shortwave receivers, or maps. As the war progressed, however, restrictions were relaxed. Aliens could work in factories having defense contracts if the aliens first obtained permission, and most applications were approved. Citizens of German and Italian extraction encountered little hostility. Spokespersons for the Italian community, testifying before a congressional committee, were treated with kid gloves. Congressmen asked about the nation's baseball idol, who was also an Italian American: "Tell us about the DiMaggios. Tell us about DiMaggio's father." On Columbus Day in 1942, Attorney General Francis Biddle announced that Italian aliens would no longer be classified as aliens of enemy nationality. "For a long time," Biddle recalled, "I was not permitted to pay for a meal at an Italian restaurant."

Similarly, the Communist party supported the government during World War II and therefore did not find its liberties abridged. Under the leadership of Earl Browder, Communists opposed strikes that might impede production and benefit Hitler's forces. "We have to find out how to make the capitalist system work," Browder said, and this required a willingness to compromise and work for gradual, peaceful change. In 1944 Browder dissolved the party, replacing it with the more informal Communist Political Association. The contrast with the years 1917–18 was stark. During World War I the government had imprisoned Socialist party leader Eugene Debs; but in 1942 Roosevelt commuted the sentence of Earl Browder, convicted earlier of passport fraud, in an effort to foster national unity. Under Woodrow Wilson the government had deported radical aliens; but in 1943 the Supreme Court restored the citizenship of a man who had been denaturalized for belonging to the Communist party at the time he swore allegiance to the Constitution.

During World War II the government was more interested in curbing the far right than the far left. The administration persuaded the Catholic church to silence Father Charles Coughlin, whose magazine, in effect, was asserting that Jews and Communists had tricked America into entering the war. The Justice Department also indicted twenty-six "native fascists" for engaging "in a mass propaganda campaign spreading hatred against the Jews, prejudice against the Negroes, fear of the communists and distrust of our public officials." After courtroom turmoil marred several trials extending over two years, the case was dropped. In 1942 the Federal Bureau of Investigation captured eight German saboteurs who were planning to dynamite railroad terminals and war plants. Roosevelt denied the saboteurs access to the civil courts and arranged a trial by military commission. The Supreme Court, meeting in special session, decided reluctantly that *Ex parte Milligan* —the case in which it had ruled unconstitutional Abraham Lincoln's use of military commissions to try civilians in areas remote from combat—did not apply. Six of the saboteurs were executed and two were given long prison terms.

The government provided conscientious objectors with several alternatives to military service. The Selective Service Act (1940) provided that no one should serve as a combatant who "by reason of religious training and belief, is conscientiously opposed to war in any form." Conscientious objectors usually performed noncombatant duties. Perhaps 25,000 men, most of them Quakers and Mennonites, served in the Medical Corps and related branches of the military. Those who objected to military service in any form could do "work of national importance under civilian direction." Some 11,950 men worked in civilian public service camps, where they engaged mainly in forestry and conservation, building roads, clearing trails, fighting forest fires, and digging irrigation ditches. About five hundred objectors volunteered to be subjects of medical experiments to find cures for typhus, malaria, and other illnesses. Alternatives to the draft, however, did not satisfy everyone. Those whose conscience did not permit them to register with the Selective Service System, and those whose objection to war rested on political rather than religious grounds, were imprisoned. About 5,500 men went to jail, more than three-fourths of them Jehovah's Witnesses who were denied the ministerial exemptions they sought.

Significantly, the only group of immigrants to lose its rights—Japanese Americans on the West Coast—was politically powerless. Foreign-born Japanese who had migrated before 1924 were barred from citizenship, and most of their children, although born in the United States and therefore citizens, were too young to vote. Japanese Americans were vulnerable for other reasons as well. They formed a relatively small group, were concentrated in a few states, were largely confined to nonessential occupations (such as vegetable farming), and could be easily singled out. Powerless and poorly assimilated, Japanese Americans were the victims of a collective view of white Americans that the Japanese Americans were guilty simply because of their race. During the spring of 1942 more than 110,000 people, two-thirds of them citizens, were herded into relocation centers. There most of them remained until 1945.

*American citizens spent 3 yrs. in camps.*

The decision to relocate Japanese Americans reflected racial, military, and political considerations. General John DeWitt, who headed the Western Defense Command, expressed a widely held view when he claimed that racial attributes made all Japanese a menace. "Racial affinities are not severed by migration," he said. "The Japanese race is an enemy race." Military leaders believed the Japanese Americans would commit sabotage at the first opportunity. The absence of any such overt acts was merely taken as proof that an "invisible deadline" was drawing near. Although some undoubtedly believed that military necessity justified relocation, others used the argument as a convenient pretext. Nativist groups had long agitated for Japanese exclusion, and some agricultural interests also expected to profit by the removal of Japanese competitors. West Coast congressmen badgered government agencies, urging drastic action. "There's a tremendous volume of public opinion now developing against the Japanese," DeWitt reported in January 1942. He added that this was the opinion of "the best people of California."

*unfair*

*BULLSh?t*

Throughout the war the Supreme Court often defended the rights of unpopular groups. It set aside the denaturalization of a German-born citizen charged with continued loyalty to the Third Reich; it protected a Fascist

Japanese Americans in California, 1942. *(National Archives.)*

sympathizer who savagely denounced Roosevelt; and it struck down a law compelling schoolchildren to salute the flag. Yet the Supreme Court did not challenge the government's policy toward Japanese Americans. In June 1943 the Court unanimously held, in the Hirabayashi case, that military officials could impose a curfew that applied only to Japanese American citizens. In time of war, the Court reasoned, "residents having ethnic affiliations with an invading enemy may be a greater source of danger than those of different ancestry." In December 1944, in *Korematsu* v. *U.S.*, the Court upheld the exclusion of Japanese American citizens from the West Coast. One of the three dissenting justices branded the decision a "legalization of racism." At the same time, however, the Court ruled that the government could not hold citizens in relocation centers beyond a reasonable time without evidence of disloyal behavior. The decision, though, was handed down a day after the government had revoked the order banning Japanese Americans from the coast.

# LABOR AND POLITICS

Organized labor was the linchpin of the Democratic coalition. If proof were needed, it was furnished by the 1942 congressional elections. Democrats suffered a severe defeat primarily because war workers who had moved to new states often could not meet residency requirements. The Republicans captured forty-four additional seats in the House of Representatives and nine in the Senate. Roosevelt's policies took account of this dependence on labor. During the war, workers significantly improved their standard of living. Hourly wage rates rose by 24 percent, and weekly earnings (which included overtime) spurted by 70 percent. But as the war progressed, the President was confronted with two politically explosive problems: how to deal with strikes and tighten manpower controls without antagonizing labor.

*Republicans held the majority*

Late in December 1941 spokespersons for labor and business had agreed to refrain from strikes and lockouts. But the pledge was not legally binding, and workers who suspected that they were being shortchanged ultimately proved willing to violate the agreement. During 1943, 3.1 million workers took part in stoppages compared with fewer than 1 million the year before. The most serious was a strike by four hundred thousand members of the United Mine Workers under the leadership of John L. Lewis. Dissatisfied with federal wage controls, miners of bituminous coal refused to accept the decisions of the NWLB. The strike caused severe public indignation. By mid-1943 Lewis had apparently become the most hated figure in the United States. Roosevelt remarked privately that he would be glad to resign as President if only Lewis would commit suicide.

Neither man resorted to such extreme measures. Even though Congress in June 1943 passed the War Labor Disputes Act, making it a crime to encourage strikes in plants taken over by the government, Roosevelt understood that a harsh response—such as an attempt to draft miners or send them to jail—might easily boomerang. Coal could not be mined without the union's cooperation, and besides, drastic measures would offend most of organized labor. Roosevelt had to avoid taking any step that might cause labor to close ranks behind the coal miners yet not allow so attractive a settlement that other workers would follow them to the picket lines. The task, one official noted, was "to isolate Mr. Lewis and his assistants from other more responsible labor leaders."

Pulled in one direction by a desire to appease his labor constituency and pushed in the other by public opinion, the President charted a hazardous course between the two. He had the government take over the coal mines but placed them under Secretary of the Interior Harold Ickes, whose relationship with Lewis was reasonably cordial. He appealed to the miners to return to work but permitted bargaining to proceed even while they stayed off the job. He approved a settlement granting the miners a substantial raise, but which did so through a new system of computing working time that did not technically violate hourly wage ceilings. He vetoed the War Labor Disputes Act but requested authority to draft strikers (up to the age of 65) as noncombatants. Roosevelt managed to retain the goodwill of most labor leaders, who

*Gov. hated strikes. Tried to quell them*

applauded his veto—which was promptly overriden by Congress—and paid little attention to his alternative proposal.

The need to adopt more stringent work-force controls also jeopardized FDR's alliance with labor. In January 1944, faced with a deepening labor deficit, Roosevelt came out for national service. In its original form this proposal would have placed all citizens, men and women alike, at the government's disposal for assignment to whatever job seemed necessary. Roosevelt favored a less drastic version, but labor detested national service in any form. Union leaders termed the plan a disguised form of "involuntary servitude." In coming out for the measure, Roosevelt had carefully protected himself by insisting that Congress also impose higher taxes on corporations, scale down profits on defense contracts, and authorize effective consumer price ceilings. Congress showed little inclination to do any of these things. Consequently, Roosevelt's advocacy of national service, although it annoyed labor, did not cause many workers to desert the Democratic party.

So successfully did Roosevelt cultivate labor that it provided massive assistance to his 1944 campaign. Inasmuch as two of every three union members considered themselves Democrats, labor knew that a light turnout, such as had occurred in 1942, would be a disaster. The Congress of Industrial Organizations (CIO), therefore, set up a Political Action Committee that undertook large-scale registration drives and distributed 85 million pieces of campaign literature. On election day, committee volunteers made telephone calls reminding union members to vote, provided baby-sitters so that housewives could get to the polls, and arranged transportation for those who needed it. The CIO eventually spent $1.5 million, and labor's total contribution to the Democratic campaign—over $2 million—made up 30 percent of the party's expenditures. Although unions had taken part in past campaigns, never had they done so much for any candidate.

Roosevelt nailed down the labor vote by stressing economic themes. He reminded audiences that the Republicans were the party of Hoovervilles and breadlines, the Democrats the party of collective bargaining and social security. Roosevelt endorsed an Economic Bill of Rights, which recognized each person's right to work at a job that would "provide adequate food and clothing and recreation," to live in a decent home, to receive adequate medical care, to obtain a good education, and to be protected against the hazards of sickness, accident, and unemployment. Ironically, Republican candidate Thomas E. Dewey of New York, although critical of FDR's management of the war, endorsed much of the reform program of the New Deal, at least that portion already on the statute books. He supported social security, unemployment insurance, relief for the needy, and collective bargaining. Some Democrats dubbed him "Little Sir Echo." The 1944 campaign helped place the welfare state beyond the range of partisan dispute.

Roosevelt, although carrying 36 states, won his most slender victory. The President obtained 53.4 percent of the popular vote, compared with 54.7 percent in 1940. He won by a margin of 3.6 million votes as against 5 million in 1940. The key to FDR's win was the labor vote in the big cities. In cities with a population over one hundred thousand, Roosevelt garnered 60.7 percent of the vote. In seven states with enough combined electoral strength to have reversed the outcome—New York, Illinois, Pennsylvania, Michigan, Missouri, Maryland, and New Jersey—FDR's plurality in each state's largest city overcame a Republican majority in the rest of the state. The Democrats picked up twenty-two seats in the House and lost one in the Senate. Without the help of the CIO's Political Action Committee, Roosevelt would not have done so well. That help, in turn, reflected Roosevelt's ability to contend with the potentially disruptive issues posed by the war economy.

## WAR AND SOCIAL CHANGE

World War II acted as a catalyst for social change. It increased the power of the federal government and of the presidency in an enduring way. During the war the government employed more people and spent more money than ever before. From 1940 to 1945 the number of civilian employees of the government climbed from 1 million to 3.8 million, and expenditures soared from $9 billion to $98.4 billion. When peace returned the government reduced its operations, but they remained well above prewar levels. The war also accelerated the growth of executive authority and a corresponding erosion of legislative influence. Congress delegated sweeping powers to the President, who in turn delegated them to administrators in war agencies. The big decisions during the war were usually made by men responsible to the President, not by congressional leaders. The Supreme Court, which had in the past scrutinized delegations of legislative authority, refused even to review such cases during the war.

War transformed the economic arrangements under which Americans lived. The huge outlay of funds for military purposes (which at the height of the war reached $250 million a day) enormously inflated industrial capacity. Manufacturing output doubled during the war, and gross national product rose from $88.6 billion in 1939 to $198.7 billion five years later. New industries, including synthetic rubber and synthetic fabrics, came into being. But the desire to obtain the greatest output in the shortest time resulted in awarding a predominant share of military contracts to large corporations and fostering the tendency toward business consolidation. Two-thirds of all military contracts went to one hundred firms; nearly one-half went to three dozen corporate giants. From 1941 to 1943, half a million small businesses disappeared. In 1939 firms with more than ten thousand workers employed 13 percent of the manufacturing labor force, but in 1944 they accounted for fully 31 percent.

Since war contracts were awarded by Army and Navy procurement officers, close ties developed between business and the military. Corporation executives and military officers found that they had much in common, particularly in 1944, when they joined to oppose a plan providing for early reconversion to peacetime production. The military feared that reconversion would lull people into believing the war was already won and would adversely affect war production. Large war contractors feared that small competitors who were not tied

*small business disappear*

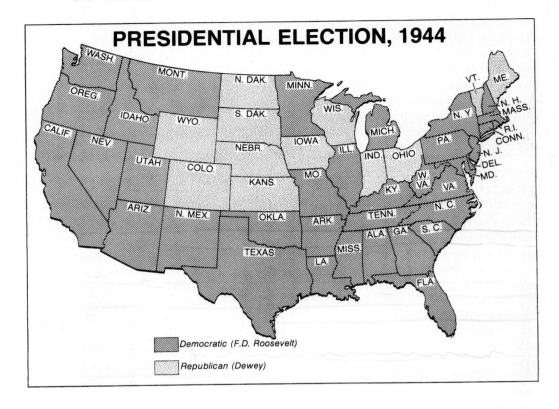

## PRESIDENTIAL ELECTION, 1944

Democratic (F.D. Roosevelt)

Republican (Dewey)

up with military orders would get a jump on them in manufacturing consumer goods. The mutuality of interest between the military and big business was underscored by Charles E. Wilson, who had left General Electric for a top post in the War Production Board. In January 1944 Wilson spoke to the Army Ordnance Association and proposed a long-term arrangement under which business would maintain permanent liaison with the military. This would keep the nation prepared for any future emergency. The military-industrial complex reached maturity later, but it had its origins in World War II.

*military-industrial Complex*

Just as the war modernized and consolidated industry, so it helped create big agriculture and big labor. The farm population declined by 17 percent from 1940 to 1945 as people left the countryside for jobs in factories and shipyards. But farmers' output and productivity climbed sharply as a result of good weather, the increased use of fertilizers, greater mechanization, and the consolidation of small farms into large ones. A million more tractors were in use at the end than at the beginning of the war. Not only did the war hasten the appearance of large-scale, mechanized farming, but it also increased the strength of organized labor. Trade unions attracted millions of members, gained a foothold in new industries, and made collective bargaining accepted practice.

The United States emerged from the war a more highly urban and technological society. The government greatly expanded its role in supporting

Manufacturing 155-millimeter shells in Hammond, Indiana, 1942. *(Torkel Korling/ Library of Congress.)*

scientific research and training. Wartime advances in medicine, particularly in the production of penicillin, saved countless lives. Some 12 million men entered the armed services, and many later received a college education or technical training under the GI Bill of Rights. More than 15 million civilians moved to new homes. Cities with shipyards, aircraft plants, or munitions factories grew at a staggering rate. Six large cities attracted 2 million migrants; California alone received 1.4 million people. As one observer noted, "the whole pattern of our economic and social life is undergoing kaleidoscopic changes, without so much as a bomb being dropped on our shores."

## TRUMAN'S TROUBLES: THE POLITICS OF INFLATION

On April 12, 1945, a stunned nation heard that Franklin Roosevelt had suddenly died of a stroke at his retreat in Warm Springs, Georgia. Harry S. Truman, who succeeded to the presidency, was quite unlike his predecessor. Roosevelt had been born to wealth and status on a Hudson River estate; the Delano family traced its lineage back to William the Conqueror. Truman came from a

## MARTHA GRAHAM AND MODERN DANCE

Martha Graham in *Chronicle. (Dance Collection, The New York Public Library for the Performing Arts. Reprinted with permission.)*

In the late 1930s and early 1940s a central theme in the work of writers, artists, photographers, composers, playwrights, filmmakers, and dancers was a fascination with America itself—its history, folklore, heritage, and even geography. This was nicely revealed in Pare Lorentz's documentary film, *The River* (1938), which described the Mississippi's course: "Down the Rock, the Illinois, and the Kankakee/The Allegheny, the Monongahela, Kanawhy, and Muskingum." Appreciation of the values associated with the American past reached a culmination during World War II when those values seemed to offer a hopeful, decent, and humane alternative to totalitarian doctrine. The success of Frank Sinatra's "The House I Live In"—and, even more, that of the Broadway musical *Oklahoma!*—attested to the depth of those sentiments. They were also reflected in modern dance, most notably in the work of Martha Graham.

Born in 1894, Martha Graham had spent her youth in California where, in 1916, she began to study dance with Ruth St. Denis and Ted Shawn. She eventually became dissatisfied with the "Denishawn" style, which stressed gossamer motion, oriental pageantry, and silken costumes. Graham was, however, equally dissatisfied with traditional ballet, with its graceful lifts, elegant postures, and classical themes. She sought to develop a new dance vocabulary in which movement was stark and down-to-earth, the costumes simple and severe. One critic noted: "Her idiom of motion has little of the aerial in it, but there's a lot of rolling on the floor." By 1926 she had moved to New York City, organized her own troupe, and given her first recital. Graham infused all she did with a fierce intensity. One student described her as "all tension—lightning. Her burning dedication gave her spare body the power of ten men."

Graham, who believed that dance should be relevant to contemporary concerns, was by the mid-1930s affirming American values and denouncing Fascist brutality. In *Chronicle* (1936), she sympathized with the Loyalist cause in the Spanish Civil War. *American Document* (1938) provided a capsule version of the nation's history—including sections on Puritanism, the Indian, and the Declaration of Independence—ending in what

the *New York Times* described as "a final tableau in celebration of democracy." Graham's purpose, noted one critic, was to "bring to bear upon today's perplexities all that was sturdy and upright and liberating in the American dream." For the first time, Graham used a male dancer, Erick Hawkins, who created something of a sensation by performing bare-chested. Also, she was the first to utilize a narrator who, by explaining events, made modern dance forms comprehensible to many who had previously found them mystifying.

Graham's celebration of American values reached a peak in the 1944 production of *Appalachian Spring,* which told the story of the marriage of a young couple in rural Pennsylvania in the mid-nineteenth century. The dance was set in a farmyard, the dancers incorporated portions of the Virginia reel, and the music, by Aaron Copland, was based partly on the Shaker hymn *Simple Gifts.* *Appalachian Spring* vibrated with a spirit of resilience and optimism.

After the war Graham gradually lost her place as the dominant figure in the world of

*American Document* —"We hold these truths to be self-evident: That all men are created equal." *(Barbara Morgan.)*

Martha Graham and Erick Hawkins in *Appalachian Spring. (Dance Collection, The New York Public Library for the Performing Arts. Reprinted with permission.)*

modern dance, but those who replaced her— Merce Cunningham, Paul Taylor—had been her students. She performed for the last time in 1969 at the age of 75, but still remained actively involved in choreography until her death in 1991. Martha Graham's extraordinary career epitomized one of her maxims: "The only freedom in life is that of the discipline one chooses."

Merce Cunningham rehearsing, 1954.  *(Dance Collection, The New York Public Library for the Performing Arts. Reprinted with permission.)*

family in modest circumstances; like FDR, he had a middle initial, but since his parents could not agree what the S stood for, he had no middle name. Roosevelt had attended Groton, Harvard, and Columbia Law School. Truman, upon graduation from high school, worked as a railroad timekeeper, in a newspaper mailroom, as a bank clerk, and on a farm. After a stint in the Army during World War I, Truman entered the haberdashery business and then took evening courses for two years at the Kansas City Law School. Later, Boss Tom Pendergast of Kansas City chose him to run for county judge and in 1934 picked him for the U.S. Senate. Roosevelt selected Truman as his running mate in 1944 because he was the second choice of each faction in the Democratic party—labor, city bosses, the South—and the only candidate they all found acceptable. Roosevelt seldom made a rash decision; Truman often acted on impulse. Associates usually described FDR as "sphinx-like"; Truman told everyone just what he thought.

*FDR*

Truman, like Roosevelt, had to contend with the problem of inflation, but in a different and less favorable context. During the war Roosevelt fought inflation with wage ceilings, price controls, rationing, and taxes. This worked for several reasons: accepting sacrifices seemed the patriotic thing to do; the system left room for improved living standards; the draft removed millions of servicemen from the consumer-goods market; and many were content to save money and pay off old debts. Yet a day of reckoning had to come, and it arrived in 1946, the first full year of peace. Truman endeavored to keep a lid on wages and prices, but he found that people who had postponed buying consumer goods for several years were no longer willing to accept government controls. The longer those controls lasted the more oppressive they seemed. Moreover, Truman faced a legislature that, having taken a back seat during the war, was anxious to reassert its prerogatives.

*Truman →*

A battle soon developed over Truman's attempt to preserve the powerful wartime OPA. The OPA faced criticism from businessmen who wanted to raise prices and, ironically, from consumers who were tired of doing without certain items. In 1946, responding to these pressures, Congress extended the OPA but stripped it of much authority. Truman recognized that if he signed the measure he would be expected to keep prices down even though the OPA would lack the means of doing so. He vetoed the bill; controls expired on July 1, 1946; and prices skyrocketed. The cost-of-living index rose 6 percent in just one month. The administration employed a few stopgap measures to curb inflation but none worked. The consumer price index rose more than twenty-four points from July 1946 to July 1947, compared with less than four points in the preceding year. Prices continued their upward spiral through 1948.

Labor difficulties plagued the Truman administration no less than rising prices. A rash of strikes broke out in 1946 as automobile, steel, electrical, and communications workers walked off their jobs in an effort to win higher wages and consolidate wartime gains. In 1946, 4.6 million workers went on strike, more than ever before in the nation's history. Strikes by railroad workers and coal miners presented especially severe challenges to the administration. In both cases, unions refused to accept arbitrated settlements. Truman, believing that the walkouts jeopardized national security, intervened by taking over the railroads and mines. When the unions persisted, the President was furious. He harshly denounced the railroad workers, called for legislation authorizing him to draft strikers, and spoke of the need to "hang a few traitors and make our own country safe for democracy." He sought and obtained an injunction against the United Mine Workers which, after the Supreme Court upheld the President, had to pay a stiff fine. Although both disputes were ultimately settled, Truman's proposal to draft strikers and his willingness to use an injunction enraged organized labor.

*Truman didn't get along w/unions unlike FDR*

By November 1946 the various strands in the old New Deal coalition were unraveling, and the Democrats suffered a sharp setback in the congressional elections. Running on the slogan "Had Enough?" the Republicans gained eleven seats in the Senate and fifty-six in the House, thereby capturing control of Congress for the first time since 1928. Democrat J. William Fulbright of Arkansas even suggested that Truman provide what the voters obviously wanted by appointing a Republican as secretary of state (at that time the position that was next in order of presidential succession) and then resigning from office. Truman did nothing of the sort. Instead, by capitalizing on the behavior of the Republican Congress, he began to reconstruct a viable political coalition.

First, Truman made a peace offering to organized labor by vetoing the Taft-Hartley Act in June 1947. Congress had passed the measure in response to postwar labor turmoil and opinion polls showing that two out of three people favored tighter control of union activities. The bill outlawed the closed shop, banned such union activities as secondary boycotts, provided for an eighty-day cooling-off period before calling a strike if the President thought it would cause a national emergency, barred union contributions to political parties, and required labor officials to sign affidavits attesting that they were not subversive. It also permitted states to pass "right to work" laws outlawing the union shop. (In a closed shop, only union members could be hired; in a union shop, anyone hired had to join the union.) Truman declared the act unworkable, unfair, and arbitrary, but a coalition of Republicans and Southern Democrats easily overrode his veto. Truman's message nevertheless went far toward mending fences with the labor movement.

*- Tries to make up w/union*

Next, Truman appealed to religious and ethnic minorities by urging a liberal entrance policy toward refugees. More than 1.2 million "displaced persons," mainly Catholics and Jews from Eastern Europe, were living in camps in American-held zones. Many had been seized by the Germans during the war and used as forced laborers. Others had fled from areas that had fallen under Russian control. Truman admitted 42,000 displaced persons in 1945, and he then urged Congress to revise the immigration laws in order to admit 400,000 displaced persons a year. The old restrictionist argument—that immigrants were dangerous radicals—hardly made sense when applied to people fleeing Communist rule. Yet Congress did nothing in 1947. The following year it passed a lukewarm measure admitting 200,000 displaced persons over a two-year period but excluding most Jews and many Catholics. Terming the bill "flagrantly discriminatory," Truman signed it reluctantly.

Finally, Truman attempted to allay any suspicion that his administration was "soft on communism," a theme successfully exploited by Republicans in the 1946 congressional elections. Public opinion polls that year revealed that most Americans considered communism an internal menace. Fear was reinforced when the Canadian government announced that it had broken a Soviet espionage ring and again when the House Committee on Un-American Activities began a new round of hearings into alleged subversion in government. In 1947 Truman responded. The Justice Department instituted deportation proceedings against aliens with Communist affiliations and began drawing up a list of subversive organizations. The administration also introduced a comprehensive loyalty program under which all federal employees would undergo security checks. The program was couched in loose, and potentially dangerous, language. An employee could be fired if "reasonable grounds exist for belief that the person involved is disloyal." Those grounds included acts of treason or espionage, advocacy of violent revolution, or "membership in, affiliation with or sympathetic association with" any organization on the attorney general's list.

These initiatives were closely related to the hardening of cold war positions. By 1947, as relations with the Soviet Union deteriorated, Americans came increasingly to accept the view (which had earlier been held during the period of the Nazi-Soviet pact) that Russian communism closely resembled German fascism. Both were characterized by purges, concentration camps, secret police, and one-party rule. Both fomented subversion abroad. Both were aggressive and expansionist. Both understood only one thing: force. "A totalitarian state is no different whether you call it Nazi, Fascist, Communist," Truman told his daughter. "The oligarchy in Russia . . . is a Frankenstein dictatorship worse than any of the others, Hitler included." In 1941 the American people had developed an image of Germany that sustained them through four years of hot war. By 1947 they were developing an image of Russia that would prepare them for four decades of cold war.

## Suggested Reading

Wartime policies are analyzed in Richard Polenberg, *War and Society: The United States, 1941–1945* (1972); James M. Burns, *Roosevelt: The Soldier of Freedom* (1970); John M. Blum, *V Was For Victory: Politics and American Culture During World War II* (1976); William L. O'Neill, *A Democracy at War* (1993); and Lewis A. Ehrenberg and Susan E. Hirsch (eds.), *The War in American Culture* (1996).

Important monographs include William M. Tuttle, *Daddy's Gone to War* (1993), an analysis of the impact of the war on children; Clayton R. Koppes and Gregory D. Black, *Hollywood Goes to War* (1987); Allan Berube, *Coming Out Under Fire: The History of Gay Men and Women in World War II* (1990); and Marilynn S. Johnson, *The Second Gold Rush* (1993), an examination of Oakland and the East Bay during the war. For the White House during the war, see Doris Kearns Goodwin, *No Ordinary Times* (1994).

Women's roles during the war years are examined in Susan M. Hartmann, *The Home Front and Beyond: American Women in the 1940s* (1982); Karen Anderson, *Wartime Women: Sex Roles, Family Relations, and the Status of Women during World War II* (1981);

Ruth Milkman, *Gender at Work: The Dynamics of Job Segregation During World War II* (1987); and D'Ann Campbell, *Women at War with America: Private Lives in a Patriotic Era* (1984).

For the civil rights movement during the war, consult Neil A. Wynn, *The Afro-American and the Second World War* (1975); Herbert Garfinkel, *When Negroes March* (1959); Louis Ruchames, *Race, Jobs, and Politics* (1948); and August Meier and Elliott Rudwick, *CORE: A Study in the Civil Rights Movement, 1942–1968* (1973). Racial policies of the military are analyzed in Richard M. Dalfiume, *Desegregation of the U.S. Armed Forces, 1939–1953* (1969); and racial tensions are analyzed in Dominic J. Capeci, Jr., *The Harlem Riot of 1943* (1977); *Race Relations in Wartime Detroit: The Sojourner Truth Housing Controversy of 1942* (1984); and Beth Bailey and David Farber, *The First Strange Place: The Alchemy of Race and Sex in World War II Hawaii* (1992).

The Supreme Court and civil liberties are discussed in C. Herman Pritchett, *The Roosevelt Court* (1948); Alpheus T. Mason, *Harlan Fiske Stone* (1956); and Sidney Fine, *Frank Murphy: The Washington Years* (1984). Two excellent studies of conscientious objectors are Mulford Sibley and Philip Jacob, *Conscription of Conscience, 1940–1947* (1952); and Lawrence Wittner, *Rebels Against War: The American Peace Movement, 1941–1960* (1969). The evacuation and relocation of Japanese Americans are explored in Roger Daniels, *Concentration Camps: USA* (1971); Audrie Girdner and Anne Loftis, *The Great Betrayal* (1969); and Bill Hosokawa, *Nisei: The Quiet Americans* (1969). See, in addition, Jacobus ten Broek et al., *Prejudice, War and the Constitution* (1954); and Peter Irons, *Justice at War* (1984).

Government policies concerning labor and manpower are considered in Melvyn Dubofsky and Warren VanTine, *John L. Lewis: A Biography* (1977); Byron Fairchild and Jonathan Grossman, *The Army and Industrial Manpower* (1959); Albert A. Blum, *Drafted or Deferred* (1967); and Nelson Lichtenstein, *Labor's War at Home* (1982), on the CIO.

For the problems confronting Harry Truman, see Alonzo Hamby, *Beyond the New Deal: Harry S. Truman and American Liberalism* (1973); Bert Cochran, *Harry S. Truman and the Crisis Presidency* (1973); Robert Donovan, *Conflict and Crisis* (1977). Two more specialized studies are R. Alton Lee, *Truman and Taft-Hartley* (1966); and Susan Hartmann, *Truman and the 80th Congress* (1971).

Martha Graham's contribution to modern dance is explained in Don McDonagh, *Martha Graham* (1973); and Agnes DeMille, *Martha* (1991).

GIs getting their first warm rations after fifteen days of fighting in the Hurtgen Forest, Germany. *(BETTMANN.)*

# CHAPTER TEN

# 1941–1947
## One World into Two

This chapter discusses:
- How world war led to cold war
- The personalities of Roosevelt, Churchill, and Stalin
- Harry Truman's policies and insecurities
- The advent of the bomb
- Rebuilding from the rubble: The Marshall Plan

On the home front Americans were single-minded in their pursuit of victory. On the battlefield they waged campaigns with the same determination. Diplomatically, however, U.S. policies were divided, even contradictory. On the one hand, the Roosevelt administration sought a united world, devoid of exclusive economic or political spheres, in which open access to all areas could be enjoyed by every nation that could compete. This vision was embodied in the Atlantic Charter of 1941. But on the other hand, Roosevelt had to come to an agreement with his two great allies, Great Britain and Russia, who feared that they had been so weakened by war that they could not compete peacefully against the gigantic American power. The British and Soviets therefore sought their own exclusive spheres of influence. Washington finally made Great Britain abandon its policies of spheres, but could never force Joseph Stalin to do so. In 1945 Franklin D. Roosevelt, then Harry S. Truman, finally opted for an open world and so opposed a Soviet sphere of influence in Eastern Europe. The confrontation thus began, slowly at first, then through a series of crises, until in 1947 the Truman Doctrine and the Marshall Plan publicly signaled the beginning of nearly a half-century in which the two great powers divided and nearly destroyed the world.

## CHURCHILL AND STALIN VERSUS ROOSEVELT

Even before Pearl Harbor, the United States had begun preparing for the postwar peace. The planning took on new urgency on June 23, 1941, when Adolf Hitler suddenly invaded the Soviet Union. Except for a brief honeymoon period in late 1933, Russia and the United States had been opponents since the 1890s. The 1941–45 alliance provided only a brief interlude in this history of confrontation. Some Americans thought Hitler could quickly defeat the Soviets. Secretary of War Henry Stimson told Roosevelt that Germany might need no longer than one to three months to conquer Russia. Senator Harry S. Truman, Democrat of Missouri, unfortunately made public his hope that Hitler's and Stalin's forces would bleed each other white on the plains of Russia. Roosevelt took a different course. He ordered immediate aid to Stalin and then began a lend-lease program, which by 1945 had pumped $11 billion worth of goods into Russia. He managed to do this despite strong anti-Soviet opposition in Congress. FDR and his top advisors hoped that Russia would stop the German armies, and as the summer passed, it seemed that Russia was succeeding. Roosevelt acted on a principle that Churchill had stated: he would make a pact with the devil himself, the prime minister declared, if this would help defeat Hitler.

Roosevelt then focused on another danger. After Hitler's invasion of Russia, Churchill and Stalin had exchanged messages that the State Department feared involved deals on postwar boundaries, possibly even a division of

288

Europe into British and Russian spheres. To clarify this explosive problem, Roosevelt and Churchill secretly met off the coast of Newfoundland in August. In the "Atlantic Charter" issued publicly after the meeting, two key provisions gave the President what he demanded. One clause pledged "respect [for] the right of all peoples to choose the form of government under which they will live." These words applied to victims of Germany and Japan, but they could relate to the Baltic states and to areas of Finland and Eastern Europe that the Soviets had claimed since 1939. The phrase could also mean that parts of the British Empire (such as India and Hong Kong) could leave the Empire—as Washington had long hoped they would.

Another provision of the charter declared that Churchill and Roosevelt "will endeavor with due respect for their existing obligations, to further the enjoyment of all States, great or small, victor or vanquished, of access, on equal terms, to the trade and to the raw materials of the world which are needed for their economic prosperity." Churchill strongly objected to this clause, for he knew that it aimed at destroying the exclusive British Commonwealth preferential trading system. The Prime Minister yielded only when "with due respect for their existing obligations" was added. But he finally had to lend his endorsement, owing to British dependence on American aid. In February 1942, the United States turned the screws tighter. In return for a long-term lend-lease pledge from FDR, the British had to promise to discuss the dismantling of their Imperial Preference system after the war.

Roosevelt and Hull were elated. The key to postwar planning lay in Anglo-American cooperation, for before the war these two powers accounted for half the world's trade. Postwar trade would now be conducted on American, not British, terms. As Hull had long believed, moreover, economic success could be quickly translated into a political triumph. In mid-December, British Foreign Secretary Anthony Eden visited Stalin, who immediately demanded Anglo-American agreement to cutting up postwar Germany and giving Russia control of the Baltic states and a large slice of eastern Poland. Eden refused, arguing that he would have to clear the matter with Roosevelt. Stalin angrily replied, "I thought the Atlantic Charter was directed against [Hitler and Tojo]. It now looks as if the charter were directed against the U.S.S.R." Eden would not budge, but the following month when FDR asked Russia to agree to the Atlantic Charter, Stalin did so only after adding the formal reservation that "the practical application of these principles will necessarily adapt itself to the circumstances, needs, and historic peculiarities of particular countries. . . ." Behind these words lurked the causes of the cold war: Soviet refusal to allow anyone to claim a right to interfere in Eastern Europe, an area which the Germans had twice used as an avenue to invade Russia during the previous twenty-five years.

Roosevelt and Hull had brought the British to heel. Stalin, however, refused to accept the American vision of the postwar world when he added the reservation to the Atlantic Charter. He had given warning.

## ONE WORLD—OR GULLIBLE'S TRAVELS

The central issues of the cold war were thus in plain view as early as 1942. The question was how FDR and Stalin would deal with them. Washington officials agreed that the most important priority must be a global economic program, resting on Atlantic Charter principles, that would remove the danger of another worldwide depression. Assistant Secretary of State William Clayton put it starkly: if Americans could not be assured of an orderly and secure postwar world, the United States itself would become an "armed camp," living "by ration books for the next century or so." Vice-President Henry Wallace warned that without comprehensive planning, "a series of economic storms will follow this war. These will take the form of inflation and temporary scarcities, followed by surpluses, crashing prices, unemployment, bankruptcy, and in some cases violent revolution." Wendell Willkie capsulized the solution to such dangers in the title of his best-selling book of 1943, *One World*. Willkie's blasts at exclusive spheres (particularly those in the British Empire) led Churchill sarcastically to suggest that Willkie's book be subtitled "Gullible's Travels." But the phrase "one world" said it all: haunted by the ghost of Depression Past, Americans determined to find markets for their inevitable postwar surpluses in a one world undivided and indivisible.

Point

Of course this required, as Hull told Roosevelt in early 1942, that the United States oppose any "arrangement which would make the Soviet Union the dominating power of Eastern Europe if not the whole continent." The last part of Hull's admonition was crucial. The Eastern European market itself was not of great importance to Americans, but Soviet control would present a grave danger as a precedent. If Stalin succeeded there, he might use it as a lever to gain influence in the remainder of Europe. If he did forge a private sphere, moreover, his success might encourage the British to repudiate the Atlantic Charter and reestablish their own spheres. Instead of one world, there would again be, as in the 1930s, a world divided economically and politically. Roosevelt and his countrymen would be back in the dark days of 1938. As Wallace, Clayton, and many others warned, that simply could not be allowed to happen.

In early 1942 Roosevelt tried to bring the Russians around. In one sense his position was weak, for American military forces were inactive in the European theater and retreating in the Pacific. The Japanese mopped up the Philippines, humiliating captured Americans by driving them on a horrible "death march" on the Bataan Peninsula. General Douglas MacArthur, American commander in the Pacific, fled the Philippines to establish headquarters in Australia. The Japanese would not be stopped until midyear at the gigantic naval battle of Midway, and then in hand-to-hand fighting at Guadalcanal. In Russia, Soviet troops only slowed Hitler's forces. This added to Roosevelt's problems, for Stalin pushed hard for Anglo-American armies to open a second front in Western Europe to relieve the German pressure.

Against this background, Soviet Foreign Minister V. M. Molotov arrived in Washington in May 1942. He wanted to discuss postwar boundaries, but FDR avoided embarrassing conversations by suggesting instead that after the war "four policemen" (the United States, the U.S.S.R., Great Britain, and China) should patrol the world. Molotov and later Stalin readily agreed, for they believed that as a "policeman," Russia would be able to take what it needed in Eastern Europe. This was not at all what Roosevelt had in mind, but the contradictions in the "four policemen" concept would not be faced for another three years. Despite the idea's problems, Roosevelt wanted to avoid discussing specific postwar settlements. Such a discussion could lead to Soviet-American arguments and disillusionment at home. Moreover, the longer he waited, the more financial and military power FDR thought he could bring to bear on Stalin.

A second remark to Molotov had immediate repercussions. Roosevelt promised a second front by late 1942. He probably did this to quiet Molotov on the boundary question. Whatever the reason, Molotov and Stalin were elated. They believed that the Soviet people would shortly no longer be alone in engaging Hitler's main forces. But there was no second front in 1942. Churchill killed the plan by refusing to agree that such a campaign could be safely opened so soon.

The prime minister instead urged that Anglo-American forces invade North Africa, where the Nazis and their French collaborators, the Vichy French government, held strategic positions in the Mediterranean. Roosevelt realized that Churchill was advancing this plan in part because North Africa had long been vital to the British and French empires, but he finally acquiesced in order to get American soldiers engaged in the European theater. The operation also led Roosevelt into a closer working relationship with the Vichy French. If the Vichyites would cooperate, the invasion might be bloodless and a large part of the French fleet turned over intact to the Allies. Roosevelt's working with Nazi collaborators has since been roundly condemned, particularly after the invasion of November 1942 turned out to be not at all bloodless. FDR survived this mistake, but he could not overcome Stalin's bitterness that the second front had been promised—and then repudiated. It almost looked as if Churchill and Roosevelt preferred reclaiming the British and French empires while leaving Stalin alone to endure the full might of Hitler's armies.

*Broken Promises*

## 1943—TURNING OF THE TIDE

The Grand Alliance of the United States, Great Britain, the Soviet Union, and their allies was in trouble by early 1943. Roosevelt tried to repair the damage by asking Stalin and Churchill to meet him at Casablanca in January. Stalin refused, pleading that the climactic struggle at Stalingrad required his constant attention. He asked only that the second front be opened immediately. FDR replied that this certainly could be done in 1943. At Casablanca, however, Churchill once more refused, insisting that since the Allies were not yet militarily prepared, they instead should move from North Africa into Sicily and then Italy. Roosevelt again reluctantly acquiesced, but tried to soften the blow for Stalin by announcing that unlike the case in 1918, when the Germans were

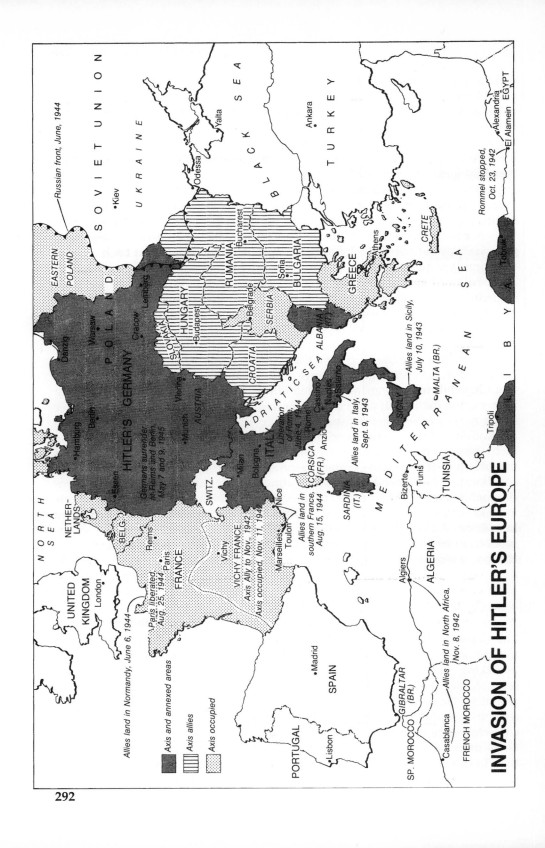

# INVASION OF HITLER'S EUROPE

Legend:
- Axis and annexed areas
- Axis allies
- Axis occupied

Map labels and annotations:

UNITED KINGDOM, London

NORTH SEA

NETHER-LANDS

BELG.

Allies land in Normandy, June 6, 1944

Paris liberated, Aug. 25, 1944 • Paris

Reims • Reims, Germans surrender at Reims and Berlin, May 7 and 9, 1945

FRANCE

Vichy • VICHY FRANCE, Axis Ally to Nov. 1942, Axis occupied Nov. 11, 1942

SWITZ.

Marseilles, Toulon, Nice

Allies land in southern France, Aug. 15, 1944

SPAIN, • Madrid

PORTUGAL, Lisbon •

GIBRALTAR (BR.)

SP. MOROCCO, Casablanca •

FRENCH MOROCCO

Allies land in North Africa, Nov. 8, 1942

ALGERIA, Algiers •

MEDITERRANEAN SEA

TUNISIA, Bizerte, Tunis •

SARDINIA (IT.)

CORSICA (FR.)

Allies land in Italy, Sept. 9, 1943

Anzio, ITALY, Cassino, Rome, Liberation of Rome, June 4, 1944, Naples, Salerno, Bologna, Milan

SICILY, Allies land in Sicily, July 10, 1943

MALTA (BR.)

Tripoli •

L I B Y A, Tobruk

Rommel stopped, Oct. 23, 1942

El Alamein, Alexandria, EGYPT

HITLER'S GERMANY, Essen •, Hamburg •, Berlin •, Munich •, Vienna, AUSTRIA

Danzig, Warsaw •, P O L A N D, Cracow •, Lemberg

EASTERN POLAND

Russian front, June, 1944

S O V I E T   U N I O N

U K R A I N E, Kiev •, Odessa, Yalta

BLACK SEA

SLOVAKIA, HUNGARY, Budapest •

RUMANIA, Bucharest •

CROATIA, SERBIA, Belgrade •

ADRIATIC SEA, ALBANIA

BULGARIA, Sofia •

GREECE, Athens

CRETE

TURKEY, Ankara •

292

not thoroughly defeated, the Allies this time would accept only "unconditional surrender." This sudden announcement was risky, for it threatened to lengthen the war by driving the German people into a last-ditch resistance. Roosevelt and Churchill were willing to take that chance in order to placate Stalin. By insisting on unconditional surrender they assured Russia that although no second front was in sight, they would nevertheless continue the war until a defeated Germany would no longer threaten the Soviets.

It was interesting diplomacy, but also increasingly irrelevant. A week after Roosevelt made his pledge, Russian armies stopped the Germans at Stalingrad, capturing hundreds of thousands of Hitler's finest troops. By midsummer the Soviets had regained two-thirds of their lost territory. They had successfully battled 80 percent of Hitler's total force and were now driving it back without the often promised, but never delivered, second front. Stalin's need for his Western allies was still great, but dropping markedly. Indeed Roosevelt was becoming the supplicant, for he wanted the Soviets to promise they would fight Japan after the conclusion of the European struggle. The military campaigns of 1943 drastically changed the diplomatic relationships between Russia and her two allies.

And so did a political crisis in Italy. After invading that country, the Americans and British refused to allow the Soviets to have any influence in reconstructing the Italian government. Fearful that Stalin would help Italy's large Communist party gain power, Churchill argued, "We cannot be put in a position where our two armies [the American and British] are doing all the fighting but Russians have a veto and must be consulted." Roosevelt agreed, observing that the Allied military commander, General Dwight D. Eisenhower, must have complete authority. The Russians were thus excluded, but at a tremendous cost. For Stalin would repeatedly use the Italian precedent to justify Russian control of postliberation policies in Eastern Europe. If the Russians were not to have "access" to Italy as the Atlantic Charter seemed to promise, then, Stalin could argue, the charter might as well not apply to Eastern Europe either. He was indeed perfectly willing to accept such a division. Stalin believed that each ally had its own security interests. The question was whether the Americans would accept this splitting of Europe into political spheres or try to have it both ways: exclude the Soviets from Italy but insist that the United States have a voice in Eastern Europe. That key issue was becoming sharper.

Churchill, Roosevelt, and Stalin met for the first time at Teheran, Iran, in late November 1943 to bind together the splintering alliance. On the surface, discussions went smoothly. The three men established easy personal relationships, doubtlessly helped along by Churchill's and FDR's firm pledge that a second front would be opened in France within six months. Stalin in turn promised he would fight Japan after Hitler's defeat. Roosevelt himself raised the crucial question of Russia's western boundary, telling Stalin that he "did not intend to go to war with the Soviet Union" over Russian absorption of the Baltic States. It was also quickly agreed that the Polish-Russian boundary must be moved westward at the expense of Poland.

But the conference floundered on a pivotal question of the Polish postwar government. Since 1940 a pro-Western Polish government-in-exile had operated in London, while a pro-Communist Polish regime worked out of Russia. When the London group refused to accept a new Polish-Russian boundary, Stalin would not recognize the group. The hatred burst into the open in mid-1943, when the bodies of 4,200 Polish soldiers were discovered in Poland's Katyn Forest. The London Poles immediately—and correctly—charged Russia with having slaughtered the men during the fighting in 1940. These charges added a tragic dimension to an already explosive problem. The Big Three could not reach agreement on either the composition of a postwar Polish government or a Polish-German boundary. Stalin wanted the boundary moved westward, but Churchill particularly resisted this move on two grounds: it would unduly weaken postwar Germany (a prospect that did not at all displease Stalin), and it would repeat the mistakes of 1919 by giving the Germans a cause for future aggression. For the next eighteen months the sore of Poland festered, spreading a cancerous infection within the Grand Alliance.

Two acts of wartime diplomacy had now been played. The first had set the theme with the Atlantic Charter and the British and Russian opposition to its principles. The second act, played out in Italy and Teheran, had brought into the open the dilemmas that would wreck the postwar peace. The third act, which in traditional theater resolves the crises of Act II, would occur with the Yalta conference and its aftermath. Instead of resolving the crises, however, Act III was to become a nerve-wracking, multibillion-dollar, forty-year-long serial.

## ONE WORLD BECOMES TWO: YALTA AND AFTERWARD

On June 6, 1944, Allied troops under the command of General Eisenhower swept ashore on the Normandy beaches in the largest amphibious operation in history. Led by General George Patton's Third Army, the forces broke through German resistance, liberating Paris in late August and crossing into Germany in mid-September. Devastating air raids hit German war industries, while an unsuccessful attempt to assassinate Hitler in July by some of his closest military advisors indicated the extent of the Nazis' internal weakness. Stalin meanwhile launched a major offensive that conquered much of Eastern Europe in 1944.

Churchill now faced a dilemma. The British had important economic and political interests in Hungary, Yugoslavia, and particularly Greece. The Greek situation was especially sensitive, for that nation bordered the Eastern Mediterranean (one of the so-called lifelines of the British Empire to Egypt and India). But Churchill's attempt to restore the Greek king's power had produced a civil war in which Greek Communists helped the antimonarchical forces. The prime minister flew to Moscow and in a dramatic meeting with Stalin worked out, on a half-sheet of scrap paper, a deal that would give Russia control of Rumania and Bulgaria, grant Churchill full power in Greece, and divide Yugoslavia and Hungary equally. Roosevelt warned that he would not be bound by this division. But Churchill went ahead, over violent American objections, to quell the

D day: the Normandy invasion, June 6, 1944. (*Robert Capa/Magnum.*)

Greek civil war with force. Stalin kept his part of the bargain by staying out of that situation and clamping firm control over Rumania.

As they made plans for the Big Three conference scheduled at the Soviet resort city of Yalta in February 1945, gloom was settling over Washington officials. It became even gloomier when in December 1944 the Germans launched a last-ditch counteroffensive that drove a huge bulge into Eisenhower's lines. At Bastogne, Belgium, only heroics by General Patton and a surrounded American force—which refused to surrender—delayed the German onslaught and finally ended the "Battle of the Bulge." The rapidly advancing Soviets were meanwhile only fifty miles from Berlin. As Roosevelt sat down at Yalta to reconstruct the world, he held few high cards. Roosevelt nevertheless managed to work out agreements on four major problems.

First, the Big Three decided to flesh out a postwar United Nations organization. The Big Three had concluded in 1944 that the United Nations, like the League of Nations, would have a Security Council dominated by the four great powers, a General Assembly, a Secretariat, and an International Court of Justice. Roosevelt agreed to give the Soviet Union three votes in the General Assembly (in order, so Stalin urged, to offset Great Britain's half-dozen votes of the Commonwealth nations), but only if the United States might, if it wished, also have three votes. Each of the Big Four (the United States, the U.S.S.R., Great Britain, and China) would have a veto in the Security Council in regard to substantive issues. Roosevelt had maneuvering room here, for both Stalin

General George Patton, General Dwight Eisenhower, and U.S. servicemen, Germany, 1945. *(Dwight D. Eisenhower Library.)*

and the United States insisted on preserving maximum national power through possession of a veto. The United Nations, however, would be able at the most to *maintain* the peace. The question at Yalta was whether the Big Three would be able to *construct* a peace.

A second point of discussion offered some hope, for Roosevelt and Stalin quickly settled Far Eastern questions. In return for Russia's promise to fight Japan within three months after Hitler's surrender, FDR secretly agreed that Stalin could have influence in Manchuria, possession of southern Sakhalin and the Kurile Islands (located off the tip of northern Japan), and a lease on the base of Port Arthur. American military advisors, including General MacArthur, had warned Roosevelt that Russian warfare against Japan was necessary if he were to avoid the 1 million Allied casualties that would probably result from an invasion of the Japanese home islands. Given such warnings, and the probability that, once in the Pacific war, Stalin would take by force what FDR had already promised, the Yalta agreements on the Pacific were realistic.

A third discussion at Yalta did not end as amicably, for it involved Poland. The Teheran decision on a new Polish-Soviet border was quickly reaffirmed, but again no agreement could be reached on the Polish-German boundary. Stalin wanted the border moved to the Oder and Neisse rivers, so that Poland would incorporate large areas of prewar Germany. Churchill objected: "It would be a pity to stuff the Polish goose so full of German food that it died of indigestion." (Stalin later provided the necessary medicine simply by removing

*[handwritten margin note:] Russia will help fight Jap.*

hundreds of thousands of Germans from the area and giving it to Poland. The West would not recognize the boundary until the early 1970s.)

The major argument, however, centered on the composition of the Polish government. In late summer 1944, a new controversy had further embittered this issue. When Russian troops drove to the outskirts of Warsaw, Polish underground fighters attacked the Nazis within the city. The Soviet attack then stalled, in part for military reasons, although Stalin was forthright in calling the anti-Soviet underground "a handful of power-seeking criminals." The Nazis then turned and exterminated the Poles. Stalin would not allow American planes to attempt dropping supplies to the underground fighters until it was too late. In January 1945, after the Soviets had finally captured Warsaw, Stalin moved in his own Polish regime as the legitimate government.

Churchill and Roosevelt refused to go along. They finally obtained Stalin's agreement that the government was to be "more broadly based" and "recognized with the inclusion of democratic leaders from Poland itself and from Poles abroad." The new government would hold "free and unfettered elections" as soon as possible on the basis of universal suffrage and a secret ballot. (Such an election was not held.) Shortly after Yalta, FDR and Churchill exchanged angry notes with Stalin over the meaning of "reorganized." Stalin insisted this meant simply adding a few pro-Western Poles to the Communist regime in Warsaw. Roosevelt, however, demanded a complete restructuring of the government. He was on weak ground. At Yalta his military chief of staff, Admiral William Leahy, had remarked that the Polish agreement was "so elastic that Russians can stretch it all the way from Yalta to Washington without technically breaking it." Roosevelt understood, but insisted that this was the best he could do. The President made only one other halfhearted effort to straighten out his policies when he asked Churchill and Stalin to sign a "Declaration on Liberated Europe," which pledged application of Atlantic Charter principles to liberated countries. Stalin accepted only after inserting an amendment that made the declaration meaningless.

The failure to reach an agreement on Poland made this issue the "symbol" of the Russian-American conflict. But that struggle increasingly focused on Germany, the fourth question discussed at Yalta. Roosevelt had been torn on this issue. He wavered between fixing the Germans once and for all ("they should be fed three times a day with soup from Army soup kitchens" he commented, and once even mentioned the possibility of mass castration), and rebuilding Germany under tight controls so it could be the core of a healthy Europe. He finally chose the second alternative under strong pressure from Hull and Stimson. They argued that American prosperity depended on a prosperous Europe, which in turn required a rebuilt Germany. That nation, after all, had been the industrial hub of the continent for nearly a century.

To Stalin, however, this policy looked suspiciously like 1919 all over again. "I will not tolerate a new *cordon sanitaire*," he announced pointedly in the spring of 1945. Nor, above all, did he want a united, prosperous Germany as the cornerstone of such a *cordon*. When at Yalta Stalin tried to gain agreement on dismemberment of Germany, Roosevelt and Churchill refused to agree. Stalin then attempted to obtain $20 billion in German reparations (half for the Soviet Union), in order to limit Germany's industry and help rebuild Russia. FDR referred this to a study commission with instructions that the $20 billion figure be only a "basis for discussion."

The disagreement over reparations was a clue to the failure of the Yalta Conference. Stalin had two primary objectives: dismembering German power so that it never again could threaten Russia, and acquiring great quantities of industrial machinery to reconstruct the Soviets' own war-devastated economy. Large German reparations would help Stalin gain both objectives. When Roosevelt and Churchill refused to agree on reparations, Stalin faced two alternatives: either obtain large loans and credits from the United States to rebuild Russia quickly, or impose such absolute control over Eastern Europe (including East Germany) that Eastern Europe would serve as a Russian-dominated buffer zone between Germany and the Soviet Union and also be forced to surrender its industry for Russia's benefit.

Stalin tested the first alternative several times between 1943 and 1946. The critical moment came in January 1945, when Molotov asked Washington for a $6 billion credit. W. Averell Harriman, the American ambassador in Moscow, advised Roosevelt that the Russians "should be given to understand" that financial aid would "depend upon their behavior in international matters." Harriman's advice was accepted. The United States refused to discuss postwar aid to Russia unless the Soviets essentially opened Eastern Europe as the Atlantic Charter asked. This Stalin refused to do.

Within six weeks after Yalta, an iron curtain descended over parts of Eastern Europe. In Rumania, which had been an ally of Hitler, a Soviet official gave the king two hours to establish a government acceptable to the Communists, accentuating his demand by slamming the door so hard that the plaster cracked around the door frame. In Poland, Stalin refused to make radical changes in the pro-Russian government. Amid this rapid deterioration, Roosevelt died on April 12, 1945. His legacy to Vice-President Harry S. Truman was not a Grand Alliance but the beginnings of the cold war, caught perfectly by FDR in a comment made privately during his return from Yalta: "The Atlantic Charter is a beautiful idea." It was nothing more.

## THE HOLOCAUST

In February 1945, as the Big Three were concluding their discussions at Yalta, Allied troops reached the Nazi concentration camps and began liberating the survivors. Over the next few months, photographs of the gas chambers and the crematoria at Auschwitz, Buchenwald, Bergen-Belsen, Dachau, Theresienstadt, and other camps were published. The evidence of Hitler's extermination campaign, which claimed the lives of between 4 million and 6 million European Jews, shocked the civilized world. In fact, the U.S. government had known of the Nazis' "final solution" since at least mid-1942. For two years, however, the Roosevelt administration had done virtually nothing to try to stop it.

Many proposals to aid Jews in the concentration camps had been made, but State Department and War Department officials always found reasons why they were "impractical." Some suggested that efforts be made to ransom Jews by offering money or supplies (such as trucks or tractors) in return for their release. However, this suggestion would require negotiating with Nazi leaders and ran an additional risk of strengthening the German war effort, so it was rejected. Another suggestion was that the United States announce it would undertake reprisal air raids against German cities if the murders continued. But retaliatory bombing, it was said, would lower the United States to the moral level of the Nazis and would so anger the German leaders as to provoke an even more vindictive response.

The most concrete proposal was that the United States bomb the gas chambers and crematoria at Auschwitz, or at least the railroad lines that were carrying additional victims there. Located in southwestern Poland, Auschwitz was the scene of mass exterminations of Jews; by the summer of 1944, it was within easy range of American airplanes. Indeed, the Air Force was routinely dropping thousands of bombs on industrial sites within a few miles of the camp. In June 1944, a plea to bomb the rail junctions leading to Auschwitz was transmitted to the War Department. Without seriously investigating its merits, the department rejected the idea on the grounds that such a bombing mission was of "very doubtful efficacy" and would divert air support from more crucial operations. The historian David Wyman has concluded that all these explanations were simply excuses: "To the American military, Europe's Jews represented an extraneous problem and an unwanted burden."

By January 1944, even some American officials recognized that the Roosevelt administration's policy was a disgrace. A report prepared for Secretary of the Treasury Henry Morgenthau, "On the Acquiescence of This Government in the Murder of the Jews," charged the State Department not only with a "wilful failure to act" but also with "wilful attempts to prevent action from being taken to rescue Jews from Hitler." Morgenthau and others took the report to the President, who immediately established the War Refugee Board in order to "rescue the victims of enemy oppression who are in imminent danger of death and otherwise to afford such victims all possible relief and assistance consistent with the successful prosecution of the war." The board worked to evacuate Jews from Axis-occupied territory, set up refugee camps, and send relief supplies to concentration camps. Despite its accomplishments, the War Refugee Board did not receive full cooperation from either the State Department or the War Department and lacked either the funds or the power to save many lives.

The United States was not the only Allied government to fail to act. Great Britain turned down requests from the War Refugee Board for cooperation, as did the Soviet Union. British officials in the air ministry and the foreign office rejected appeals to bomb Auschwitz by saying "this idea would cost British lives and aircraft to no purpose. . . . it is fantastic and should be dropped." Winston Churchill understood more clearly than most Allied leaders the enormity of the Nazi campaign to exterminate European Jews. In July 1944, he commented privately: "There is no doubt that this is probably the greatest and most horrible single crime ever committed in the whole history of the world." But Churchill's government, like Roosevelt's and Stalin's, remained aloof. For all the differences between the three Allied leaders over foreign policy, one thing they agreed on was that action to aid European Jews was not a priority.

# TRUMAN

After Roosevelt's death in April 1945, a very different figure entered the scene. Harry Truman had been a Missouri judge, politician, and U.S. senator, but he had no experience in foreign affairs. He entered the White House at precisely the time American policy was hardening against the Soviets. Truman was never confronted with the alternatives that Roosevelt had struggled with between 1942 and Yalta. FDR had tried to handle the dilemma—whether to try to enforce the Atlantic Charter or accept political-economic spheres—by delaying until, as in the Polish question, the problem had to be confronted. Truman's temperament was more impulsive and decisive. He disliked delays, preferring to decide on a policy and then make it work. This decisiveness was reinforced by a second influence: his jealousy of, and determination to protect, his presidential powers. This jealousy, indeed Truman's enormous personal insecurity during 1945, resulted in part from his realization that he was an accidental President following in the hallowed footsteps of Roosevelt. Truman was adamant in not allowing these circumstances to weaken the presidential powers. This determination easily led him to be as tough as the toughest of his advisors.

Twenty-four hours after entering office, and before he was thoroughly briefed on incredibly complex foreign policies, Truman told his secretary of state, "We must stand up to the Russians at this point and not be easy with them." This view was reinforced by advisors—Ambassador to the Soviet Union Averell Harriman, Leahy, Secretary of the Navy James Forrestal, Secretary of War Stimson—all of whom harbored deep suspicions about even negotiating with Russia. By late spring Truman was convinced that he might not get "100 percent of what we wanted; but that on important matters . . . we should be able to get 85 percent." He fully realized how American economic and military power, including the possibility of a newly developed atomic bomb, might obtain that 85 percent.

The restraints on Truman were few but significant. The Red Army controlled Eastern Europe and had been the first to reach Berlin. Eisenhower's troops might have raced the Soviets to the German capital, but the American commander wisely calculated that it would not be worth the lives lost. The political division of Germany and Berlin for occupation purposes, moreover, had been determined at earlier conferences. The mighty Russian force, astride the eastern half of Europe, was the most formidable barrier conceivable to Truman's hope for realizing "85 percent."

But the President also had problems at home. Between 1940 and 1944, American industrial production rose 90 percent; total production of goods and services rose 60 percent. Some place had to be found to sell the products of this system or Americans would relive the horrors of the 1930s. Many, particularly those in the business community, believed that the Soviets could become the great market. "Russia will be, if not our biggest, at least our most eager, consumer when the war ends," predicted the president of the U.S. Chamber of Commerce in 1944. Pro-Russian sentiment also had such other roots as the propaganda about the valor of "our Russian allies"; the movies sentimentalizing the Soviets (for example, *Mission to Moscow*); and the sanguine statements at the end of the conferences, which failed to mention the deep divisions separating the two nations. These Roosevelt also bequeathed, along with an increasingly anti-Russian policy. Truman could not get tough with Stalin until Americans were ready to move straight from hot war against a common enemy to cold war against a former ally. Very few were ready to do that in 1945. The President therefore had to educate the country about the "85 percent." He received help from Stalin.

## STALIN

The Soviet dictator, in the words of a fellow Communist who knew him well, combined "the senselessness of a Caligula with the refinement of a Borgia and the brutality of a Czar Ivan the Terrible." Nevertheless, this observer continued, "Viewed from the standpoint of success and political adroitness, Stalin is hardly surpassed by any statesman of his time." Seizing control after Lenin's death in 1924, Stalin became supreme through blood purges. He brutally collectivized Soviet agriculture, ruthlessly shaped Russia into a growing industrial power, and through luck and skill survived the hatreds of both the Western powers and Germany between 1931 and 1945. The impact of World War II alone was incalculable: more than 15 million—perhaps 20 million—Russian dead (six hundred thousand civilians starved to death in the battle of Leningrad alone); thousands of cities and villages decimated; and agriculture and, to a lesser extent, industry destroyed. During the war, moreover, Stalin knew that his countrymen would fight harder for Mother Russia than for his Communist party, so he loosened some internal controls. But as the Nazi threat disappeared, he quickly reimposed an iron grip. He was Russian power in person.

In an attempt to explain why Stalin would not come to terms with the United States, a few historians have since blamed the dictator's paranoia which, indeed, made him increasingly deranged. This is slippery territory, but several facts are beyond dispute. No foreign diplomat—not even those dealing frequently with him—suggested that Stalin showed any signs whatsoever of paranoia during 1945–46. More important, the substantive issues dividing Russia from the West were more than sufficient to start the cold war. In the Soviet mind, East–West animosity was natural, for East was Communist, West capitalist, and therefore, according to Leninist teachings, conflict was inevitable. Woodrow Wilson and other Western leaders had earlier made Lenin appear to be a prophet when they sent troops into Russia. And during the 1930s the Soviets were convinced that the West, particularly at Munich, was trying to drive

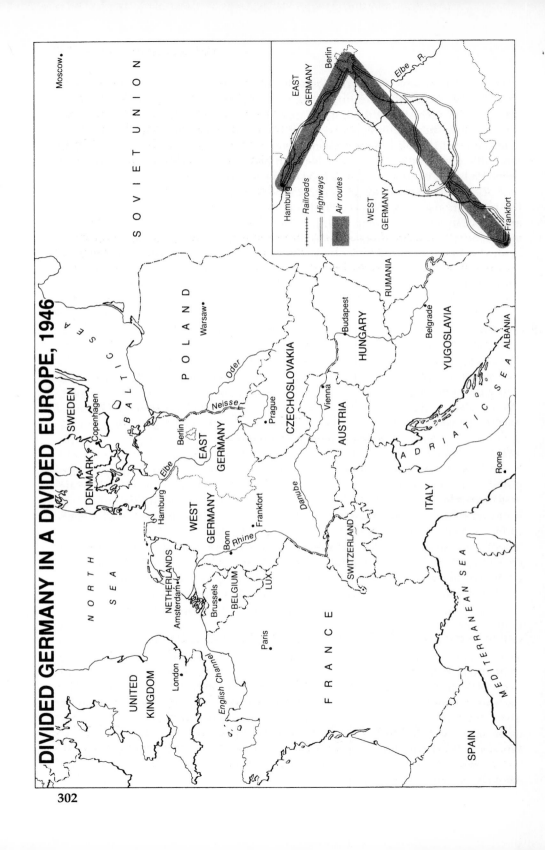

# DIVIDED GERMANY IN A DIVIDED EUROPE, 1946

Hitler to war against Russia. These historical events were little emphasized by Americans after 1945, but they were stamped indelibly on the Soviet mind. Stalin determined that history would not repeat itself. So after Truman prevented him from obtaining access to German industrial plants by dividing Germany and, in 1947, integrating Western Germany into the U.S. camp, Stalin used the Red Army to dismantle Eastern Germany and clamp his control over Eastern Europe. This was hardly classic Communist revolution "from the bottom up." Instead, Stalin imposed control from the top down.

But he did so selectively at first. Hungary, Finland, Bulgaria, and Czechoslovakia remained independent to a considerable extent throughout 1946 and 1947. Eastern Europe did not fall behind the iron curtain with one loud clang, but instead disappeared bit by bit as the victim of an escalating Soviet-American argument between 1945 and 1948. Nor did Stalin attempt to overthrow Western European governments during this time. The State Department told Truman in June 1945 that the Russians "are not too greatly concerned about developments in Western Europe so long as the Western European countries do not show signs of ganging up on them." Stalin had broken away decisively from the Marxist-Leninist ideal that world revolution be given top priority. He would settle for "socialism in one zone"—a zone of Eastern Europe, which would protect Russia strategically and help reconstruct it economically. In this zone Stalin would tolerate no intervention. After all, Churchill and Roosevelt had tolerated none in their Italian zone. Consequently, when Truman vigorously urged democratic elections in Poland and Rumania, Stalin blandly replied, "If a government is not Fascist, a government is democratic." But on another occasion he was more candid with Truman: "A freely elected government in any of these countries would be anti-Soviet, and that we cannot allow." He would not complain if the West controlled Italy or Latin America, but, Stalin told the President bluntly, he expected Truman to show similar consideration for Soviet interests.

Put simply, Russia's attention focused on Eastern and Central Europe, while America, as a worldwide, expansive economic power, took the entire globe as its province—including the Soviet sphere. For these reasons, the cold war erupted not over questions in the Americas, Asia, or even Western Europe. It broke out because of American demands in Eastern and Central Europe, that is, in the areas that the Russians were determined to dominate brutally.

## POTSDAM: THE TURN IN AMERICAN POLICY

The Soviets, so Washington officials thought, might not become capitalists overnight, but at least they might tolerate the economic plans that underlay the U.S. postwar program. "Nations which act as enemies in the marketplace cannot long be friends at the conference table," Assistant Secretary of State William Clayton announced in 1945. When this was applied to Communists and capitalists, Clayton was actually asking for oil and water to mix. Truman was meanwhile demanding at least an 85 percent dissolubility. But the President believed that there was no alternative.

In late April he had a stormy session with Molotov over the Polish issue, which produced only more mistrust. In June Stalin inserted several pro-Western Poles into a government that remained staunchly Communist. Making the best of a bad situation, Truman recognized the Warsaw regime, hoping that over time he could use American financial aid to change the government's policies. The Big Three then concentrated on the conference at Potsdam (on the outskirts of obliterated Berlin), where, it was hoped, German questions would be handled more satisfactorily than had those concerning Poland.

It was not to be. After acrimonious debates, the two central questions—the German-Polish boundary and reparations—were lumped together and compromised. Stalin and the Poles received permission to govern part of East Germany de facto (although the area was not formally given to Poland), but Truman in turn required Stalin to accept a reparations package that gave Russia almost nothing out of the German industrial sectors controlled by the British and American armies. The United States therefore retained the power to reindustrialize West Germany (and in late 1945 and 1946 this was accomplished in rapid steps), but at the price of dividing the country. For if Stalin could not get reparations from the West, he would cordon off and exploit East Germany. Truman's policy, therefore, helped ensure the division of Germany.

The deal also marked a significant turn in American policy. A divided Germany meant a divided Europe. It meant giving up trying to apply Atlantic Charter principles everywhere. Truman did not fall back immediately. Throughout 1945 and early 1946, his new secretary of state, James F. Byrnes, worked on peace treaties that would open Eastern Europe; but the Soviets refused to agree. Potsdam was a portent. It demonstrated the abyss separating the Allies on the central issue of Germany, shook Truman with the realization that he would not get his "85 percent" after all, destroyed the hope for an immediately united and open Europe, and, therefore, forced American officials to return to the drawing board and devise new postwar plans.

## CHINA: ANOTHER REVOLUTION AMID THE COLD WAR

At Potsdam, Truman and Stalin did extend earlier agreements on Asian affairs. The Asia that they discussed, however, was changing radically and rapidly. Japan, which had dominated the area for a half-century, reeled from military defeats. In 1944 American forces took Saipan and Guam in bloody fighting, providing bases from which the U.S. Air Force devastated Japanese cities. Japan's industrial plants suffered (although not nearly as much as the Air Force claimed at the time), but the raids proved especially effective as a terror weapon. In one attack on Tokyo, windswept fires killed more than eighty thousand Japanese.

As Japan tottered, American officials hoped that China might replace the Japanese as the balance-wheel of Asia. Roosevelt pursued this dream, for he clearly realized that if China became dominant in Asia, then it, in turn, would be dependent on American economic and military aid and, he hoped, advice.

# MARGARET BOURKE-WHITE AND PHOTOJOURNALISM

If Edward R. Murrow's radio broadcasts brought the sound of war to Americans, then Margaret Bourke-White's photographs brought them its awful sight. Bourke-White's career had especially prepared her to document the terrible consequences of modern technology gone berserk. After graduating from Cornell University in 1927, Bourke-White, like many other artists at the time, became fascinated with the aesthetic of the machine. She photographed industrial plants and equipment because she thought them "sincere and unadorned in their beauty." In 1930, when Henry Luce began publishing *Fortune* magazine—which believed that "any modern estheticism must embrace the machine"—he invited Bourke-White to

Margaret Bourke-White, 1943. (*Margaret Bourke-White*, Life Magazine © *Time Inc.*)

serve as associate editor and photographer. Not only did she photograph examples of American technology, but she also documented military rearmament in Germany and the construction of huge dams and bridges in Russia.

By the mid-1930s Bourke-White had shifted her focus from the triumph of industry to the human anguish it produced. She began to photograph the depression's impact on America: the dust bowl, with its parched land and skeletons of dead animals; Southern prisons, with their potbellied guards and black chain gangs; tenant farms, with their tar-paper shacks and emaciated children. She published many of these photographs in *You*

Winston Churchill sitting for Margaret Bourke-White, London, 1940. *(Margaret Bourke-White, Life Magazine © Time Inc.)*

*Have Seen Their Faces* (1937), with commentary by Erskine Caldwell (to whom she was married for three years). Bourke-White was not associated with the Farm Security Administration, which accumulated 200,000 photographs of rural America, but was, in the words of her biographer, "virtually a one-woman FSA photographic project." When Luce introduced *Life* magazine in 1936, Bourke-White became a major contributor. She was instrumental in the development of photojournalism—structured photo-essays that told a logically ordered story.

During World War II, Bourke-White was at the height of her creative power. As an accredited Air Force photographer, she observed the assembling of airplane squadrons in England, flew with bombing missions over Africa, and documented American Army operations in Italy. She accompanied General George Patton in his final drive along the Rhine, so was able to photograph

Joseph Stalin smiling for Margaret Bourke-White, Moscow, 1941. (*Margaret Bourke-White,* Life *Magazine © Time Inc.*)

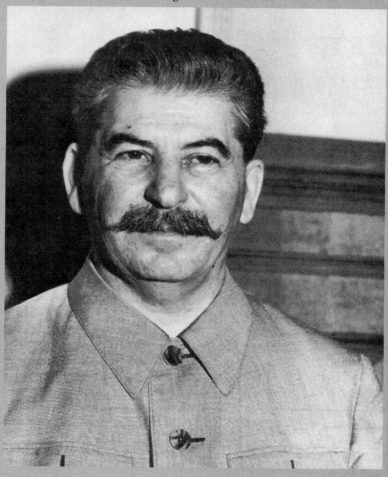

the survivors of the concentration camp at Buchenwald and the charred corpses at the Leipzig-Mochau labor camp. When Patton ordered two thousand German civilians to walk through Buchenwald, Bourke-White photographed them attempting to avert their eyes from the piles of dead bodies. She also photographed Nazi officials who, fearing Allied retribution, had committed suicide along with their wives and children. Her account of all this appeared in *Dear Fatherland, Rest Quietly* (1946).

After the war Bourke-White photographed people and events in India and South Africa, and, when the Korean War began, she returned to the battlefield. She was one of the first to appreciate the possibilities for aerial photography provided by the newly developed helicopter. Then, during the 1950s, Bourke-White was stricken with Parkinson's disease, an illness that gradually deprived her of the ability to hold a camera steadily. She believed the disease had been triggered by the hardships she had experienced in Korea, but added: "If I had been in a position to make a choice between getting my photographs in the fog, rain and wild mountains of Korea set against the risks involved, I would still choose to get my story—Parkinson's or no Parkinson's." She battled the disease valiantly—a struggle she described in *Portrait of Myself* (1963)—until her death in 1971.

Nazi concentration camp, 1945. (*Margaret Bourke-White*, Life *Magazine © Time Inc.*)

FDR's schemes even went beyond this. He believed that China and the United States in tandem could dismantle the British and French empires in Asia (including Hong Kong, India, Singapore, Burma, and French Indochina), allow China either to absorb or to police these areas, and then have China and the United States develop them. This vision explains why throughout 1943–44 Roosevelt refused to agree that after the war France should be allowed to reenter Indochina. The President hoped that this area—comprising Vietnam, Cambodia, and Laos—would become a United Nations trusteeship under the day-to-day control of China.

In mid-1944 FDR's dream collapsed when a crisis ripped apart Sino-American relations. The focal point was Chiang Kai-shek, China's leader and the pivot for Roosevelt's plans. Harry Hopkins, Roosevelt's closest advisor, had commented that China could be one of the postwar Big Four, but only "if things go well with Chiang Kai-shek." During the spring of 1944 Chiang's government was gravely beset from two directions. The Japanese launched an attack on South China in an attempt to destroy airfields from which American planes (including the famed "Flying Tigers") were bombing Japan's bases. FDR pleaded with Chiang to throw his armies and American-supplied equipment fully into the battle, but Chiang stalled.

Roosevelt then urged him to name the American commander in China, General Joseph Stilwell, as head of the Chinese armies. Chiang and Stilwell had never gotten along; "Vinegar Joe" condescendingly called Chiang "Peanut" because of his bald head, but also because of his refusal to fight the Japanese. Chiang interpreted FDR's request as an insult and seized the opportunity to throw Stilwell out of the country in September 1944. Roosevelt lost his illusions about China. At Yalta and Potsdam, Americans and Russians settled Asian problems without bothering to consult with the Chinese.

Chiang refused to fight the Japanese because he was saving his troops for a struggle-to-the-death with the Chinese Communists. Since 1927 this battle had raged, primarily in the north, where Mao Tse-tung's Communist armies had taken refuge after their famous "long march" to escape Chiang's wrath in the mid-1930s. By 1944 Mao had consolidated and expanded his power, gaining support among the peasants (by 1945 he controlled one-quarter of China's population), and effectively fighting guerilla wars against both Chiang and the Japanese.

## THE BOMB

In early 1945 the United States had decided to stick with Chiang and not deal seriously with Mao. By the time of the Potsdam conference in July, however, this policy was insufficient. Stalin's armies would be in the Pacific theater within a month, raising the unattractive prospect that his and Mao's forces might link up in Manchuria. At Potsdam Truman worked diligently to remove that threat. He gained from Stalin the promise that the Soviet dictator would recognize Chiang as the official government of China. After a private lunch with Stalin, moreover, Truman told his advisors that he had "clinched" the

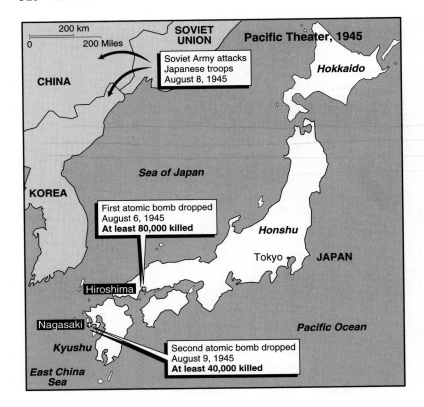

Pacific Theater, 1945

Soviet Army attacks Japanese troops August 8, 1945

First atomic bomb dropped August 6, 1945 **At least 80,000 killed**

Second atomic bomb dropped August 9, 1945 **At least 40,000 killed**

*had felt was atomic bombs were good for policing the world*

*no end of war point for paper*

Russian acceptance of an open door in Manchuria. In return, the President reaffirmed the promises of Far Eastern territory made by Roosevelt to Stalin at Yalta. Truman was elated, but not satisfied. By dropping an atomic bomb on Japan on August 6 and again on August 9, he tried to end the war as soon as possible, before American troops had to die in an invasion of the home islands and preferably before Russian troops were able to gain control of large chunks of Japanese-occupied territory.

The terrible weapon that Truman now held before the world had resulted from a series of breakthroughs in physics during the interwar era. In 1939 Albert Einstein, the greatest and best-known of the physicists, wrote a simple one-page letter to Roosevelt urging him to begin development of the unknown weapon. Fearful that Hitler might obtain it first, FDR poured $2 billion into the secret Manhattan Project. (The fears were fortunately misplaced; German scientists ran into numerous dead ends and received little understanding from Hitler.) From the beginning, the bomb was built to be used only under American control. Roosevelt evidently saw the bomb as giving him the military power he would need to police the postwar world without having to take the politically unpopular step of sending American armies overseas. At no time did he ever seriously consider sharing the bomb's secrets with Stalin. The President considered it a diplomatic as well as a military weapon. Again, Truman fully accepted Roosevelt's policies. Scientists from the University of Chicago sug-

Hiroshima, two hours after the atomic blast, two miles from the center of the explosion. The photographer later died of injuries from the explosion. *(Culver Pictures.)*

gested to Truman that demonstrating the bomb in an uninhabited area would be considerably more humane than devastating a city, and might convince the Japanese to surrender. But the President sided with his Scientific Advisory Panel, which rejected the suggestion on the grounds that the bomb might not work properly or, if it did, it should be used for maximum military effect. Besides, only two bombs could be built by August.

In mid-July 1945 the bomb was tested, successfully, for the first time. Truman was at Potsdam having difficulty with Stalin, but was greatly "pepped up" by news of the test. The President now began to assume an even tougher position with the Soviets. The Americans, as Churchill privately remarked at Potsdam, "do not at the present time desire Russian participation in the war against Japan." Truman no longer needed or wanted Stalin's help in the Far East. The Big Three urged Japan to surrender unconditionally, including abdication of the emperor, or face "utter devastation." The Japanese government refused the ultimatum. Hiroshima was obliterated on August 6, killing, searing, and infecting with deadly radiation more than one hundred thousand people. Two days later Russia declared war and invaded Manchuria. On August 9 a second bomb destroyed Nagasaki. Stimson now pushed Truman to accept a Japanese surrender that would keep the Emperor in place, but without his traditional powers. Byrnes, however, warned that if he did so the American people would "crucify" the President. An unsure Truman hesitated while U.S.

bombers killed thousands in heavy conventional air attacks between August 10 and 14. The militarists continued to hold out, but on August 14–15, the emperor took the virtually unprecedented step of overruling the government and accepting surrender if the terms did not completely destroy his role in Japanese society. Truman now accepted the condition. World War II was over. It might have ended days before had Truman earlier accepted the emperor's role.

The atomic bomb had helped end one conflict, and throughout the summer of 1945 Truman, Stimson, and other top officials discussed how it might be used as a negotiating weapon against Russia to preclude a third world war. In June, according to Stimson's diary, he and the President had talked of possible concessions that the bomb might bring from Russia, and Truman "mentioned the same things that I was thinking of, namely the settlement of the Polish, Rumanian, Yugoslavian, and Manchurian problems."

By September, however, Stimson had changed his mind. He warned the President that if the United States refused to cooperate with the Russians in controlling the bomb, but merely talked to them while "having this weapon ostentatiously on our hip, their suspicions and their distrust of our purposes and motives will increase." Truman refused either to negotiate the issue or to use the bomb as an explicit threat against the Soviets. Perhaps he felt that he did not have to, for Stalin well knew that the President had used it without qualms against the Japanese.

## BACK TO THE 1920s

To drive home his concern over postwar Asia, Truman ordered American planes and troops to help Chiang's forces reach Manchuria ahead of Mao's Communist troops. By the end of 1945, 110,000 American soldiers were in China, many of them in the north. But all this was of no avail. Chiang was unable to consolidate his power, the Russians remained in Manchuria until they took out $2 billion worth of plant and equipment, and American officials failed to work out an agreement between Chiang and Mao.

Truman now turned to General George Marshall, the man primarily responsible for planning and coordinating the entire American military effort during the war. Marshall hoped to find a third faction in China that was "liberal" and middle of the road, then construct a political solution embracing Mao's Communists, Chiang's Nationalists, and the third group. It was hoped that after a period of time Chiang would be able to absorb the third group and subordinate the Communists. During the spring of 1946 Marshall nearly pulled off the miracle, but by summer civil war had reopened.

China was too polarized between reactionaries and Communists to develop any third force. Chiang cared no more for Marshall's telling him—the leader of China—how to run the country than he had for Roosevelt's advice. Marshall reported home that he was confronted by "the incompetence, inefficiency, and stubbornness of the Central government—qualities which made it very difficult to help them." Chiang and Mao, moreover, hated each other.

When skirmishes erupted between their forces Chiang decided that, with his superiority in men (two to one over Mao's) and firepower (nearly three to one), he could destroy the Communists militarily. Chiang persisted despite Marshall's warning not to try to settle the problem on the battlefield. After initial defeats, the Communists inflicted a series of losses on the Nationalists in mid-1947. Truman privately berated Chiang, but stuck with him to the bitter end. As Admiral Leahy explained the cruel dilemma, "If we break with [Chiang's] Central Government the result will be that we will have no friends in either of the Chinese factions and no friends in China."

But Chiang was past help. In 1947 Washington officials seized the only alternative. They assumed that if Mao won, China would be too chaotic to govern and the Soviets too poor to provide major help. The United States decided to stay out of a situation it could not control. Truman instead turned to Japan to create once again the stability in Asia that Chiang could not provide. During 1947–48 Japanese industrial and political controls were lifted by the American occupation authorities. Stalin did not relish the idea of a revived Japan, but he had nothing to say about it, for the United States had frozen Russia completely out of the Japanese occupation. Japan was on the road back. Truman's approach to Asia smacked of the American policy at the Washington Naval Conference of 1921–22, not of 1943. And it fit in perfectly with the new American approaches in Europe.

## NEW SCIENCE—NEW DANGERS

World War II produced not only the greatest slaughter in history but, ironically, advances in technology and medicine that saved millions of lives and made life more decent for millions of others. Much of the new technology, such as the atomic bomb and the increased size and firepower of air force bombers, aimed at greater and more efficient killing. But Charles Lindbergh, for example, quietly conducted dangerous experiments with new fuel mixtures that eventually doubled the range of warplanes and, later, commercial airliners. Engineers also developed jet propulsion to drive planes not with the old, complex, and less efficient piston engines, but with a great jet of air created by a gas turbine. Before the war, German and British scientists had raced to see who would build the first jet plane. The Germans won one week before World War II erupted, but they could not get planes into operation until 1944. Then American engineers took over. They and the British built jet airliners that, after several disasters, resulted in the Boeing 707. This airplane revolutionized transoceanic flights when it appeared in 1958. Airtime between New York and London was cut in half, to only six hours. A new phrase, "jet-setters," described the wealthy who flew around the world as easily as their grandparents had traveled from New York to Chicago.

Other than atomic energy, no discovery proved more important than penicillin. This miracle drug was first glimpsed in 1889, when European scientists discovered "good" bacteria that killed "bad," life-threatening bacteria. In

1928 a British scientist, Alexander Fleming, accidentally discovered a broth on which mold *(Penicillium notatum)* grew. This mold possessed powers to kill bacteria without harming the body's healthy cells. A decade later Americans finally appeared in the story. Only their huge chemical companies had the resources (especially the expensive distilling and fermentation facilities) required to develop penicillin. By 1944 these companies produced enough of the drug to treat all Allied battle casualties, so the danger of infection could be dramatically reduced. By 1950, the companies exported enough to meet world demand. The breakthroughs in developing penicillin and sulfa drugs radically changed worldwide health care. Half the drugs used in 1947 had been unknown in 1937.

DDT (dichloro-diphenyl-trichloro-ethane) became a miracle worker in destroying deadly insects. During World War I, more people had died of typhus (carried by lice) than had died of battlefield injuries. But when a typhus epidemic appeared in Italy during late 1943, Allied physicians quickly stopped it by spraying DDT on seventy thousand people in a single day. One expert, Trevor I. Williams, estimates that within the following twenty-five years about 1.5 billion people were for the first time in history free of malaria because DDT destroyed the deadly mosquito carrying the disease. A Swiss scientist had discovered DDT's powers in 1939 as he worked in the new field of synthesizing chemical agents. (This was the same field that during the 1920s and 1930s had produced the first plastics, synthetic rubber, nylon, and rayon.) Again, however, U.S. plants took the European discovery, then refined and mass-produced it for the world's health, and America's wealth.

But there was a flip side. As penicillin and DDT extended life expectancy and reduced infant deaths, world population increased until observers feared that starvation, even political revolution, would result from overcrowding. Others worried that these scientific miracles saved lives only by altering nature's order. For example, animals that fed on mosquito larvae could be endangered when DDT destroyed the larvae. Traces of the deadly drug began to appear in foods eaten by humans. The new sciences of atomic physics, synthetic chemistry, and drugs altered the world by helping the Allies win World War II and by improving living standards, but they also raised new possibilities of destruction.

## CRISES IN THE MEDITERRANEAN—AND AT HOME

There was no peace at the end of World War II. Instead of a world of the Atlantic Charter, Americans witnessed the failure of a settlement in Europe, the refusal of Russia to leave Austria (on the grounds that it was a conquered, not a liberated, state), and Soviet rejection of a plan to control atomic energy on American terms. In February 1946, Stalin warned the Russians that because of the outside threats they would have to revert to rigid state control and make additional sacrifices under new five-year plans. He was tightly closing off the Soviet Union and its sphere in Eastern Europe.

Washington buzzed with ominous rumors that Stalin's speech was the "declaration of World War III," since the world could not exist "half free and half slave" any more than it had in the 1930s. In March, former Prime Minister Churchill traveled to Truman's home state of Missouri to announce that "an iron curtain has descended across the continent." He pleaded for a joint Anglo-American atomic force to confront the Soviets, especially since "God has willed" that Anglo-Saxons, not Communists or Fascists, should first have the bomb. Stalin, in reply, compared Churchill's "racial theory" with Hitler's and called Churchill a warmonger. For his part, Truman had no intention of tying American power to a declining Great Britain, but he believed, like Churchill, that the Soviets respected only superior strength.

The first test came in Iran during March 1946. During the war the United States, Great Britain, and Russia had occupied Iran to assure a route for the delivery of supplies to the Soviets. The Big Three agreed to leave six months after the war ended. But in February 1946, Russia refused to evacuate its troops, claiming that under Western pressure the Iranians were not honoring earlier agreements with the Soviets on oil and security along the Iranian-Russian border. The security issue was of most importance; Stalin did not want to move his troops if the vacuum was to be filled by British oil and political interests. The United States swiftly reacted. It first took the issue to the United Nations. Then, as Stalin moved reinforcements toward the border, Secretary of State Byrnes issued a warning to stop the troop movement or the United States would take countermeasures. The Russians stopped, settled directly with Iran (on Iranian terms), and withdrew their forces.

Truman had won a significant victory. But the Russians continued to press for advantages and additional security around their southwestern borders, and especially pushed Turkey for a new treaty on the Dardenelles, the vital passage between the Black Sea and the Mediterranean. With American encouragement, including the beefing up of the U.S. fleet in the Mediterranean, Turkey refused to negotiate. In Greece, the civil war against the British-supported king picked up steam, with Yugoslavia's Communist regime funneling aid to the revolutionaries. The cold war had expanded from Central Europe through the eastern Mediterranean.

In February 1947 the British suddenly informed the State Department that they could no longer afford to support the antirevolutionary forces in Greece. Decimated by two world wars, Great Britain's economy was suffering through one of the coldest and most destructive winters in history. The British Empire had reached the end of the line. The question became whether the United States would assume the British role. This question was actually academic, for in Iran and Turkey the United States had already taken the lead. The Truman administration had been waiting for this opportunity.

Here was a chance to create a long-term anti-Soviet policy. Equally important, Washington officials needed to mobilize the United States for an all-out cold war effort. This became urgent as they realized that such an effort would cost large sums of money, but that Congress was considerably more interested in budget balancing and tax cutting than in another expensive overseas commitment.

Somehow, the American people's benign view of world affairs had to be transformed and brought into accord with the tough policies that Washington had actually been following since at least early 1945.

## "SCARING HELL" OUT OF THE AMERICAN PEOPLE

Truman encouraged the American people, in four stages during late 1946 and early 1947, to commit themselves to an anti-Communist crusade. The first stage occurred in September 1946, when Secretary of Commerce Henry Wallace attacked American policies for alienating the Soviets. He urged a more conciliatory approach along economic lines that would open Russia to American goods. Wallace advocated much the same policy that Hull and others had pushed during the war. That approach, however, had not worked. Truman and Byrnes had moved to the next step: political and military confrontation. When Byrnes demanded Wallace's resignation, Truman fired his secretary of commerce. Some pro-Wallace support appeared, but of greater significance was the number of former New Dealers (led by a new organization called "Americans for Democratic Action") who attacked Wallace as being naive and defended Truman's policies. The President purged the Cabinet of his leading critic and in the process discovered important political support.

The second stage of intensified anticommunism occurred during the 1946 congressional elections. The Republicans scored a stunning victory by capturing both houses of Congress for the first time since 1928. Truman was humiliated; one poll showed his support, which had stood at 87 percent of the electorate in 1945, sinking to only 32 percent. The President, however, turned the defeat to his own advantage. Many of the newly elected senators had advocated tax cuts but had also taken a tough line against subversives at home and abroad. Since Canada had just uncovered a spy ring that had apparently been sending atomic secrets to Russia, attacking subversives promised rich political rewards. Leading members of the Senate's new "Class of '46," including Joseph McCarthy of Wisconsin, John Bricker of Ohio, William Jenner of Indiana, and William Knowland of California, exemplified this Republican line.

Truman tried to undercut their position by proposing a government loyalty program under executive control that would ferret out subversives in Washington. The President was taking the lead in the hunt for Communists. The loyalty program would not pry the needed monies from a tightfisted Congress for a major foreign policy offensive, but it did enable Truman to play on Congress's fear of communism. The British retreat from Greece provided the opportunity for the President bluntly to inform Senate and House leaders that this was the moment to put up or shut up.

The third stage of Truman's program was magnificently handled by Under Secretary of State Dean Acheson when, in a private session, he told the congressional leadership that "like apples in a barrel infected by one rotten one, the corruption of Greece would infect Iran and all to the east." Asia Minor, Egypt, and then Europe would be next, as the dominoes would inevitably fall.

Believing personally that "we were met at Armageddon," Acheson eloquently concluded that "the Soviet Union [is] playing one of the greatest gambles in history at minimal cost. . . . We and we alone [are] in a position to break up the play." After a stunned silence, the key Republican senator on foreign policy issues, Arthur Vandenberg of Michigan, admitted that he had been persuaded. But he later warned Truman and Acheson that they would have to "scare hell" out of the American people if they hoped to get necessary public support for their new foreign policies.

Truman did just that with two speeches in the fourth stage of his program. The first address, at Baylor University in Texas on March 6, 1947, provided the classic explanation of why Americans must embark on a new crusade. "Peace, freedom, and world trade are inseparable," Truman began. "Our foreign relations, political and economic, are indivisible," he stressed. Then: "We must not go through the thirties again." Freedom of worship and freedom of speech are related to freedom of enterprise, for the first two "have been most frequently enjoyed in those societies" hospitable to free enterprise. And "least conducive to freedom of enterprise" is government intervention. Yet, the President warned bluntly, unless the world marketplace were quickly reconstructed and opened, even the U.S. government would soon have to step in to control American society in order to allocate goods and resources. Such government intervention "is not the way to peace," Truman concluded. The President's meaning was clear: his administration defined the state-controlled Russian economy as the deadly enemy of American prosperity, and he would do everything possible to save the world on this side of the iron curtain for the American form of "freedom of enterprise." If Americans did not join him, they risked losing all their most precious freedoms.

Six days later he issued the call to action with the "Truman Doctrine" speech. To make the case as forcefully as possible, Truman presented a world divided simply between "free peoples" and areas where "the will of a minority [is] forcibly imposed upon a majority." He included Greece and Turkey in the first group, but unless Congress immediately appropriated $400 million for their aid, they would slide into the second. Only the United States could now save the free world: "If we falter in our leadership, we may endanger the peace of the world—and we shall surely endanger the welfare of our own nation."

The speech "scared hell" out of many people. Senator Robert Taft (Republican of Ohio and the Republican leader) disliked it because "I do not want war with Russia." Doubts existed even within the State Department. Some officials had argued that Turkey, which had been pro-Hitler and was not at all democratic, hardly ranked as a "free people." It shared, moreover, a very sensitive boundary with Russia. But Truman nevertheless decided to use the opportunity in Greece to send arms to Turkey. "Turkey was slipped into the oven with Greece because that seemed to be the surest way to cook a tough bird," as one official observed. More generally, the speech was notable because it defined the Communist threat as ideological, and therefore asked Americans to commit themselves against that threat globally. This request has been the most explosive part of the Truman Doctrine, for once the threat was defined ideologically, Americans had to be ready to intervene anywhere in the world where that threat was perceived, regardless of whether the area in question was in fact directly threatened by Russia or, later, China. Soon presidents could use the doctrine as a rationale for American military intervention in Southeast Asia as well as in Europe.

It was "the most fundamental thing that has been presented to Congress in my time," Vandenberg rightly observed, and so Congress wanted to examine Truman's proposal carefully. On March 21, the President gave it a major push when he issued the executive order that set in motion the loyalty program to find Communists in the government. It was the first such program ever established by a President (Congress had earlier legislated the hunts), the first ever established in peacetime, and—most important—the first under which a person could be dismissed for political beliefs. Truman had defined the issue, created a growing consensus, and outflanked congressional opponents. One Truman supporter in Congress chuckled at the trap the President had sprung on Republicans who wanted to fight communism, but not spend money: "Course they don't want to be smoked out. . . . They don't like Communism, but still they don't want to do anything to stop it. But they are all put on the spot now and they all have to come clean." The $400 million was soon appropriated, allowing American military advisors and equipment to aid the Greek government. The revolution finally subsided, however, only after Yugoslavia defected from the Russian bloc in 1948 and quit sending aid to the Greek rebels.

## AVOIDING THE 1930s: THE MARSHALL PLAN

Aid to Greece and Turkey was only a bandage on a large, festering wound that cut to the heart itself, the economy of Western Europe. Confronted with deteriorating economies, the Europeans were responding as Truman feared they would. A British Labour government, for example, nationalized leading industries, while in Italy and France large Communist and radical socialist factions gained strength. The American economy maintained its pace, but primarily because of a booming $15 billion in exports during 1946. If Europe could not continue to take its share of these exports, the United States would, in the President's words, "go through the thirties again."

The key to the problem was the lack of dollars that Europeans had to spend for American goods. Moreover, they could derive little from their war-ruined economies to sell to the United States in order to acquire dollars. Great Britain, France, Italy, and the Benelux countries immediately needed about $5 billion if they hoped to buy goods from the United States to maintain a minimum standard of living.

In June 1947, the United States announced its plan to save itself and Western Europe. Newly appointed Secretary of State George Marshall offered massive economic aid but attached two conditions. First, the initiative in formulating a long-term program would have to come from the Europeans. They would have to commit themselves. Second, the program would have to be cooperative and open. This worked against Russian participation, for although the Soviets

George Marshall and V. M. Molotov, 1947. *(George C. Marshall Foundation.)*

*Marshall plan*

attended the first planning session in Paris, they quickly repudiated the Marshall Plan when they saw that they would have to accept American conditions, including the disclosure of Russian economic information. The Soviets claimed that the Truman Doctrine and the Marshall Plan had irretrievably divided the world into "two camps." To solidify their own camp, they announced a "Molotov Plan" to provide economic links for their East European empire.

The Western Europeans finally asked for $29 billion, but the United States cut this to $17 billion for four years, with $5 billion the first year. The figures are revealing, for they show that the decision to give aid was not based merely on anticommunism. More immediately, officials planned to provide the $5 billion they had long before calculated as the amount needed to keep American exports to Europe at necessary levels. When the aid was distributed, moreover, it went not primarily to Italy or France, where the Communist threat was most immediate, but to Great Britain and Germany, the potential industrial powerhouses for Europe. The Marshall Plan was publicly explained as part of the fight against communism, which it was to the extent that officials believed that poverty and unemployment in Europe would produce radicalism there and perhaps even in the United States. Most important, however, the plan aimed at averting a repeat of the 1930s by rebuilding the great market for American products and molding Western Europe into a long-term partner.

The United States had emerged from World War II as the greatest power in world history. Its incredible economic prowess, monopoly of atomic energy, and success as the world's oldest republic seemed to indicate that Americans were truly embarked on an "American Century," as *Life* magazine proclaimed in 1941. But by 1947 the Truman administration had shifted from trying to create a free world (particularly in China and Eastern Europe) to rebuilding nations this side of the iron curtain. The Marshall Plan seemed an intelligent, manageable, and limited plan for maintaining "freedom of enterprise" in the West. On the other hand, the Truman Doctrine proposed worldwide ideological and even military warfare. Truman had beautifully built a public consensus around both.

It now remained to be seen which road Americans would choose: the path that was more modest and whose terminus could be clearly seen, or the one that required commitment without an apparent limit on dollars, energy, and perhaps even lives. As the ancient Greeks understood, the essence of human tragedy is choice. But then they too discovered this after it was too late.

## Suggested Reading

Begin by consulting R. D. Burns, ed., *Guide to American Foreign Relations Since 1700* (1983); the relevant entries and bibliographies in Bruce Jentleson and Thomas Paterson, eds., *Encyclopedia of American Foreign Relations,* 4 vols. (1997); and the interpretations and bibliographies in Akira Iriye, *The Globalizing of America, 1913–1945* (1993). Military strategy is well analyzed in Ronald H. Spector, *Eagle Against the Sun* (1984); and H. P. Willmott, *The Great Crusade: A New Complete History of the Second World War* (1990). More specific problems are well treated in Mark A. Stoler, *The Politics of the Second Front* (1977); Mark A. Stoler, *George Mashall* (1989); and David Wyman, *The Abandonment of the Jews: America and the Holocaust 1941–1945* (1984). Randall B. Woods, *Fulbright* (1995), is helpful on the rise of internationalism. Robert C. Hilderbrand, *Dumbarton Oaks: The Origins of the U.N.* (1990) is standard. Important interpretations are Gabriel Kolko, *The Politics of War, 1943–1945* (1967); Joyce and Gabriel Kolko, *Limits of Power, 1945–1954* (1970); John L. Gaddis, *U.S. and Origins of the Cold War, 1941–1947* (1972); and Daniel Yergin, *Shattered Peace* (1990). The best detailed analyses of the politics surrounding the atomic bomb are Martin J. Sherwin, *A World Destroyed* (1975); and Richard Rhodes, *The Making of the Atomic Bomb* (1987).

For helpful overviews on the eruption of the Cold War, see Warren Cohen, *America in the Age of Soviet Power, 1945–1991* (1993), with good bibliography; Dennis Merrill, ed., *Documentary History of the Truman Presidency,* 10 vols. (1995); Melvyn Leffler, *Preponderance of Power* (1992); Lloyd Gardner, *Architects of Illusion* (1970); Richard Freeland, *The Truman Doctrine and Origins of McCarthyism* (1971); Dean Acheson's classic autobiography, *Present at the Creation* (1970); George Kennan's alternative views in *Memoirs, 1925–1950* (1967); Edward M. Bennett, *FDR and the Search for Victory: American-Soviet Relations 1939–1945* (1990); and Lawrence Wittner, *American Intervention in Greece, 1943–1949* (1982). Louis Fisher, *Presidential War Power* (1995), is standard. Blanche Wiesen Cook's essay on Eleanor Roosevelt's influence during and after the war is in Edward P. Crapol, ed., *Women and American Foreign Policy* (1992). Carolyn Eisenberg,

*Drawing the Line: The American Decision to Divide Germany, 1944–1949* (1996) is important and provocative. Michael Hogan, *The Marshall Plan* (1987), is the standard account.

The era's economic policies can be found in Richard N. Gardner's splendid *Sterling Dollar Diplomacy* (1956); its Latin American affairs in David Green, *The Containment of Latin America* (1971). For Asian relations, Christopher Thorne, *Allies of a Kind: The United States, Britain and the War Against Japan, 1941–1945* (1978) is classic; Akira Iriye, *The Cold War in Asia* (1974), an influential interpretation; and Michael Schaller, *The U.S. Crusade in China, 1938–1945* (1979), a good overview.

Theodore Brown has done a definitive study in *Margaret Bourke-White, Photo Journalist* (1972).

General Douglas MacArthur. *(Library of Congress.)*

# CHAPTER ELEVEN

# 1947–1952
## The America of the Cold War

This chapter discusses:
- The postwar boom in babies and wealth
- How Truman scored the greatest political upset of the century
- Why Americans and Chinese became mortal enemies
- Why the plague of McCarthyism spread across America

Two events in March 1947—the announcement of the Truman Doctrine and the institution of a federal loyalty program—set the tone for American foreign and domestic affairs in the cold war era. For a time Truman managed to turn cold war tensions to his own advantage, won reelection in 1948, and formed the North Atlantic Treaty Organization in 1949. With the outbreak of the Korean War in June 1950, however, the Truman administration became a victim of its own policies. In the President's view the North Korean attack closely resembled the Fascist aggression of the 1930s, but he found that waging a long, limited war imposed strains on society quite unlike those of World War II. Those strains—political, economic, social, and military—nourished a mood of hysteria in which the Truman administration could itself be charged, by Senator Joseph McCarthy and others, with being "soft on communism" at home and overseas. It seemed odd for a superpower to be so insecure.

## THE PHYSIQUE OF A SUPERPOWER: THE AMERICAN ECONOMY

By the late 1940s, as the battlefields cooled, the war dead were buried, and the world faced the unknown nuclear age, Americans were the richest people on the globe—indeed, the richest in recorded history. In merely five years after 1940, their gross national product (the GNP, or the sum of all goods and services they produced) doubled from $100 billion to $200 billion. With 6 percent of the world's population, the United States produced 50 percent of the world's goods. In 1946, the average American received $1,262 in annual income, compared with $653 in Great Britain and $45 in India. Half the world's population clustered around India's level.

Several reasons explained the incredible superiority. Two former competitors, Western Europe and Japan, had been largely destroyed by war. In the poorest nations, moreover, population increased faster than wealth. One United Nations (UN) expert believed "that the average and median standard of living of the world as a whole is actually lower today than in 1913." The British economist Thomas Malthus (1766–1834) had calculated that population would increase faster than food production until widespread poverty and starvation would result. "The multiplying Malthusians drag [the living standard] down faster than the horsepowerful Americans can raise it," worried one U.S. business observer in 1950.

The United States, however, was so rich and efficient that after a century of declining birthrates, it had a "baby boom" between 1946 and 1960 but still created ever-greater wealth. The immediate basis of the wealth was an economic empire developed during World War II. The government played a key role in the empire's creation. Of some $25 billion worth of new and expanded factories built during the war, the government built three-quarters of this amount. Most of this wealth resulted from government spending for the military effort. During the conflict itself, Americans enjoyed good incomes but had many fewer civilian goods available to buy. Two results became clear in 1946. First, Americans had a huge $140 billion savings pool to spend when goods were again in the stores (triple the savings in 1940); and second, war taxes and the general prosperity had redistributed incomes for the only time in the post-1900 era. The rich got relatively poorer; the poor richer between 1941 and 1945. Before the great crash of 1929, fewer than one-third of Americans qualified as "middle class" (that is, received incomes of $3,000 to $10,000). After the war nearly two-thirds qualified. This meant that the demand for automobiles and new homes would be deep and widespread. Wartime New Dealers created more new wealth and a more equitable distribution of that wealth than the peacetime New Dealers had thought possible.

Even as government peacetime spending dropped from $79.7 billion in 1946 to $55 billion in 1948 (due mostly to defense cuts), spending doubled on education (to 7.7 billion) and on highways ($3 billion). These figures included local, state, and national government expenditures. After the Korean War began in 1950, national government expenditures shot up, mostly on the military side, from $70 billion in 1950 to $151 billion in 1960. In addition, the GI Bill of Rights, passed by Congress in 1944, gave veterans money for attending school, starting businesses, and buying houses. In 1946 Congress also passed the Employment Act, which pledged in general terms to use government powers to keep unemployment low (about 6 percent seemed to be maximum). The act also created the President's Council of Economic Advisers to help assure that full employment measures would be followed. From now on, the American economic machine would have the government's hand near the steering wheel and its feet near the brake or accelerator, as the need arose.

Business and labor made the most of this help. For example, in the synthetic-rubber industry, government built expensive plants, then leased them to businesses during the war for $1 a year. As production rose, Americans had their own rubber supply, instead of depending on Asian or African producers, for the postwar automobile boom. The all-important rate of U.S. productivity (the amount of goods a worker produced each hour) had long led the world. During the war the productivity rate of American workers rose at about 7 percent annually, but after 1945 jumped to nearly 10 percent a year—the result of new technology and capital expenditures. Despite the economic expansion, the number of factory workers actually dropped in the late 1940s and early 1950s by about 4 percent, while new entrants into the labor market moved more into the expanding service and clerical sectors that oversaw the more efficient industrial complex.

A stunning example of this new technology was the chemical industry. Virtually unknown in 1920, it had since expanded three times faster than the rest of industry. As *Life* magazine bragged in 1953, "the $9 billion-a-year chemical industry has transformed American life. It has scrubbed the modern world with detergents, doctored it with synthetic drugs, dressed it in synthetic textiles, cushioned it with synthetic rubber, and adorned it from head to toe with gaudy plastics." Another example could be found in the rich farmlands. During the war agricultural income rocketed from $4 billion in 1940 to $12.3 billion in 1945, but acreage harvested rose only 4 percent. Not more land but new machinery and fertilizers made American farms the world's breadbasket. In 1947 one in six families lived on a farm; three decades later only one in twenty-six would do so, although an amazingly successful U.S. agriculture increased crop and livestock production nearly six times during those years.

After the war, much of the non-Communist world depended for survival on U.S. producers, but those producers also depended on the world. The nation's exports and imports amounted to only about 8 percent of its GNP, but that figure—around $12 to $20 billion—placed Americans behind only the British as the world's greatest traders. Exports of oil, iron and steel, and food were critical for U.S. prosperity. When America's best customers in war-devastated Western Europe lacked dollars to pay for these exports, the Truman administration created the Marshall Plan to pump billions of dollars quickly into Europe so it could purchase U.S. goods. After the Marshall Plan was ended in 1952, foreign aid nevertheless continued. In all, between 1945 and 1970 the U.S. government sent $125 billion overseas; most of it was used for buying American goods. Europeans received more than one-third of the figure, Asians about one-fifth, and Latin Americans only one-twelfth.

U.S. private firms meanwhile profited from investing directly in this reviving global economy. Between 1945 and 1950 they increased their overseas investment by 33 percent, to nearly $16 billion. Ten giant companies led the drive, with Standard Oil of New Jersey (later Exxon) in front. Standard Oil put about $1 billion into Venezuelan and Middle East oil development. Coca-Cola expanded so rapidly that, as one observer noted in 1950, "The Communists have made a propaganda point of the 'Coca-colonization' of the world. This has not stopped the wine-drinking Italians, among others, from taking heartily to Cokes" and enjoying wages from a bottling industry "worth several thousand jobs." *Fortune* magazine even bragged about "the spectacular export of American ideas to foreign minds." *Reader's Digest,* it pointed out, "is now printed in eleven languages, manufactured in fourteen foreign countries, sold in sixty-one." New York City, the world's money center, helped finance this expansion. U.S. banks had 95 branches overseas in 1950 and 536 in 1970.

Seldom in their history had Americans enjoyed such a chance to get rich. In early 1950, their steel industry worked at 98 percent of capacity, back orders for refrigerators were the largest on record, and the Christmas shopping weeks of 1949 had been the biggest in retailing history. Henry Luce, who had coined the phrase "the American Century" in his *Life* magazine in 1941, asked in 1950 why the world should—and would—be led by U.S. business: "First of all . . . American business" produces "more food, more houses, more doctors, . . . more amusements. . . ." Second, it "*has* licked the most serious problem of the economic cycle, namely, real want in the midst of plenty." Luce believed there might be economic downturns, but "the needy will be taken care of; they will be the first charge on the economy." In the American Century, the new superpower would do not only well, but good.

# CRISIS DIPLOMACY: 1947–1948

But Americans could do little good in Eastern Europe. Under Secretary of State Dean Acheson later observed that by 1948 the Truman administration had concluded that negotiations with Russia were useless, for "the world of the last half of the twentieth century was, and would continue to be, a divided world. The [decision] was to make the free—that is, the non-Communist–dominated—part of that divided world as secure and flourishing as possible." In 1947 Acheson wrote that because negotiations were not successful, "we must use to an increasing extent our second instrument of foreign policy, namely economic power," to protect the free world. The Marshall Plan indicated how the nation's tremendous economic strength would be used to create a postwar world on American terms. As Truman liked to put it, he was "tired of babying the Soviets."

The Republican-controlled Congress passed the $400 million Truman Doctrine appropriations for Greece and Turkey but proved extremely reluctant to legislate the nearly $12 billion, four-year program that Truman was asking for the Marshall Plan. Secretary of State Marshall and other officials warned that without the plan the American economy would lose its European markets, then shrivel. This decline, Marshall predicted, "would drive us to increased measures of government control." Such threats did not move Congress, for it believed that lowering taxes and encouraging private investment to go overseas would do the job. The administration vainly retorted that there was not enough time for such solutions and that private investors would not help until government monies rebuilt the infrastructure (roads, communications, banking facilities) of Western Europe. Congress refused to budge. Then came Czechoslovakia.

Although the Czechs survived as an independent people in 1945, their geographic position (bordering on both Russia and West Germany) forced them to be cautiously neutral in 1946. The Czech Communist party's power grew steadily, however, and by 1947 American diplomats had given up hope of bringing the nation into the West's camp. No one was prepared, though, for the sudden demand by Czech Communists, in March 1948, for key government posts nor for the threat that this demand would be enforced by the Red Army, then camped on the border. The government surrendered. Foreign Minister Jan Masaryk, long a hero in the West because of his opposition to Nazism, fell to his death from an upper-story window. The Communists claimed that he committed suicide. Truman and many other Americans believed that the Czech leader had been murdered. Whatever the cause, Russia was tightening its grip in response to the challenge of the Truman Doctrine and the Marshall Plan. Like Acheson and Truman, Stalin also neglected negotiations. He relied instead on the Soviet army. Rumania fell under complete Communist control in February; Czechoslovakia followed; then non-Communist leaders in Bulgaria, Hungary, and Poland either disappeared or fled to the West.

Truman, comparing these events to those that had triggered world war in 1939, rapidly moved to a tougher military position, which had long been urged by Secretary of the Navy James Forrestal and other officials. Forrestal was the most fervent anti-Communist of the President's close advisors. He became especially powerful in mid-1947, when Truman named him the first secretary of defense. In the new position Forrestal was head of all the military services, now centralized in the Department of Defense. A former investment banker, Forrestal had entered government service early in World War II and soon issued scathing warnings about postwar cooperation with Stalin. As he wrote to a friend in 1944:

> Whenever any American suggests that we act in accordance with the needs of our own security he is apt to be called a goddamned fascist or imperialist, while if Uncle Joe [Stalin] suggests that he needs the Baltic Provinces, half of Poland, all of Bessarabia and access to the Mediterranean, all hands agree that he is a fine, frank, candid and generally delightful fellow who is very easy to deal with because he is so explicit in what he wants.

Events after 1945 strengthened Forrestal's fears. He concluded that the United States and Russia would conflict politically, militarily, ideologically, and spiritually around the globe. To support this conclusion, he arranged that American diplomat George Kennan be brought back from the U.S. Embassy in Moscow so that Kennan could work out a long analysis of Soviet intentions that verified Forrestal's suspicions. Published in mid-1947 under the mysterious pseudonym of "Mr. X," Kennan's "The Sources of Soviet Conduct" concluded that two factors—Communist revolutionary beliefs and Stalin's need to create an external enemy as an excuse for tightening his dictatorship over the Russian people—made Russia like a "toy automobile" that, when wound up, would move inexorably onward until it struck a superior force.

Some Americans disputed this view. Walter Lippmann, the nation's most respected journalist, argued that traditional national interests, not a vague revolutionary mentality or Stalin's personal needs, governed Soviet policy. Therefore, Lippmann concluded, sincere negotiations could end the cold war by reconciling Russian and American national interests. Forrestal, however, found Kennan's analysis exactly suited to his own views and urged Truman to build the worldwide counterforce needed to stop the toy automobile. With the fall of Czechoslovakia, the President publicly advocated Forrestal's arguments.

On March 17, 1948, just seven days after Masaryk's death, Truman appeared before Congress to deliver a tough speech that urged restoration of selective service, universal military training for all young men (long a pet Forrestal project), and immediate passage of the Marshall Plan. A frightened Congress rushed the plan through, although the legislators moved more slowly on the draft and rejected universal military training. But the President had gained a triumph and, as in the case of the Truman Doctrine, had done so by frightening Congress, this time with claims that Stalin had monstrously subjugated another nation without any provocation from the United States. Americans were being conditioned to respond instantly whenever Truman rang out the Forrestal-Kennan version of Soviet policy. And Stalin was giving Truman ample opportunity to do so.

# DR. KINSEY AND SEX RESEARCH

In 1938 Alfred C. Kinsey began offering a course on marriage at Indiana University. Trained at Harvard as a zoologist, and a specialist in the behavior of the gall wasp, Kinsey had been teaching biology at Indiana for nearly two decades without causing a ripple. This abruptly changed when he introduced his new course. Dismayed at the lack of scientific evidence concerning human sexual behavior, Kinsey set out to compensate by taking the sexual case histories of anyone willing to cooperate. Kinsey assembled these data with the same compulsive care he had once devoted to collecting gall wasps, and soon found that people were volunteering information faster than he could transcribe it. By January 1948, when *Sexual Behavior in the Human Male* appeared, Kinsey's staff had accumulated more than 5,000 case histories. Supported by a small grant from the Rockefeller Foundation, the Institute for Sex Research ultimately acquired 17,500 case histories, although it never reached Kinsey's goal of 100,000.

Viewing himself as a scientist, Kinsey attempted to exclude all moral judgments from his work. He trained interviewers to ask direct questions, telling them that "evasive terms invite dishonest answers." One of his associates recalled: "We also never asked *whether* a subject had ever engaged in a particular activity; we assumed that everyone had engaged in everything, and so we began by asking *when* he had first done it." Kinsey presented his findings in cold, clinical language: 86 percent of American males had engaged in premarital sexual intercourse, 37 percent had on some occasion engaged in homosexual

Dr. Alfred C. Kinsey conducting an interview, 1948. (*Wallace Kirkland*, Life *Magazine* © *Time Inc.*)

activity to the point of orgasm, and 40 percent had carried on extramarital affairs. Kinsey concluded that existing laws were violently at odds with prevailing practices, that, indeed, better than nine of every ten American men at some time in their lives engaged in some form of sexual activity punishable as a crime. The book, in many respects, was a resounding plea to end hypocrisy by bringing public moral codes into line with private behavior.

The report was hailed by most psychologists and sociologists. One writer even claimed that Kinsey had done for sex "what Columbus did for geography." But many criticized Kinsey's methodology, pointing out that his statistical sample was drawn too heavily from underworld characters (because it was easy to obtain their case histories) and that his interview technique did not allow for faulty recall. Others believed that Kinsey took an overly mechanistic approach. Lionel Trilling, professor of English at Columbia University, attacked the report for assuming that "the whole actuality of sex is anatomical and physiological" and thereby ignoring emotional and affective considerations. Yet the book proved amazingly popular. It went through six printings in ten days, sold one hundred thousand copies in three months, and remained on the best-seller list for twenty-seven weeks.

In 1953 Kinsey published a sequel, *Sexual Behavior in the Human Female*. He claimed that since "the anatomic structures which are most essential to sexual response and orgasm are nearly identical in the human female and male," any dissimilarities in response reflected psychological and hormonal rather than physiological differences. Kinsey also reported "a marked, positive correlation between experience in orgasm obtained from premarital coitus, and the capacity to reach

Drs. William Masters and Virginia Johnson using dolls to illustrate their findings, 1970. (*Leonard McCombe,* Life *Magazine © Time Inc.*)

orgasm after marriage," and he found that women took part in premarital and extramarital affairs more often than was commonly supposed. The second report triggered even sharper criticism than the first, partly because of the double standard concerning sexual behavior but also because of growing conformity in the nation. One congressman denounced the book as "the insult of the century against our mothers, wives, daughters, and sisters," and a clergyman feared it "will in time contribute inevitably toward Communism."

In 1954, frightened by this public outcry, the Rockefeller Foundation (under its new president, Dean Rusk) cut off further support for Kinsey's institute. The man who had no difficulty probing the most intimate details of a person's behavior was virtually incapable of asking wealthy individuals for money. Bitter and disillusioned, Kinsey died in 1956 at the age of 60. His work, however, paved the way for many others, most notably William H. Masters and Virginia E. Johnson. Their books, *Human Sexual Response* (1966) and *Human Sexual Inadequacy* (1970), reported the results of laboratory experiments that measured the physiological changes in the human body during all phases of sexual stimulation. Yet their volumes, which also made the best-seller lists, caused little commotion, partly because Kinsey's pioneering work had made sex research respectable.

Dr. Ruth Westheimer providing sex counseling to viewers during her cable television program, "Good Sex." On hand to help her field call-in questions is actor Burt Reynolds. *(BETTMANN.)*

## STALIN'S RESPONSE: THE BERLIN BLOCKADE

The Marshall Plan aimed at rapidly rebuilding Western Europe for two purposes: to make it a market for American farms and factories and to erect a bastion against Soviet expansion. To accomplish these objectives, the reconstruction of West Germany was necessary, for Germany had been the industrial core of Europe. Unless West Germany rebuilt there was little chance Western Europe could recover. The West Germans, however, suffered from inflation in early 1948, primarily because they had printed paper money in such volume that the currency had become almost worthless. In the weeks following the Czech crisis, the United States decided to cure West Germany's economic ills with drastic surgery. The Truman administration pushed for a currency reform program that would replace the bad money with new, better-supported bills. Despite Soviet objection that this had not been discussed with them, the program went ahead without their approval. Then in June 1948 the Western allies asked West Germany to form a federal republic, that is, an independent nation comprised of the American, British, and French occupation zones. The new nation, which would include West Berlin (located deep within the Soviet zone), would be rebuilt and closely tied to the West through the Marshall Plan.

These moves directly threatened Stalin's plans to keep Germany so weak that it could never again threaten Russia. At the same time, he was challenged from within the Soviet bloc itself. Yugoslavia's Communist leader, Josip Broz (Marshal Tito) broke with Stalin, rooted out Russian attempts to assassinate him, and declared Yugoslavia a Communist but independent state. Tito had complete control of the nation, and his army was strong enough to make Russian troops pay dearly if they attempted to invade. "Titoism" became a new, hopeful sign to the West. The United States soon sent aid to the Yugoslavians.

Confronted with these threats in Germany and Yugoslavia, Stalin retaliated by trying to squeeze the West out of Berlin, thus removing that listening post within the Russian zone and weakening the entire Western position in Europe. In 1945 the Allies had made only oral agreements about the right to use railroads and highways through the Soviet zone to reach West Berlin. On June 24, 1948, the Russians stopped all surface traffic into West Berlin. The city stood isolated.

Truman correctly viewed Stalin's action as a challenge to American policy toward all of Germany. The President had three alternatives: pull out; use force to open access to Berlin, perhaps starting World War III in the process; or fly over the blockaded routes with supplies. Truman never seriously considered the first point. When the question arose in a Cabinet meeting, he interrupted to say, "There [is] no discussion on that point, we [are] going to stay, period." But he wanted no war and so followed the last alternative. The 2.5 million West Berliners required four thousand tons of food and fuel every day. With a massive airlift that landed a plane almost every minute of the day and night in the small West Berlin airport, the West soon delivered more than twelve thousand tons each day. For more than three hundred days pilots flew through impossible conditions, with some losing their lives in crashes during bad weather, in

Berlin airlift, 1948. *(Walter Sanders,* Life *Magazine © Time Inc.)*

order to carry out "Operation Vittles." West Berlin held on, and in the early summer of 1949 Stalin agreed to lift some of the road blockades.

The President's tough responses to the Greek, Czech, and Berlin crises won support at home. So also did his foreign policy in the Middle East. Since 1945 hundreds of thousands of Jews, many of them survivors of Nazi concentration camps that had become slaughterhouses, flooded into Palestine. For many decades Palestine had been British controlled, but since 1917, British officials had intimated that someday the territory could become the homeland that Jews had sought for centuries. As the Jews moved into Palestine, they met bitter resistance from Arabs already settled on the land. After a bloody conflict, the Jews proclaimed their new nation on May 14, 1948.

Fifteen minutes after the announcement, Truman recognized the new state of Israel. He did so over vigorous opposition from Cabinet advisors (particularly Forrestal), who feared recognition would turn the rich oil-producing Arab states against Washington. British Prime Minister Clement Attlee and other Western Europeans, who were utterly dependent on Arab oil, also opposed Truman's action. The President nevertheless listened to his political advisors. He acted because of his great admiration for what the Jews had accomplished in Palestine, but his recognition also assured Jewish political support in the 1948 presidential election. Attlee later observed, "There's no Arab vote in America, but there's a very heavy Jewish vote and the Americans are always having elections."

Whatever Truman's motivation, his handling of foreign crises during 1947–48 accelerated his triumphant run for the White House. In Europe Stalin had been especially helpful in this regard. Truman's closest political advisor told him that there was "considerable political advantage to the administration in the battle with the Kremlin."

## COLD WAR POLITICS: THE 1948 ELECTION

In 1948 Truman's Fair Deal program combined two features: promises to bolster American defenses against the perceived Communist menace and an expansion of New Deal benefits. On the domestic front, he appealed for civil rights legislation, federal aid to education, national medical insurance, power development in river valleys, increases in unemployment compensation and the minimum wage, higher taxes on corporations, and lower taxes on just about everyone else. Truman did not expect the Republican Congress to enact these measures, but he recognized that, in the words of one advisor, recommendations "must be tailored for the voter, not the Congressman." On the other hand, the Truman administration stepped up its attack on suspected subversives. Early in 1948 the Justice Department arrested a dozen aliens who belonged to the Communist party and instituted deportation proceedings against them. The attorney general also drew up a list of subversive organizations. None of these groups had an opportunity to contest their listing, and most then experienced difficulty in renting meeting halls or recruiting members.

Yet despite Truman's brand of liberal anticommunism, Democratic prospects in 1948 appeared bleak. When the party convention met that summer, newsmen reported that delegates looked like "mourners," caucus rooms resembled "weeping chambers," and the affair reminded them of a "wake." The *New York Times* observed: "The delegates drank bourbon, scotch, and rye as if it were so much embalming fluid—and with about the same effect." The reasons for such pessimism were apparent. The Republicans had captured Congress in 1946, and in the past when the party out of power had won control of Congress in an off-year election—Republicans in 1894, Democrats in 1910, Republicans in 1918, Democrats in 1930—it had gone on to victory in the next presidential election. Even worse, the Democratic party seemed to be coming apart at the seams. Henry Wallace was leading a defection on the left into the Progressive party, and Strom Thurmond was leading a defection on the right into the States' Rights Democratic party.

Henry Wallace announced his willingness to run on an independent ticket in December 1947. In the year since he had left the Cabinet, Wallace's differences with Truman had sharpened. Wallace considered the President too cautious in defending the civil liberties of radicals and the civil rights of blacks. But the major source of disagreement concerned foreign policy. Truman regarded the Soviet Union as inherently aggressive, but Wallace believed that Soviet moves often came in response to an American military buildup. Truman condemned Soviet control of Eastern Europe, but Wallace held that Stalin had legitimate reasons for establishing a political sphere of influence in that area, provided that such a sphere remained open to American trade and investment. Wallace maintained that the American plan for controlling atomic energy was bound to be unacceptable to the Russians. He criticized the Marshall Plan for turning Western Europe into a "vast military camp" and believed that universal military training would persuade people of the inevitability of war. Fearing that "we are whipping up another holy war against Russia," Wallace accepted the Progressive party nomination in the summer of 1948.

"We're on the march. We're really rolling now," Wallace told a friend after a speech before 32,000 cheering admirers. But his candidacy, itself a product of the cold war, soon became a casualty of that conflict. Wallace was widely denounced as a Communist dupe, in part because American Communists backed his candidacy, in part because he refused to repudiate their support, and in part because his views concerning the Soviet Union often coincided with the Communist party line. The Americans for Democratic Action, a group of anti-Communist liberals, claimed that the Progressive party represented "a corruption of American liberalism" for it had "lined up unashamedly with the force of Soviet totalitarianism." Democrat Lyndon B. Johnson of Texas remarked that Wallace drew his following from "the sallow, deluded lunatic fringe that bores and scavenges like termites eating away at the foundations of a strong building." Wallace, a devout man who never subscribed to the Communist position, failed to repudiate Communist backing, although to have done so might well have helped his candidacy. He probably believed that the number of votes to be gained was not worth the price—that is, contributing to what he considered anti-Communist hysteria.

Even had a majority of Americans not come to believe that Communists ran the Progressive party, events in Europe—particularly the coup in Czechoslovakia and the Berlin crisis—would surely have undercut Wallace's candidacy. As it was, the Progressives suffered a disastrous defeat. Wallace received only 1.1 million votes, or 2.4 percent of the total. The party received no electoral votes, and elected only one member, Vito Marcantonio of New York City, to the House of Representatives. Wallace made his best showing in New York, where he obtained 8 percent of the vote, and in California, where he received 5 percent. Nor did the Progressives have the murderous impact on the Democrats that had been predicted. Although Wallace garnered enough Democratic votes to deprive Truman of three states—New York, Michigan, and Maryland—his candidacy also acted as a lightning rod for anti-Communist sentiment. Wallace, not Truman, became the target, with the result that the Democrats could solidify their hold on voters, particularly ideologically conservative but staunchly Democratic Irish Catholics, who were motivated by such sentiment.

Just as the Progressive party hurt Truman in some respects and helped him in others, the States' Rights Democratic party cost Truman electoral support in the South but strengthened his position with black voters in the North.

Henry A. Wallace campaigning, August 1948. *(AP/WIDE WORLD PHOTOS.)*

The States' Rights party (labeled "Dixiecrats" by some and "Dixiebrats" by others) was created when the Democratic convention narrowly adopted a civil rights plank calling on Congress to support the President in guaranteeing blacks political and economic equality. A number of Southern delegates stormed out, called a convention in Birmingham, Alabama, and nominated J. Strom Thurmond, governor of South Carolina, for the presidency. The Dixiecrats did not imagine that Thurmond could win. Rather, they believed that his campaign would teach the Democrats not to take the South for granted and that it would possibly throw the election into the House of Representatives, where some sort of bargain might be struck with the Republicans.

The Dixiecrats bitterly criticized every attempt by the federal government to ensure racial justice. "We stand for the segregation of the races and the racial integrity of each race," they proclaimed. Proposals to outlaw the poll tax, to permit federal trials of lynch-mob participants, to provide economic opportunity for blacks—all were said to violate states' rights. Attempting to turn cold war rhetoric back on the Truman administration, Dixiecrats denounced the Fair Deal for its "totalitarian" features. The Fair Employment Practices Committee, Thurmond noted, was "patterned after a Russian law written by Joseph Stalin about 1920, referred to in Russia as Stalin's 'All-Races law.'" Although the party gained support chiefly for its stand on race, it also attracted Southern conservatives who had held a grudge against the welfare state since the late 1930s but had lacked a political vehicle for expressing their displeasure.

Dixiecrats and Progressives stood at opposite poles on the issue of civil rights. Wallace was assailed by Southern whites for his vigorous advocacy of racial equality and his refusal to speak before segregated audiences. Nevertheless, the two parties faced problems that were in some respects analogous. Just as Wallace failed to win the backing of most liberals, so Thurmond found that many Southern politicians, even those who shared his outlook, would not risk forfeiting their patronage and seniority by abandoning the Democratic party. Both candidates found the electorate enormously reluctant to "waste" a vote on a third party. Progressives and Dixiecrats wanted to bring the Democratic party around to their way of thinking, but their withdrawals proved only that the Democrats could win without them. Thurmond, like Wallace, polled 1.1 million votes, or 2.4 percent of the total. He carried four states (Mississippi, South Carolina, Louisiana, and Alabama), but by freeing the Democrats from the stigma of Southern racism he also simplified Truman's task of appealing to black voters. Blacks provided the Democrats' margin of victory in the crucial states of California, Illinois, and Ohio.

At the Republican convention, delegates were confident of victory. But the defection of the Progressives and Dixiecrats silenced two guns in the Republican arsenal. Republican candidate Thomas E. Dewey—who, according to one observer, sought the presidency "with the humorless calculation of a Certified Public Accountant in pursuit of the Holy Grail"—hardly made the most effective use of the weapons still at his disposal. Dewey often spoke in generalities, emphasizing national unity and avoiding harsh personal attacks. He did so for several reasons: his sharp criticism of Roosevelt in 1944 had not paid off; public opinion polls all declared him an easy winner if he did not alienate voters already committed to the Republicans; and growing international tensions meant that voters might resent sharp attacks on Truman. Confident of victory, Dewey spent much time campaigning for other Republican candidates in states that were not crucial to his own election.

The same polls that helped convince Dewey to pull his punches persuaded Truman to wage a bare-knuckled campaign. The Democrats emphasized welfare state liberalism but also exploited anticommunism. Truman endeavored to resurrect the Roosevelt coalition by promising to extend the Fair Deal and by charging that Dewey's election would usher in a depression as surely as did Herbert Hoover's. Truman peppered his speeches with references to "Republican gluttons of privilege," "bloodsuckers with offices on Wall

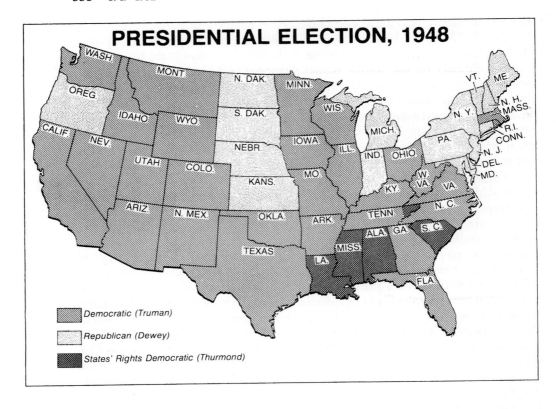

## PRESIDENTIAL ELECTION, 1948

Democratic (Truman)

Republican (Dewey)

States' Rights Democratic (Thurmond)

Street," who had "stuck a pitch fork in the farmer's back" and had "begun to nail the American consumer to the wall with spikes of greed." Truman not only denounced the Progressive party as a Communist front, but he also claimed that Communists supported the Republican party "because they think that its reactionary policies will lead to the confusion and strife on which communism thrives." The Republican party was, therefore, at the same time a spokesman for "powerful reactionary forces" and an "unwitting ally of the Communists in this country."

Truman's strategy paid rich dividends in November 1948. The pollsters made the dual mistake of ending their interviews a few weeks before election day and assuming that the "undecided" vote would divide evenly. But many voters changed their minds at the last moment, and Truman won a disproportionately large share of the undecided vote. "I talked about voting for Dewey all summer, but when the time came I just couldn't do it," said one farmer. "I remembered the depression and all the good things that had come to me under the Democrats." Truman received 24.1 million votes to Dewey's 22 million. The Democrats, by picking up seventy-five seats in the House of Representatives and nine in the Senate, regained control of Congress. Having successfully navigated the rapids of cold war electoral politics, it remained for Truman to guide his Fair Deal program through Congress.

# THE FAIR DEAL: CIVIL RIGHTS

What Truman managed to do, however, was to extend and codify New Deal measures already on the statute books. Congress accepted his recommendations to expand three programs, all sorely in need of modernization: social security benefits, considerably increased, were extended to 10 million people; the minimum wage was raised from 40 cents to 75 cents an hour; and the federal housing program was further developed. The National Housing Act (1949), a modest measure calling for the construction of 810,000 low-cost units over a six-year period, won bipartisan support in the Senate. Where the New Deal had been innovative, the Fair Deal was more often imitative.

But Congress rebuffed Truman when he attempted to go beyond New Deal initiatives in agricultural policy, federal aid to education, health insurance, and civil rights. In 1949 Truman proposed the Brannan plan for agriculture, named after Secretary of Agriculture Charles Brannan from Colorado. This plan would have substituted an "income support standard" for the concept of farm parity and would have limited the payments available to large, corporate farmers. When organized farm groups denounced the plan, Congress defeated it. The President's $300 million aid-to-education bill was strangled in the House Committee on Education and Labor, whose members were hopelessly divided on the issue of aid to parochial schools. Similarly, Truman's program for health insurance and medical care never got to the floor of Congress. Although the plan allowed patients to choose their own physician and hospital, leaving physicians free to participate or not, it was widely and inaccurately condemned as socialized medicine. Fair Deal programs stood no chance when they antagonized entrenched interest groups, offended influential congressmen, or could be labeled Communistic.

Of all these Fair Deal setbacks, however, none was more revealing than the defeat of civil rights. That Harry Truman should have been the first President to support such legislation was surely ironic. Although Missouri was one of the slave states that did not secede from the Union in 1861, Confederate sentiment was strong, and Truman's family had favored the Southern cause. His uncle had fought in the Confederate army. Years later his grandmother had expressed dismay when she first saw young Harry in his National Guard uniform, remarking, Truman recalled, "that it was the first time a blue uniform had been in the house since the Civil War, and she said please not to come in it again." Truman described his mother as an "unreconstructed rebel" who, when visiting her son at the White House, warned that if he put her up in the room with Lincoln's bed, "I'll sleep on the floor." Truman observed, "she was just the same Mama she had always been." Yet as senator from Missouri, Truman supported civil rights measures, and as President, he did so even more strongly.

This reflected not only his own convictions, but also his recognition of the importance of the black vote. Large numbers of blacks had migrated north and west during World War II. Strategically located in such states as Illinois and California, they exerted more political leverage than ever before. The more evenly balanced the Republicans and Democrats, the more influential the black vote. Truman's victory in 1948, when he received close to 70 percent of that vote in large cities, illustrated this. His pluralities in the black wards of Los Angeles, Chicago, and Cleveland enabled him to carry California, Illinois, and Ohio. In addition, cold war requirements influenced Truman's policies. Since Soviet propagandists never failed to exploit racial discrimination in the United States, Truman argued that such discrimination alienated millions in Africa and Asia. The achievement of racial justice, therefore, could strengthen American diplomacy.

The administration took action on a number of fronts. First, the President appointed a Civil Rights Commission whose report, in October 1947, called for an end to segregation in every area of American life and recommended that steps be taken to implement political, economic, and social equality. Truman endorsed the report, although his own legislative proposals did not go nearly so far. Second, Truman issued executive orders in July 1948 designed to end discrimination in government hiring and to eliminate segregation in the armed forces. Third, the Department of Justice filed briefs in support of groups challenging the legality of segregated housing, education, and transportation. In October 1949 one such brief argued that "'separate but equal' is a constitutional anachronism which no longer deserves a place in our law." Finally, Truman asked Congress to pass legislation creating a Civil Rights Division in the Department of Justice with authority to protect the right to vote, providing harsh penalties for members of lynch mobs, abolishing the poll tax in federal elections, and setting up a Fair Employment Practices Committee with the power to prevent discriminatory hiring.

Southern Democrats made mincemeat of this legislative package. They threatened a filibuster that would bring the Senate to a standstill. Senate rules required approval by two-thirds of the total membership (sixty-four votes) to close debate. Liberals attempted to amend the rules to permit cloture either by a simple majority or by two-thirds of those present and voting, but they met with no success. Southern Democrats also held crucial committee posts by virtue of seniority. A subcommittee of the Senate Judiciary Committee had authority over the antilynching bill; it was headed by James Eastland of Mississippi (who believed that Truman's endorsement of the Civil Rights Commission report "proves that organized mongrel minorities control the Government"). A subcommittee of the Senate Rules Committee was responsible for poll tax legislation; it was headed by Mississippi's other senator, John Stennis. Southerners ultimately offered a compromise: a Fair Employment Practices Committee with no enforcement powers, an antilynching bill giving jurisdiction to the states rather than the federal government, and a constitutional amendment outlawing the poll tax that would require approval by three-fourths of the states. Truman rejected the deal.

The Supreme Court proved more responsive to demands for racial justice than did Congress. In *Shelley* v. *Kraemer* (1948), the Court held that state courts could not enforce restrictive housing covenants. These covenants, under which a group of homeowners agreed not to sell or lease property to non-Caucasians, played an important part in maintaining residential segregation. In St. Louis, 5.5 square miles were closed to blacks; in Chicago, 11 square miles were off lim-

Grant Reynolds and A. Philip Randolph testifying before the Senate Armed Services Committee, 1948. *(AP/WIDE WORLD PHOTOS.)*

its. If a non-Caucasian family—black, Asian, or American Indian—moved into a home in a restricted area, a state court would issue an injunction requiring it to leave. Those who favored covenants reasoned that homeowners had the right to protect their neighborhood against "elements distasteful to them" and that covenants, as private agreements, did not violate the Fourteenth Amendment's ban on discrimination. The National Association for the Advancement of Colored People (NAACP), which argued the other side, held that court enforcement of the covenants constituted state action within the meaning of the Fourteenth Amendment. In May 1948 the Supreme Court, by a 6-to-0 vote, accepted the NAACP's reasoning. The decision allowed homeowners to make convenants but not to seek injunctions to enforce them. The ruling by no means removed all the obstacles to integrated housing, but it removed one of them.

If the restrictive covenant decision vindicated the NAACP, A. Philip Randolph's campaign against segregation in the armed forces proved the worth of a more militant approach. In 1948 Randolph and Grant Reynolds demanded integration of the military, first through legislation and then, when that failed, through an executive order. Insisting that blacks would not fight for democracy abroad if they did not enjoy it at home, Randolph threatened a massive civil disobedience campaign. "I personally pledge myself to openly counsel, aid and abet youth, both white and Negro, to quarantine any Jim Crow conscription system." Asked if this did not border on treason, Randolph replied, "we are serving a higher law than the law which applies to the act of treason." On July 26, 1948, after protracted negotiations with Randolph, the President issued Executive Order 9981, asserting that equality of treatment and opportunity for all members of the armed services would be effected "as rapidly as possible." Randolph expressed satisfaction, and Truman later set up a committee to implement the new policy. The Navy and Air Force quickly agreed to integrate. The Army, however, raised one objection after another until in January 1950 it finally accepted a plan of gradual integration. The plan suddenly moved into high gear when American soldiers landed in South Korea.

## NATO: MULTIPURPOSE MILITARISM

In early 1949, fresh from his triumphs over the Republicans at the ballot box and over the Russians in West Berlin, Harry Truman was at the peak of his powers. Some leading senators even believed that the cold war had been "won." But Truman determined to march on, using these victories to consolidate American power in Western Europe. In early 1949, after close consultation with Senate leaders, the President asked for a military alliance between the United States and Western Europe. Called the North Atlantic Treaty Organization (NATO), it became the first United States political tie with Europeans since 1778, when a treaty with France enabled the American revolutionaries to survive.

Truman urged this major break with the American past for several reasons. American officials worried that the Marshall Plan was not working as effectively as they had hoped because of widespread fear among Europeans, and among American investors, that Russia could swarm over Western Europe at will. Such fears were much overdrawn. Half the transportation of the standing Russian army was still pulled by horses. U.S. experts concluded that Stalin would not chance a major war for at least fifteen years. Truman's new secretary of state, Dean Acheson, nevertheless observed that "economic measures alone are not enough," for their success depends "upon the people being inspired by a sense of security." One would not work without the other. Not for the first or last time in their history, Americans had to make a military commitment in order to gain economic benefits. But NATO also vastly increased American leverage in Western Europe. The European armies required American supplies, and the United States would be in a position to exact political and economic concessions in return for providing the supplies. The European armies, moreover, were ultimately dependent on the American atomic bomb. As Truman's closest military advisor noted, in case of war with Russia, U.S. plans were "completely dependent upon full use of atomic bombs for success." Again, the United States held the high card and could ask Europeans to cooperate with its policies in return for atomic protection.

Secretary of State Acheson eloquently took the lead in urging the new policies. He became Truman's chief foreign policy advocate. Acheson took that role from Forrestal, who had resigned from the Defense Department and then

Harry S. Truman and Dean Acheson in 1955. *(AP/WIDE WORLD PHOTOS.)*

committed suicide after his fears and suspicions about communism deepened until he became mentally ill. The son of an Episcopal minister and a graduate of Yale, the elegant, mustachioed, subtle, and brilliant Acheson was a conservative who believed that the American future depended on close cooperation with Europe. To build this community, Acheson determined to deal with Russia only on American terms, which, given Stalin's views, meant not dealing with Russia at all. Acheson similarly dismissed public opinion at home: "If you truly had a democracy and did what the people wanted," he later declared, "you'd go wrong every time." As secretary of state, he initially handled Congress as successfully as he had during the crises of 1947. His only allegiance was to Truman, a man completely different in appearance, background, and nearly every other respect except their common mistrust of Stalin and their mutual desire to enhance presidential power. An associate of Acheson recalled that the secretary once looked over a speech drafted for Truman, then "said with that magnificent manner of his: 'You can't ask the President of the United States to utter this crap.'" Demanding a typewriter, Acheson pecked out his own draft of the speech. It was clear who made foreign policy in Washington. When the bubble burst, Acheson would be a highly visible target for his enemies.

# THE BURSTING OF THE BUBBLE: 1949–50

Creating NATO marked the high point of American postwar policy. In April 1949 twelve nations (United States, Canada, Great Britain, France, Italy, the Netherlands, Belgium, Norway, Denmark, Iceland, Portugal, and Luxembourg) pledged that each would consider an attack on one as an attack on all and that each would respond as it deemed necessary, including the possible use of force. But within six months a series of events rocked the Truman administration.

Overseas the Soviets exploded an atomic bomb and China fell to the Communist forces of Mao Tse-tung. American officials knew that the Russians would have the bomb soon, but few expected it this early. Similarly, the fall of nationalist leader Chiang Kai-shek in China had been expected, but the actual Communist proclamation of victory shocked Americans. Acheson correctly argued that the United States had no power to stop the Chinese Communists unless millions of Americans were sent to fight, and this not even the most vocal supporters of Chiang Kai-shek were willing to urge. The only hope had been Chiang himself, but despite American advice and $2 billion of aid between 1945 and 1949, his regime had become so corrupt and inefficient that it could not save itself. As Acheson phrased it, Chiang's armies "did not have to be defeated; they disintegrated." The fact remained that the world's two largest nations were Communist, and one of them had the atomic bomb. Senate Republican leader Arthur Vandenberg said it best: "This is now a different world."

Truman also faced dangerous conditions at home. The American postwar depression, which many prophesied and everyone feared, seemed to be approaching. The unemployment figure of 1.9 million in 1948 shot up to 4.7 million, or 7.6 percent of the labor force, by early 1950. The Marshall Plan helped keep the economy buoyant, for almost every dollar appropriated by Congress had to be spent by Europeans in the United States for American goods. (This would be the case with nearly every dollar of the $125 billion Congress appropriated for "foreign aid" during the next quarter-century.) The Marshall Plan, however, would last only a few more years. When Congress stopped spending these monies—that is, when Americans had to return to a peacetime economy with more "free enterprise" and less government spending—the nation could find itself in conditions resembling those of the 1930s. Republican congressional leaders who had followed Truman in a bipartisan spirit began to have second thoughts. The administration became fair game for political attacks.

As the nation settled down into a winter of deep discontent, Truman and Acheson prepared to counterattack. The President ordered a complete review of American policy. The review was completed in April 1950 and was termed "NSC-68" (National Security Council Paper No. 68). This document set American cold war policy for the next twenty years. It assumed that only the United States could save Western Europe and Japan, which, along with North America, constituted the globe's great industrial centers. The United States would have to take the lead, letting its friends simply follow (much as satellites revolve around a primary planet, as NSC-68 phrased it), while Americans reorganized the "free world." According to NSC-68, reorganization meant militarization, and that, in turn, meant that the United States would soon have to accept a $50 billion defense expenditure instead of the $13 billion budgeted for 1950. Such spending would of course also pump up the deflating domestic economy.

Even as Truman planned a massive escalation of military strength, he and Acheson responded cautiously to developments in Asia. While refusing to recognize the Chinese Communists immediately, throughout early 1950 the secretary of state maintained that the real danger to China came not from Washington but from Stalin's desire to control all Communists, including Mao. U.S. trade with China continued into late 1950. In January 1950 the President's military advisors concluded that the island of Formosa (to which the Chiang regime had fled) would shortly fall to Mao's troops, and the United States should not lift a finger. Acheson clearly was flirting with the idea of recognizing the Chinese Communists. The flirtation cooled only after the Chinese seized U.S. property, mistreated American citizens, and signed a friendship pact with Stalin in February 1950.

At the same time, Acheson took steps to ensure that Japan would replace China as the American outpost in Asia. As early as 1947, when Washington officials saw the hollowness of Chiang's regime, they had encouraged Japan to rebuild more rapidly than the 1945 surrender terms allowed. Following this lead, U.S. businesses trooped into the promising Japanese market, increasing their investment from $96 million in 1946 to nearly $500 million in 1949. With Japan recovering and an independent government at work in Tokyo in 1949, the question became how the United States could be assured that Japan would stay on Washington's side for the indefinite future. This question became pressing when China fell, for Japan had looked to China for decades as a market and source of raw materials. If something were not done, the Japanese might well fall into the Chinese Communist orbit.

Acheson's answer was a NATO-like device for Japan: the United States and Japan would sign a treaty ending American occupation but allowing U.S. military bases to remain. While the Japanese themselves would not possess a large military establishment, their islands would become an American outpost on Russia's Asian rim. Stalin did not care for this. As early as 1947 the Soviets had warned against any "intention to restore the economy of Germany and Japan on the old [pre-1939] basis provided it is subordinated to interests of American capital." Acheson had done much more, making Japan both an economic and a military outpost. Faced with NATO to the west and long-term American military bases on his eastern flank, Stalin decided to act.

## KOREA: JUNE 1950

His opportunity lay in Korea. That nation had been divided along its 38th parallel between American and Russian forces in 1945 in order to facilitate the surrender of Japanese troops. After the surrender, however, neither power would leave. Korea was vital because whoever controlled it also controlled strategic entrances to Japan, China, and the Soviet Union itself. Russian troops finally retreated in early 1949, but left behind a Communist North Korean government possessing a strong Soviet-equipped army. The United States exited from South Korea several months later; it left behind strongman Syngman Rhee and an army useful primarily for eliminating Rhee's domestic political opponents.

Acheson believed that Rhee's troops and the American presence in Japan sufficed to protect South Korea. On January 12, 1950, the secretary of state spoke at the National Press Club in Washington. He defined the U.S. defense perimeter in the Pacific as running from the Aleutians through Japan to the Philippines. That was the same defensive line that General MacArthur had agreed to in 1949. Acheson carefully added, however, that any aggression against Korea would be opposed by the UN. That statement alone would not serve to make Stalin quake in his boots. For his part, Stalin had little to lose and much to gain. His North Korean allies were eager to attack southward to reunite their country. A successful invasion could endanger Acheson's attempt to rebuild Japan. It would also show Mao, with whom Stalin was having difficulties over Sino-Russian border and economic problems, that Russia remained the dominant Communist power. Stalin could accomplish all this, moreover, without any direct Soviet involvement in the attack. In the spring of 1950 he flashed the green light to the North Koreans, while sending them supplies and advisors. But he also warned them that if they got into trouble, he would not help. Stalin was not going to start World War III over South Korea. He wanted only Asians and Americans killed.

On June 25 North Korean troops moved across the 38th parallel. Truman quickly responded. On June 27 he sent in American air and naval forces. When these proved insufficient and South Korea faced certain defeat, he ordered U.S. combat troops into battle. Meanwhile Acheson obtained the support of the UN. On June 27 the UN resolved that its members should help repel the aggressors so that "peace and security" could return to the area. Angry over the American refusal to allow the Chinese Communists into the world organization, the Russians had been boycotting UN sessions and were not present when Acheson rushed the resolution through. The struggle against North Korea was to be fought by a UN army under General MacArthur.

But this was misleading. The United States actually controlled operations through MacArthur, and the UN simply followed Truman's lead. Americans contributed 86 percent of the naval power, more than 90 percent of the air support, and, along with the South Koreans, nearly all the combat troops. The President made these drastic decisions, moreover, without going before Congress to ask for a declaration of war as the Constitution required. He termed the struggle a "police action," not a war, hoping that this would limit the conflict before it expanded with atomic weapons and Russian participation. The President merely consulted and informed congressional leaders, of whom only Senator Robert Taft, the Ohio Republican, raised major objections. This procedure was clearly unconstitutional and later, when the war went badly, proved to be a political error as well, for it left Truman exposed to bitter partisan attack. The President's decision set a precedent for the later Kennedy-Johnson-Nixon commitment of American troops to Vietnam, a commitment again taken without a congressional declaration of war.

## CHANGING "CONTAINMENT" TO "LIBERATION": THE UNITED STATES ON THE OFFENSIVE

Truman and Acheson used the Korean War as an opportunity to take the initiative against communism not only in Asia but in Europe too. The remaining months of 1950 were the most active and crucial ones in the cold war. During this time the President decided to change his policy of "containment," as  defined in the 1947 Truman Doctrine, to the more active policy of actually trying to liberate a Communist-controlled area. Several motivations shaped the new approach. The war gave Acheson a perfect opportunity to build great military bastions in Asia and Europe as he had long desired. After all, he could argue, if the Communists struck in Korea, they might strike anywhere. In a larger sense, the war was the chance to put the global ideas of NSC-68 into effect. Driving back communism would also silence growing criticism at home. These critics, whom Acheson acidly called "primitives" and "animals," attacked the administration for merely containing, instead of eliminating, communism. Truman and Acheson used the Korean War as a springboard to launch a worldwide diplomatic offensive.

In Asia this offensive included the first full-fledged American support to Chiang Kai-shek's rump regime on Formosa. Truman sent the Seventh Fleet to protect Chiang and signed large-scale economic and military aid pacts. By August 1950, the United States had bedded down with Chiang to establish a new American military outpost on Formosa. In Southeast Asia, Acheson agreed to help France reimpose its control over the Indochinese peoples in May, a month before Korea erupted. By midsummer the United States sent large military assistance and a military mission to aid the French. Here lay the beginning  of the American involvement in Vietnam. Acheson also hurried plans to sign the Japanese security treaty, doing so over strong objections from the Soviets and also from such friends as Australia and New Zealand, who feared the threat of a revived Japan.

The secretary of state similarly took the diplomatic offensive in Europe. He used the Korean crisis as the opportunity to achieve goals that had been impossible to gain earlier because of opposition from allies and the Congress. Above all, Acheson determined to lock West Germany firmly to the West by rearming it and integrating the new German forces into NATO. France and England voiced strong opposition to any revival of German militarism, but Acheson refused to listen. Simultaneously, Truman, again without consulting Congress, tied the United States closer to Western Europe by stationing American troops on European soil. Both moves were completed despite strong congressional opposition. In 1949 Acheson had told Congress, "We are very clear

**CONFLICT IN KOREA, 1950–1953**

that the disarmament and demilitarization of Germany must be complete and absolute." At the same time, he had guaranteed that there would be no Americans assigned to NATO duty without the assent of Congress. The shifting cold war, especially the new Soviet atomic bomb, changed Acheson's mind. The U.S. commitment to Europe was fixed for the rest of the twentieth century. Truman meanwhile increased defense spending until in 1952 it reached $50 billion, the figure envisioned by NSC-68.

Finally, Truman and Acheson decided not only to stop the North Koreans but also to drive them back until all Korea was liberated. Such a triumph would teach Stalin a lesson, silence the critics at home, ensure Japan's position, and put the United States on the border of Communist China itself. In July and August the tragic decision was taken to cross the 38th parallel. In September, General MacArthur made a brilliant landing at Inchon, trapping thousands of Communist troops. By late October, the UN forces were marching through North Korea toward the Yalu River, which separates Korea from China. At this point the Chinese issued blunt warnings that UN troops should not approach the Yalu. Acheson was not concerned. "Everything in the world" was done to assure China that its interests were not endangered, he later observed. "And I should suppose there is no country in the world which has been more outstanding in developing the theory of brotherly development of border waters [like the Yalu] than the United States."

This was an absurd statement. Such "brotherly development" of the Yalu with U.S. troops on China's borders, was precisely what Mao determined to prevent. Moreover, Stalin urged Mao to fight the Americans. It was to the Soviet interest that Americans and Chinese kill as many of each other as possible. Mao knew of Stalin's duplicity; knew (correctly, as it turned out) that Stalin would send too little help; and knew that fighting the world's greatest power could perhaps destroy his Chinese Revolution. Nevertheless, after he spent days agonizing over the decision, in late November Mao's armies swarmed southward across the Yalu. Large units of American and South Korean troops were surrounded, killed, or left to freeze to death in a bitter winter. By late December the UN forces had fled south across the 38th parallel before MacArthur could counterattack. The war then turned into a bloody stalemate. More than 140,000 Americans and more than 1 million South Koreans were killed or wounded. Most of the casualties were suffered after Truman ordered UN forces to liberate North Korea.

The casualties were only part of the high price Americans paid for the administration's 1950 diplomatic offensive. The immense and rapidly mounting war expenditures skewed the nation's economy, producing inflation and labor unrest. A renewed military-industrial alliance fattened on the defense budget, which, in turn, distorted the economy while wasting irreplaceable resources. Abroad, Americans discovered that their friends held serious doubts about U.S. stability. These allies found German rearmament so repugnant that it would be delayed for four years. Others feared a revived Japan. Some refused to follow Acheson's policy of aiding French colonialism in Southeast Asia. All were concerned about how the United States might use its incredible power, particularly its atomic weapons.

The Truman administration was also on the defensive at home. Despite the President's assurance that communism could be contained and even driven back, communism had not only survived, but large numbers of American boys were being slaughtered in Korea. The administration and indeed the entire liberal tradition it claimed to represent were embattled. The struggle at home reached a peak in early 1951, when the President, in his words, reached "a parting of the way with the big man in Asia."

# TRUMAN AND MacARTHUR

In April 1951, for the first time in twenty years, baseball fans booed the President of the United States when he threw out the ball to open the Washington Senators' season. For, a few days before, Truman had relieved General Douglas MacArthur of his command of UN forces in Korea. That action released a tidal wave of sympathy for the general, who, on his return to the United States, received a hero's welcome. When MacArthur concluded a speech to Congress by quoting an old army ballad—"old soldiers never die, they just fade away"—and then added, "like the old soldier of that ballad, I now close my military career and just fade away, an old soldier who tried to do his duty as God gave him the light to see that duty," it seemed as if the applause would never end. The Truman administration, however, regarded MacArthur as an ambitious and dangerous man, one who wanted to subvert civilian control of policymaking and plunge the United States into nuclear war. Privately, members of the President's staff revealed their bitterness by composing an imaginary tour schedule for the general: "Burning of the Constitution. Lynching of Secretary Acheson. Twenty-one atomic-bomb salute. Three hundred nude D.A.R.'s leap from Washington Monument."

The basis of the conflict between Truman and MacArthur had existed in 1950 but was concealed because American forces had been successful until late in the year, and the administration, in deciding to cross the 38th parallel, in effect had endorsed MacArthur's goal of eliminating the Communist government in North Korea. Once Chinese forces intervened, however, the options available to the United States narrowed considerably: it could either accept a stalemate or risk nuclear war. Truman chose the first alternative and MacArthur the second. The two men, therefore, rapidly moved toward a showdown. In January 1951 MacArthur demanded permission to blockade China, bomb military and industrial targets across the Yalu River, use Chinese nationalist troops in Korea, and allow Chiang Kai-shek to attack the Chinese mainland. When Truman rejected all of this, MacArthur took matters into his own hands. In March he publicly threatened to destroy China if it did not concede defeat, and he stated that there was no substitute for victory. Truman then recalled him.

MacArthur not only repudiated the very concept of limited war but also disagreed with the administration's strategic priorities. As commander of U.S. forces in the Pacific during World War II, MacArthur had declared: "Europe is a dying system. It is worn out and run down. . . . The lands touching the Pacific with their billions of inhabitants will determine the course of history for the next 10,000 years." But the Truman administration regarded Europe, not Asia, as the key to containment. Provoking a war with China, as MacArthur seemed ready to do, would antagonize the nations of Western Europe and jeopardize the NATO alliance. By funneling American forces to the Pacific, such a conflict would weaken European defenses. When General Omar N. Bradley, speaking for the joint chiefs of staff, asserted that an attack on China would involve the United States in "the wrong war, in the wrong place, at the wrong time, and with the wrong enemy," he left little doubt as to what he considered the right war, the right place, the right time, and the right enemy: a war waged to defend Western Europe against Soviet domination.

That General Bradley defended the Truman administration was of crucial significance. The conflict between Truman and MacArthur, often interpreted as one between civilian and military interests, actually involved sharp disagreement within the military. This, in turn, reflected the development of ties between the armed services and government that emerged during World War II and grew firmer during the cold war. The Truman administration, indeed, often asked military men to fill policy-making posts in government; by 1948, 150 officers held such positions. The joint chiefs of staff fully endorsed Truman's decision to recall MacArthur. So, too, did General George Marshall, who served as secretary of state (1947–49) and secretary of defense (1950–51). "The S.O.B. should have been fired two years ago," Marshall commented. On the other hand, almost all the field commanders in Korea backed MacArthur. (The lone exception was General Matthew Ridgeway, and Truman selected him to replace MacArthur.) The military establishment's support of the President's Korean policy helped him ride out the storm created by MacArthur's dismissal.

## LIMITED WAR AT HOME

The Korean War did not require the same level of economic regulation as World War II did. Since military operations occurred on a limited scale, the armed forces absorbed a relatively small proportion of industrial output and consumer goods were plentiful. Inflationary pressures, strong during the first nine months of war, subsided in the spring of 1951. World War II had produced gargantuan deficits, but the government showed a budgetary surplus in 1951 and 1952. Even so, the administration took a number of steps to control inflation and encourage production: it limited credit purchases by requiring larger down payments, restricted new housing starts, and liberalized amortization for costs incurred in plant expansion. The President established an Office of Defense Mobilization, issued an order designed to hold the line on prices and wages, and took possession of the railroads when workers threatened to strike for higher wages. Truman bitterly assailed the union leaders for acting "like a bunch of Russians," but the workers eventually won most of their demands, and the government returned the lines to private owners.

The Supreme Court's response to the President's seizure of the steel mills illustrated the problems encountered in regulating the economy during a limited war. In March 1952 a federal wage panel concluded that steelworkers deserved a raise, but the companies refused to grant the increase unless the administration approved a sizable price increase. When the administration refused, the steel firms rejected a wage hike and the union called a strike. Truman could have invoked the Taft-Hartley Act and ordered an eighty-day cooling-off period, but he did not want to use the law against workers with a legitimate grievance or risk alienating organized labor. Instead he seized the steel mills, citing as justification the existence of a national emergency, the importance of steel production in wartime, and his implied powers as commander in chief. The case rapidly moved to the Supreme Court, which, in *Youngstown Sheet and Tube Co.* v. *Sawyer* (1952), ruled against the President by a 6-to-3 margin. The majority held that the President had no constitutional authority to order the seizure and that in bypassing the Taft-Hartley Act he had ignored "the clear will of Congress." Chief Justice Fred M. Vinson, speaking for the minority, cited precedents under Abraham Lincoln, Woodrow Wilson, and Franklin Roosevelt for granting the President a broad range of discretionary authority in wartime. Obeying the Court, Truman then returned the steel mills to their owners and, when the union struck, refused to intervene. The strike lasted nearly two months and ended with the workers obtaining their raise and the administration reluctantly granting the steel companies their price increase.

Despite the limited nature of the mobilization, the Korean War greatly bolstered the American economy. Expenditures for purchasing armaments and other equipment, constructing bases, and meeting military payrolls rose sharply, from slightly more than $13 billion in the year ending June 1950 to slightly under $60 billion in the year ending June 1953. Although the percentage of GNP devoted to national security never approached the World War II level (43.1 percent), it nevertheless rose from 6.4 percent in 1950 to 14.1 percent in 1953. As government spending created millions of new jobs, unemployment dropped to its lowest level in years. Federal expenditures, together with special tax incentives, encouraged industries to expand their productive facilities. From 1950 to 1954, steel capacity increased by 24 percent, electrical generating capacity by 50 percent, and aluminum capacity by 100 percent. Finally, the government began to stockpile petroleum, chemicals, and scarce metals to protect itself against shortages in the event of a long war. By 1954 it had acquired more than $4 billion worth of critical materials.

The Korean War also led to a doubling of the size of the armed forces and, more important, to the construction of the hydrogen bomb. Truman had authorized development of the hydrogen (or "super") bomb in January 1950, but little progress was made in the next six months, and doubts about the bomb's feasibility persisted. The outbreak of the Korean War removed several obstacles to its completion. The national emergency convinced a number of scientists who had refused to work on thermonuclear weapons to put aside their moral qualms and also made it possible to justify testing within the continental United States for the first time since 1945. The war allowed Truman to pump billions of dollars into the bomb project; the Atomic Energy Commission eventually employed 150,000 people. Tests in May 1951 proved the technical feasibility of a thermonuclear weapon. Finally, the first hydrogen bomb was detonated over the Pacific on November 1, 1952, its 10.4-megaton explosion obliterating the uninhabited island of Elugelab. Russia, which produced its atomic bomb four years after the United States used its bombs, obtained a hydrogen bomb only one year after the U.S. test of its "super."

If the Korean War had the effect of accelerating the development of bombs and weapons, it had a similar effect in desegregating the armed services. By mid-1950 the Navy and Air Force had taken long strides toward desegregation, but the Army, although it had yielded to administration pressure to abolish racial quotas on enlistments, still maintained separate black and white units. Yet segregation led to a wasteful duplication of facilities and an inefficient use of personnel. Moreover, the tendency to assign black units to noncombatant duties meant that whites suffered a disproportionate share of casualties. When white troops experienced heavy losses in the early days of the war, field commanders in Korea broke with existing policy and used black soldiers as replacements. In March 1951 the Pentagon announced the integration of all training facilities in the United States. A few months later the Army received a preliminary report from a team of social scientists emphasizing the advantage of integration and denying that it would damage morale. The Army then announced that it would integrate its forces in Korea and the Far East. Later it extended this policy to troops stationed in Europe. By the end of the Korean War, nearly all black soldiers were serving in integrated Army units.

## CIVIL LIBERTIES UNDER SIEGE

The Korean conflict intensified the growing fear of Communist subversion, a fear that partly fed on the actions of the House Committee on Un-American Activities. In 1947 the committee sought to prove that Communists had infiltrated the motion picture industry. Several writers and producers who refused to answer questions concerning their political affiliations were jailed for contempt, and Hollywood adopted a blacklist barring the employment of anyone who failed to cooperate with congressional investigators. In 1948 the committee stalked bigger game: Alger Hiss, president of the Carnegie Endowment for International Peace, who was charged with perjury for denying that, while working for the State Department in the late 1930s, he had given classified papers to a Communist party member for transmittal to the Soviet Union. After his first trial resulted in a hung jury, Hiss was convicted of perjury in January 1950. By 1949 the committee was looking into espionage by scientists who had allegedly passed secret information about the atomic bomb to Russia. The Korean War, coming on the heels of all this, had a chilling effect on civil liberties. That effect could be measured by the behavior of Congress, the President, and the courts.

Three months after American troops landed in Korea, Congress passed sweeping legislation to curb subversive activities in the United States. The Internal Security Act (1950) made it unlawful to conspire to perform any act that would "substantially contribute" to establishing a totalitarian dictatorship in the United States. The measure required members of Communist organizations to register with the attorney general, barred them from employment in national defense, and denied them the right to obtain passports. The act imposed stringent controls on immigrants, aliens, and naturalized citizens. It blocked the entry of those who had belonged to totalitarian organizations, provided for the deportation of suspected alien subversives, and permitted the government to revoke the naturalization of those who joined a subversive group within five years of acquiring citizenship. Finally, the act authorized the President, in the event of war or invasion, to detain persons if there were "reasonable grounds" to believe that they might conspire to commit espionage or sabotage. This provision, first put forth by Senate liberals as a substitute measure, was, ironically, added to all the other features. On September 22, 1950, Truman vetoed the bill, declaring that it would "strike blows at our own liberties" by moving toward "suppressing opinion and belief." Congress very easily overrode the veto.

The President's blistering veto of the Internal Security Act did not prevent him from narrowing the rights of government employees under the federal loyalty program. At its inception in March 1947 this program provided for dismissal from federal employment in cases where "reasonable grounds exist for belief that the person involved is disloyal." But the Loyalty Review Board, which supervised the program, found it difficult to discover such evidence. It therefore favored a procedure that would take account of individuals "who are potentially disloyal or who are bad security risks." In April 1951 Truman issued a new executive order providing for dismissal from federal employment in cases where "there is a reasonable doubt as to the loyalty of the person involved." In effect, the burden of proof now fell on employees who, to keep their jobs, had to dispel all doubts. Since those doubts might rest on nothing more substantial than associating with persons considered to be Communists, attending meetings to raise money for suspect causes, or even subscribing to radical publications, the burden was a heavy one.

At the same time that the new loyalty program went into effect, a jury in New York found Ethel and Julius Rosenberg guilty of conspiring to commit espionage. Documents made public only in the 1990s showed that a top-secret U.S. intelligence operation, named "Venona," had cracked the most sensitive Soviet codes. "Venona" code-breakers concluded from their reading of Soviet cables that Communist agents were working in sensitive U.S. projects. The Rosenbergs were among the first to be identified (although the "Venona" expert who did the work later said he always doubled Ethel's guilt). The Rosenbergs were charged with having plotted to arrange for the transfer of atomic secrets to the Soviet Union during World War II. Ethel Rosenberg's brother, who had worked as a machinist on the Manhattan Project, testified that he had transmitted such information and received cash payments; the alleged courier supported this account. The defense denied everything, insisting that the entire story was a fabrication. On April 5, 1951, in handing down a death sentence, Judge Irving Kaufman attempted to tie the case to the Korean War. By helping Russia obtain the atomic bomb, he asserted, the couple had caused "the Communist aggression in Korea, with the resultant casualties exceeding fifty thousand. . . . We have evidence of your treachery all around us every day—for the civilian defense activities throughout the nation are aimed at preparing us for an atom bomb attack." Appeals dragged through the courts for two agonizing years, with the Rosenbergs protesting their innocence to the end, although their sentence would have been commuted to life imprisonment had they confessed. They were electrocuted on June 19, 1953. Even many who considered them guilty regarded the sentence as barbaric.

In June 1951 the Supreme Court moved with the prevailing tide by upholding the constitutionality of the Smith Act. Passed in 1940, the act made it a crime to conspire to teach or advocate the forcible overthrow of the government. In 1949 Eugene Dennis and ten other Communist leaders had been found guilty of violating the act, and the following year a court of appeals sustained their convictions. In *Dennis* v. *U.S.* (1951), the Supreme Court approved the Smith Act by a 6-to-2 vote. Chief Justice Fred M. Vinson wrote the majority opinion. To prove the American Communists presented a clear and present danger to the United States, Vinson pointed to the formation of a "highly organized conspiracy" with "rigidly disciplined members," the "inflammable nature of world conditions," and the "touch-and-go nature of our relations" with Russia. Justices Robert Jackson and Felix Frankfurter, both of whom rejected this line of reasoning, nevertheless concurred with the majority on other grounds. Justices Hugo Black and William O. Douglas dissented. Affirming the value of free speech, Douglas denied that American Communists, whom he termed "miserable merchants of unwanted ideas," posed an immediate threat. He also expected that "in case of war with Russia they will be picked up overnight as were all prospective saboteurs at the commencement of World War II." The Dennis decision cleared the way for the prosecution of other Communist leaders. Nearly one hundred of them were indicted in the early 1950s.

The Internal Security Act, the revamped loyalty program, the trials of alleged spies, the Smith Act prosecution—all trespassed to some extent on civil liberties. Of these measures, Truman's loyalty program undoubtedly affected the largest number of people. Yet of the 4.7 million jobholders and applicants who underwent rigid loyalty checks by 1952, only about ten thousand failed to gain clearance. Most of them quietly resigned or withdrew their applications; 560 people were actually fired or denied a job on the grounds of security. The Korean War's impact on civil liberties, however, would not stop at this point. With the emergence of Senator Joseph McCarthy, open season was declared on liberals. The Truman administration itself became the quarry.

## McCARTHYISM

Joseph McCarthy, elected to the Senate as a Republican from Wisconsin in 1946, had a meteoric career in the early 1950s. Although he first achieved notoriety for a speech he gave at Wheeling, West Virginia, a few months before the Korean War broke out, and although he remained a powerful political force for some time after the war ended, McCarthy's appeal derived largely from his success in exploiting the frustrations involved in waging a limited war. McCarthy declared at Wheeling that the United States, at the end of World War II, had been the most powerful nation in the world; but by 1950 it had "retreated from victory" and found itself in a "position of impotency." One thing alone, McCarthy said, was responsible: "the traitorous actions" of high government officials in the Roosevelt and Truman administrations. This explanation, as deceptive as it was simple, set the tone for all that McCarthy did and for much of what went by the name of "McCarthyism."

There was nothing new in the charge that Communists had infiltrated government. What distinguished McCarthy was his assertion that the most eminent and reputable Democrats were serving the Communist cause by waging a "caricature of a war" in Korea. To McCarthy, Secretary of State Dean Acheson was the "Red Dean of the State Department," "the elegant and alien Acheson—Russian as to heart, British as to manner." Similarly, the Wisconsin senator believed that General George Marshall had been hoodwinked into aiding "a great conspiracy, a conspiracy on a scale so immense as to dwarf any previous such venture in the history of man." Democratic Governor Adlai E. Stevenson of Illinois "endorsed and could continue the suicidal Kremlin-directed policies of the nation." McCarthy even found a trace of grim humor in the situation. "I do not think we need fear too much about the Communists dropping atomic bombs on Washington," he remarked savagely. "They would kill too many of their friends that way."

McCarthyism meant more than wild attacks on the Truman administration. It also signified a climate of all-embracing conformity. Many people became afraid to voice unpopular views or even to express controversial opinions. The drive to conform was sometimes carried to ludicrous lengths. One state required professional boxers and wrestlers to take a non-Communist oath before entering the ring. Efforts were made in Indianapolis, Indiana, to remove such "controversial" works as *Robin Hood* (whose indiscretion was stealing from the rich and giving to the poor) from public school libraries. Names themselves often took on great significance: the Cincinnati Reds were solemnly renamed the "Redlegs," and a face powder known as "Russian Sable" was marketed as "Dark Dark." Dearborn, Michigan, crowned a "Miss Loyalty" at a beauty pageant complete with loyalty oaths. Not everyone surrendered to this mood, but pressures for ideological conformity in America have seldom been stronger than during the early 1950s.

McCarthyism was also closely identified with the use of heavy-handed tactics. McCarthy presented himself as a rough-and-tumble fighter; his supporters affectionately termed him "Jolting Joe," "The Wisconsin Walloper." Never far from the surface was the suggestion that the Truman administration was infested with moral, as well as ideological, perverts. The senator, wrote one admirer, "learned that the State Department was literally crawling with so-called 'men' who wore red neckties and sometimes women's clothes—who wanted other men for lovers instead of women." McCarthy's allusions to homosexuality among government employees were hardly more circumspect. He referred to "those Communists and queers" in the State Department who wrote "perfumed notes." McCarthy insisted that the war against communism must be fought with brass knuckles, not kid gloves. The tactics he employed—from the juggling of statistics concerning the number of alleged security risks in the State Department to the browbeating of witnesses—seemed entirely legitimate to his followers.

Different critics saw in McCarthy the embodiment of their own worst fears. Socialists, who feared the intrigues of reactionary capitalists, regarded McCarthy as an agent of Texas oilmen and other new millionaires who wanted to impose a fascist order on the United States. Liberals, who feared the introduction into politics of moral issues that could not be resolved through a process of give-and-take, thought that McCarthyism represented such an issue.

Senator Joseph McCarthy and his aide, Roy Cohn, 1954. *(BETTMANN.)*

They believed that the senator played on status resentments of middle-class ethnic groups, especially the Irish and Germans, who, having achieved a measure of economic security, were seeking to prove their Americanism by attacking a social elite. A few conservatives believed McCarthy expressed the masses' hatred of aristocratic privilege and excellence. One asserted: "McCarthyism is the revenge of the noses that for twenty years of fancy parties were pressed against the outside window pane."

Support for McCarthy closely followed political, religious, and occupational lines. The senator won more backing from Republican than from Democratic voters, more from Catholics than from Jews, more from Baptists and Lutherans than from Congregationalists and Episcopalians, and more from blue-collar workers than from white-collar professionals. McCarthy also exploited his position in the Senate. Even though some Republican senators found his methods abhorrent, few dared to criticize him openly because they either feared antagonizing him or recognized his partisan value. Moreover, the Senate customarily permits its members broad latitude, relying on tradition or unwritten rules to ensure discretion. McCarthy also manipulated the mass media with great success. He developed techniques for monopolizing headlines that kept his name before the public even when his allegations had no substance.

That McCarthy could have charged the Democrats with treason, and that anyone could have taken those charges seriously seems, in retrospect, incredible.

In the years from 1947 to 1952 the Truman administration had built up Western European economic and military strength through the Marshall Plan and NATO, faced down the Russians in Berlin, taken stern measures against radicals at home, developed the hydrogen bomb, and fought a war against Communists in Korea. Nevertheless, Truman erred in supposing that the American people would be willing to make the terrible sacrifices war required without being convinced that the government was doing everything in its power to win that war. In the past, although war had sometimes been used as an instrument of diplomacy, it had always been presented as a crusade: to free Cuba in 1898, to make the world safe for democracy in 1917, to establish the four freedoms in 1941. When McCarthy asserted that the United States was "engaged in a final, all-out battle between communistic atheism and Christianity," when MacArthur claimed that "there is no substitute for victory," they were speaking the kind of language Americans had customarily spoken when waging war. If Truman was correct in believing that in the nuclear age only limited war was feasible, his opponents were surely correct in recognizing that limited war provided them an unequaled political opportunity. They would make the most of that opportunity in the 1952 election.

## Suggested Reading

Good overviews of the American economy include Stuart Bruchey, *Enterprise: The Dynamic Economy of a Free People* (1990); W. Elliot Brownlee, *Dynamics of Ascent* (1979); and, for a splendid specialized study, Harold G. Vatter, *The U.S. Economy in World War II* (1985). John Kenneth Galbraith, *The Affluent Society* (1958), offers an influential, near-contemporary view.

For Henry Wallace and the Progressive Party, see Graham White and John Maze, *Henry A. Wallace: His Search for a New World Order* (1995). In *Democrats and Progressives* (1974), Allen Yarnell discusses the election of 1948. On the Dixiecrats' candidate, see Nadine Cohodas, *Strom Thurmond and the Politics of Southern Change* (1993). The Truman administrations' civil rights program is explored at length in William Berman, *The Politics of Civil Rights in the Truman Administration* (1970); and Donald McCoy and Richard Ruetten, *Quest and Response* (1973). See also Paula F. Pfeffer, *A. Philip Randolph: Pioneer of the Civil Rights Movement* (1990).

The political consequences of the Korean War are considered in John Spanier, *The Truman-MacArthur Controversy* (1959); Maeva Marcus, *Truman and the Steel Seizure* (1977), and Geoffrey Perret, *Old Soldiers Never Die: The Life of Douglas MacArthur* (1996); and, on a crucial topic, Louis Fisher, *Presidential War Power* (1995). Contrasting views of the Truman administration's position on civil liberties are presented in Alan D. Harper, *The Politics of Loyalty, 1946–1952* (1969); Athan Theoharis, *Seeds of Repression: Harry S. Truman and the Origins of McCarthyism* (1971); and Stanley I. Kutler, *The American Inquisition* (1982). On Alger Hiss, see Allen Weinstein, *Perjury: The Hiss-Chambers Case* (1978); on the Rosenbergs, see Ronald Radosh and Joyce Milton, *The Rosenberg File* (1983); and Marjorie Garber and Rebecca L. Walkowitz (eds.), *Secret Agents: The Rosenberg Case, McCarthyism, and Fifties America* (1995). Important studies of McCarthyism are David Oshinsky, *A Conspiracy So Immense: The World of Joe McCarthy* (1983); Richard M. Fried, *Nightmare in Red: The McCarthy Era in Perspective* (1990); and Ellen W. Schrecker, *The Age of McCarthyism: A Brief History with Documents* (1994). Two excellent biographies of J. Edgar Hoover are

Richard Gid Powers, *Secrecy and Power* (1987); and Athan Theoharis and John Stuart Cox, *The Boss* (1988).

For foreign relations, the important reference sources are R. D. Burns, ed., *Guide to American Foreign Relations Since 1700* (1983); Bruce Jentelson and Thomas Paterson, eds., *Encyclopedia of American Foreign Relations*, 4 vols. (1997); Warren Cohen, *America in the Age of Soviet Power, 1945–1991* (1993), with good bibliographies; and Dennis Merrill, ed., *Documentary History of the Truman Presidency*, 10 vols. (1995). A prize-winning overview is Melvyn Leffler, *Preponderance of Power* (1992); and also see Melvyn Leffler and David Painter, *Origins of the Cold War: An International History* (1994). Specific topics are well analyzed in Vladislav Zubok and Constantine Pleshakov, *Inside the Kremlin's Cold War* (1996), on Stalin's policies; Andrew Rotter, *The Path to Vietnam* (1987); Ronald Steel, *Walter Lippmann and the American Century* (1980); McGeorge Bundy, *Danger and Survival* (1988), surveys the arms race; Richard Rhodes, *Dark Sun* (1995), superb on the making of the hydrogen bomb, and on many other aspects of the era; Thomas Borstelmann, *Apartheid's Reluctant Uncle* (1993), a prize-winning account of U.S.–South African relations; Nancy B. Tucker, *Patterns in the Dust, 1949–1950* (1983), on China and the China Lobby; Harry Harding and Yuan Ming, *Sino-American Relations, 1945–1955* (1989), with both U.S. and Chinese perspectives. A most important overview on U.S.–China between 1947 and 1958 is Thomas Christensen, *Useful Adversaries* (1996).

For the Korean War, major contributions include Bruce Cumings, *The Origins of the Korean War*, 2 vols. (1981, 1990), which effectively challenged 30 years of interpretations; William Stueck, *The Korean War: An International History* (1995), which disagrees with Cumings; Sergei Goncharov, John W. Lewis, and Xue Litai, *Uncertain Partners* (1993), for the Soviet and Chinese, as well as U.S., policies; and James Matray, ed., *Historical Dictionary of the Korean War* (1991). MacArthur gives his side in *Reminiscences* (1964); but see Michael Schaller, *Douglas MacArthur* (1989); and Howard B. Schonberger, *Aftermath of War* (1989) on the U.S. occupation of Japan. The final chapters of Ronald Pruessen's *John Foster Dulles: The Road to Power* (1982) are important for both politics and diplomacy.

On the Kinsey reports, see Wardell Pomeroy, *Dr. Kinsey and the Institute for Sex Research* (1972); and Paul Robinson, *The Modernization of Sex . . . Kinsey, Masters, Johnson* (1976).

Levittown, Long Island, 1958. *(Joe Scherschel, Life Magazine © Time Inc.)*

# CHAPTER TWELVE

# 1952–1957

## Eisenhower and the
## American Consensus

This chapter discusses:
- The explosion of a new suburban America
- The hero Eisenhower and his agenda
- The beginning of the end of segregation
- John Foster Dulles's cold war—in a rapidly changing world

D wight David Eisenhower, reared on the Kansas frontier and the plains of West Point Military Academy, became famous as the commander of Allied forces in Western Europe during World War II. In 1952, campaigning for the presidency as a spokesman for traditional American values, he offered reassurance and hope to a people soured by the trials of the cold war. Within two years of his election, the Korean War had ended and Joseph McCarthy had fallen from power. Americans then settled down to enjoy the piping prosperity that they believed they so richly deserved. It was, one critic observed, a classic case of "the bland leading the bland." Yet appearances deceived, for beneath a placid surface society was in ferment. At home, pressures were building that later would produce the massive civil rights movement. Abroad, the United States approached the Suez crisis of 1956, a turning point of the cold war. Not even the smiling, waving golfer in the White House was always what he seemed. Widely perceived as passive and even deferential, Eisenhower, behind the scenes, employed presidential power in an energetic and assertive fashion.

## THE SUBURBAN SOCIETY

The most distinctive demographic development in the United States at midcentury was the expansion of the suburbs. During the 1950s, the population of "standard metropolitan statistical areas"—defined by the Census Bureau as places containing a city with at least fifty thousand inhabitants—jumped from 95 to 120 million. That growth took place primarily in the suburbs. Central cities grew by 11 percent, from 54 million to 60 million, while suburbs grew by 46 percent, from 41 million to 60 million. Much of the urban growth in the South and West, however, occurred through the extension of cities' boundaries to incorporate suburban tracts instead of through an increase in the existing population. In the North and Midwest this kind of expansion was uncommon. From 1950 to 1960, fourteen of the fifteen largest cities in the nation experienced a population decline even as their suburbs underwent a population explosion: New York City's suburbs grew by 58 percent, Chicago's by 101 percent, Detroit's by 131 percent, and Cleveland's by 94 percent.

Suburban development depended, in the first instance, on the expansion of the automobile industry and the construction of new highways. The postwar years were boom years for American car manufacturers. Passenger car output rocketed from 2 million in 1946 to 8 million in 1955, and registrations jumped from 25 million in 1945 to 51 million in 1955. For nearly all suburbanites, the automobile was a necessity; indeed, by 1960, nearly one-fifth of suburban families owned two cars. At the same time, states and municipalities built or improved many thousands of miles of new roads. The federal government made an essential contribution. The Interstate Highway Act of 1956 provided for the construction of 41,000 miles of express highways at a cost of more than $100 billion. The new roads made it easier to commute and made it more feasible than before to commute over much longer distances.

The government aided suburban growth in other ways as well. The Veterans Administration offered to insure the mortgages of former servicemen on highly advantageous terms. More than 3.75 million veterans bought homes under Veterans Administration programs that, typically, required only a token down payment and provided long-term, low-interest mortgages. The Federal Housing Administration also insured millions of mortgages, giving preference, in all instances, to buyers of single-family, detached dwellings. Those who wanted to buy a home in the suburbs could therefore count on a much more favorable response from federal agencies than those who wished to purchase an older home. Insuring mortgages in the central cities, the Veterans Administration and Federal Housing Administration believed, represented a much higher risk, and a risk not worth taking. Government programs tipped the balance in favor of middle-income buyers, those looking at homes in the $7,000 to $10,000 range, and those seeking a suburban location.

The burgeoning suburbs began to lure commerce and industry from the cities. The trend toward plant relocation meant that employment in trade and manufacturing declined in the nation's largest cities and rose dramatically in the suburbs. The appearance of giant shopping centers also heralded the economic transformation of suburbia. At the end of World War II there were only eight shopping centers; by 1960 the number had risen to 3,840. In a three-month period in 1957, no fewer than seventeen regional shopping centers opened for business, leading one observer to note that "at times it seemed they must be coming off a hidden assembly line."

The migration from cities to suburbs was predominantly a migration of whites; black Americans characteristically moved from farms to cities. In the decade of the 1950s, the twelve largest central cities lost 3.6 million whites and gained 4.5 million nonwhites. By 1960 more than half the black population, but only one-third of the white population, resided in central cities. In the suburbs, however, whites outnumbered blacks by a ratio of more than 35 to 1. The number of blacks residing in the suburbs did increase, from 1 million in 1950 to 1.7 million in 1960, but most of that increase occurred in older, all-black communities. Few blacks bought homes in the new, postwar suburban tracts. Either they could not afford to do so or they were excluded by real estate brokers who would not show them homes, bank officers who would not grant them mortgages, or suburban zoning ordinances that artificially boosted home construction costs in order to restrict entry.

The word *suburbia* brought to mind images of small children, and with good reason. The 1950s saw an unusually high marriage rate and a truly extraordinary increase in the birthrate. The postwar "baby boom" crested in 1957, when the fertility rate reached the highest level since the government first began to compile statistics in 1917. At the rate prevailing in 1957, one thousand women could be expected to give birth to 3,767 children. At the same time, improvements in medical care led to a steady increase in life expectancy. In 1954, for the first time in American history, life expectancy for white men and women reached 70 years. (Black men and women could expect to live an average of 64 years.) The rapid increase in the over-65 age bracket led one enterprising publisher to market a magazine designed exclusively for those preparing to retire. During the 1950s the population of the United States increased from 152.3 to 180.6 million. That represented an annual growth of 1.7 percent, the highest rate of change in four decades. Far from worrying about scarcity or overpopulation, most Americans confidently assumed that growth would trigger further economic expansion. As one business periodical happily proclaimed: "More People: It Means New Trade, Good Times."

## DOMESTIC IDEALS IN POSTWAR AMERICA

"No job is more exacting, more necessary, or more rewarding than that of housewife and mother," journalist Agnes Meyer wrote in the *Atlantic* in 1950, and the decade that followed seemed to support her claim. Affluence and suburbanization shaped the aspirations of postwar women. When pollsters George Gallup and Evan Hill surveyed the views of "The American Woman" for the *Saturday Evening Post* in 1962, they had reason to conclude, after 2,300 interviews, that "few people are as happy as a housewife." Indeed, 96 percent of the women surveyed declared themselves extremely happy or very happy, though most wished that their daughters would marry later and get more education. "The suburban housewife was the dream image of the young American woman," Betty Friedan would write in 1963. As wife, mother, homemaker, and consumer, "she had found true feminine fulfillment."

The domestic ideals that flourished in the 1950s were part of a larger phenomenon, a surge of postwar upward mobility, and part of the prevalent national mood, a turning away from public affairs toward private goals and family life. "Togetherness," a *McCall's* slogan of 1954, meant early marriages, large families, and "sharing a common experience." The accompanying article described a young suburban couple who "centered their lives almost completely around their children and their home," while the father served as "a link with the outside world." The homemaker's role, though limited, was imbued in the press with higher purpose. Her presence in the household provided security for other family members in a changing world that seemed full of unstable if not threatening elements. "Two World Wars and a depression have uprooted family life and created a nationwide turmoil," Meyer told her *Atlantic* readers. "The mounting divorce rate, the appalling number of youthful crimes, the deliberate neglect of children in many homes, and the looseness of sexual morality among young and old—these are only some of the inescapable signs of a decaying moral structure in areas for which women have a prime responsibility."

When questioned about their aspirations in moving to the suburbs, women in New Jersey's Levittown cited more personal, material goals—privacy, freedom, comfort, roominess, quality of life, and a chance to enjoy a "normal family role, being a homemaker." They also looked forward to "furnishing and decorating the home." If women's roles as consumers increased in the postwar decade, this was hardly a surprise after the deprivations of the

1930s and the scarcities of the war years. During the 1950s, the median family income almost doubled. Stores were now full of electrical appliances that had been unavailable during the war, from electric mixers to dishwashers, and a gamut of new products from aluminum foil to room deodorants. Postwar consumerism was abetted by an eightfold expansion of consumer credit and by advertisers' ingenuity in tapping the growing household market, where women made three out of four family purchases. "It's nice to be modern," a young housewife told a postwar survey of women's attitudes towards electric appliances. "It's like running a factory in which you have the latest machinery." Advertisers stressed the psychological dimensions of purchasing. "Just as producing once served as an outlet for social tension," reported a 1957 study of consumer motivation, "now consumption serves the same purpose."

While higher incomes provided a dramatic rise in living standards, the baby boom evoked new interest in child rearing. This paved the way for the extraordinary success of Dr. Benjamin Spock's *Baby and Child Care* (1946). No child-rearing manual had ever been published at so propitious a time or geared to such a boom market. During the late 1940s and 1950s, Dr. Spock's book sold over a million copies a year. Though widespread in appeal, his message was directed toward the new suburban family, where each child could be expected to have its own room, and where mothers could be expected to devote full-time to answering their children's needs. Parents seemed to appreciate Dr. Spock's upbeat tone and down-to-earth manner. "You make me feel as if I were a sensible person," one mother wrote. Most of the voluminous correspondence

Homemakers shopping for household appliances, 1956. *(Burton Glinn/Magnum.)*

Refreshments being served to Young Men's Christian Association father-son group, 1956. (*Ralph Crane,* Life *Magazine © Time Inc.*)

Dr. Spock received also managed to recreate his cheerful tone, even when children refused to eat vegetables or speak in sentences, or got caught in pieces of household machinery. But parents were often unable to meet the demands of "permissive" child rearing. Some letters were from physicians with practices too busy to pay attention to their own children, from parents who accused themselves of "selfishness," from couples who found child care "an unbearable drain," and from guilt-ridden mothers who reproached themselves. "I know that a lot of my problem is personal," one mother wrote.

Although early marriage, "togetherness," and child rearing appeared to be the dominant themes of women's lives in the 1950s, the decade also witnessed other developments. One was the massive expansion of higher education that followed World War II. Between 1940 and 1960, the percentage of college-age Americans who went to college more than doubled. The proportion of women attending college fell during the late 1940s, when the GI bill sent millions of veterans back to school, but the educational gender gap was only temporary; during the 1950s, women began to catch up in percentages. Going to college, now a middle-class perquisite, seemed to have no noticeable impact on the domestic goals of most women college students in the postwar era. "The average college girl views her future through a wedding band," the *New York Times* reported. But colleges remained relative enclaves of equality, and they also prepared thousands of alumnae for eventual entry into the labor market.

The decade of domesticity, paradoxically, was one in which the contemporary female work force took shape. Between 1940 and 1960, the number of women in the work force doubled. By 1952, 2 million more women than during World War II were at work. The postwar woman worker, moreover, was likely to be married, middle class, and middle-aged; during the 1950s, women from middle-class families entered the labor market at a higher rate than any other segment of the population. Since second incomes were now needed to maintain middle-class family status in an inflationary economy, wives, not older children, became the major supplementary wage earners. The needs of the labor market also changed. Economic expansion increased the demand for low-paid, qualified workers in service jobs, sales jobs, and especially office jobs. Elementary school teachers were needed to accommodate the baby boom population. The pool of young, single women, usually the mainstay of the female labor force, had diminished, due to low birthrates in the 1920s and 1930s. Postwar employers therefore turned to the older, married white-collar worker. By the early 1960s, one worker in three was a woman, one out of three married women worked, and three out of five women workers were married. Significantly, during the 1950s, women's numbers rose more than 40 percent in many occupations, from professional work to clerical work. Equally significant, as a government commission concluded, "Most jobs that women hold are in the low-paid category." Postwar women provided an inexpensive and available new labor pool.

The contradictions between domestic ideals and women's new roles in the labor force would not emerge until the mid-1960s. During the postwar years, most Americans, women included, were relieved to be done with the war and out of the depression, and looked forward to enjoying the benefits of the 1950s—security, prosperity, and unprecedented social mobility.

## THE MOOD OF THE 1950s

During the 1950s, many social critics diagnosed American society as suffering from a terminal case of conformity. The suburbs, they claimed, best illustrated the symptoms. In *The Organization Man* (1956), William F. Whyte described an emerging group of Americans, primarily middle-class junior executives, who accepted "a belief in 'belongingness' as the ultimate need of the individual." Organization men and women, Whyte reasoned, found their natural habitat in the new suburbia, with its emphasis on participation in community affairs, sociability for its own sake, and conformity to group values. To residents of Park Forest, Illinois, for example, the lack of privacy was itself a virtue. "I never feel lonely, even when Jim's away," beamed one young woman. "You know friends are near by, because at night you hear the neighbors through the walls." Suburban public schools stressed life adjustment and relied on peer-group disapproval to maintain discipline. "The teacher strives not to discipline the child directly but to influence all the children's attitudes so that as a group they recognize correct behavior."

Whyte concluded that the organization man "is not only other-directed" but "is articulating a philosophy which tells him it is the right way to be."

David Riesman had first discussed the concept of "other-direction" in *The Lonely Crowd* (1950), one of the most influential books ever written by an American sociologist. Riesman argued that Americans were in the process of moving from an inner-directed to an other-directed society, one in which the peer group replaced parents as the dominant source of authority and in which those who failed to conform experienced anxiety rather than guilt. If the typical nineteenth-century American had a system of values implanted early in life which thereafter acted as a psychological gyroscope, then twentieth-century Americans had built-in radar systems tuned to the sounds around them. Riesman detected the emergence of this other-directed personality chiefly "in the upper middle class of our larger cities." The children's story *Tootle* epitomized the new view. Tootle was a little engine who was taught to "always stay on the track no matter what" and who, when he strayed off the track to frolic in the fields, was pressured into returning. "The children who read Tootle," Riesman said, "are manipulated away from rebellion and taught the lesson of obedience to signals."

As sociologists found evidence of conformity in the American present, historians discovered evidence of consensus in the nation's past. Many historians in the 1950s minimized conflict and emphasized continuity. David Potter's *People of Plenty* (1954) held that material abundance—the product of "human ingenuity, human initiative, human adaptability, and human enterprise"—had shaped American character. Potter admitted the existence of some inequality (although the word *poverty* did not appear in his index), but noted that social inequality violated the nation's most cherished ideals. He concluded that "in every aspect of material plenty America possesses unprecedented riches and . . . these are very widely distributed."

Unprecedented affluence and the broad acceptance of middle-class liberal values meant that American society had escaped the bitter class antagonism that had plagued Europe, or so argued Louis Hartz in *The Liberal Tradition in America* (1955). Daniel Boorstin asserted that Americans had always shown a lack of interest in ideology. They had been concerned, rather, with finding practical solutions to everyday problems. That, to Boorstin, constituted "the genius of American politics." In the view of these historians, the American past was as free of doctrinal clashes as of widespread suffering or sharp class rivalry.

Boorstin believed that this historical tradition fitted Americans "to understand the meaning of conservatism." During the 1950s a group of self-styled "new conservatives" attempted to clarify that meaning. They reiterated the importance of religion, tradition, hierarchy, property rights, and the organic conception of society. The conservatives pointed to their own "sense of human limitation and frailty, as opposed to the megalomaniac faith in limitless progress through mass-movements and material reforms." They continued in varying degrees to oppose the expansion of the welfare state, which they thought rested on the dangerous premise that "justice is identical with equality." If anything identified the new conservatives, it was their assault on "relativism," that is, on the unwillingness of society to uphold correct moral values and stamp out evil ones. This idea was carried furthest, perhaps, in William F. Buckley's *God and Man at Yale* (1951). Buckley, then a recent Yale graduate, condemned the university for hiring professors who caused students to doubt Christianity and the virtues of free enterprise. Buckley claimed that a private university had the duty to inculcate the values held by its financial backers. Professors who did not wish to teach those values, of course, had the right to seek employment elsewhere. The book went through five printings in the first six months of publication.

## REPUBLICANS ON THE POTOMAC

In Dwight Eisenhower the American people found a figure who perfectly suited their mood. In the 1952 campaign Eisenhower exploited the issues identified by the formula "$K_1C_2$"—Korea, communism, and corruption. Of the three, Korea was the most critical. By the fall of 1952 slightly more than half the electorate regarded the war—or, more accurately, how it might be ended—as the single most important issue. Democratic candidate Adlai E. Stevenson of Illinois fully endorsed Truman's war policies, even suggesting that the nation brace itself for years of additional sacrifice. "The ordeal of the twentieth century is far from over," Stevenson said in accepting the nomination. Eisenhower, who also had backed the decision to wage a limited war in Korea, nevertheless seemed to offer a way out of the quagmire. Two weeks before the election he said, "I shall go to Korea," and though he did not say what he would do when he got there, his pledge, coming from a man identified with victory in World War II, was a masterful stroke. Popularly regarded as the candidate best able to end the war, Eisenhower was politically irresistible. It was appropriate that the last word of his last campaign address was "peace."

The two other issues also worked to Eisenhower's benefit. Republican charges that the Truman administration was infested with Communists and that Stevenson was himself dangerously "soft" came not only from Joseph McCarthy but also from Eisenhower's running mate. Richard Nixon spoke of "Adlai the Appeaser," who lacked "backbone training" because he was a "Ph.D. graduate of Dean Acheson's cowardly college of Communist containment." Stevenson was vulnerable because he had once given a deposition attesting to Alger Hiss's good reputation. As governor of Illinois, moreover, he had courageously vetoed a bill requiring loyalty oaths of all state employees.

The issue of corruption hammered a last nail into the Democrats' coffin. In its last years the Truman administration was plagued by scandals, many of them involving money-making schemes or influence peddling by the President's cronies. Promising to "drive the crooks and the Communists from their seats of power," Eisenhower embarked on a moral crusade for decent government. Electing a Democrat to replace Truman, an Indiana Republican suggested, would be equivalent to "putting a new pin on a soiled diaper." On the eve of the inauguration one supporter told Eisenhower that "for the first time in many years the country feels clean again."

What was striking about the election was not so much the magnitude of Eisenhower's victory—he received 55 percent of the vote and carried thirty-nine states—as the high level of voter interest. In 1948 only 51.5 percent of those eligible had voted, but in 1952 the turnout was 62.7 percent. Eisenhower broke through traditional Democratic strongholds, winning nearly half the popular vote in the South (doing particularly well in the cities) and carrying Virginia, Florida, Texas, and Tennessee. Stevenson's reluctance to campaign on the old New Deal slogans and Eisenhower's reputation as a liberal Republican combined to mute economic issues. The Republicans, therefore, did better than they had expected in working-class wards. Whether as a result of his promise to end the war, his crusade for clean government, or his reputation as a family man (in contrast to the divorced Stevenson), Eisenhower was even more popular among women (58.5 percent) than men (52.5 percent). Most significant of all was his showing among the middle class in the burgeoning suburbs. Stevenson captured New York City, Chicago, Cleveland, and Boston, but in each case Eisenhower won the surrounding suburbs by even larger pluralities, thereby offsetting the Democrats' advantage. These expanding areas also had exceedingly high turnout rates.

Critics of Eisenhower interpreted the 1952 election as a popularity contest involving no real issues beyond Ike's famous grin and twinkling blue eyes. They were mistaken. So, too, were those who saw him as a babe in the woods who did not understand politics or the use of power. If Eisenhower seemed to remain above political battles it was because he recognized that his reputation for nonpartisanship was an important political asset. As one advisor explained to him, "The people want another George Washington. They really think of you as a modern George Washington." If Eisenhower urged his program on congressional Republicans cautiously, it was because he knew that his party was torn between a liberal and conservative wing. He wanted to heal rather than widen the rift. If Eisenhower adopted a more restrained view of presidential authority than his Democratic predecessors, it was because of his belief in the separation of powers and his distaste for emotionally charged disputes. None of this, however, prevented him from manipulating his powers to influence legislation or from using patronage to reward loyal followers. He also fashioned an orderly administrative system based on a clear chain of command.

To staff his Cabinet, Eisenhower relied primarily on successful businessmen, many of whom had some political experience. Secretary of the Treasury George M. Humphrey, a staunch fiscal conservative, had headed a successful steel company in Ohio. Three other Cabinet members—Secretary of the Interior Douglas McKay, Postmaster General Arthur Summerfield, and Secretary of Defense Charles E. Wilson—had made their fortunes in the automobile industry, giving some point to Adlai Stevenson's quip that the New Dealers were making way for the car dealers. Wilson, who had served as president of General Motors since 1940, once explained his reluctance to use defense contracts for the purpose of reducing unemployment in words that few workers appreciated: "I've always liked bird dogs better than kennel dogs myself. You know, one who will get out and hunt for food rather than sit on his fanny and yell." The rhetoric of the automobile industry even crept into Cabinet discussions. On one occasion, explaining why large cuts in defense spending were necessary,

Humphrey said to Wilson: "Charley, . . . you just got to get out the best damn *streamlined model* you ever did in your life. . . . This means a *brand new model*—we can't just patch up the old jalopy."

These appointments fairly reflected Eisenhower's own outlook. The new President was determined to reverse the direction taken by the New Deal and Fair Deal or, in his words, to remove "the Left-Wingish, pinkish influence in our life." Referring to the Tennessee Valley Authority, which symbolized such intervention in the economy, Eisenhower once blurted out: "By God, if ever we could do it, before we leave here, I'd like to see us *sell* the whole thing, but I suppose we can't go that far." The President demonstrated his economic orthodoxy by removing the moderate wage and price controls Truman had instituted, and by closing down many small federally operated establishments that appeared to compete with private business. In addition, Eisenhower cut the government payroll by two hundred thousand workers and trimmed federal spending by 10 percent—or $6 billion—in his first year. In 1954 Congress enacted an administration measure lowering price supports for farm products.

His position on natural resource development clearly revealed Eisenhower's desire to limit federal involvement. The President consistently favored private rather than public development of hydroelectric power plants. He reversed Truman's decision to proceed with federal construction of such a plant in Hell's Canyon, Idaho, licensed a private firm to build the dams, and threatened to veto any legislation looking toward federal development. Eisenhower opposed the Tennessee Valley Authority's request to build a new plant to furnish power for the Atomic Energy Commission. The commission instead awarded the contract to a private concern known as Dixon-Yates. When a 1955 congressional investigation revealed that the consultant who advised the commission to accept this arrangement was connected with an investment firm that marketed Dixon-Yates securities, a scandal erupted and Eisenhower had to cancel the contract. Finally, the President favored granting the states control of offshore oil deposits within their historic boundaries (usually a distance of three miles). Truman had twice vetoed such legislation on the grounds that tidelands oil belonged to the federal government. In May 1953, much to the delight of Texas, California, and Louisiana, Eisenhower signed the Submerged Lands Act, turning these rights over to the states.

But despite Eisenhower's inclination, he in fact presided over a further enlargement of the welfare state. The social security system was expanded to include more workers, to increase benefits, and to lower the age of eligibility for old-age pensions. In 1954 an additional 4 million workers were brought under the unemployment insurance program. In 1955 Congress raised the minimum wage from 75 cents to $1.00 an hour (although Eisenhower had favored a 90-cent limit). The administration supported, unsuccessfully, a modest program to provide $200 million over three years to assist school construction in impoverished districts. The President also won authorization for building an additional 35,000 public housing units. Finally, the Interstate Highway Act (1956) provided for the construction of a modern interstate highway system. In urging its enactment, Eisenhower pointed out that new roads could reduce traffic accidents, relieve the massive congestion sure to develop as automobile use increased, and provide for quick evacuation "in case of an atomic attack on our key cities."

In expanding government benefits the Eisenhower administration was responding, in part, to congressional pressure. Although the Republicans won a slim victory in Congress in 1952 (they controlled the Senate by one vote and the House by ten), the Democrats recaptured control of both houses in 1954 and retained it throughout the remainder of Eisenhower's presidency. The administration was also taking account of economic realities. Sharp recessions in 1954 and 1958 led the President to abandon his budget-balancing efforts and to accelerate spending. The government therefore ran a deficit in five of his eight years in office. The people had not elected Eisenhower to dismantle the welfare state, the President's brother observed. Conveying the results of a public opinion poll, Milton Eisenhower said: "Please note the 'new conservatism' really means that we should keep what we have, catch our breath for a while, and improve administration; it does not mean moving backward." In the main, that was the prescription the Eisenhower administration followed.

## THE WANING OF McCARTHYISM

The President was as determined to step up the campaign against internal subversion as he was to curb the expansion of the welfare state. Eisenhower succeeded in toughening the government loyalty program. He turned responsibility for loyalty investigations over to departmental security officers who evaluated all employees and submitted reports to each department head for action. The administration also introduced stricter standards for measuring loyalty. The old criteria—reasonable grounds for believing an employee disloyal (1947) or reasonable doubt as to an employee's loyalty (1951)—no longer sufficed. As of 1953 the government would dismiss any "security risk," which meant that it would seek information concerning "any behavior, activities, or associations which tend to show that the individual is not reliable or trustworthy." Partly to appease right-wing Republicans, the State Department appointed an ardent McCarthyite, Scott McLeod, as security officer. Within a year, McLeod had ousted 484 persons, including several career officials whose only crime had been to tell the truth about the relative strength of the Communist and nationalist forces in China. Even Joe McCarthy seemed satisfied, commenting that the new loyalty program was "pretty darn good, if the administration is sincere."

Perhaps the most famous alleged "security risk" was Dr. J. Robert Oppenheimer, who had headed the project to develop the atomic bomb during World War II. A man of profound intellect who exerted a charismatic hold on his fellow physicists, Oppenheimer had associated with left-wing causes and individuals during the late 1930s. The government compiled a massive dossier on him during the war but knew him to be loyal, considered him indispensable, and regarded his activities as merely indiscreet. Disturbed by the nuclear arms race, Oppenheimer unsuccessfully opposed the decision to proceed with a

Dr. J. Robert Oppenheimer. *(Henri Cartier Bresson/Magnum.)*

hydrogen bomb in 1949. By 1953 he was head of Princeton's Institute for Advanced Study, retaining only a consultant's contract with the Atomic Energy Commission. When his old dossier was dragged out, Eisenhower directed that a "blank wall" be erected between Oppenheimer and sensitive material. When Oppenheimer refused to resign his contract, a hearing was held in the spring of 1954 that deteriorated into a judicial farce. A special panel found, by a vote of 2 to 1, that reinstating Oppenheimer's clearance would be inconsistent with national security. The Atomic Energy Commission upheld the ruling because Oppenheimer's association with radicals had exceeded the "tolerable limits of prudence and self-restraint," because his attitude toward the hydrogen bomb was "disturbing," and because of fundamental defects in his "character." Nine years later the government implicitly conceded the injustice by presenting the

Fermi Award for distinguished contributions to American science to Oppenheimer at a White House ceremony.

Congress, too, joined the continuing hunt for domestic radicals in 1954.
When a conservative Republican endeavored to amend the Internal Security
Act (1950) by requiring Communist-infiltrated (as well as Communist and
Communist-dominated) organizations to register with the attorney general, a
liberal Democrat offered a counterproposal: that the Communist party itself be
defined as an "agency of a hostile foreign power" and stripped of the privileges
political groups usually enjoyed. Hubert Humphrey of Minnesota, who proposed the change, declared: "I do not intend to be a half-patriot." In the end,
the Communist Control Act (1954) incorporated both provisions, and it passed
the Senate with but one dissenting vote. The act asserted that the Communist
party was "an instrumentality of a conspiracy to overthrow the Government"
and declared that its existence constituted a "clear, present and continuing danger." The measure was seldom invoked, although it once served to deny a
Communist candidate a place on the ballot in a New Jersey election.

The new security program, the Oppenheimer case, and the mood in Congress all revealed the persistence of anticommunism. But by 1954 the worst of
the hysteria was beginning to fade, and with it ebbed the power of Joseph
McCarthy. Eisenhower, who strongly disapproved of McCarthy's tactics, had
been reluctant to challenge the junior senator from Wisconsin. Campaigning in
Wisconsin in 1952, Eisenhower had agreed not to make a speech defending
General George Marshall, whom he admired greatly, on the grounds that to do
so would alienate McCarthy's followers and hurt the Republican ticket. As one
worried politician informed an Eisenhower aide, "When a man calls on the
Pope, he doesn't tell him what a fine fellow Martin Luther was." After the election Eisenhower refused to criticize McCarthy publicly. Privately he said he
would not "get into the gutter with that guy," although he confessed that "at
times one feels almost like hanging his head in shame when he reads some of
the unreasoned, vicious outbursts of demagoguery that appear in our public
prints." Then, in 1954, McCarthy crossed swords with two institutions—the
Army and the Senate—and they proved too powerful for him.

The Army seemed a most unlikely target, but McCarthy accused it of promoting and giving an honorable discharge to a dentist who, in filling out loyalty forms, had refused to answer questions about his political affiliations.
McCarthy criticized the man responsible, General Ralph Zwicker, as not having
"the brains of a five-year-old." The senator warned Secretary of the Army
Robert Stevens: "I am going to kick the brains out of anyone who protects Communists!" The Army retorted that McCarthy had tried to pull strings to obtain
preferential treatment for a recently inducted member of his staff. Stevens and
McCarthy then lumbered toward a showdown. Congressional hearings into the
controversy began before a nationwide television audience in April 1954 and
continued for two months. Toward the end, enraged by the attempt of attorney
Joseph Welch to poke fun at his allegations, McCarthy savagely attacked a
lawyer employed by Welch's law firm for having once belonged to a left-wing
organization. Welch then berated McCarthy, concluding, "Have you no sense of

decency, sir, at long last? Have you left no sense of decency?" That the congressional committee found some of the Army's allegations well founded was less important than that many Americans, offended by McCarthy's tactics, had begun to ask the same question.

By hurling wild accusations, McCarthy managed to alienate almost all Senate Democrats and a considerable number of Republicans. "The hard fact is that those who wear the label—Democrat—wear with it the stain of an historic betrayal," he thundered in 1954. McCarthy called Democrat J. William Fulbright "halfbright" and termed Republican Senator Ralph Flanders "senile. I think they should get a man with a net and take him to a good quiet place." In June 1954 Flanders introduced a motion to censure McCarthy. It was referred to a special committee that in September recommended censure on two counts: showing contempt for the Senate by refusing to testify before a subcommittee investigating the use of campaign funds in 1952, and abusing General Zwicker. In December, with the midterm elections safely past, the Senate censured McCarthy on the first count only. The vote was 67 to 22, with Democrats voting unanimously for censure and Republicans dividing evenly. Terming the action a "lynch party," McCarthy apologized to the people for having supported Eisenhower two years earlier. McCarthy retained his committee assignments but suffered a great loss of prestige. His popularity continued to diminish until his death three years later.

Eisenhower made his most significant contribution to civil liberties through his Supreme Court appointments. His choice of Earl Warren to replace Fred Vinson as Chief Justice in September 1953 was especially important. In 1956 Warren delivered an opinion in which the Court ruled that the federal Smith Act preempted the field of sedition, thereby rendering state sedition laws invalid. The Court upheld a lower-court decision that overturned the conviction of a Communist sentenced to twenty years in prison for having violated a Pennsylvania ordinance. A year later the Court dealt a crippling blow to the Smith Act in *Yates* v. *U.S.* (1957). John Marshall Harlan, another Eisenhower appointee, ruled for the majority that the Smith Act's injunction against conspiring to advocate the forcible overthrow of the government applied to the advocacy of concrete actions but not abstract principles. If one did not call for direct revolutionary acts, one could lawfully urge the overthrow of the government. The *Yates* decision rendered further prosecutions under the Smith Act all but impossible.

## DESEGREGATION AND THE SOUTH

If the Supreme Court took a leading role in defending civil liberties, it came close to revolutionizing patterns of race relations. On May 17, 1954, in *Brown* v. *Board of Education,* the Court unanimously overturned the "separate but equal" doctrine. That doctrine, first elaborated in *Plessy* v. *Ferguson* (1896), had allowed states to provide segregated facilities as long as they were of the same quality. It provided the legal foundation for the intricate Jim Crow system in the South, which included everything from separate schools, hospitals, and railroad cars to separate football fields, drinking fountains, and restrooms. By 1950, the Court had supported the right of blacks to attend white universities or law schools, but on the grounds that those facilities could not be duplicated. In the *Brown* decision, however, the Court met the issue squarely, holding that separate public schools were inherently unequal and therefore unconstitutional. Unanimity was possible only because of the influence of Chief Justice Earl Warren. One member of the Court admitted that had the decision come a year earlier, four justices would have dissented and the majority would have written separate opinions. That, he believed, "would have been catastrophic," for only a unanimous decision stood much chance of winning public approval.

To achieve unanimity, however, Warren avoided claiming that the framers of the Fourteenth Amendment had intended to bar segregated schools, for the evidence was at best "inconclusive." Instead, the Court relied on the work of sociologists and psychologists. Even though the buildings might be of similar quality, Warren asserted, racially segregated schools had a harmful effect on black children by creating "a feeling of inferiority as to their status in the community that may affect their hearts and minds in a way unlikely ever to be undone." In asserting that this conclusion was "amply supported by modern authority," the Court relied largely on studies that indicated black children often placed a higher value on white skin color than on black, thereby revealing what one psychologist termed "basic feelings of inferiority, conflict, confusion in the self-image, resentment, hostility toward himself, hostility toward whites." The Court's reliance on evidence of this kind led such critics as Senator Sam J. Ervin of North Carolina to claim that the justices had "substituted their personal political and social ideas for the established law of the land."

Recognizing that its decision required a monumental change in Southern life and was sure to provoke intense opposition, the Supreme Court decided to allow ample time for implementation. In May 1955, in a second school decision, it asked local federal courts to determine the pace of desegregation. Insisting only that a "prompt and reasonable start" be made and that desegregation proceed "with all deliberate speed," the Court acknowledged that it would take time to iron out problems relating to administration, school size, transportation, and personnel. A "declaration of unconstitutionality is not a wand by which these transformations can be accomplished," one justice noted privately. "Not even a Court can in a day change a deplorable situation into the ideal. It does its duty if it gets effectively under way the righting of a wrong." The Court, fearing that the inability to enforce a decision would discredit the judicial process, was as committed to gradualism as to integration.

Public opinion polls indicated that most white Southerners—perhaps more than 80 percent—opposed the *Brown* ruling. In March 1956, 101 of the 128 Southern senators and congressmen echoed this sentiment by signing a "Southern manifesto," which blasted the Supreme Court. This much the Court may have anticipated, but no one was prepared for the wave of massive resistance that followed. In states of the Deep South, "White Citizens' Councils" were formed that applied economic pressure on blacks (and white businessmen) who were known to favor integration. In addition, measures of "interposition" were adopted whereby the states placed their authority behind local school board officials who defied federal court orders. Various states hounded the National Association for the Advancement of Colored People (NAACP) by demanding its membership lists, using such membership as a basis for dismissal from state employment, and making it a crime to incite a disturbance by attacking local segregation ordinances. In some cases, rock-throwing mobs prevented black children from attending classes with whites.

Of all the techniques of evasion and defiance, none was more effective than the pupil placement laws. Enacted in many states after 1954, these laws provided for the assignment of students on an individual basis. The criteria established by Georgia were typical. They permitted school boards to consider "the psychological qualification of the pupil for the type of teaching and associations involved," "the psychological effect upon the pupil of attendance at a particular school," "the ability to accept or conform to new and different educational environments," "the morals, conduct, health, and personal standards of the pupil," and "mental energy and ability." The result was that black and white children were invariably assigned to different schools. In 1958 the

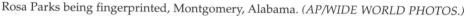

Rosa Parks being fingerprinted, Montgomery, Alabama. *(AP/WIDE WORLD PHOTOS.)*

Supreme Court accepted the constitutionality of such laws. Consequently, ten years after the *Brown* ruling, the vast majority of black children in the South still attended segregated schools.

Nevertheless, the forces unleashed by the Supreme Court helped inspire Southern blacks to adopt a more militant posture. In December 1955 blacks in Montgomery, Alabama, began a boycott of city buses to protest Jim Crow seating practices which required blacks to vacate seats and move to the rear to make room for whites who had boarded after them. The boycott began when seamstress Rosa Parks, a long-time NAACP member and well-known member of Montgomery's black community, was arrested for refusing a bus driver's request to vacate her seat for a white male passenger. The protesters demanded courteous treatment by bus drivers, employment of black drivers in black districts, and seating on a first-come, first-served basis with "Negroes seated from the back of the bus toward the front, [and] whites seated from the front toward the back."

The boycott's leader was 27-year-old Martin Luther King, Jr., who, after having received a divinity degree and a doctorate in theology from Boston University, had become pastor of the Dexter Avenue Baptist Church. King considered his task that of "combining the militant and the moderate." He preached a philosophy of nonviolent resistance, declaring: "We must meet the forces of hate with the power of love; we must meet physical force with soul force." By arranging car and taxi pools and sometimes walking long distances, Montgomery's blacks made the boycott effective. They also adhered to King's teachings even when whites retaliated with mass arrests and intimidation. The movement finally achieved victory in May 1956, when a district court ruled segregation on the city buses illegal, and when the Supreme Court affirmed the ruling six months later. After another flurry of violence, beatings, and bombings, desegregation was carried out. In 1957 King also established the Southern Christian Leadership Conference, which served thereafter as his organizational base.

Turmoil in the South ultimately had repercussions in Washington. Eisenhower personally regretted the 1954 desegregation ruling, believing that law could not alter age-old customs overnight and that, in his words, "we can't demand perfection in these moral questions." The President also opposed federal infringement on states' rights. Yet in the District of Columbia, where the states' rights problem did not arise, Eisenhower moved swiftly to comply with court orders. His administration ended segregation in Washington's restaurants, hotels, theaters, and public schools. Although Eisenhower approached the matter of legislation gingerly, he eventually concurred with Attorney General Herbert Brownell, who favored legislative action. In 1957 Congress passed the first civil rights act in eighty-two years, empowering the Justice Department to seek injunctions against interference with the right to vote and creating a Commission on Civil Rights to investigate such occurrences. Although clothed only with fact-finding powers, the commission viewed its chief task as "restoring the franchise to all American citizens." In its report, which demonstrated beyond any doubt that a pattern of discrimination barred blacks from voting in

## JACK KEROUAC AND THE BEAT GENERATION

Jack Kerouac's novel *On the Road* was published in 1957 and instantly became a bestseller. It had taken Kerouac six years to find a publisher, but that was hardly surprising since the manuscript, in its original form, violated all literary conventions. Typed as an unbroken, seldom-punctuated, single-spaced paragraph, on a 250-foot roll of shelf paper (the last six feet of which were rewritten when a pet cocker spaniel chewed them up), the

Beat writers William Burroughs, Peter Orlovsky, Gregory Corso, and Allen Ginsberg. (*Burton Glinn/Magnum.*)

novel appeared only after it had been heavily edited by the publisher. According to Kerouac's biographer, Ann Charters, *On the Road* "captured the spirit of his own generation, their restlessness and confusions in the years immediately following World War II." Centering on a series of cross-country automobile trips taken by Kerouac and his friends in the late 1940s, the novel popularized the lifestyle associated with the major figures in the Beat Movement. The fictional characters—Sal Paradise, Dean Moriarty, Carlo Marx, and Old Bull Lee—had real-life counterparts in Kerouac, Neal Cassady, Allen Ginsberg, and William Burroughs.

To say, as one critic has, that *On the Road* depicted "an underground subculture that departed entirely from the dominant middle class mores of the fifties" is to understate the matter. Beat writers, rejecting socially prescribed roles and socially approved forms of behavior, exhibited more contempt than pity for the "square" world, for "the middle-class non-identity which usually finds its perfect expression . . . in rows of well-to-do houses with lawns and television sets in each living room with everybody looking at the same thing and thinking the same thing at the same time." The Beats most admired those who in their view were the least tied down by obligations to career or country—the poets, the hoodlums, the junkies, the hoboes, the jazz musicians, and the blacks. Those groups, generally regarded as among the most deprived in the nation, were from the Beat perspective among the most fortunate: free to take life as it came, to act with abandon, to appreciate the intensity of each experience, to "dig everything."

Though Beat writings contained a critique of conformity, technology, and mechanization, Beat writers shared no single political outlook. Allen Ginsberg (whose poem *Howl* began "I saw the best minds of my generation destroyed by madness, starving hysterical naked/dragging themselves through the negro streets at dawn looking for an angry fix") offered a thoroughly radical indictment of American society, its anti-Communist paranoia, and a reliance on nuclear weapons. Yet William Burroughs, the author of another Beat classic, *Naked Lunch* (1959), believed that "increased government control leads to a totalitarian state." In 1956 Kerouac declared that if he were to vote it would be for Dwight Eisenhower. The key word was *if*. What united the Beats was a conviction that politics held few answers to life's most crucial problems. Those problems required personal rather than social solutions. The characteristic Beat stance was one of political disengagement.

Beat authors received much acclaim in the 1950s (a reviewer in the *New York Times* hailed publication of *On the Road* as a "historic occasion"), but they more commonly encountered hostility. *Time* magazine, denouncing the Beats as "disorganization" men concerned only with self-gratification, labeled Ginsberg "the discount-house Whitman of the Beat

Jack Kerouac, 1958. *(BETTMANN.)*

Allen Ginsberg at Kerouac's gravesite, 1969. *(Peter Simon/Stock, Boston.)*

Generation." Another reviewer, in a blistering assault on "the Know-Nothing Bohemians," remarked on Kerouac's "simple inability to say anything in words." The Customs Bureau seized copies of *Howl*, attempting to repress it on the grounds of obscenity. In 1957, however, a judge in San Francisco cleared the poem of those charges. William Burroughs spent years in self-imposed exile to avoid indictment for drug possession, and Neal Cassady went to jail in 1958 for marijuana possession. Kerouac, a victim of alcoholism, died at the age of 47 in 1969. He had been too ill in his final years to realize that the cultural rebellion then sweeping across the nation owed much to the Beat generation.

the South, the commission recommended the appointment of temporary federal registrars as a solution.

The Eisenhower administration faced its most explosive civil rights crisis in Little Rock, Arkansas. Desegregation of Central High School was scheduled to begin in September 1957. But many whites wished to obstruct the plan, and the state's ambitious governor, Orville Faubus, believed that supporting desegregation would mean political suicide. To avert violence when school opened, Faubus sent the National Guard to Little Rock with instructions to prevent integration. The guardsmen, bayonets at the ready, turned back nine blacks who sought admission and maintained segregation for nearly three weeks until a federal judge ordered them to desist. When Faubus removed the troops, a howling mob overwhelmed the police who tried to protect the black students. With the level of tension rising by the hour, the mayor appealed to Eisenhower, informing him that the "situation is out of control and police cannot disperse the mob." Eisenhower responded by sending federal troops to uphold the court order. The President told one unhappy Southern senator that "failure to act in such a case would be tantamount to acquiescence in anarchy and the dissolution of the union." Troops patrolled the high school for months, but the controversy over desegregation convulsed the city for two more years.

## ACHESON TO DULLES

As massive change began at home, so similar rumbles began to shake a world supposedly divided rigidly into only "two camps." Secretary of State John Foster Dulles had difficulty comprehending the rumbles partly because of his own unbending anti-Communist views. The deeply religious son of a Presbyterian minister, Dulles hated atheistic communism. As the senior partner of a great New York law firm, Dulles had formed ties during the interwar period with Western nations that were staunchly anti-Soviet. His diplomatic experience reached back to 1919, and this long background plus his religious beliefs led Eisenhower to remark, "To me he is like a patriarch out of the Old Testament."

Several other convictions were perhaps most important in shaping Dulles's policies. He had served under Dean Acheson, notably as the negotiator for the Japanese security treaty. If anything, Dulles believed Acheson had not been tough enough, certainly not anti-Communist enough publicly to quiet such critics as Joseph McCarthy. Dulles therefore proclaimed in 1952 that his policies would aim at "peaceful liberation" of Communist areas, not mere containment. This meant no negotiations with the Soviets. Even after Stalin's death in March 1953 and Winston Churchill's public plea for a summit conference to reduce cold war tensions, Dulles assured Americans that he would continue to fight rather than negotiate. Churchill disgustedly remarked that Dulles was "the only bull I know who carried his china shop with him." The secretary's belief that he had to appease McCarthy and other congressmen also resulted in a purge of Foreign Service officers that crippled the American diplomatic corps for the next decade.

Atomic bomb test in Yucca Flat, Nevada, 1953. (*J. R. Eyerman*, Life *Magazine © Time Inc.*)

Finally, Dulles assumed that for economic and strategic reasons, the United States had to intensify Acheson's drive to integrate the free world within a system controlled by Americans. Dulles constantly worried that Communists would gain control of such third-world areas as Southeast Asia and the Middle East, which contained rich raw materials, and thus be able to slowly strangle the U.S. economy.

Despite Dulles's fears, American policies were usually restrained because Eisenhower kept a firm leash on the State Department. The President once remarked, "There's only one man I know who has seen more of the world and talked with more people and knows more than [Dulles] does—and that's me."

Eisenhower rejected Dulles's advice to end the Korean conflict "by giving the Chinese one hell of a licking." Instead, the President, knowing military victory impossible, obtained an armistice in mid-1953 by using a combination of diplomacy and military threat (including the deployment of atomic-tipped missiles in Korea when China and North Korea refused to make peace). Eisenhower's primary concern was to balance the budget and thereby, he believed, invigorate the economy. He cut Truman's military budget, especially the expensive ground combat forces. Informing his Cabinet that "peace rests squarely on, among other things, productivity," the President emphasized that "unless we can put things in the hands of people who are starving to death we can never lick communism." His concern heightened when in the mid-1950s Russia's economy grew at the rate of 7 percent annually while America's economy increased at about half that figure. Eisenhower nevertheless retained faith in the free-market system, refused to inject massive monies for defense during his first term, and left office warning about the dangers of "a military-industrial complex."

Dulles's diplomacy therefore had to rely not on conventional ground troops, but rather on nuclear "massive retaliation," or, as he defined it, the ability "to retaliate instantly against open aggression by Red Armies . . . by means of our own choosing." Dulles and new military strategists, such as 30-year-old Henry Kissinger of Harvard, declared that atomic weapons could be refined so that they could be effectively used in conventional wars. Cheaper than troops, such weapons could give the country "more bang for a buck." Meanwhile, Dulles flew around the globe establishing new alliances with nations on the Communist borders. These countries, especially those in the Middle East (where the Central Treaty Organization, or CENTO, was formed) and in Southeast Asia (where the Southeast Asia Treaty Organization, or SEATO, developed), would, it was hoped, provide the personnel while the United States would provide atomic support if necessary. The secretary might have proclaimed "peaceful liberation," but Eisenhower was in effect following Truman's "containment" idea.

To establish these policies, Eisenhower worked effectively with Congress. Yet the new President fought back hard and successfully in 1954 when conservatives, led by Republican Senator John Bricker of Ohio, tried to pass the "Bricker Amendment" to the Constitution. This proposal gave Congress additional power over the President's constitutional right to make treaties. It especially struck at executive agreements (those made by the President with a foreign power which would be binding only for the President's term in office, but which usually remained in effect much longer—as had Roosevelt's executive agreements at Yalta). Eisenhower refused to compromise his power. Overcoming strong Southern Democratic and Republican support for the amendment, he defeated it by a narrow margin.

## CRISES IN A THIRD CAMP: IRAN, GUATEMALA, AND SOUTHEAST ASIA

Fate tricked Eisenhower and Dulles. They were prepared to deal with Stalinist Russia, but Stalin died in March 1953. The new Soviet leadership, soon headed by Nikita Khrushchev, changed some policies, concentrated on internal development, and made overtures to Tito and Mao Tse-tung—leaders whom Stalin had angered with his iron-fisted methods. Eisenhower and Dulles had also planned to concentrate on European affairs, the area they knew best. In 1954 the secretary of state and British officials finally pressured France to agree to German rearmament and membership in the North Atlantic Treaty Organization (NATO). The following year Dulles could claim a victory for "liberation" as Soviet troops finally left Austria after the Austrians promised they would not join any anti-Soviet alliance. Washington's European policies seemed firmly in place.

But American energies soon had to switch to the newly emerging nations. The focal point of the cold war was changing. Dulles understood the importance of this "third camp." "To oppose nationalism is counterproductive," he declared. He worked to remove British and French colonialism from the Middle East and Asia before the foreign domination triggered further radical nationalism. But he also expected the new nations to be pro-American and anti-Communist: hence his famous remark that "neutrality . . . is an immoral and short-sighted conception." Fearing that Khrushchev's economic and ideological power might woo the third world to the Soviets, Dulles grimly warned NATO leaders of the possible consequences: "The world ratio as between Communist dominated peoples and free peoples would change from a ratio of two-to-one in favor of freedom to a ratio of one-to-three against freedom. That," the secretary of state emphasized, "would be an almost intolerable ratio, given the industrialized nature of the Atlantic community and its dependence upon broad markets and access to raw materials."

Within eighteen months after entering office, Eisenhower scored two triumphs in the third world. In Iran, a nationalist government under Mohammed Mossadegh in 1951 had taken over the nation's rich oil wells from British companies that had long exploited them. Mossadegh's action set a dangerous precedent, for the Middle East held nearly 90 percent of all non-Communist oil reserves, and his success could lead to similar seizures elsewhere. In 1953 the U.S. Central Intelligence Agency worked with Iranian army officers to overthrow Mossadegh, give full powers to the friendly Shah of Iran, and restore the oil wells to the companies. But henceforth British oil firms had to share the profits with American companies.

Eisenhower performed an encore in Latin America. Since 1947 the United States had kept its southern neighbors in line by military aid, channeled through the Rio Pact of 1947 (a hemispheric military alliance that was a precursor of NATO), and the establishment of the Organization of American States (OAS) in 1948. In the OAS Charter, each nation promised not to intervene in one another's internal affairs, to consult frequently, and to resolve disputes peacefully. The United States, however, refused to give economic aid that the Latin Americans desperately needed, particularly when their raw materials dropped steeply in price during the mid-1950s.

Guatemalan officials took matters into their own hands. In this desperately poor nation, roughly the size of Tennessee, a 1944 revolution had weakened the dictatorial rule of a few wealthy Guatemalans who had long dominated affairs. During 1953 Colonel Jacobo Arbenz Guzmán accelerated the reform, seizing vast properties held by the American-owned United Fruit Company. Dulles demanded prompt payment for the property. Guatemala was obviously unable to pay immediately. In May 1954, as U.S. threats grew more ominous, the Arbenz government received a shipment of arms from the Communist bloc. Dulles responded swiftly. In April he had obtained a general anti-Communist resolution from the OAS clearly aimed at Guatemala. Now he armed an anti-Arbenz force that had gathered in neighboring Honduras. In June 1954 this unit of Guatemalans marched into their country, overthrew Arbenz, and restored United Fruit's property. Dulles lied in publicly disclaiming any connection with the coup. He had little choice, for the United States had broken its own OAS pledge not to intervene in another nation's internal affairs. When Arbenz tried to obtain a hearing at the United Nations, Dulles blocked it. The United States had overthrown a constitutional government, and guerrilla warfare soon erupted again in Guatemala, but Eisenhower and Dulles believed that they had saved the hemisphere from communism.

The administration's next crisis was different. It occurred in Southeast Asia and required the delicate operation of removing French colonialism from Indochina (Cambodia, Laos, and Vietnam) while preventing Ho Chi Minh, who was both nationalist and Communist, from obtaining power in Vietnam. Since 1950 American aid to France had multiplied until by 1953 it accounted for 80 percent of the French war budget for Indochina. France nevertheless suffered defeat after defeat at the hands of Ho's troops. In early 1954 the French made a catastrophic blunder by committing main forces to the indefensible area of Dienbienphu. Paris appealed for help. Dulles wanted to intervene, as did Vice-President Richard Nixon, and the administration even discussed the use of atomic weapons. Eisenhower's military sense stopped what could have been a tragedy. He refused to intervene with conventional forces unless congressional leaders approved and Great Britain agreed to join the effort. Neither would go along. The opposition of the Senate Democratic leader, Lyndon Johnson of Texas, was especially strong.

The defeated French then met with Ho's government and other interested nations at Geneva, Switzerland. Two agreements emerged in July 1954. The first, signed only by France and Ho's regime, worked out a cease-fire arrangement. To carry out this agreement, a temporary dividing line was drawn across Vietnam at the 17th parallel. The second document, the "Final Declaration," provided for reuniting the country under procedures that were to climax with elections in 1956. The document further stated that the 17th parallel line "is provisional and should in no way be interpreted as a political or territorial boundary." The United States would not directly endorse this agreement. Ho could obviously win the election (Eisenhower later estimated he would have received 80 percent of the vote), and Dulles did not want to be a party to a pact giving Vietnam to a Communist regime. Instead, Eisenhower brought in Ngo Dinh Diem to head a new South Vietnam government. Diem had been living in an American Roman Catholic seminary. Dulles and Diem readily agreed that no national elections should be held. American aid rapidly flowed to Diem, and the United States now replaced France as the key foreign power in Southeast Asia.

John Foster Dulles and Dwight D. Eisenhower. *(Dwight D. Eisenhower Library.)*

The American commitment was neither accidental nor abrupt. The State Department had concluded in 1951 that Indochina had to be controlled for its "much-needed rice, rubber, and tin" and because its fall "would be taken by many as a sign that the force of communism is irresistible." A secret National Security Council paper in 1952 reiterated these points, adding that the loss of Southeast Asia would "make it extremely difficult to prevent Japan's eventual accommodation to Communism." Japan, which was the centerpiece of American policies in Asia, required Southeast Asia's markets and raw materials. Eisenhower publicly warned in 1954 that if Vietnam fell, the rest of non-Communist Asia could follow like a "fallen domino."

In late 1954 Dulles tried to keep the dominoes in place by establishing SEATO. The signatories (United States, France, Great Britain, Australia, New Zealand, the Philippines, Thailand, and Pakistan) promised to "consult immediately" if aggression occurred in the area. It was a weak alliance, made weaker by India's, Indonesia's, and Burma's refusal to join, but it would provide a major pretext for the American involvement in Vietnam during the 1960s. The Senate overwhelmingly ratified the SEATO pact. Meanwhile, when Communist China threatened small islands around Formosa, which China claimed were rightfully its own, Eisenhower warned that any move would be countered by the U.S. fleet. The President was even prepared to use nuclear weapons against China if it attacked the offshore islands. Dulles and Chiang then worked out a military alliance that assured long-term American support. To show its enthusiasm for these measures, the Senate vastly increased presidential powers by passing the "Formosa Resolution." This resolution gave Eisenhower the right to respond to crisis in regard to Formosa without consulting Congress. To fight the cold war more effectively, the Senate was surrendering its constitutional power to declare war.

## THE TURN: SUEZ AND HUNGARY, 1956

Centralized power had dangerous implications, particularly if it could be used irresponsibly in a world made up not simply of two camps, but rather of "gray areas," as the nations that disavowed both camps came to be known. The rapid emergence of such gray areas caused two momentous crises in 1956.

The first occurred early in the year when Nikita Khrushchev launched an attack against the ghost of Joseph Stalin by condemning him as a repressive ruler and military blunderer. Khrushchev hoped to consolidate his own power, remove Stalinists who opposed him, and gain room to carry out his own policies. The results, however, were quite different. Soviet-controlled nations of Eastern Europe seized on the speech as an opportunity for throwing off Stalinist policies and seeking their own nationalistic goals. Riots occurred in Hungary and Poland as crowds demanded the removal of Stalinist leaders. In early autumn, a confused Khrushchev bent to some demands, but the dissolution of the Soviet bloc continued.

Meanwhile the United States was also clashing with several of its client states. In 1952 the British had been forced by Egyptian nationalism to surrender their long hold on that country. Two years later, the government of General Abdul Nasser demanded that Britain turn over the vital Suez Canal to Egypt. Nasser's plans also included building a great Aswan dam on the Nile River to provide badly needed electric power. Dulles offered to help fund the dam, hoping that this would pull Nasser closer to the West. But Egypt then made an arms agreement with the Soviet bloc and recognized Communist China. Dulles retracted his offer, punishing Nasser before the world for dallying with the Communists. The Egyptian leader retaliated by seizing the Suez Canal in July 1956 so he could use the canal tolls to build the dam himself.

Dulles rushed across the Atlantic to work out a compromise. Before he could succeed, the British and French made a final effort in late October to restore their old imperial dreams by sending a military force into the Suez. They were joined by Israel, which hoped to improve the dangerously insecure borders it had lived with since 1948. Dulles and Eisenhower were aghast. They feared that the conflict would turn the Arabs against the West, lead to seizure of the vast Western-controlled oil resources in the area, and give Khrushchev the chance to inject Russian power into the Mediterranean theater. The United

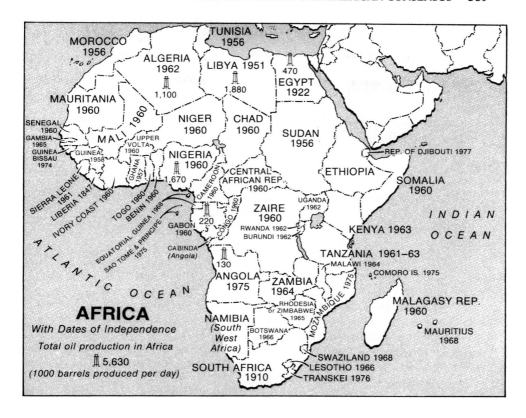

States demanded an immediate withdrawal by Anglo-French-Israeli forces and turned off large amounts of oil to England and France until they pulled back. Deserted by the Americans, the Europeans retreated, followed by the Israelis.

Khrushchev seized this opportunity to dispatch the Red Army and execution squads to end the anti-Stalinist uprisings in Hungary. Order was reimposed in Eastern Europe. The United States offered no aid to the Hungarian resistance—so ended Dulles's vaunted policy of "peaceful liberation." Russia then offered Nasser funds and experts to build the Aswan dam project. The Soviets were indeed a new presence in the Mediterranean. Equally important, Nasser had successfully defied one of the two superpowers, and the Poles, Hungarians, British, and French had vividly demonstrated that the world was no longer comprised of two monolithic camps. The second Eisenhower administration would begin in a radically altered world.

## Suggested Reading

Useful accounts of the Eisenhower administration are Charles C. Alexander, *Holding the Line: The Eisenhower Era* (1975); H. W. Brands, Jr., *Cold Warriors* (1988); Fred I. Greenstein, *The Hidden-Hand Presidency: Eisenhower as Leader* (New York, 1982); Chester J. Pach, Jr., and Elmo Richardson, *The Presidency of Dwight D. Eisenhower* (1991); and Gunter Bischof and Stephen E. Ambrose (eds.), *Eisenhower: A Centenary Assessment* (1995). On the 1952 election, consult Steven E. Ambrose, *Nixon . . . 1913–1962* (1987), and John Bartlow Martin, *Adlai Stevenson of Illinois* (1977). Important specialized studies include Gary Reichard, *The Reaffirmation of Republicanism* (1975); Duane Tananbaum, *Bricker Amendment Controversy* (1988); and Jeff Broadwater, *Eisenhower and the Anti-Communist Crusade* (1992).

For women's roles in the 1950s, see Betty Friedan, *The Feminine Mystique* (1963); Elaine Tyler May, *Homeward Bound: American Families in the Cold War Era* (1988); and Joanne Meyerowitz, ed. *Not June Cleaver: Women and Gender in Postwar America* (1994). The growth of the female labor force is described in Alice Kessler-Harris, *Out to Work: A History of Wage-Earning Women in the United States* (1982). The literature on the suburbs, while uneven, is indispensable. The more valuable studies include Herbert Gans, *The Levittowners* (1967); Kenneth T. Jackson, *Crabgrass Frontier: The Suburbanization of the United States* (1985); Robert Fishman, *Bourgeois Utopias* (1987); and Barry Schwartz, ed., *The Changing Face of the Suburbs* (1976). Michael N. Danielson, *The Politics of Exclusion* (1976), discusses the exclusion of blacks. For conservatism, see John P. Diggins, *Up from Communism: Conservative Odysseys in American Intellectual History* (1975); and Richard Pells, *The Liberal Mind in a Conservative Age* (1985).

Supreme Court decisions in the area of civil liberties are explored in Harry Kalven, *A Worthy Tradition: Freedom of Speech in America* (1988). For McCarthy's difficulties with the Army and the Senate, see Robert Griffith, *The Politics of Fear: Joseph R. McCarthy and the Senate* (1970); and Fred Cook, *The Nightmare Decade* (1971). Two fine studies of the most famous case involving science and national security are Philip Stern, *The Oppenheimer Case* (1969); and John Major, *The Oppenheimer Hearing* (1971).

For the 1954 desegregation ruling, its origins and consequences, see Mark V. Tushnet, *The NAACP's Legal Strategy against Segregated Education* (1987); and Richard Kluger, *Simple Justice* (1976); for a critique, see Lino A. Graglia, *Disaster by Decree* (1976). The Southern response is examined in Numan Bartley, *The Rise of Massive Resistance* (1969); and Francis M. Wilhoit, *The Politics of Massive Resistance* (1973). For Martin Luther King, Jr., and the Montgomery bus boycott, see Stephen B. Oates, *Let The Trumpet Sound: The Life of Martin Luther King, Jr.* (1982); and Taylor Branch, *Parting the Waters* (1988). Robert B. Burk, *The Eisenhower Administration and Black Civil Rights* (1984), is a more general account.

For further reading and research on foreign policy, one must start with R. D. Burns, ed., *Guide to American Foreign Relations Since 1700* (1983); the relevant entries in Bruce Jentleson and Thomas Paterson, eds., *Encyclopedia of American Foreign Relations*, 4 vols. (1997); and Warren Cohen, *America in the Age of Soviet Power, 1945–1991* (1993), with good bibliographies. Highly readable overviews of the era's diplomacy include Robert Divine, *Eisenhower and the Cold War* (1981); Lloyd Gardner's *Approaching Vietnam* (1988); and Richard Immerman, ed., *John Foster Dulles* (1989). For specific crises, a recent overview of Vietnam is George Herring, *America's Longest War* (1996); and see the essays and documents in William Appleman Williams, et al., *America in Vietnam* (1985); a fresh perspective on Iran is Mark Lytle, *Origins of the Iranian-American Alliance, 1941–1953* (1987). See also Burton Kaufman's *Trade and Aid, Eisenhower's Foreign Economic Policy* (1982). African policy is discussed in Madeleine Kalb, *The Congo Cables* (1982). There are several superb accounts of the Guatemalan intervention: Piero Gleijeses, *Shattered Hope* (1991); Richard H. Immerman, *The CIA in Guatemala* (1982), which takes the story to 1961; and Blanche Wiesen Cook, *The Declassified Eisenhower* (1981), ranging far beyond Guatemala. For the 1956 Suez crisis, see Diane Kunz, *The Economic Diplomacy of the Suez*

*Crisis* (1991); Burton Kaufman, *The Arab Middle East and the United States* (1996), for the framework; and William Roger Louis and Roger Owen, eds., *Suez 1956* (1989). For nuclear policy, see especially Lawrence Freedman, *The Evolution of Nuclear Strategy* (1983); and Robert Divine, *Blowing on the Wind* (1978). The shock effect of Eisenhower policies on the West and Japan is noted in Richard Barnet, *The Alliance* (1983). The Soviet view is in Nikita Khrushchev's remarkable two-volume memoir; see especially *Khrushchev Remembers* (1970). Superb insight into the Cold War mentality, Eisenhower, and the CIA is in Audrey R. and George McT. Kahin, *Subversion as Foreign Policy: The Secret Eisenhower and Dulles Debacle in Indonesia* (1995).

For analyses of the Beat Generation, consult Ann Charters, *Kerouac: A Biography* (1973); and John Tytell, *Naked Angels: The Lives and Literature of the Beat Generation* (1976).

John Kennedy, Pierre Salinger, and John Kennedy, Jr. *(Library of Congress.)*

# CHAPTER THIRTEEN

# 1957–1963
## New Frontiers at Home and Abroad

This chapter discusses:
- A new Africa, a new neighborhood, for Americans
- Eisenhower's and Kennedy's different views of the military-industrial complex
- A march on Washington, D.C.
- John Kennedy's tragic failure in Cuba and Vietnam

The Suez and Hungarian crises transformed the cold war. They demonstrated that the two great powers no longer monopolized global affairs and especially could no longer control the newly emerging areas. Confronted with this new world, American policymakers could respond in one of two ways: either continue to focus on Europe and relationships with Russia or begin to concentrate attention on such less industrialized areas as Vietnam and Latin America. The Eisenhower administration chose the first alternative; John F. Kennedy, the second. Kennedy's fateful choice determined the nation's foreign policy for the next ten years. And like the 1950s crises in foreign affairs, so too would domestic decisions of the Eisenhower years reshape the future choices in domestic politics. The Supreme Court ruling of 1954 outlawing school segregation, for example, provided a legal foundation for the massive civil rights movement of the early 1960s. Both abroad and at home Americans faced a transformed world.

## AFTER SUEZ: EUROPE

Although the Suez and Hungarian crises reshaped world affairs, the transformation did not occur overnight. The most dramatic international event in the late 1950s was the Russian-American confrontation over Berlin, a city that had long symbolized the hostility between East and West. Situated inside Communist-controlled East Germany, Berlin had been divided into Russian and Western sectors since 1945. As Khrushchev bluntly remarked, West Berlin was a "bone in my throat," for it served as a display of Western wealth and power as well as a listening post deep within the Soviet empire.

In 1958 Khrushchev decided to dislodge the bone. He believed that the launching of Sputnik in late 1957 gave him a military advantage. Projecting this earth satellite into the upper atmosphere demonstrated that the Soviet missile capability was greater than the American. Moreover, in early 1958 Western Europe, with American encouragement, created a large economic "Common Market" (the European Economic Community) by agreeing gradually to abolish tariffs and other restrictions on trade. The European Economic Community included France, Italy, Belgium, the Netherlands, Luxembourg, and—most crucial to Khrushchev—West Germany. With this decision, the Europeans had gone far to lessen the nationalisms that had produced two world wars. But they had also tied West Germany more firmly within the Western camp. Faced with a rejuvenated, West Germany—always a fearful sight to Russians—and believing that his new missile capacity gave him the necessary diplomatic leverage, Khrushchev struck at the Western powers by demanding in November 1958 that they surrender control of West Berlin. Eisenhower and the European leaders rejected the demand and stood firm.

Khrushchev backed off, proposing that visits be exchanged with Eisenhower for personal discussions. The United States eagerly accepted, particularly because a visit would allow the President to see previously closed areas of

Russia and spread the Eisenhower charm. "The name Eisenhower meant so much" to the Russians, one State Department official noted. "I mean, you could send [Vice-President] Nixon over, but the average Ivan wouldn't know who the hell he was. But Eisenhower meant something. It was victory. It was World War II and all that." Khrushchev arrived in the United States in mid-1959, visiting American farms and a movie set of *Can-Can* (whose uninhibited dancing girls appalled him), and discussing foreign policy with the President. Eisenhower, however, was never to see Moscow. He had planned to do so after a summit conference in early 1960 in Paris. But before world leaders could fly to the French capital, Khrushchev angrily announced that the Soviets had shot down an American spy plane, a U-2, which had been taking aerial photographs more than a thousand miles inside Russia.

At first Washington denied involvement. Khrushchev then produced evidence that the denials were lies, and Eisenhower hastily assumed full responsibility for sending the plane over Russia. The Soviet leader heatedly refused to talk with the President. The summit was over before it had begun. The United States was embarrassed, but it is probable that neither Khrushchev nor Eisenhower had originally wanted to go to Paris, for neither side was willing to budge on the key Berlin question. Of equal significance, U-2 planes had been flying over Russia for four years. They brought back information that convinced Washington officials that despite Khrushchev's bragging about his missiles, he did not have missile superiority or even military equality with the United States. Khrushchev realized that he had been found out and therefore was not displeased to avoid talking with the President. Publicly, the Soviet began softening his stand by downplaying the importance of missiles: "They are not like cucumbers, you know—you don't eat them, and more than a certain number are not required." The real loser was U-2 pilot Francis Gary Powers. He was imprisoned in Russia for two years until exchanged for a captured Soviet spy.

## AFTER SUEZ: NEWLY EMERGING AREAS

Berlin captured world attention, but the effects of the 1956 crises were already working profound changes elsewhere. For the Suez episode had demonstrated new and unexpected features of the cold war. Despite its awesome power, the United States had been unable to control its junior partners, the British and French. The Soviets, meanwhile, had needed tanks and planes to keep their supposed ally, Hungary, within the Russian bloc. The old bipolar globe—the world divided and controlled by the two superpowers—was disappearing. This disappearance was hastened as China and the Soviet Union became enemies in 1960 because of differences over Communist ideology and their 1,200-mile common boundary.

The effects of these changes were especially noticeable in the newly independent nations in Asia and Africa, which had recently freed themselves from European colonialism. The leaders of these countries often refused to join either

# CENTRAL AND SOUTH AMERICA
# IN THE 1954–1970 ERA

UNITED STATES

**CUBA**
*Batista overthrown 1959*
*Attempted anti-Castro invasion 1961*
*Soviet military aid, U.S. quarantine 1962*

Miami

BAHAMAS
(Br.)

**DOMINICAN REP.**
*U.S. broke diplomatic ties 1960*
*Trujillo assassinated 1961*
*Diplomatic ties restored 1962*
*U.S. and O.A.S. intervention 1965*

MEXICO

Havana

Mexico City•

BR.
HONDURAS
JAMAICA

HAITI

**GUATEMALA**
*Arbenz overthrown 1954*
*Castillo Armas assassinated 1957*

HONDURAS
*Diaz overthrown 1956*

BARBADOS
*Pérez Jiménez overthrown 1958*
*Anti-Nixon riots 1958*

EL SALVADOR

NICARAGUA
*Canal Zone*

COSTA RICA
PANAMA
*Anti-U.S. riots 1959*

Caracas•
VENEZUELA

TRINIDAD AND TOBAGO

GUYANA
SURINAM *(Neth.)*
FR. GUIANA

*Rojas Pinilla forced out 1957*

•Bogota
COLOMBIA

*P A C I F I C*

EQUADOR  Quito•

*O C E A N*

PERU

B R A Z I L

*Anti-Nixon riots 1958*
*Military coup 1962*
*Military coup 1968*  •Lima

BOLIVIA
La Paz•

•Brasilia

*Average annual per capita income*
*late 1960's*

| | |
|---|---|
| Argentina | $800 |
| Barbados | 428 |
| Bolivia | 165 |
| Brazil | 350 |
| Chile | 465 |
| Colombia | 262 |
| Costa Rica | 380 |
| Cuba | 310 |
| Dominican Rep. | 212 |
| Ecuador | 183 |
| El Salvador | 245 |
| Guatemala | 264 |
| Guyana | 250 |
| Haiti | 75 |
| Honduras | 209 |
| Jamaica | 431 |
| Mexico | 600 |
| Nicaragua | 347 |
| Panama | 477 |
| Paraguay | 192 |
| Peru | 241 |
| Trinidad & Tobago | 515 |
| Uruguay | 537 |
| Venezuela | 902 |

PARAGUAY
Asuncion•

Rio de Janeiro•

*Salvador*
*Allende*
*elected 1970*

CHILE

Santiago•
Buenos Aires•
ARGENTINA

URUGUAY
Montevideo•

*Punta del Este Conferences*
*1961, 1962*

*A T L A N T I C*

*O C E A N*

| | |
|---|---|
| ▨ | *Under $200* |
| ▦ | *$200-399* |
| ▨ | *$400-599* |
| ▨ | *Over $600* |

the Soviet or the American side. They instead tried to play Washington off against Moscow in order to acquire aid from both camps. This had been Nasser's policy in Egypt, and although he suffered a military setback in 1956, he had retained control of the Suez Canal while receiving aid from both Americans and Russians. Nasser set an example that sparked nationalist revolutions in the Middle East.

Eisenhower and Dulles feared that the new nations would be unstable, anti-Western, and, therefore, pro-Communist. As Dulles once blurted out, neutrality was "immoral." These changes in turn could threaten the supply of oil which Europe and the United States required from the Middle East. The results could be disastrous. "In my view," Dulles remarked in early 1957, "we are in a war situation right now." Consequently, in the spring of that year Congress passed a resolution proposed by Eisenhower that allowed him to commit American power to stop "overt armed aggression" by Communists in the Middle East if a nation in the area asked for such help. This "Eisenhower Doctrine" was unfortunate. It angered some Middle Eastern nations, divided others, and forced some to choose between East and West, something they did not want to do.

The doctrine, moreover, was largely irrelevant. The area was threatened not by overt Communist invasion but by intense internal nationalism, which the proclamation did not cover. Yet when the monarchy in Iraq was suddenly overthrown by an internal coup led by pro-Nasser nationalists in 1958, the government of neighboring Lebanon asked for American protection. No "overt" Communist threat was apparent; indeed, Eisenhower knew the Lebanese president needed help against *internal*, not external, opposition. Eisenhower nevertheless immediately landed fourteen thousand American troops in Lebanon to display his muscle. The bikini-clad bathers on the shore scarcely moved as the Marines waded in, and the effect on Iraq was equally slight. Despite the Eisenhower Doctrine and the Lebanon landings, Middle Eastern nationalism continued to flourish and unsettle the area. As the Suez crisis had demonstrated, foreign troops only worsened the situation. The world could not be rolled back to the pre-1956 years.

## THE GOOD NEIGHBOR AND A CHANGING NEIGHBORHOOD

Nationalism also threatened American policies in Latin America, where the United States had seemed to have sure control. By 1955 United States firms produced 10 percent of Latin America's products, 30 percent of its export goods (and in such nations as Venezuela and Cuba, two or three times that percentage), invested more that $3 billion directly, and dominated the continent's great oil and mineral resources. That domination, however, had brought no prosperity to most Latin Americans. With little industrialization, the area depended on world market prices for its oil and other raw materials, but most of these prices declined in the late 1950s. Foreign investment worsened this drain of money, for Americans took more profits out of Latin America than they put back in.

This economic trap was aggravated by the highest population growth rate in the world. In other words, the key sections of Latin America's economy were largely exploited by foreign capital, and that economy was scarcely growing fast enough to keep up with the population increase.

Washington officials understood this, but since 1947 had poured their resources into Europe while taking Latin America for granted. During these years Belgium and Luxembourg alone received three times more economic aid than the twenty Latin American nations combined. More than two-thirds of the aid that did go south was for military purposes, not economic growth. The political results were all too obvious: instability, frequent changes of government, repressive right-wing dictatorships, and a heightened anti-American nationalism among intellectuals and jailed politicians. Between 1930 and 1965, 106 illegal and often bloody changes of government occurred throughout the continent. Only Mexico of all twenty Latin American governments had peaceful presidential changes through this period. (Woodrow Wilson, who had bitterly opposed the Mexican Revolution between 1913 and 1916, would doubtless have been surprised but pleased.)

Latin America differed fundamentally from Africa or Southeast Asia, for it had been free of direct colonial control for more than a century, and was politically more experienced. Latin Americans knew that their problems could not be solved by throwing off foreign rulers as Egyptians, Vietnamese, and others were doing, for there was no such formal colonialism in the area. Instead, they had to control and develop their internal resources, that is, loosen the economic grip that the United States held on their countries. The question was whether Washington would help or hinder that aspiration. In 1954 Dulles had given his answer by helping overthrow a nationalistic left-wing government in Guatemala. The area then quieted somewhat. In early 1958 a high State Department official was asked whether he thought there was much anti-Yankee feeling among Latin Americans. "No sir, I do not," he promptly replied.

Two months later Vice-President Nixon traveled south. From Uruguay to Venezuela crowds hurled eggs and stones at his car, nearly tipping it over in Caracas, Venezuela. Eisenhower ordered a thousand Marines to prepare to rescue Nixon, who escaped to Washington before the troops were dispatched. The outburst shocked the United States. The President ordered a review of Latin American policies. He finally initiated economic aid programs, which, after 1961, the Kennedy administration would enlarge and attempt to glamorize with the title "Alliance for Progress." But this was too little and too late to prevent anti-American nationalists from working fundamental, revolutionary changes.

It was, for example, too late to insulate Cuba from such a revolution. This was striking, for nowhere had U.S. control been so complete. Americans controlled 80 percent of the island's utilities and 90 percent of the mines, ranches, and oil; owned half the great sugar crop; and surrounded Cuba with military might. The island had one of the highest per capita income figures in the southern hemisphere, but the wealth fell into the hands of foreign investors and a few Cubans, while the mass of the people suffered in poverty. In 1952 Fulgen-

cio Batista overthrew a moderately liberal regime and created a military dictatorship. He received support from highly unlikely bedfellows—the U.S. military (which helped train and equip Batista's forces) and a well-behaved Communist party, which sought to survive by whipping up local support for the
dictator. The U.S. Air Force pinned the Legion of Merit on Batista's breast, calling him "a great president."

That sentiment was not shared by most Cubans. In 1953 a young, middle-
class lawyer (unemployed, as were most Cuban lawyers) started a revolt. Fidel
Castro was captured and imprisoned, but by 1957 he was again free. Collecting
a force of peasants and middle-class Cubans, he successfully resisted the police
units sent out to destroy the guerrillas. The Communists refused to cooperate
with Castro until late 1958, when Batista was preparing to escape with millions
from the Cuban treasury for a luxurious exile in Spain. On January 1, 1959, Castro marched triumphantly into Havana. Washington officials, an authoritative
journalist reported, generally agreed that "there was no dominant Communist

Fidel Castro at the United Nations, 1960. *(BETTMANN.)*

influence. . . . One official went so far as to say that there was very little trace of Communism in the movement."

As Castro moved to change the distribution of wealth, and especially of land ownership, his relationships with the Communists and the United States altered. The Communists provided disciplined organization and an ideology, which Castro required. When the Cuban leader visited the United States, Eisenhower left Washington to go golfing. There was little to talk about. Castro insisted that American companies and landholdings be placed in Cuban hands. He could not pay for these without borrowing money from abroad and again becoming indebted to foreigners. As the *New York Times* editorialized in mid-1960, "So long as Cuba is in the throes of a social revolution directed by her present leaders, she is going to be in conflict with the United States. We think it is wrong, but it is a fact of life. The revolution harms American interests in Cuba and in Latin America generally." Castro turned to the Soviet Union for credits, machinery, and military equipment. Eisenhower first cut back Cuban sugar imports, then authorized the secret training of 1,400 anti-Castro Cubans by the Central Intelligence Agency, although the President never did decide when—or even whether—they might be used. Assuming that Castro was "beyond redemption," as a State Department official commented, the United States and Cuba broke diplomatic relations in January 1961.

## THE EISENHOWER LEGACY AND THE NEW FRONTIER

Eisenhower presided during a decade that many Americans would later recall with nostalgia. The generation that came of age during the 1950s seemed quiet, apolitical, and more concerned about personal security than international crises. It would later be tagged as "the generation that never showed up." This was how Eisenhower wanted it. Despite provocations in Korea, the Middle East, and Berlin greater than those that later faced Presidents Kennedy and Johnson, Eisenhower, unlike his successors, did not involve the country in war. His use of power was restrained. He frequently remarked that he had seen enough war. Moreover, Eisenhower cared more about balancing the budget and strengthening the American economy than he did about creating a great military force that might intervene at will in the post-1956 world.

He did not disavow anti-Communist policies, but neither did he think that those policies were worth undermining the American economic, political, and even educational systems. Between 1950 and 1960, for example, such leading universities as Harvard, Chicago, Columbia, Pennsylvania, California, and Johns Hopkins had obtained large amounts of money, both from such private foundations as Ford and Carnegie and from the federal government, to establish defense-policy centers. Instead of questioning governmental power, many American intellectuals were justifying that power. With this in mind, Eisenhower issued a warning in his farewell address of January 1961. He spoke of "the prospect of domination of the nation's scholars by Federal employment, project allocations, and the power of money" and noted that too often "a government contract becomes virtually a substitute for intellectual curiosity." Eisenhower believed that two "threats, new in kind or degree," had appeared:

> This conjunction of an immense military establishment and a large arms industry is new in American experience. The total influence—economic, political, even spiritual—is felt in every city, every state house, every office of the federal government. We recognize the imperative need for this development. Yet we must not fail to comprehend its grave implications. . . . In the councils of government, we must guard against the acquisition of unwarranted influence, whether sought or unsought, by the military-industrial complex. The potential for the disastrous rise of misplaced power exists and will persist. . . . We should take nothing for granted.

In part this warning expressed Eisenhower's fear that the incoming Kennedy administration would try to control world affairs by spending even greater sums on arms. His fear was well founded. In accepting the Democratic presidential nomination in 1960, John F. Kennedy called not for caution, but for "sacrifices" on "the New Frontier." He spoke in Los Angeles in late afternoon as the sun went down on what had been the last of the old American frontier territory. The New Frontier, Kennedy declared,

> sums up not what I intend to offer the American people but what I intend to ask of them. It appeals to their pride, not to their pocketbook; it holds out the promise of more sacrifice instead of more security.

> But I tell you the New Frontier is here whether we seek it or not . . . uncharted areas of science and space, unsolved problems of peace and war, unconquered pockets of ignorance and prejudice, unanswered questions of poverty and surplus.

This call to action was most eloquently stated in Kennedy's inaugural speech of January 1961. His words sharply contrasted with Eisenhower's farewell address. Kennedy proclaimed:

> Let every nation know, whether it wishes us well or ill, that we shall pay any price, bear any burden, meet any hardship, support any friend, oppose any foe to assure the survival and the success of liberty.

> This much we pledge—and more. . . .

> In the long history of the world, only a few generations have been granted the role of defending freedom in its hour of maximum danger. I do not shrink from this responsibility; I welcome it. . . .

> And so, my fellow Americans, ask not what your country can do for you; ask what you can do for your country.

# JOHN F. KENNEDY

In April 1960 Richard E. Neustadt, a political scientist at Columbia University, published *Presidential Power.* Neustadt believed that a strong President

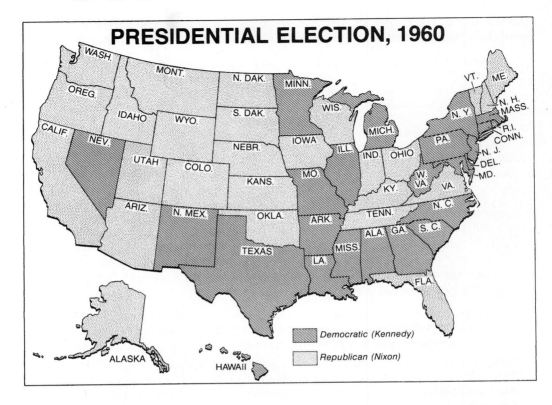

PRESIDENTIAL ELECTION, 1960

Democratic (Kennedy)

Republican (Nixon)

"contributes to the energy of government and to the viability of public policy." He attempted, therefore, to show how a chief executive could exercise power effectively. "The Sixties, it appears, will be a fighting time," Neustadt predicted. "It follows that our need will be the greater for a Presidential expert in the Presidency." Shortly after the book appeared, John F. Kennedy, the Democratic nominee for President, recruited Neustadt as an advisor. In truth, the two men held similar views. Kennedy thought that the President "must serve as a catalyst, an energizer, the defender of the public good and the public interest." He must "place himself in the very thick of the fight," for he was "the vital center of action in our whole scheme of government."

"Energy," "fight," "vitality," "public interest"—the words were temperamentally congenial to Kennedy. But while he was President his approach to domestic policies could more accurately be described by a different vocabulary: "caution," "prudence," "compromise," "interest group." Kennedy believed that politics was the art of the possible, that politicians were most likely to succeed if they dealt with concrete rather than abstract issues, and that a give-and-take process in resolving those issues was not only inevitable but also desirable. For a President to safeguard the national interest translated, in the pluralist world of American politics, into arranging mutually acceptable trade-offs between such competing interest groups as business and labor, farmers and consumers, blacks and whites. "Politics and legislation," Kennedy once said, "are not matters for inflexible principles or unattainable ideals."

Kennedy was elected to the House of Representatives in 1946, to the Senate in 1952, and, at the age of 43, to the presidency. His rise to political eminence was so swift and his personal qualities were so attractive that his virtues were exaggerated by the public, by the media, and especially by his inner circle of friends and admirers. A vigorous man who enjoyed sports such as sailing, Kennedy felt it necessary to deny that he suffered from Addison's disease (an adrenal insufficiency requiring cortisone treatments) so as not to jeopardize his career. In World War II Kennedy had been a naval officer who courageously rescued members of his crew after their PT boat had been sunk in the South Pacific. Although he was widely regarded as a hero, Kennedy's poor seamanship was partly responsible for the disaster. A person of impressive intellect, Kennedy was awarded a Pulitzer Prize in 1957 for *Profiles in Courage,* a book written primarily by an aide. The truth about these incidents, however, was not widely known or accepted until after Kennedy's death.

## CONGRESS AND THE NEW FRONTIER

Unlike Franklin D. Roosevelt and Dwight Eisenhower, Kennedy did not take office with a resounding popular mandate. He barely edged out Richard Nixon, winning by the smallest margin of any President in the twentieth century. Kennedy, who received 49.7 percent of the popular vote to his opponent's 49.6 percent, actually carried fewer states than did Nixon. Although Kennedy secured a 303-to-219 majority in the electoral college, had 4,500 people in Illinois and 28,000 people in Texas voted Republican instead of Democratic, Nixon would have emerged the victor in the electoral college. President by a razor-thin margin, Kennedy was not in a position to make demands on Congress.

Nor could Kennedy turn for support to first-term congressmen carried into office on his coattails. In 1960 Kennedy invariably trailed the Democratic ticket; furthermore, his party lost twenty-two seats in the House and two in the Senate. Although the Democrats maintained comfortable majorities in both houses of Congress, those majorities were deceptive, consisting largely of Southerners who regarded many New Frontier programs with distaste. The seniority system gave Southern Democrats representing rural constituencies control of key committees: Wilbur Mills of Arkansas headed the House Ways and Means Committee, Harry Byrd of Virginia chaired the Senate Finance Committee, and Howard Smith of Virginia ran the House Rules Committee. Kennedy barely won a bitterly contested struggle to liberalize the Rules Committee by enlarging its membership, and then only because he had the backing of Speaker Sam Rayburn of Texas. Even the Kennedy style appeared to offend some congressmen. "All that Mozart string music and ballet dancing down there," said one; "he's too elegant for me, I can't talk to him."

In some respects religion acted as another constraint on the President. Kennedy's Catholicism had played an important role in the 1960 election.

Many Protestants bolted the Democratic party, but Kennedy received 80 percent of the Catholic vote (rather than the 63 percent a Democrat could ordinarily expect). On the whole, the religious issue appears to have cost Kennedy votes. However, his loss of support occurred primarily in the South, where the Democrats could afford it; meanwhile he gained support in such critical states as Illinois and Michigan. As the first Catholic President, Kennedy leaned over backward to dispel any suspicion that he was under church influence. He did not favor sending an American ambassador to the Vatican, and he similarly opposed "unconstitutional aid to parochial schools." It was easier to prove that a Catholic could be elected President than to convince skeptics that a Catholic President could be scrupulously fair.

The conflict over federal aid to education illustrated Kennedy's difficulties with Congress. Early in 1961 Kennedy proposed spending $2.3 billion over three years to build new schools and to raise teachers' salaries. The wealthiest states would receive $15 per child; the poorest, nearly twice that amount. A separate program to aid college students would bring the package to $5.6 billion. But federal aid to education raised divisive issues. In a vain effort to appease Southern Democrats, the administration agreed not to withhold aid from segregated school districts. The religious issue proved more difficult to resolve. Kennedy declared that the Constitution prohibited aid to parochial schools, but the Catholic church replied that the Constitution did not prohibit long-term, low-interest loans to help such schools improve their facilities. An arrangement was seemingly worked out restricting the federal aid bill to public schools, but attaching an amendment to the National Defense and Education Act authorizing loans to parochial schools for expanding their mathematics, science, and language facilities. At the last minute, a Northern Catholic Democrat on the Rules Committee, fearing that Congress would renege on aid to religious schools, joined Republicans and Southern Democrats to oppose the education bill. In July 1961 the President watched helplessly as the Rules Committee, by a one-vote margin, buried the measure.

A second New Frontier proposal—Medicare—met a similar fate. In February 1961 Kennedy asked Congress to extend social security benefits to people over the age of 65 to cover hospital and nursing home costs. This would be financed by a small increase in the social security tax. The President pointed out that the elderly had, on the average, half the income of people under 65 but medical expenses that were twice as high. Kennedy insisted that his plan, which would not cover surgical expenses or physicians' fees, ensured "absolute freedom" in the choice of a doctor and hospital. The American Medical Association, however, viewed Medicare as a giant step toward socialized medicine. Physicians foresaw a "bureaucratic task force" invading "the privacy of the examination room." The twenty-five-member House Ways and Means Committee was the real hurdle. Its chairman, Wilbur Mills, opposed the plan, as did ten Republicans and six Southern Democrats. They easily bottled up the bill. In July 1962 the Senate defeated the measure by a vote of 52 to 48, with twenty-one Democrats opposing the administration. The limitation of presidential leadership in domestic affairs was rapidly becoming clearer.

# THE NEW ECONOMICS

Yet the picture of a stodgy, conservative Congress frustrating the hopes of an energetic, liberal President is accurate only in part. Kennedy set certain domestic priorities, and in the process he often sacrificed reform programs. This was true even in the case of Medicare, for Kennedy, recognizing that he needed Wilbur Mills's support for tax reform and trade expansion, did not press the Ways and Means Committee too hard. Moreover, to attract Southern Democratic support for economic proposals, Kennedy postponed introducing civil rights legislation for as long as possible. He always put first things first, and in his view what came first was the economy. In January 1961 the nation was in the throes of a recession: unemployment stood at 5.4 million, more than 6 percent of the labor force. Kennedy's goal was to stimulate economic growth and reduce unemployment while at the same time balancing the budget and preventing inflation.

The administration applied a number of remedies to the sluggish economy. To aid jobless workers, Kennedy extracted from Congress, though usually in a diluted form, legislation that increased unemployment compensation, created retraining programs, and provided for public works in depressed areas. Congress also raised the minimum wage from $1.00 to $1.25 an hour and brought an additional 3.6 million workers under the law's protection. To stimulate business expansion, Congress granted a 7 percent tax credit to firms investing in new equipment. Kennedy attached the greatest significance to the Trade Expansion Act (1962). This facilitated the export of American goods to the European Common Market by authorizing the President to arrange mutual tariff reductions of 50 percent on certain categories of goods and, in other cases, to eliminate tariffs completely. To assist industries threatened by foreign competition, the government would help businesses change or diversify their products and retrain workers who lost their jobs.

The keys to curbing inflation were labor's willingness to limit wage demands to an amount justified by gains in productivity and industry's corresponding readiness to keep prices down. Early in 1962 Kennedy helped persuade the steelworkers to accept a noninflationary wage settlement. Then, in April, United States Steel announced a price hike of $6 a ton, and other steel companies immediately followed suit. Furious at what he termed this "utter contempt for the public interest," Kennedy mustered every ounce of executive authority to salvage his economic program. He pressured smaller steel companies into holding the price line, threatened to take government contracts away from the offending concerns, and hinted that the Justice Department would determine whether the price increases violated the antitrust laws. Faced with massive presidential and public pressure, United States Steel backed down and rescinded the increase.

Kennedy's stance earned him the lasting resentment of the business community. The remark attributed to him at the time—"My father always told me that all businessmen were sons-of-bitches, but I never believed it till now"—did nothing to allay suspicion. When, in May 1962, the stock market hit the skids,

# DAVID SMITH: THE MACHINE SHOP AND SCULPTURE

David Smith transformed twentieth-century sculpture by combining the American machine shop with radical versions of modern art. Reaching the peak of his powers between 1958 and 1965, Smith's work exemplified the new American leadership in world art at precisely the same time John F. Kennedy proclaimed in his inaugural address that a "new generation" of Americans would assume world political leadership.

Smith learned about machines in Decatur, Indiana, where he was born in 1906. One of his ancestors had been a frontier blacksmith. Leaving home at 16, he enrolled briefly at Ohio State and Notre Dame before learning to weld in the Studebaker automotive works in South Bend. Smith then traveled to New York City, encountering the work of leading European artists who were fleeing Nazism to live in the United States. As these emigrés helped make New York City the center of the art world, Smith lived among them, beginning as a painter, then moving into "constructivism," whereby objects other than paint (for example, bits of newspaper, glass, or metal) were placed on the picture to change it from a painting to a construction. At that point, Smith recalled, "I was then a sculptor." To develop his craft he believed he needed nothing "outside of factory knowledge," which he had gained as a welder.

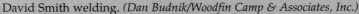

During the 1930s, as many artists protested the drift toward war, Smith became politically involved and saw Nazism up close in 1935–1936 during a stay in Europe. He expressed his vision in fifteen horror-filled, yet magnificently designed "Medals for Dishonor." These depicted scenes of such

David Smith welding. *(Dan Budnik/Woodfin Camp & Associates, Inc.)*

David Smith with *Cubi I*, 1963. *(Dan Budnik/Woodfin Camp & Associates, Inc.)*

"dishonors" as *War-Exempt Sons of the Rich, Munitions-Makers,* and *Elements Which Cause Prostitution.* In the 1940s his work became increasingly abstract, and for the first time he combined painting with sculpture so that the colors seemed to change the form of his pieces. One critic noted that Smith was among the first to practice "drawing in space," and called some of his work "a graceful abstract drawing that has leaped off the page into three-dimensional life."

Smith was soon exploring all forms, from overpowering monoliths to light, lyrical creations that, although made from heavy steel, seemed to float in air. His greatest work was done at his studio on the shore of Lake George in upper New York State, where he could display his works outdoors, the only place he thought large enough for them. Here he extended and transformed European art styles, particularly cubism, which drew natural subjects in simplified lines and basic geo-

*Medal for Dishonor No. 9: Bombing Civilian Populations,* 1939. *(Estate of David Smith, Courtesy of M. Knoedler and Company, New York.)*

metric shapes, usually to show the subject simultaneously from several points of view. In 1958 he began his spectacular *Cubi* series, shaping great slabs of stainless steel in pure geometric construction and then polishing and arranging them so their three dimensions reflected changing sunlight—sometimes with dazzling intensity, sometimes with a delicacy that one critic called "purely optical poetry." In these new forms, Smith expressed the essence of cubism. He indeed worked with

steel, he declared, because it was at once "so beautiful" while "also brutal: the rapist, the murderer, and the death-dealing giants are also its offspring." In *Cubi* he brought the beauty and brutality into one.

A burly man who lived life to the full, Smith had by the 1960s not only created an American sculpture, but shaped world art as well. Yet in 1965 he could declare, "I'm 20 years behind my vision." In the spring of that year he was killed in an automobile crash.

David Smith in his sculpture garden. (*Dan Budnik/Woodfin Camp & Associates, Inc.*)

dropping 35 points in a day and 100 points in two weeks, Wall Street attributed the disaster to a lack of confidence in the administration. Whatever businessmen may have thought, their fears were illogical. Not only did Kennedy's tax and trade policies favor business interests, but the administration also sponsored a plan, bitterly resented by Senate liberals, that conceded a dominant interest in the newly developed communications satellite to the American Telephone and Telegraph Company. (The satellite, launched into outer space, relayed television and radio signals around the world.) In addition to this, during his first eighteen months in office Kennedy worked hard to achieve a balanced budget. So orthodox did the New Frontier's fiscal program appear that journalist Walter Lippmann commented, "It's like the Eisenhower administration 30 years younger."

Not until late 1962 did Kennedy endorse the planned use of budget deficits as the only certain means of spurring further economic growth. In January 1963 the President called for a $13.5 billion reduction in corporate and personal taxes over three years. With the closing of loopholes, this would inject $10 billion into the economy, but it would also produce a $12 billion deficit in a total budget of $98.8 billion. Kennedy's plan, while thoroughly Keynesian in its assumptions, did not satisfy all liberals. John Kenneth Galbraith, the Harvard economist whom Kennedy had appointed ambassador to India, believed that "money from tax reduction goes into the pockets of those who need it least; lower tax revenues will become a ceiling on spending." Galbraith wished to create a deficit by expanding programs to aid the needy rather than by cutting taxes. On the other hand, Kennedy's proposal shocked conservatives. Dwight Eisenhower offered a homely bit of economic wisdom: "Spending for spending's sake is patently a false theory. No family, no business, no nation can spend itself into prosperity."

Unfortunately for Kennedy, more congressmen, and particularly more members of the House Ways and Means Committee, preferred Eisenhower's brand of economics to Galbraith's. Once again, as in the case of Medicare and federal aid to education, a House committee blocked consideration of a key New Frontier proposal. But by 1963 Kennedy had somewhat lowered his sights, at least with respect to domestic matters. The exercise of power proved a sobering experience. Although he never repudiated his activist view of the presidency, Kennedy came to see the office in terms of its limitations as well as its opportunities. "The problems are more difficult than I had imagined they were," he conceded. "Every President must endure a gap between what he would like and what is possible."

## KENNEDY AND CIVIL RIGHTS

The same practical considerations that modified Kennedy's view of presidential authority also affected his stand on civil rights. In 1960 Kennedy declared that the President should throw the full moral weight of his office behind the effort to end racial discrimination. "If the President does not himself wage the struggle for equal rights—if he stands above the battle—then the battle will inevitably be lost." Once in office, however, Kennedy found himself torn between the claims of white Southerners, whose support he needed, and the pressure applied by an increasingly militant civil rights movement. Not until 1963 did Kennedy cease standing above the battle, and he then acted only after segregationist resistance to demands for racial equality provoked massive turmoil.

Unlike Eisenhower, Kennedy relied heavily on the black vote. In the 1960 campaign he expressed agreement with the Supreme Court ruling on desegregation, but perhaps nothing did more to solidify his support among blacks than his intervention on behalf of Dr. Martin Luther King, Jr. Late in October a Georgia judge jailed King for taking part in a protest demonstration. In a well-publicized move, Kennedy telephoned King's wife, both to express his concern and to offer assurances regarding her husband's safety. The next day, Robert F. Kennedy, the candidate's brother, helped arrange King's release on bail. Kennedy's phone call, a symbolic act at best, nevertheless had the right personal touch. When Nixon remained silent, the Democrats printed two million copies of a pamphlet titled *No-Comment Nixon versus a Candidate with a Heart, Senator Kennedy.* In 1960 black voters provided Kennedy's margin of victory in Texas, Illinois, New Jersey, and Michigan. Had only white people voted, Nixon would have received 52 percent of the vote and gone to the White House.

Kennedy understood this, yet he placed civil rights lower on his legislative agenda than other New Frontier measures. To introduce a civil rights bill, Kennedy believed, would alienate Southerners, split the Democratic party, snarl Congress in a filibuster, and dissipate administration energies. He considered the chance of passage too slim to justify these risks. So the President turned instead to other techniques. He issued an executive order designed to pressure federal agencies and government contractors into hiring more black workers. In addition, Kennedy sought to achieve through litigation what he doubted was possible through legislation. Under Attorney General Robert F. Kennedy, the Justice Department attempted to speed the pace of school desegregation by entering court cases on the side of those challenging separate facilities. The policy had some success. In Eisenhower's last three years, 49 school districts had begun the process of desegregation. In Kennedy's three years, 183 did so.

In the eyes of New Frontiersmen, the franchise held the key to racial equality. Litigation to win the vote seemed crucial, for if blacks attained political strength commensurate with their numbers, politicians would accord them justice and the Jim Crow system would topple. Many states in the Deep South systematically excluded blacks from the polls. In Mississippi, where blacks constituted more than 40 percent of the population, they made up less than 4 percent of the eligible voters. To attack this system, the Justice Department utilized the Civil Rights Act of 1957, which authorized the department to seek injunctions against interference with the right to vote. The Eisenhower administration had brought only ten suits under the act. The Kennedy administration filed forty-five such suits.

Yet the reliance on litigation had three fatal defects. First, it assumed that the law sanctioned racial equality, which, in much of the South, it did not. Second, it assumed a degree of judicial impartiality that did not exist. A number of judges in Southern district courts held harshly segregationist views and stymied moves toward integration. Judge Harold Cox, a Kennedy appointee, informed a Justice Department official: "I spend most of my time in fooling with lousy cases brought before me by your Department in the Civil Rights field." Cox could find no pattern of discrimination in Clarke County, Mississippi, although only one black, a high school principal, had succeeded in registering to vote in thirty years. Even where successful, litigation was a glacial process, and this proved to be a third source of weakness. Many blacks were no longer willing to let the law run its course. They insisted that equality was a moral as well as a legal issue. By taking direct action to end segregation, they forced Kennedy to choose sides.

The first such case involved the "freedom rides," which were themselves an offshoot of the sit-in movement. In February 1960 a group of black college students in Greensboro, North Carolina, sat down at a Woolworth's lunch counter and refused to leave until served. Within a year, fifty thousand people had participated in similar demonstrations in more than one hundred cities and had succeeded in desegregating many hotels, stores, theaters, and parks. The freedom ride seemed a logical extension of this tactic. In May 1961 white and black students boarded buses in Washington with plans to travel through the Deep South, desegregating depots as they went. Angry mobs met the buses, though, and attacked the riders with chains and rocks. The President finally sent five hundred marshals to Montgomery, Alabama, to prevent further violence. Kennedy then asked the Interstate Commerce Commission to ban segregation at all bus and train stations. In November 1961 such an edict took effect, although some Southern communities continued to evade it. The Justice Department also persuaded airlines to desegregate their terminals. The freedom riders had, in effect, created the conditions under which Kennedy was willing to use executive authority on behalf of civil rights.

Kennedy's hand was forced a second time in September 1962, when James Meredith tried to integrate the University of Mississippi law school. The controversy originated when a U.S. court of appeals found that the university had rejected Meredith solely on the basis of race and ordered his admission. After a segregationist judge stayed the ruling, Supreme Court Justice Hugo Black ordered its enforcement. Meredith flew to Oxford, Mississippi, in a federal plane and was escorted to the campus by federal marshals. Governor Ross Barnett tried to convince Robert Kennedy that Southern sentiment would never tolerate the integration of Ole Miss. Barnett thought Meredith was "being paid by some left-wing organization to do all this. He has two great big Cadillacs, no income, riding around here. . . . We never have trouble with our people, but the NAACP, they want to stir up trouble down here." The attorney general responded that "if we don't follow the order of the federal court, we don't have anything in the United States." In the end, white students and outside troublemakers, massed behind Confederate battle flags, attacked the federal marshals. A fifteen-hour riot ensued in which two men were killed and the campus was shrouded in tear gas. The President dispatched thousands of federal troops to restore order, to protect Meredith's right to attend class, and to demonstrate that, in Robert Kennedy's words, only the rule of law permitted a nation "to avoid anarchy and disorder and tremendous distress."

The nine months following the Mississippi crisis saw the administration move haltingly toward an affirmative civil rights posture. In November 1962 the President issued a long-awaited executive order banning segregation in all new housing subsidized by the federal government. In February 1963 Kennedy introduced a civil rights bill designed to prevent biased registrars from using spurious tests to deprive blacks of the vote. The bill provided that the completion of six grades of public school would automatically constitute proof of literacy. Yet civil rights activists now considered these steps inadequate. They pointed out that the executive order did not affect housing that was already built or that would be privately financed. They noted that Kennedy, while favoring a civil rights bill, refused to support an effort to amend the Senate rules to make easier the termination of debate. Without such a change, a Southern filibuster seemed certain to block passage of any civil rights measure. Assessing Kennedy's record in March 1963, Martin Luther King, Jr., found that the administration had settled for "tokenism." Nearly a decade after the Supreme Court decision, only 7 percent of black children in the South attended classes with white children, and two thousand districts remained segregated. King concluded: "The administration sought to demonstrate to Negroes that it has concern for them, while at the same time it has striven to avoid inflaming the opposition."

In the spring of 1963 civil rights demonstrations in Birmingham, Alabama, made further fence straddling impossible. Black leaders in the city—where blacks constituted 40 percent of the population—launched a drive to end segregation in stores and to pressure businesses to hire black sales and clerical help. Adhering to King's philosophy that "you can struggle without hating; you can fight war without violence," blacks engaged in protest marches, sit-ins, and even kneel-ins at white churches on Good Friday. The city government reacted savagely. Police Commissioner Eugene "Bull" Connor met the marchers, many of them schoolchildren, with fire hoses and snarling police dogs and threw thousands into jail. The mayor, who had lost the previous election but was contesting the result in court, called white businessmen who favored some form of accommodation "a bunch of quisling, gutless traitors." He said of Robert Kennedy: "I hope that every drop of blood that's spilled he tastes in his throat, and I hope he chokes on it." In May, riots and bombings rocked the city. The following month, with the crisis in Birmingham still unresolved, Governor George C. Wallace challenged an attempt by two black students to integrate the University of Alabama. To safeguard their entrance, the President federalized the National Guard.

In June 1963, responding directly to these events in Alabama, Kennedy endorsed a sweeping civil rights bill. It would outlaw segregation in hotels, restaurants, theaters, and other public places; permit the Justice Department to file suits for school desegregation; prohibit discrimination in state programs receiving federal aid; and remove racial barriers to employment and trade-union membership. "We are confronted primarily with a moral issue," the President asserted. The demand for racial justice had grown so loud, the "fires of frustration and discord" had begun to burn so brightly, that government could no longer stand aside. Indeed, the government must prove that revolutionary changes in race relations could occur in a "peaceful and constructive" way.

Even as Kennedy came to support civil rights, his administration decided to wiretap Martin Luther King, Jr.'s, home and office. J. Edgar Hoover, director of the Federal Bureau of Investigation, was convinced that King was associating with Communists and put unrelenting pressure on Attorney General Robert F.

Birmingham, Alabama, 1963. (*Black Star. Reprinted with permission.*)

Kennedy to use wiretaps. In October 1963, he authorized the use of taps. Ironically, the administration's new identification with the civil rights movement was partially responsible for the invasion of King's civil liberties. Robert Kennedy evidently believed that if Communists were involved in the movement, and if opponents publicized that, then the President himself could be discredited; besides, the opportunity to know in advance what moves King was planning to make was a temptation the attorney general could not resist. While they never accepted Hoover's view that King was under Communist influence, the Kennedys fully accepted the cold war view that communism was a menace at home as well as abroad. This was clearly illustrated when John F. Kennedy, justifying the use of federal authority to support the movement for racial equality, noted: "Today we are committed to a worldwide struggle to promote and protect the rights of all who wish to be free. And when Americans are sent to Vietnam or West Berlin we do not ask for whites only."

## THE WORLDWIDE NEW FRONTIER

The problems afflicting Americans at home deeply influenced Kennedy's foreign policies. His diplomacy assumed a united homefront that would unquestioningly support the President in Asia as it had in Europe, and that would see racism and poverty at home as less important than using national resources to fight communism overseas. Kennedy, like most of his generation, was the product of World War II and the cold war. As a young congressman in 1949, he attacked Truman for "losing" China, refused as a senator to take a public position on Senator Joseph McCarthy's vicious attacks, and in 1956 justified American support to Ngo Dinh Diem's autocratic regime in South Vietnam. By 1960 Kennedy had focused on the newly emerging areas as the key to victory in the cold war. The new President believed that Americans must confront communism everywhere. "What is at stake in the election of 1960 is the preservation of freedom all around the globe," he proclaimed during the campaign, and he made this the central theme of his administration's foreign policy.

That remark seemed to make little-known countries in Southeast Asia, for example, as important to American interests as Western Europe. But as Kennedy saw it, the global battle would be to the finish. "Freedom and communism are locked in a deadly embrace," he believed in 1960, and later declared, "The world cannot exist half slave and half free." In a speech in May 1961 he was specific: "The great battleground for the defense and expansion of freedom today is the whole southern half of the globe—Asia, Latin America, Africa, and the Middle East—the lands of the rising peoples." His famous inaugural was a trumpet call to that battle. It was also a speech that never mentioned domestic problems. Those could be assumed as secondary to the "historic mission" of America abroad. Nor did Kennedy set any limits on that mission. "I don't believe that there is anything this country cannot do," he declared during his television debates with Vice-President Nixon in 1960.

A strong presidency was required to carry out the mission, one even stronger than that developed by Roosevelt, Truman, and Eisenhower. Kennedy declared that the President "must be prepared to exercise the fullest powers of his office—all that are specified and some that are not." He even believed that the office not only spoke for all Americans, but represented "all of the people around the world who want to live in freedom." Kennedy established a separate foreign affairs group in the White House under his national security advisor, McGeorge Bundy, former dean at Harvard University. Bundy would be followed by Walt W. Rostow and then in 1969 by Henry Kissinger. All three used their office to drain power from the Department of State and congressional foreign affairs committees. In diplomacy, the President had become a virtual king—only more so, for he was an elected king, complete with advisors who did not have to be responsible to Congress or to anyone but the President.

## ICBMs AND GREEN BERETS

As commander in chief, Kennedy had at his disposal the most powerful military force in history. During the campaign he had charged Eisenhower with allowing a "missile gap" to develop in favor of the Soviets. Having seen the U-2 and other intelligence reports, Eisenhower knew that there was no gap.

At a Green Berets training camp. *(Bruno Barbey/Magnum.)*

Kennedy also soon learned this, but refused to believe that American power was sufficient. Without evidence of Russian intentions, the new President assumed that Khrushchev would try to build new missiles as rapidly as possible. The Soviets had in fact decided to move slowly in this area, but Kennedy nevertheless accelerated American missile building. Khrushchev interpreted this to mean the Americans wanted a first-strike capability (that is, forces sufficient to wipe out Russia in one strike without fear of a return salvo), so he ordered a step-up of Russian production and began nuclear testing at an increased rate. The most expensive arms race in history had begun, with China and France rushing to build their own nuclear weapons. Secretary of Defense Robert McNamara later believed that the Kennedy decision was "not justified" but was "necessitated by a lack of accurate information." By 1964 the U.S. force of 750 ICBMs (intercontinental ballistic missiles) was four times greater than that of the Soviets.

Kennedy, however, determined that since nuclear weapons would be of little use in the jungles and hamlets of the newly emerging areas, he would need conventional forces. Eisenhower, the foremost American military figure of the post-1950 era, believed that such power would be too expensive and ineffective, but Kennedy assumed that it was crucial if the new nations were to be saved from communism. He increased the number of conventional Army troops, created the Special Forces (and suggested the "Green Berets," by which they would be known) to fight guerrilla wars, and spent billions increasing the nation's helicopter and weapon capacity for fighting in the third world. The Kennedy administration indeed tended to define the world primarily in military terms. Rostow told Special Forces troops in mid-1961: "I salute you, as I would a group of doctors, teachers, economic planners, agricultural experts, civil servants, or others who are now leading the way in fashioning the new nations."

## THE NEW FRONTIER CONTAINED: 1961–62

Kennedy had determined on these policies before entering office, but in early January 1961 Khrushchev delivered a speech that spurred on the new President. The Soviet leader declared that revolutions, such as the "national liberation war" in Vietnam, were "not only admissible but inevitable." He asserted that the Communists did not have to start such wars, for nationalists within each country would fight to drive out imperialism. Communists would, however, "fully support" such conflicts. Khrushchev then focused, perhaps unfortunately, on Cuba by saying that Castro's victory was a herald of what was to come.

Kennedy interpreted this speech as a direct challenge. One reaction was to announce with great publicity the Alliance for Progress. Over a ten-year period the Alliance was to use $100 billion of U.S. and Latin American funds to develop and stabilize the southern continent, that is, to prevent any more Castros from appearing. The Alliance quickly encountered innumerable problems. In Washington these included bureaucratic mix-ups, lack of funds, and the growing involvement in Vietnam, which absorbed money and attention. In Latin America there were few funds, mistrust of Yankees, entrenched interests refusing to budge, and disputes between nations. Washington too often forgot that the region consisted of twenty very different countries. Worst of all, the rich in Latin America used the money to make themselves richer and the poor poorer. The gap between rich and poor widened. Political crises followed. In Central America, for example, only one revolutionary band existed in 1960. But after ten years of the Alliance for Progress, revolutions threatened El Salvador, Nicaragua, and Guatemala.

A serious blow struck the Alliance's dream at the beginning, when Kennedy agreed to allow the Cuban exile force, with American air cover, to invade Cuba at the Bay of Pigs in an attempt to overthrow Castro. It was a disaster from the start. Afraid that the aircraft would too deeply involve the United States, Kennedy recalled them at the last minute, leaving the small exile army at the mercy of Castro's planes and tanks. The invaders were either killed or captured. Washington had assumed that the invasion would trigger a massive uprising against Castro, but Cubans instead rallied to his side. Contrary to the expectations of the Central Intelligence Agency and the White House, there would not be a successful replay of the 1954 invasion of Guatemala. By supporting the exiles, Kennedy had broken numerous American pledges not to use force in inter-American affairs. It marked a terrible start for the Alliance for Progress and Kennedy's struggle to win over the newly emerging peoples. But it redoubled his determination. He secretly ordered an immediate review of policy in other areas and soon sent five hundred more special "advisors" to

Vietnam. Publicly, he tried to rebuild American prestige by announcing that the country would develop the missile and technological power to land a man on the moon within the decade. (Eight years and $24 billion later, Neil Armstrong walked on the moon, but by 1969 riots at home and interventions in newly emerging areas had gone far toward destroying that prestige.)

In June 1961 Kennedy and Khrushchev met in Vienna. They worked out a cease-fire for one part of Indochina (Laos) but engaged in a heated debate on "wars of liberation." Khrushchev's next move, however, was not to support such wars, but to resolve the Berlin question. Russia had become deeply embarrassed as thousands of East Germans fled the Communist zone to find new homes in the West. Announcing that this outward flow of talent would have to stop, Khrushchev demanded an immediate Berlin settlement. Kennedy responded by adding $3 billion more to the defense budget, calling up some national reserve units to prepare for battle and warning Americans to begin building civil-defense shelters. This last idea was questionable—there was no way to protect even half the population from being killed in a nuclear war—but Kennedy had at least replied to Khrushchev. As Russian and American tanks faced one another in Berlin, the Russians brutally solved the problem by building high concrete walls along the East German borders and ordering guards to shoot anyone who tried to escape.

## THE BRINK: THE CUBAN MISSILE CRISIS

The dangers of the Berlin confrontation paled in comparison with the threat of nuclear war that seemed possible during the Cuban missile crisis of October 1962. On October 14, a high-flying U-2 plane took pictures of Soviet medium- and long-range ground-to-ground missiles being emplaced in Cuba. President Kennedy summoned a special fourteen-man executive committee (the "ExCom") to meet secretly and advise him on a response.

Khrushchev had begun sending the missiles to Cuba during the spring of 1962 for three reasons. First, since the disaster at the Bay of Pigs, U.S. officials had made plans to overthrow Castro. The plans, code-named "Operation Mongoose," proposed covert actions and apparently discussed using American mob figures to kill the Cuban leader with poison pills or explosives. Part of the plans called for a U.S. invasion of Cuba, if necessary, to finish the job. During mid-1962 thousands of troops were deployed on maneuvers in the southeastern United States, and some practiced amphibious invasions around Puerto Rico. Khrushchev pledged that the Soviets would protect Cuba from such an invasion. Second, Americans enjoyed an overwhelming superiority over the Russians in deliverable nuclear warheads and bombs, and top Washington officials not only publicly discussed this superiority, but noted that their most awesome nuclear weapon, the ICBM, would double in number during 1963. Khrushchev planned to set up his own missiles in Cuba to partially offset the American superiority. Third, Kennedy had deployed fifteen Jupiter (intermediate-range) missiles in Turkey. They were within easy range of key

Soviet cities. As the Jupiters became operational in 1962, Khrushchev came under heavy pressure from the Soviet military to respond. He not only sent his missiles to Cuba, but accompanied them with 42,000 Soviet troops and technicians who were in Cuba when the crisis erupted.

After six days of top-secret ExCom discussions, on October 22 Kennedy dramatically demanded in a nationwide television speech that the Soviet missiles be immediately removed. He announced that a U.S. naval blockade around Cuba would search Soviet ships carrying missiles and prevent them from reaching Havana. The President warned that if any missile were fired from Cuba, the United States would respond—by attacking the Soviet Union. "KENNEDY READY FOR SOVIET SHOWDOWN," the *New York Times* headline proclaimed the next morning. American forces went on full alert. Airborne U.S. bombers were filled with fuel and nuclear weapons. Khrushchev, however, never put his strategic forces in high-readiness alert. He did not want to test the superior U.S. conventional or nuclear forces in combat. Nevertheless, for six days the Soviet leader refused to remove his missiles from Cuba. As the crisis heated up, the ExCom split. Some urged Kennedy to stay with the blockade. Others wanted a "surgical strike" on the missiles, which would doubtless have killed Russian advisors. Others urged a full-scale conventional attack to remove both the missiles and Castro. Attorney General Robert Kennedy later wrote that this was "probably the brightest kind of group that you could get together," but "if six of them had been President . . . I think the world might have been blown up."

Just hours before the U.S. attack was planned, a U-2 plane was shot down over Cuba by a Soviet officer who acted without Moscow's instructions. The plane's pilot was killed. Khrushchev later claimed that Castro demanded that "we should launch a preemptive strike against the United States." The Soviet leader turned down the demand. Fighting reportedly broke out between Cubans and Russians over who would control the missile sites. In this superheated atmosphere, a deal emerged October 26–27. Khrushchev agreed to remove the missiles. "We're eyeball to eyeball, and I think the other fellow just blinked," Secretary of State Rusk remarked. But in turn, Kennedy publicly pledged not to invade Cuba, and his brother privately informed the Soviets that the United States would pull the Jupiter missiles out of Turkey. Indeed, Kennedy was ready to offer further concessions to Khrushchev to avoid a nuclear showdown.

The crisis was over. As Rusk noted to another ExCom member, "We have a considerable victory. You and I are still alive." The reverberations of the crisis were nevertheless felt long after. Kennedy emerged as a hero for apparently facing down Khrushchev, although some suggested that the President overreacted, and did so not because of a military threat but for political reasons at home. He could not suffer another Bay of Pigs or Berlin setback, this argument went, particularly after some Republicans had warned weeks before about the missiles being shipped into Cuba. The Soviets, moreover, had lied to Kennedy about their plans for putting in the missiles; this deception, together with the U.S. public's belief that the missiles threatened the nation with extinction, forced Kennedy to act or else, his brother Robert warned, he would be impeached. Whatever their motivations, Khrushchev and Kennedy decided to install a "hotline" telephone between Washington and Moscow so that future crises could be handled more intelligently. They next negotiated a nuclear test-ban treaty in 1963 prohibiting aboveground testing. This treaty stopped further creation of deadly radiation that was building in the earth's atmosphere from earlier tests, but it did not stop all testing. The bombs were taken underground, and more nuclear tests were conducted during the next ten years than had occurred during the previous ten. The U.S. military and some members of Congress demanded that Kennedy allow such expanded testing as the price for their support of the treaty. The two great powers had nevertheless taken a first, if small, step toward arms control. Another by-product of the crisis occurred in Southeast Asia, and it was not as constructive.

## VIETNAM

American involvement in Vietnam had begun between 1950 and 1954. Kennedy transformed that involvement. When he became President, 675 American military advisors helped the South Vietnam government of Ngo Dinh Diem; the number had been determined by the 1954 Geneva agreements. When Kennedy was assassinated, 17,000 American troops were in South Vietnam.

Kennedy's commitment is easily understood. He had repeatedly declared that the cold war would be determined in the newly emerging areas, and Washington officials saw Vietnam as the key to the Asian struggle. A worse place for such a commitment could hardly be imagined, for Americans and Vietnamese lived in worlds so totally different that each easily misunderstood the other. In *Fire in the Lake,* a history of the Vietnam War, Frances FitzGerald noted, "There was no more correspondence between the two worlds than that between the atmosphere of the earth and that of the sea."

Americans thought in terms of expansion, open spaces, limitless advance, and reliance on technology. They preferred to stress the future rather than think about their past, especially if that history showed their limitations, as it often did. They liked a society that was mobile, competitive, and individualistic. But Vietnamese life depended on self-contained villages that had remained unchanged for centuries. Vietnamese considered individualism destructive to the integrated, settled, and rural life that centered on the family and the memories of ancestors. Habits were carefully handed down through generations, and when old Vietnamese died they would often be buried in the rice field to help provide sustenance for their grandchildren. Vietnam's economy depended on rice, for the country shipped large amounts to other Asian nations besides using it for its own staple diet. The people developed sophisticated growing methods, but they did not depend on technology. Change was to occur over centuries, and order, not change, was most highly desired. Otherwise the village could be disrupted, ancestral ties neglected, society torn apart. More than

80 percent of the Vietnamese were Buddhists, and their religion was tightly integrated with their everyday life.

If society did fail to work properly, if its order did disintegrate, the Vietnamese expected their leaders to step down, committing suicide if necessary, so that new leaders could make necessary changes to restore order. These changes could be radical as long as the village life retained its wholeness. For this reason, the Vietnamese could accept the revolutionary doctrines of Communist leader Ho Chi Minh, for he carefully worked through the villages to drive out French colonialism between 1946 and 1954. The Communists later used the same tactic against the Americans. The United States, on the other hand, fought Communist successes in the villages by destroying the villages. In so doing, Americans destroyed the very foundation of the society they thought they were saving.

The people of Southeast Asia had long dealt with foreign invaders. For more than a thousand years China controlled much of the area, but in the eleventh century A.D. the Chinese were driven out. During the next eight hundred years vigorous societies developed in present-day Vietnam, Laos, Cambodia, and Thailand, while the peoples continued to repulse Chinese attempts to control the area. In the nineteenth century France established a colonial empire over Cambodia, Laos, and Vietnam, but its control had been strongest in the area of South Vietnam and weakest in the north. During the 1920s a strong nationalist movement under Ho Chi Minh developed. His great opportunity appeared when Japan defeated and humiliated the French during 1940–45. With American help, French power reappeared in 1946. Ho believed that a settlement could be worked out and preferred dealing with France than with closer, more threatening neighbors: "It is better to smell the French dung for a while than eat China's all our lives." The settlement, however, broke down in late 1946, and war ensued until Ho's victory in 1954.

The Geneva agreements of 1954 temporarily divided the country along the 17th parallel until elections could be held in 1956. Historically, South Vietnam had not been a separate nation. But with American support, South Vietnamese President Diem, who had been installed in Saigon during late 1954 with Washington's aid, refused to hold the elections. He knew that his own weakness in the south, Ho's reputation as a nationalist, and Ho's iron hand in the north would result in a lopsided victory for the Communists. Believing that American support made his own position secure, Diem cut back drastically on promised land reforms. He concentrated power within his own family. That family was Roman Catholic, a religion adopted by only 10 percent of the Vietnamese. Elections were rigged and the South Vietnamese constitution forgotten.

Civil war finally erupted against Diem in 1958. In March 1960 the National Liberation Front was organized by Communists to lead the rebellion. Guerrilla warfare accelerated. In the fall of 1960 Diem's own army tried to overthrow his government but failed. As Diem approached the brink, he called for help. Kennedy responded.

## THE NEW FRONTIER IN VIETNAM: 1961–63

The United States tried to build a nation where none had existed by supporting a ruler who was under attack by his own people. Kennedy nevertheless thought the effort necessary. Secretary of State Dean Rusk fully supported the policy. Rusk had been an army officer in Asia in 1944–45 and assistant secretary of state for Far Eastern affairs during the Korean War. He fervently believed that the 1960s would test whether Americans could contain communism in Asia as they had in Europe. Utterly loyal to Kennedy and, later, to President Johnson, Rusk remained dedicated to winning in Vietnam even after Kennedy's policies had failed and White House officials tried to blame their own mistakes on Rusk.

In the Department of Defense, Secretary Robert McNamara quickly built the armed force needed by Kennedy and Rusk. A brilliant product of the Harvard Business School and former president of the Ford Motor Company, McNamara used computer and other new quantitative techniques to build and demonstrate the superiority of American power. "Every quantitative measurement we have shows we're winning this war," he declared in 1962. But in Vietnam, numbers were not enough. They could even be misleading, for the war involved a struggle in the villages that required political and cultural judgments. McNamara's computers could not make such judgments.

As a consequence, Kennedy continued to try to prop up Diem even as Diem's support was dwindling. During 1961–62, ten thousand Americans departed for Vietnam. Kennedy made the commitment even though he fully realized it was nothing more than a start. He compared aiding Diem with being an alcoholic: "The effect [of one drink] wears off and you have to take another." But given his own call to action against communism, he believed that he had no alternative. Diem saw clearly what was happening. The weaker he became, the more he could expect Kennedy's help. Diem could consequently pay little attention to American advice. He could do as he pleased since Kennedy had no alternative but to support the South Vietnamese regime. Meanwhile Diem's generals dreamed up statistics to feed McNamara's computers, and the computers told McNamara and Kennedy what they wanted to hear.

After the Cuban missile crisis, Kennedy's determination increased. He believed that the crisis had forced Khrushchev to retreat in the world struggle but that Russia's place would be taken by Mao Tse-tung's China. Mao, the President privately believed, was the true revolutionary, and when China developed nuclear weapons, that country would be the great threat to world stability. It was only a short step for Kennedy to conclude that since Vietnam bordered on China, and since Mao aided Ho Chi Minh, the Vietnamese struggle would decide whether Chinese communism would triumph in the newly emerging nations. All of Kennedy's assumptions were doubtful: Ho and the Vietnamese feared China and would not cooperate politically with Mao; Chinese communism had little to do with Vietnamese communism, which was highly nationalistic; and above all, Vietnamese nationalism, not communism, was the main fuel for the war against Diem. As nationalists, Vietnamese were

Secretary of Defense Robert McNamara, General Maxwell D. Taylor, and General Paul Harkins stroll by a barbed-wire barricade near Saigon, South Vietnam, September 1963. *(BETTMANN.)*

determined to be free of all foreigners, whether French, American, or Chinese. But Kennedy, who too easily defined the world as simply "half slave and half free," seemed unable to see these differences.

Despite Washington's help, Diem's forces lost ground in 1962. Kennedy was reluctant to admit this publicly, but Americans learned of Diem's setbacks through American newspaper correspondents in Vietnam. Washington officials tried to silence these reports. The American commander in the western Pacific shouted at one critical journalist, "Why don't you get on the team?" Kennedy even privately suggested to the publisher of the *New York Times* that he give a "vacation" to one reporter who was telling the story accurately but not the way Kennedy wanted it reported. To the publisher's credit, he rejected the President's advice. American-Vietnamese relations worsened as Diem would not take U.S. suggestions concerning political and land reforms.

The turning point came in mid-1963. Buddhist leaders celebrated Buddha's 2,587th birthday with flags and religious demonstrations. Diem had banned such displays. He ordered his troops to fire on the Buddhist leaders. Anti-Diem forces immediately rallied to the Buddhists, and civil war threatened within the principal cities. Several Buddhists responded by publicly burning themselves to death, an act that the government ridiculed as a "barbecue show." The deaths, however, dramatized the growing opposition. Kennedy decided to move.

In late August, American officials told South Vietnamese military leaders that there would be no objection if Diem were deposed. On November 1 the South Vietnamese president and his brother were captured and shot by army leaders. Although they had not known about, and indeed had disapproved of, the assassination, American officials had encouraged Diem's overthrow. In doing so, they had again demonstrated their deep involvement in the Vietnamese conflict and their determination to "save" the country even if this required helping overthrow the government. The Kennedy administration was now fully committed to the war and to a new government. What the President would have done next is unknown. On November 22, 1963, while on a political junket to Dallas, Texas, John F. Kennedy also fell victim to an assassin's bullet.

A later government investigation headed by Chief Justice Earl Warren concluded that the murderer was probably Lee Harvey Oswald, young, embittered, and, it seems, especially angered by Kennedy's anti-Castro policies. But Oswald never told his story, for shortly after his arrest he was shot—on national television and while surrounded by police guards—by a small-time nightclub owner, Jack Ruby. In the following years many self-appointed investigators produced evidence suggesting that Oswald was innocent, or that he was only one of several killers, or that he was the front man for a powerful secret group still at large. Loving mysteries of this kind, especially when it involved a glamorous President, Americans debated at length the circumstances of the tragedy. While they focused on Dallas and the shattered dreams of the Kennedy promise, a new tragedy was growing twelve thousand miles away that would destroy more than 57,000 American lives.

## Suggested Reading

For a comprehensive analysis of John F. Kennedy's career, see the two volumes by Herbert S. Parmet: *Jack: The Struggles of John F. Kennedy* (1980) and *JFK: The Presidency of John F. Kennedy* (1983). Other useful accounts of the New Frontier are provided in James N. Giglio, *The Presidency of John F. Kennedy* (1991); Irving Bernstein, *Promises Kept: John F. Kennedy's New Frontier* (1991); and Richard Reeves, *President Kennedy: Profile of Power* (1993). On the election of 1960 see Christopher Matthews, *Kennedy and Nixon: The Rivalry that Shaped Postwar America* (1996).

Economic policy is considered in Amy Davis, *The Kennedy Presidency and the Politics of Prosperity* (1997); Jim Heath, *John F. Kennedy and the Business Community* (1969); and Daniel Knapp and Kenneth Polk, *Scouting the War on Poverty: Social Reform Politics in the Kennedy Administration* (1971). Lawrence Fuchs, *John F. Kennedy and American Catholicism* (1967), is a useful work, as is David J. O'Brien, *The Renewal of American Catholicism* (1972). For a critique of the New Frontier's approach to civil rights, see Victor Navasky, *Kennedy Justice* (1971); for a more sympathetic view, see Carl M. Brauer, *John F. Kennedy and the Second Reconstruction* (1977). Aspects of the civil rights movement are considered in William H. Chafe, *Civilities and Civil Rights: Greensboro, North Carolina and the Black Struggle for Freedom* (1981); and David J. Garrow, *The FBI and Martin Luther King, Jr.* (1981).

On foreign policy, first consult the indexes and appropriate sections of R. D. Burns, ed., *Guide to American Foreign Relations Since 1700* (1983); Bruce Jentleson and Thomas Paterson, eds., *Encyclopedia of American Foreign Relations,* 4 vols. (1997); and Warren Cohen, *America in the Age of Soviet Power, 1945–1991* (1993). Useful overviews include Thomas G. Paterson, ed., *Kennedy's Quest for Victory* (1989); Warren Cohen, *Dean Rusk* (1980); Desmond Ball, *Politics and Force Levels* (1981), on the military buildup. For special topics see Montague Kern et al., *The Kennedy Crises: The Press, the Presidency and Foreign Policy* (1983); Richard D. Mahoney, *JFK: Ordeal in Africa* (1983); Marilyn Young, *The Vietnam Wars* (1991), on Vietnam; Bernard J. Firestone, *The Quest for Nuclear Stability* (1982), on the nuclear test ban treaty; Richard Barnet, *The Alliance* (1983), on relations with Japan and Western Europe; Walter LaFeber, *Inevitable Revolutions: The United States in Central America* (1992), on the Alliance for Progress; Michael R. Beschloss, *Mayday: The U-2 Affair* (1986); and, on Cuba, start with Thomas Paterson's excellent *Contesting Castro* (1994); Jules R. Benjamin, *The U.S. and the Origins of the Cuban Revolution* (1989); Morris Morley, *Imperial State and Revolution* (1987); Trumbull Higgins, *The Perfect Failure* (1987), on the Bay of Pigs fiasco; Raymond Garthoff, *Reflections on the Cuban Missile Crisis* (1989); J. G. Blight and D. A. Welch, *On the Brink* (1989); and Gerard T. Rice, *The Bold Experiment: JFK's Peace Corps* (1985).

For David Smith's importance, Stanley E. Marcus, *David Smith: The Sculptor and His Work* (1983), is informative.

Martin Luther King, Jr., September 1967. *(Benedict J. Fernandez.)*

# CHAPTER FOURTEEN

# 1963–1968
## The Great Society and Vietnam

This chapter discusses:
- Lyndon Johnson's dreams of a Great Society
- How the Supreme Court moved to change America
- The feminists, NOW
- Martin Luther King's dreams, urban realities
- The many tragedies of the Vietnam War

John Kennedy bequeathed to Lyndon Baines Johnson (often referred to as "LBJ") a legacy of social reform at home and a policy of military interventionism in Vietnam. That was a highly combustible mixture. Johnson, who wanted to be regarded as "president of all the people," also wanted to achieve a consensus in favor of his Great Society programs. But while he succeeded in implementing those programs in the fields of civil rights, education, and welfare, his escalation of the war in Vietnam led to unprecedented tensions and divisions. The consequences were disastrous. The war undermined social reform, stimulated the growth of irresponsible presidential power, triggered ruinous inflation, eroded fundamental civil liberties, and strained crucial diplomatic alliances. The war led, finally, to violence at home, which, if not so destructive as the violence in Vietnam, was a political turning point. It forced Johnson to withdraw from the presidential race in 1968 and paved the way for the victory of Richard M. Nixon.

## THE 1964 ELECTION

Lyndon Johnson knew as much about the exercise of political power as any American in the post-1945 era. He had grown up in central Texas, learning state and national politics during the New Deal era from such masters as fellow Texan Sam Rayburn, Speaker of the House of Representatives. During the 1950s Johnson became leader of the Senate Democratic majority, where he wheeled and dealed, whipped and cajoled, flattered and intimidated until he became one of the strongest of all Senate leaders. Johnson often gathered votes by subjecting fellow senators to intense, person-to-person harangues. Such encounters became known as the "treatment"; it was described by one victim as "a great overpowering thunderstorm that consumed you as it closed in around you." When he moved into the White House, Johnson was perfectly prepared to use the vast powers of the executive branch. Almost nothing could stop him from having his way, and he wanted his way on every issue. "When we made mistakes, I believe we erred because we tried to do too much too soon and never because we stayed away from challenge," he later wrote. "If the Presidency can be said to have been employed and to have been enjoyed, I had employed it to the utmost, and I had enjoyed it to the limit."

In the 1964 presidential campaign Johnson ran against Republican nominee Barry Goldwater, a conservative senator from Arizona. Goldwater never had a chance. Johnson had been masterful in assuring continuity of government after Kennedy's murder. The Republicans' choice of Goldwater reflected a persistent belief in the existence of a "hidden vote," that is, a truly conservative vote that the Republican party could never obtain so long as it nominated liberal candidates. Goldwater made few concessions to Republican liberals, but he made an explicit overture to those on the right when, in accepting the nomination, he declared: "Extremism in the defense of liberty is no vice; moderation in the pursuit of justice is no virtue."

Goldwater voiced several themes during the campaign. "The moral fiber of the American people is beset by rot and decay," Goldwater asserted. He traced this largely to the "political daddyism" of Lyndon Johnson and other politicians whose only concern was "the morality of get, the morality of grab." Goldwater noted ominously: "You will search in vain for *any reference* to God or religion in the Democratic platform." The Republican candidate promised to apply a carving knife to welfare state programs, thereby seeming to be cautious and negative while the Texan was pushing the country forward. "I just want to tell you this," Johnson told a cheering crowd during the campaign, "we're in favor of a lot of things and we're against mighty few."

Goldwater then made the mistake of appearing to be tougher than Johnson by asserting that the Democrats had dallied in Southeast Asia instead of winning a total victory. He further suggested that such a triumph would be hastened if military commanders in the field, rather than the President, had the final word in using nuclear weapons. Johnson effectively seized on these remarks to score Goldwater for being irresponsible and bloodthirsty. As for Vietnam, "We don't want our American boys to do the fighting for Asian boys," LBJ announced on September 25, 1964. "We don't want to get involved in a nation with 700 million people [Red China] and get tied down in a land war in Asia."

It was, therefore, as easy for the Democrats to argue that Goldwater would propel the nation into an all-out war in Vietnam as it was to portray him as an extremist on domestic issues. Johnson humiliated his opponent in the election, winning 61.1 percent of the popular vote and carrying forty-four states to Goldwater's six. One of every five people who had voted Republican in 1960 switched to the Democrats in 1964. When asked why, many said of Goldwater, "He's too radical for me." Prospects for the Johnson administration could hardly have been more promising.

## LYNDON JOHNSON AND THE GREAT SOCIETY

Lyndon Johnson had greater success than any President since Franklin Roosevelt in putting across his legislative program. After his sweeping triumph in 1964, Johnson could work with comfortable Democratic majorities in Congress. The Democrats—with majorities of 294 to 140 in the House and 68 to 32 in the Senate—enjoyed their largest margin of control since 1937, the year Johnson entered Congress. The 71 freshman Democrats in the House, many of whom owed their election to the Johnson landslide, vied with one another in their willingness to cooperate with the White House. Then too, Johnson's Southern background and reputation as a moderate allowed him to enact far-reaching programs without losing his broad popular backing. Those programs often broke sharply with prevailing practice. The Revenue Act (1964) cut taxes by a whopping $11.5 billion even while the government was operating at a deficit. Advocates of an expansionary fiscal policy predicted correctly that the resulting boost in purchasing power would spur economic growth. The Housing Act

(1965) provided rent supplements for low-income families displaced by urban renewal or otherwise unable to find suitable public housing. The government would subsidize that portion of their rent which exceeded 25 percent of their income. In 1965, too, Congress renovated the immigration laws, removing quotas based on race or national origin that had existed in some form for more than fifty years. The Great Society, however, channeled most of its energies into four other areas: the war on poverty, aid to education, medical care, and civil rights.

Publication of Michael Harrington's *The Other America* (1962) had done much to focus public attention on the problem of poverty. Harrington documented the existence of an "economic underworld" of some 40 to 50 million Americans, inhabited "by those driven from the land and bewildered by the city, by old people . . . and by minorities facing a wall of prejudice." He also explained how that world—which was off the beaten track of interstate turnpikes, insulated from the view of suburban commuters, and politically impotent—had become "socially invisible." Harrington believed that existing social welfare legislation bypassed the poor. Asserting that the welfare state was "not built for the desperate, but for those who are already capable of helping themselves," Harrington called for a comprehensive federal assault on poverty. This would require the extension of welfare benefits to the poor by expanding social security and minimum wage laws, providing medical care and new housing, and eliminating racial prejudice.

In January 1964 Lyndon Johnson called for an "unconditional war on poverty," and later that year Congress approved the Economic Opportunity Act as the chief weapon in that war. The measure created an Office of Economic Opportunity (OEO), which sought to provide education, vocational training, and job experience for impoverished youths. The OEO also sponsored community action programs with a view toward improving employment opportunities, health care, housing, and education in poor neighborhoods. These programs were supposed to elicit "the maximum feasible participation of residents of the areas and members of the groups served." The OEO, which spent $750 million in 1965 and $1.5 billion in 1966, succeeded in reducing poverty but not in eliminating it. Government statistics indicated that 15.4 percent of the American people lived in poverty in 1966, compared with 22.1 percent in 1959. Funds for the OEO were always inadequate, and powerful local interests, anxious to get their hands on antipoverty money and patronage, often gained control of the community programs and used them for their own advancement.

The war on poverty was closely linked with federal aid to education. In the past such legislation had bogged down over the issue of assisting religious schools, but in 1965 the Johnson administration discovered an antipoverty rationale for school aid programs. The Elementary and Secondary Education Act (1965), which Congress passed in much the same form as Johnson requested, provided funds to local school districts according to a formula involving the number of children from low-income families in the county. The act also appropriated funds for the purchase of textbooks and other instructional materials that could be used by private as well as by public schools. Under this legislation, U.S. Office of Education expenditures soared from under

$50 million in 1960 to $5.6 billion in 1973. Congress also followed Johnson's recommendation in approving the Higher Education Act (1965), which provided college scholarships for needy students, subsidized interest costs on loans to college students, and helped fund classroom construction.

In the case of health insurance, as in that of federal aid to education, Johnson enacted a program first proposed by Harry Truman twenty years earlier. To appease those who saw the specter of socialized medicine in any national plan, the administration tied health care to the existing social security system and allowed participating physicians to charge their "usual and customary fees" if these were reasonable. Moreover, it limited coverage to the poor and elderly, who were least able to afford medical care and least likely to be protected by private insurance plans. Medicare provided benefits covering approximately 80 percent of hospital expenses for all persons over age 65. Medicaid provided assistance in meeting doctors' bills for poor people, regardless of age, who qualified for public assistance. By July 1967, at the end of its first year of operation, 17.7 million of 19 million elderly Americans had enrolled in Medicare, one in five had entered a hospital under the law, and 12 million had used it to defray medical expenses.

Civil rights legislation rounded out the Great Society agenda. Early in 1964 the Senate passed a civil rights bill already approved by the House. The act, which grew out of John F. Kennedy's recommendations, barred discrimination on the basis of race in all public accommodations. These included restaurants, gas stations, places of entertainment, and hotels (except for private residences renting fewer than five rooms for overnight lodging). Almost all such enterprises were held to affect interstate commerce—a gas station, for example, if its customers drove across state lines. The act also authorized the Justice Department to bring suit against state facilities, such as parks and auditoriums, that remained segregated. Finally, the act included an equal opportunity clause making it unlawful for firms with more than twenty-five employees to discriminate in hiring on the grounds of race, religion, sex, or national origin.

The measure also included provisions to safeguard the right to vote, but these were soon superseded by the Voting Rights Act (1965), which the President urged Congress to enact after violence erupted in Alabama. Early in 1965 Dr. Martin Luther King, Jr., led a demonstration in the town of Selma, in a county where more than fifteen thousand blacks were eligible to vote but only 335 had been able to register. When state troopers attacked King's followers and extremists murdered a civil rights worker, Congress responded with a drastic measure. It affected counties that prescribed literacy or other tests for voting and contained a substantial nonwhite population, but in which relatively few blacks actually cast ballots. In those counties, located primarily but not exclusively in South Carolina, Georgia, Mississippi, Alabama, and Louisiana, the right to vote would no longer depend on literacy or character fitness. The only valid criteria would be age, residence, and citizenship. The attorney general could appoint federal examiners to register voters, and the states, if they wished to protest, would have to appeal to a federal court in Washington, D.C.

Selma, Alabama, March 1964. *(Danny Lyon/Magnum.)*

Lyndon Johnson never passed up a chance to point out the historical significance of his legislation. To sign the education bill he traveled to the one-room schoolhouse he had attended as a child and asked his former teacher, 72-year-old "Miss Katie," to sit beside him. He journeyed to Independence, Missouri, to present the pen used to sign the Medicare bill to Harry Truman. He signed the Voting Rights Act in the same room that Lincoln had used more than one hundred years before to free the slaves conscripted into the Confederate army. Similarly, Johnson used grandiose terms in defining his objectives. He proclaimed that the Great Society "rests on abundance and liberty for all. It demands an end to poverty and racial injustice." Despite its impressive accomplishments, few would claim that the Great Society achieved that much. Michael Harrington, whose book had inspired much of the antipoverty program, applauded Johnson's initiative but concluded sadly: "What was supposed to be a social war turned out to be a skirmish and, in any case, poverty won."

## THE WARREN COURT: JUDICIAL ACTIVISM

In seeking new remedies for the nation's problems, the President and Congress were joined by the third branch of government. Far from inhibiting reform, as it had often done in the past, the Supreme Court acted as a catalyst for social change. Of the justices most closely identified with the new activism, two—Hugo Black and William O. Douglas—had been appointed by Roosevelt; two others—Earl Warren and William Brennan—had been named by Eisenhower.

John Kennedy's appointment of Arthur Goldberg in 1962 further tipped the scales toward judicial activism. Goldberg replaced Felix Frankfurter, who had long been the most articulate spokesman for the theory of judicial restraint. Frankfurter believed that judges must guard against the temptation to write their own biases into law and that society must not expect the Supreme Court to solve all its problems. After his retirement the Court moved boldly into areas it had once avoided.

In several important decisions, the Court curbed the erosion of civil liberties that had been under way since the 1950s. It found that membership in the Communist party did not alone constitute proof that an individual knew that the organization advocated the forcible overthrow of the government. Unless the government could demonstrate that a party member had such knowledge, conviction under the Smith Act was impossible. In 1965 the Court declared that the government could not require an individual to register as a member of a subversive organization, for to do so violated the constitutional prohibition against self-incrimination. The power of the House Un-American Activities Committee to force witnesses, under threat of a contempt citation, to answer questions about their acquaintances was sharply curtailed. Finally, the Court affirmed the right of a Communist party member to obtain a passport for foreign travel. These civil liberties rulings were, ironically, among the Court's least controversial.

The Supreme Court, 1965: *(standing, left to right)* Justices Byron R. White, William J. Brennan, Jr., Potter Stewart, and Abe Fortas; *(seated, left to right)* Justices Tom C. Clark and Hugo L. Black, Chief Justice Earl Warren, and Justices William O. Douglas and John M. Harlan. *(Black Star. Reprinted with permission.)*

Following the path it had charted in the school desegregation decision of 1954, the Court threw its weight behind the civil rights movement. In 1963 the Court was forced to rule on cases stemming from a refusal to seat blacks at lunch counters. It found that local ordinances upholding segregation in private business establishments were unconstitutional, for they involved state action within the meaning of the Fourteenth Amendment. Even if no such ordinances existed, public statements upholding de facto segregation by city officials were held to constitute such action and were therefore enough to invalidate Jim Crow practices. In *Cox* v. *Louisiana* (1964) the Court reversed the conviction of black demonstrators in Baton Rouge who had refused to disperse when so ordered by the police. The justices decided that breach-of-the-peace laws could not serve as a pretext for preventing peaceable speech and assembly. The Court quickly sanctioned the civil rights acts of 1964 and 1965. It also ruled that delays in school desegregation were "no longer tolerable," and in *Loving* v. *Virginia* (1967) it struck down a state law barring marriage between persons of different races.

Religious dissenters, no less than civil rights workers, received new forms of legal protection. In the early 1960s, twelve states required Bible reading in public schools, and thirty others encouraged such exercises. Children in New York State recited a nonsectarian prayer: "Almighty God, we acknowledge our dependence upon Thee, and we beg Thy blessings upon us, our parents, our teachers and our country." A state court saw no objection to this. Although recitation might cause discomfort to nonbelievers, there was no need to "subordinate the spiritual needs of believers to the psychological needs of nonbelievers." But the Supreme Court, in *Engel* v. *Vitale* (1962), ruled the New York prayer unconstitutional on the grounds that it was a religious activity which placed an "indirect coercive pressure upon religious minorities." Then, in 1963, the Court took up the case of Edward Schempp, a Unitarian, whose children attended a school in which biblical passages were read over the loudspeaker and students recited the Lord's Prayer. Those who did not wish to participate could wait outside the classroom. Schempp argued that this arrangement would penalize his children and make them feel like "oddballs." The Supreme Court agreed: "Through the mechanism of the State, all of the people are being required to finance a religious exercise that only some of the people want and that violates the sensibilities of others." The justices ruled that public schools could not show the slightest preference for any particular religion.

Nowhere did the Court break more decisively with the past than in the area of obscenity. In the mid-1950s, explicit sexual references in books, magazines, and motion pictures were illegal, and even such classics as D. H. Lawrence's *Lady Chatterley's Lover* were proscribed. The Supreme Court began to change all this in *Roth* v. *United States* (1957). Although ruling that obscenity did not deserve constitutional protection, the Court nevertheless felt it necessary to propose a test of obscenity, which became "whether to the average person applying contemporary community standards, the dominant theme of the material taken as a whole appeals to prurient interest." Thus began years of controversy over the meaning of such terms as "prurience." In 1961 the Court decided that a magazine could indeed appeal to prurient interest so long as it did not reveal "patent offensiveness." The justices went a step further in *Jacobellis* v. *Ohio* (1963), asserting that "material dealing with sex in a manner that advocates ideas . . . or has literary or scientific or artistic value or any other forms of social importance may not be branded as obscenity and denied the constitutional protection." In 1966 the Court extended such protection to *Fanny Hill,* an eighteenth-century novel usually considered pornographic. A book could not be banned unless "it is found to be utterly without redeeming social value." Under that standard, nearly all restrictions on the right of an adult to obtain sexually explicit material vanished.

This expansion of individual freedoms also characterized other areas of Court action. Three classic decisions revolutionized criminal justice procedures. In *Gideon* v. *Wainwright* (1963) the Court decided that an indigent person charged with a felony—in this instance, entering a pool hall and committing theft—was entitled to representation by a state-appointed attorney, although Florida law provided legal aid only for capital offenses. In *Escobedo* v. *Illinois* (1964) the Court ruled in favor of a man who, when interrogated on a murder charge, was not informed of his right to remain silent or permitted to see an attorney. Five justices believed that when the police centered their investigation on one individual and sought to extract a confession, they must allow the suspect to see a lawyer. Four members of the Court dissented: "Supported by no stronger authority than its own rhetoric, the Court today converts a routine police investigation of an unsolved murder into a distorted analogue of a judicial trial." A similarly close and bitter division prevailed in *Miranda* v. *Arizona* (1966), which involved a man who, after a two-hour interrogation, had confessed to charges of kidnapping and rape. The majority held that a confession could not be introduced as evidence unless the defendant had been informed at the outset of the interrogative process that he could see an attorney or remain silent, and that any information he provided would be used against him. The burden of proof was placed on the prosecution to show that a defendant knowingly waived the privilege against self-incrimination and the right to counsel. Four dissenting judges gravely warned that the ruling "will return a killer, a rapist or other criminal to the streets . . . to repeat his crime whenever it pleases him."

Judicial activism reached a culmination in decisions concerning legislative reapportionment. The Court in the past had skirted this issue, reasoning that if district lines were drawn unfairly, citizens should seek political, not judicial, redress. But in *Baker* v. *Carr* (1962) the Court entered the "political thicket." The case involved a resident of Memphis, Tennessee, who complained that because of malapportionment his vote for a member of the state legislature was worth less than the vote of a rural resident. The Supreme Court agreed that reapportionment was a proper question for judicial determination. Federal district judges were to set guidelines, and in 1963 the Supreme Court provided a clue as to what those guidelines should be when it overturned the county-unit voting system in Georgia, under which the candidate winning a majority in a county received all its votes. Justice William O. Douglas explained that political equality "can mean only one thing, one person, one vote." The Court applied this doctrine in *Reynolds* v. *Sims* (1964). Earl Warren, speaking for the majority, said that just as a state could not give a citizen two votes, so it could not permit any person's vote to count twice as much as anyone else's. Both houses of state legislatures had to be apportioned on the basis of population. Substantial equality, if not mathematical precision, was needed in determining the size of districts. Within a few years, the great majority of states had reapportioned their legislatures to conform with these rulings.

Most of the Warren Court's decisions sparked bitter controversy. One member of Congress called the justices an "unpredictable group of uncontrolled despots," and efforts were made to overturn certain rulings, particularly those concerning reapportionment and school prayer. In 1964 the House of Representatives passed a bill denying federal courts jurisdiction over apportionment, but the Senate refused to concur. A constitutional amendment that would have permitted the states to apportion one house of their legislatures on some basis other than population (if approved by voters in a referendum) passed the Senate in 1965 and 1966, but each time fell short of obtaining the required two-thirds majority. Similarly, in 1966 the Senate approved an amendment allowing voluntary participation in prayer in the public schools, but again by less than a two-thirds vote. Critics complained that the Supreme Court had become "a general haven for reform movements." There was, however, no minimizing the social and political impact of its rulings.

## ORIGINS OF THE NEW FEMINISM

Nor was there any minimizing the significance of the revival of feminism, inspired in part by Betty Friedan's *The Feminine Mystique*, published in 1963. The book was a powerful indictment of the "housewife-heroine" of the 1950s. After World War II, Friedan contended, women had been told that "they could desire no greater destiny than to glory in their own femininity," to seek fulfillment as wives and mothers. Instilled by women's magazines, which published such articles as "Have a Baby While You're Young," "How to Snare a Male," and "Cooking to Me Is Poetry," the feminine mystique was also perpetrated by psychologists, advertisers, and educators, who dissuaded college women from seeking careers. Although women had accepted the feminine mystique because it seemed to promise a safe, secure existence, Friedan argued, it actually confined them to the home, "a comfortable concentration camp," produced feelings of emptiness, and deprived women of a sense of individualism. "I've tried everything women are supposed to do, but . . . I begin to feel I have no personality," one victim claimed. To escape the mystique, Friedan concluded, women had to develop "new life plans," establish independent careers, and pursue "goals that will permit them to find their own identity."

Betty Friedan's best-seller immediately evoked a strong response from appreciative readers. "I and other women knew we were not alone," one woman wrote. "It struck at the very center of my being," wrote another.

Friedan had not intended to create a new feminist movement in 1963. The publication of her book, in fact, did not immediately create one. But the civil rights struggle of the early 1960s provided another catalyst for feminist revival. First, civil rights advocates created a climate of protest that paved the way for other reform movements. Second, civil rights organizations demonstrated what committed pressure groups could accomplish through confrontation tactics and egalitarian arguments. Third, by demanding remedial legislation, the civil rights movement set a precedent for ending discrimination under law. Finally, and seemingly by accident, the Civil Rights Act of 1964 propelled a new women's movement into existence.

During congressional debate over Title VII of the civil rights bill, which prohibited discrimination in employment on grounds of race, a Virginia representative proposed an amendment that would prohibit such discrimination on grounds of sex as well. His goal was to discredit the bill, prevent its passage, and make its supporters look foolish. But once the new law was enacted, with its controversial amendment intact, the sex discrimination clause had an unexpected impact. When complaints about sex discrimination, sent to the Equal Employment Opportunity Commission, received little attention, a small group of women's rights advocates—including Betty Friedan—tried to spur the commission to act on women's grievances. Since success seemed unlikely unless public support was mobilized, the new group took action. In 1966, twenty-eight women's rights supporters created the National Organization for Women (NOW) "to bring American women into full participation in the mainstream of American society NOW." Some NOW founders were veterans of President Kennedy's Commission on the Status of Women, formed in 1961, or of similar state commissions. Others were union leaders or professionals, like Friedan. Defining itself as a "civil rights" organization for women, NOW was the first national women's rights organization formed since 1920.

NOW's first effort was to provide the new feminist movement with an agenda. In its manifesto, NOW demanded "a truly equal partnership of the sexes, as part of the worldwide revolution of human rights." Denouncing pay disparities, employment inequities, and educational discrimination, NOW called for new types of social roles. "We reject the current assumption that a man must carry the whole burden of supporting himself, his wife, and family . . . or that marriage, home, and family are primarily woman's world and responsibility," NOW stated. While proposing a new relationship between men and women, NOW stopped short of an attack on the institution of marriage. "We believe that a true partnership between the sexes demands a different concept of marriage, an equitable sharing of the responsibilities of home and children, and of the economic burden of their support." Under the leadership of Betty Friedan, its first president, NOW became a national political pressure group, with growing numbers of local chapters. Its members sought to end sexual inequity through legislation and court decisions. They lobbied, demonstrated, filed class-action suits to end discrimination in hiring and promotion, and insisted that newspapers stop publishing separate want ads for males and females.

Too radical for some, NOW proved too conservative for others. Its campaign was soon affected by the eruption of a younger, more radical, feminist wing, one that emerged from the ranks of civil rights activists. In the early 1960s, hundreds of college students had participated in voter registration drives in the South. During these campaigns, young women developed a new consciousness of sex discrimination, both within the civil rights movement and outside it. "Assumptions of male supremacy are as . . . crippling to the woman as assumptions of white supremacy are to the Negro," one civil rights worker concluded. Similar objections to male dominance were voiced by young women who moved on to "new left" (see "The New Left and the Counterculture," page 456) community organizing projects outside the South. By 1967, radical women had developed their own brand of feminist attack, one that bore the imprint of new left rhetoric. To radical feminists, women constituted "an oppressed class. Our oppression is total, affecting every facet of our lives. . . . We identify the enemy as man." The radical agenda, indeed, seemed to differ sharply from that of NOW. "The institution of marriage is the chief vehicle for the perpetuation of the oppression of women," the radicals contended. "It is through the role of wife that the subjugation of woman is maintained." The radical feminist recruitment technique of "consciousness raising" was also innovative. It consisted of small discussion groups, in which women reconsidered their personal experiences as political phenomena. Out of consciousness raising emerged the distinctive, all-encompassing goals of radical feminism: "women's liberation" and the eradication of "sexism." Eliminating sexism, like eliminating racism, meant changing attitudes, behavior, relationships, and institutions. The end was fundamental social change, or "revolution."

Structureless, with no headquarters, organization, or officers, women's liberation was again a contrast to NOW. "It's not a movement, it's a State of Mind," one advocate explained. But the new state of mind seemed contagious, notably among educated, younger women. During the late 1960s, women's liberation created a ferment of activity. Some radical feminists staged confrontations to gain media attention by crowning a sheep at the 1968 Miss America Pageant or invading an all-male bar in New York City. Other groups devoted their efforts to special projects—health collectives, day care centers, abortion counseling services. Still others published "position papers" explaining their new ideology or sought to promote consciousness raising among new constituencies. While women's liberation campaigns were diffuse, NOW's goals became more specific. By 1968, the core of its legislative agenda was complete. NOW supported passage of an Equal Rights Amendment, a cause that had languished for several decades. It demanded repeal of state laws that prevented women from having abortions. And it urged the creation of government-funded day care programs to ease the burden on working mothers.

The two feminist wings were apparently much at odds. Reform-minded NOW viewed liberationists as a lunatic fringe, given to wild pronouncements, while radical feminists denounced NOW members as bourgeois conservatives, whose equity goals were only minor. But the postures of the two wings were in fact complementary, as feminist successes in the early 1970s were to prove.

# BLACK POWER AND URBAN RIOTS

The differences between radicals and reformers evident in the feminist movement were also increasingly apparent in the civil rights movement. The reformist approach, with its stress on nonviolent protest as a means and integration as an end, reached its zenith with the passage of the civil rights acts of 1964 and 1965. But the mid- and late-1960s saw the emergence of many black leaders who repudiated integration and nonviolence in favor of separatism and self-defense. The result was a fragmentation of the protest movement.

The "black power" slogan was coined by Stokely Carmichael, who had for several years worked with the Student Nonviolent Coordinating Committee (SNCC). This organization had helped organize the sit-ins and freedom rides. At first it endorsed Martin Luther King, Jr.'s, approach, but in the mid-1960s many in SNCC grew disenchanted with the existing civil rights program. They felt betrayed in 1964 when the Democratic convention refused to provide adequate representation for the Freedom Democratic party, which they had founded in Mississippi as an alternative to the lily-white state organization. SNCC workers found that turning the other cheek often created deep feelings of rage and hostility. Consequently, they became more receptive to the arguments of those, like Black Muslim leader Malcolm X, who advised: "If someone puts a hand on you, send him to the cemetery." An influx of white college students into the South to assist the civil rights movement also led some in SNCC to believe that such participation reinforced feelings of inferiority in Southern blacks. In June 1966, during a demonstration in Mississippi, Carmichael shouted: "Black Power! It's time we stand up and take over! Take over! Move on over, or we'll move on over you!"

In the following months Carmichael explained his viewpoint. Instead of seeking alliances with white liberals, who, he asserted, wished to perpetuate paternalistic control, blacks should do things for themselves. Instead of adopting nonviolent methods, "black people should and must fight back." Instead of demanding integration, which Carmichael considered "a subterfuge for the maintenance of white supremacy," blacks should develop their own cultural identity, purge their communities of outside control, and thereby achieve self-determination. Black power looked toward the welding of blacks into a cohesive voting bloc capable of controlling political organizations inside the ghetto or of creating autonomous parties in the South. It meant establishing self-sufficient business and consumer cooperatives and taking over public schools in black communities. "We don't need white liberals," Carmichael told a sympathetic convention of the Congress on Racial Equality (CORE). "We have to make integration irrelevant."

Not surprisingly, the sharpest critics of this doctrine were themselves veterans of the civil rights crusade. Roy Wilkins of the National Association for the Advancement of Colored People (NAACP) branded black power "the father of hatred and the mother of violence." Bayard Rustin, an associate of Martin Luther King, Jr., pointed out that blacks, as a minority, could not hope to achieve anything of substance without allies, particularly in the labor movement, among ethnic groups, and among poor whites. The organizations that endorsed black power—such as SNCC and CORE—were primarily composed of young people who disliked compromise, distrusted whites, and wanted fast results. Those that supported integration—such as the NAACP—believed that compromise was necessary, hoped to convert whites, and did not expect overnight triumphs. When black power advocates excluded NAACP field secretary Charles Evers from a rally in Jackson, Mississippi, he replied: "I'll be here when they're all gone."

Black power advocates rejected nonviolence as well as integration. This justification of self-defense frightened many whites, but what frightened them even more was a series of explosions that rocked black ghettos across the land. From 1964 to 1968 the United States experienced the most protracted period of domestic unrest since the Civil War. In 1964 blacks rioted in the Harlem and Bedford-Stuyvesant sections of New York City. A year later the Watts district in Los Angeles came to resemble a disaster area after a week-long riot left thirty-four dead, more than a thousand injured, and hundreds of buildings in ashes. To restore order, fifteen thousand National Guardsmen were sent to the city. In 1966 more than two dozen major riots occurred, most of them marked by looting, firebombs, and sniper fire. A study group concluded that the year's events "made it appear that domestic turmoil had become part of the American scene." Dozens of riots flared in black ghettos in 1967. In Newark, police and guardsmen fired 13,326 rounds of ammunition in three days. In Detroit, 43 people were killed and 7,200 arrested; the city was thrown into chaos. The assassination of Martin Luther King, Jr., in April 1968 led to the very thing the martyred civil rights leader most abhorred: race riots broke out in Chicago, Washington, and other cities.

These disturbances seldom involved violent clashes between whites and blacks, but rather looting, burning, and physical assaults within the ghetto's boundaries. The target might be a store owned by a white merchant, or it might be a white policeman, but the black communities themselves bore the heaviest cost. The riots did not usually occur along the points of intersection between black and white neighborhoods for, in fact, recent population shifts had done much to create two separate societies. From 1950 to 1966, 98 percent of the total black population growth took place in metropolitan areas, mainly in the central cities. In the same period, 78 percent of white population growth occurred in suburban areas. The National Advisory Commission on Civil Disorders, which was appointed by the President in 1967 and headed by Otto Kerner, found that the country was increasingly divided "into two societies: one, largely Negro and poor, located in the central cities; the other, predominantly white and affluent, located in the suburbs and in outlying areas."

It was this very division that the Kerner Commission, in its February 1968 report, blamed for the outbreaks. The commission viewed the riots as a protest against conditions in the ghetto, and the ghetto as a product of white racism. The commission pointed out that 16–20 percent of black city dwellers lived in "squalor and deprivation" and that 40 percent of the nation's nonwhite residents had incomes below the poverty line ($3,335 for an urban family of four).

Ghetto riot in Washington, D.C., 1968. *(Burt Glinn/Magnum.)*

It further noted that a black man was two times as likely to be unemployed as a white man, and three times as likely to be working in a low-paid or unskilled job. Chronic poverty bred disorder: "Prostitution, dope addiction, and crime create an environmental 'jungle' characterized by personal insecurity and tension. Children growing up under such conditions are likely participants in civil disorder."

A far simpler explanation for the riots, although a much less well-founded one, appealed to officials in the Federal Bureau of Investigation (FBI). Long suspicious of the civil rights movement, FBI Director J. Edgar Hoover now attributed the racial violence chiefly to "the exhortations of 'Black Power' advocates" who had transformed "volatile situations . . . into violent outbreaks." Accordingly,

Hoover stepped up his agency's surveillance of black communities and its efforts to disrupt nationalist groups and such militant organizations as the Black Panthers. By mid-1968, the FBI's "Ghetto Informant Program" employed about 3,250 agents, and its new "Rabble Rouser Index" listed "individuals who have demonstrated a potential for fomenting racial discord."

The FBI and the Kerner Commission represented two very different approaches to the problems of racism and violence. The first emphasized surveillance of alleged agitators; the second emphasized massive government programs to improve conditions in the ghettos. By 1968, white Americans increasingly were leaning toward Hoover's approach, rather than Kerner's, partly because of a backlash against the urban riots but also because of the domestic costs of Lyndon Johnson's foreign policy.

## THE GLOBAL BACKGROUND TO VIETNAM

During his 1964 campaign against Barry Goldwater, Johnson had promised to pursue peace in Vietnam, but had also threatened wider war. In August he announced that two American destroyers had been attacked in international waters (the Gulf of Tonkin) by North Vietnamese torpedo boats. "The attacks were unprovoked," Johnson claimed. He ordered air strikes against North Vietnam's naval base, then urged Congress to pass a broad resolution giving him the authority to "take all necessary measures to repel any armed attack against the forces of the United States and to prevent further aggression." (It was later discovered that this resolution and the list of bombing targets had been drawn up by the White House two months before.) Democrats Wayne Morse of Oregon and Ernest Gruening of Alaska opposed the resolution. They argued that the circumstances of the attack were not clear. It seemed weird, they declared, that several small boats would challenge the strength of the U.S. Navy. They also believed such broad powers should not be given to the President. Senator Gaylord Nelson, Democrat of Wisconsin, urged an amendment opposing "extension of the present conflict," but this was dropped when he was assured that this was understood by Johnson. The House passed the Gulf of Tonkin Resolution 416 to 0; the Senate 88 to 2.

Four years later Secretary of Defense Robert McNamara admitted that the American people had been misled in 1964. He revealed that the American destroyers had been accompanying South Vietnamese ships and commandos that were attacking North Vietnamese bases. Shortly after the engagement, moreover, the North Vietnamese had approached the United States for peace discussions. Fearful that the South Vietnamese government was too weak even to negotiate with the North, Johnson had rejected the approach and again withheld the information from the American people.

The truth arrived much too late. Congress gave Johnson a blank check in 1964, then allowed him to cash it over and over again in the following years as he escalated the fighting into full-scale war without asking for a formal declaration of war from the legislative branch. That vital congressional restraint upon the wielding of incalculable power by a single man had disappeared. The President drew decision-making increasingly into his own hands until the fundamental choices in Vietnam—choices that would ultimately lead to hundreds of thousands of deaths—were made by four men in a regularly scheduled Tuesday luncheon group: Johnson, McNamara, Rusk, and the President's national security advisor, McGeorge Bundy (replaced in 1966 by Walt Whitman Rostow). There were few effective restraints on an imperial presidency during the next four years.

That presidential power was exercised in a rapidly changing world. In the Soviet Union Nikita Khrushchev fell from office in October 1964, victimized by his ineptness during the Cuban missile crisis and, more importantly, by his bungling of the Russian economy. He was replaced by two men, Aleksei Kosygin and Leonid Brezhnev, both of whom had risen to power under Stalin. They aimed at two objectives. First, they determined to mobilize Soviet society for rapid economic advances. This determination and their apprenticeship under Stalin led the two leaders to ruthlessly squash any internal opposition. Dissident Soviet intellectuals, particularly Jews, were harassed, imprisoned, or declared insane. Second, the Soviets vowed to keep Chinese power contained. The two leading Communist nations were at each other's throat, deeply divided over ideology and, more important, over clashing national interests. By 1965 fighting between Chinese and Soviet troops had erupted along a 1,200-mile frontier. When Kosygin visited Chinese leader Mao Tse-tung in 1965, Mao said that differences between the two nations were so profound that they would last for ten thousand years. When Kosygin protested, Mao agreed to make it only nine thousand years.

These disagreements gave the Johnson administration an opportunity to reduce cold war tensions by improving relations between the two superpowers. The Russians needed American economic aid and would welcome any easing of relations in Europe, for then they could concentrate on their more dangerous enemy in China. East-West trade did improve. Moscow and Washington, moreover, agreed in a nonproliferation treaty that they would work to prevent the spread of nuclear weapons. But no major initiative to end the cold war occurred. American officials were too preoccupied with Vietnam. They insisted, moreover, that the Soviets were not truly mellowing. Secretary of State Rusk warned that while Americans had come to see Khrushchev as "an affable old grandfather, he was 68 and a half when he put missiles in Cuba." That perception seemed verified in August 1968, when Soviet troops suddenly marched into their satellite state of Czechoslovakia to terminate a new regime that, while remaining Communist, was nevertheless becoming more liberal and pro-Western.

As the two great powers struggled to keep the status quo, much of the rest of the world struggled to survive. In 1965 the North Atlantic nations (United States, Canada, and Western Europe) accounted for only 20 percent of the world's population but 70 percent of its income. The United States *added* as much to its income each year as Latin America had in total income, and twice as much as the total income received by Africans. Lyndon Johnson's childhood and his memories of the 1930s depression made him aware of this unequal distribution of the world's wealth. When mass starvation threatened India during 1965–67, he mobilized six hundred ships to dispatch one-fifth of the gigantic American grain crop. In one especially revealing remark the President warned Americans that "there are 3 billion people in the world and we have only 200 million of them. We are outnumbered 15 to 1. If might did make right they would sweep over the United States and take what we have. We have what they want."

In dealing with such immense problems, however, Johnson increasingly resorted to guns rather than food. He was not entirely free to choose. Foreign economic-aid programs had failed to work miracles in the newly emerging nations and were increasingly unpopular in Congress. Special commissions assigned to investigate the problem reported to Johnson that because government programs had failed, he should encourage private investment in Latin America, Asia, and Africa. That approach, however, was hollow. Private investors preferred to operate in secure, expanding Europe rather than in the chaotic third world. When they did go into the newly emerging nations, their primary investment went into oil, minerals, and other raw materials, thereby further unbalancing economies that were already overly dependent on a single product.

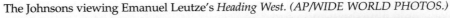

The Johnsons viewing Emanuel Leutze's *Heading West.* (AP/WIDE WORLD PHOTOS.)

Sometimes investors refused to move unless the American government assured their holdings. The Overseas Protection Insurance Corporation was thus created to insure investment against losses caused by confiscation or war. Investors who suffered such losses would be reimbursed by the U.S. government—that is, by the American taxpayers. Even this measure proved woefully insufficient to narrow the rapidly widening gap between the world's rich and poor. United Nations studies revealed in the mid-1960s that peoples in the newly emerging areas were closer to starvation than they were before World War II, and that their real income had shrunk so that it actually bought fewer goods than it had ten years earlier.

## LATIN AMERICA AND AFRICA

Latin America provided a case study of Johnson's response to these problems. U.S. business had invested $15 billion directly into American-owned firms in these southern nations by 1965. These firms accounted for one-third of Latin America's industrial and mining output, one-third of its exports, and one-fifth of its taxes. The investors, however, were taking more out of Latin America than they were putting in. Between 1965 and 1970 the southern continent sent more money to Americans than it received in every year but 1967, and in 1969 the gap amounted to more than $500 million. In 1966 Latin Americans were receiving only enough development loans and grants to pay back the interest on the massive loans that they had needed during the 1955–65 period. While money for future development disappeared back into the United States, the population increased by 3 percent a year, one of the largest rates of increase in the world.

President Johnson had few remedies for these predicaments. Kennedy's Alliance for Progress was nearly dead, the victim of too little support in both North and Latin America. And while Johnson was devoting nearly all of his attention in foreign affairs to Vietnam, private interests lobbied in Congress to profit at Latin America's expense. For example, economic aid was given only when the recipient nation promised to spend it on American goods, regardless of the cost. Thus Bolivia had to spend U.S. funds to buy American-made ore carts for its vast mines even though the carts cost three times more than Belgian-made carts.

Increasing political tension resulted. The Alliance for Progress tried to build a new middle class, for such a class, in South as well as in North America, would be least likely to be revolutionary. But the middle classes were actually losing ground in Latin America by the 1960s, for their incomes were eaten by galloping inflation. "It is significant," a United Nations report observed, "that groups falling within the narrower definitions of the middle classes, such as bank employees and school teachers, have been among the most frequent and militant participants in strikes in recent years." As those middle classes grew bitter, societies polarized between very rich and very poor. Revolution grew more likely. To stop any possibility of radical change, military governments rose to power in Brazil, Bolivia, Guatemala, and Ecuador. Latin America was being torn apart.

Lyndon Johnson responded forcefully to a rebellion in Santo Domingo. In 1961 the thirty-year dictatorship of Rafael Trujillo ended with his assassination. Three years of confusion followed until the army took control. In April 1965, however, a strange combination of liberals, radicals, and low-ranking army officers tried to replace the military rulers with a more liberal government. As the military regime crumbled, it pleaded for help from President Johnson and used the bait that supporters of Fidel Castro were gaining power. Johnson immediately dispatched 22,800 American troops into the Caribbean nation to put down the rebellion. At first the President said he only wanted to assure the safety of American citizens. It soon became clear that he intended to use force to establish a stable, pro-American government. He did this even though the United States had signed the Charter of the Organization of American States (1948), which said in part, "No state or group of states has the right to intervene, directly or indirectly, for any reason whatever, in the internal or external affairs of any other state." The administration proclaimed that the troops had prevented "the Communists . . . from taking over."

No one, however, has ever been able to demonstrate that either Communists or Castroites were important in any way in the uprising. But that did not prevent the President from announcing the "Johnson Doctrine": the United States would use force, if necessary, anywhere in the hemisphere to prevent Communist governments from coming to power. The Latin Americans did not appreciate this reappearance of Theodore Roosevelt's and Woodrow Wilson's gunboat diplomacy. "It is fall here," one reporter wrote from South America, "and U.S. flags as well as leaves are being burned."

American policies in Africa (especially in those nations south of the Sahara) were not dissimilar. Between 1945 and 1970 more than forty African nations gained independence as the old European empires fragmented. Few of the new governments had the economic or political experience to hold together national, freely elected regimes. For its part, the United States provided little help. In 1965 American development aid amounted to $200 million spread among thirty-three nations. One country received $50,000. Such a program did nothing to improve conditions internally and relations with the United States externally. Eight countries fell to army coups between 1964 and 1966 as parts of the continent seemed headed toward tribal warfare. American investment meanwhile centered on two white-dominated governments, South Africa and Southern Rhodesia. In addition, South Africa received military aid because of its strategic location at the tip of the continent. Both nations appeared prosperous and stable, but appearances were at the expense of the black population, which comprised the overwhelming majority in both countries. The blacks were victimized by *apartheid,* a white-controlled system that, through legislation and violence, brutally separated and exploited the blacks.

The Johnson administration intervened directly in the former Belgian Congo. That area of 17 million blacks had suddenly become free in 1960 despite the lack of any preparation by the former Belgian rulers. Civil war erupted, but the United Nations, with American and Russian support, stabilized the area. By 1964 the United States was the dominant foreign power in the Congo, and the vast copper and diamond mines again produced their riches. Then nationalist revolts began, with rebels massacring thousands of blacks and whites. Despite help from the Central Intelligence Agency, the Congolese government could not quell the rebellion. The United States staged a paratroop strike to free a number of hostages, including sixteen Americans, whom the insurgents had threatened to kill, and by late 1965 the situation was quieted. When it flared again in 1967, President Johnson prepared large-scale military aid for the Congo, but Senate leaders, particularly conservative Democrats from the South, forced a scaling-down of the aid. The Senators argued that the administration had enough racial problems at home and enough military activity in Vietnam. The Congolese government then settled its own internal problems.

# VIETNAM ABROAD

The President's responses in Santo Domingo and the Congo differed only in degree from those in Vietnam. In each case the United States chose armed might as a solution for the social ills that generated nationalist revolts. Johnson's preoccupation with force led humorist Art Buchwald to claim that the President wanted to alert two airborne divisions, four Marine brigades, and the Atlantic fleet—before proclaiming Mother's Day.

The Gulf of Tonkin incidents in August 1964 were followed by five months of little fighting, but the Johnson administration was exceptionally busy. The murder of President Diem in 1963 had created political chaos. Vietnamese regimes changed so frequently that Johnson twice felt that he had to reject North Vietnamese peace overtures for fear that the American-supported regime in Saigon lacked the strength to negotiate an acceptable peace. These peace feelers were kept secret from the American people.

On February 5, 1965 (two days after the final American rejection of the second North Vietnamese peace approach), the Communists killed seven Americans at a base in Pleiku. The President immediately ordered bombing of the north in carefully selected attacks aimed at cutting off supplies flowing south to the Communist National Liberation Front of South Vietnam (the NLF). The raids were also a warning that North Vietnam should not try to escalate the pressure on the rickety regime in Saigon. South Vietnamese governments, however, had fallen owing to lack of support within the country. As for supplies coming from the north, a careful study by the Department of State, written to justify the bombings, actually revealed that of fifteen thousand weapons taken from Communist soldiers, fewer than two hundred were made in Communist factories. The remainder had been captured from South Vietnamese troops, the study concluded.

The U.S. escalation, therefore, was aimed less at stopping North Vietnamese intervention in the south (for in February 1965 that intervention was not significant) than at propping up Saigon regimes, which seemed incapable of defending themselves in the civil war. In March the escalation took a drastic turn. Johnson sent in Marine battalions. He thus started a buildup of American troops who were to participate directly in the combat rather than merely be "advisors" to South Vietnamese soldiers. During the summer, over one hundred thousand more Americans poured into the country. The President tried to cover these actions by declaring that the troops would secure only American and South Vietnamese bases. In a speech in April, he announced that he would enter "unconditional discussion" with North Vietnam but that the Communists would have to begin the discussions by accepting the fact of an independent South Vietnam, something the North Vietnamese would never accept. The government of Ho Chi Minh responded with its own four-point offer. It included a return to the 1954 Geneva agreements (which stated that the boundary between north and south would only be temporary) and settlement of South Vietnam's affairs "by the South Vietnamese people themselves in accordance with the program of the [NLF] without any foreign interference." The United States replied with accelerated use of force.

With few pauses, American bombing continued for seven years. More bombs were dropped on Vietnam than on Germany, Japan, and their Axis allies combined during World War II. The bombing had little military effect. By 1966, eleven tough regiments of North Vietnamese troops were in the south to fight 200,000 Americans and 550,000 South Vietnamese. The Russians and Chinese supplied ever larger amounts of goods to the Communists. Most ominous of all, the North Vietnamese, who historically had fought and feared the Chinese, were necessarily moving closer to Beijing in order to receive aid. American policy, aimed at blocking the influence of China, seemed to be producing the opposite result.

By April 1966, more Americans than South Vietnamese were being killed in action. In July the number of American dead reached 4,440, more than the number killed in the American Revolution and ten times the number who died in the Spanish-American War. The results were discouraging. The South Vietnamese controlled less than 25 percent of their own 12,000 hamlets. But a stable government was finally established in Saigon by the army. Its leaders were Major General Nguyen Van Thieu as head and, as premier, Nguyen Cao Ky, a swashbuckling air force officer who had fought with the French against the Vietnamese nationalists and who had been overheard expressing admiration for Adolf Hitler.

The new regime failed to reverse the course of the war. Lieutenant Colonel John Vann, perhaps the most perceptive American advisor to serve in Vietnam, put his finger on one fundamental problem: "This is a political war and it calls for discrimination in killing. The best weapon for killing would be a knife, but I'm afraid we can't do it that way. The worst is an airplane. The next worse is artillery." Americans were not prepared either politically or militarily to fight such a war. They wanted to resort to their unimaginably powerful technology to blow up the enemy from the air or engage him in massive ground battles. The Communists actually had little to blow up (except their ports, where the presence of Russian ships made attacks dangerous), and they refused to stand still in large groups as targets for U.S. artillery. They fought more like George Washington's guerrilla forces of 1777 than like the Chinese in Korea during 1951. The war was confusing and frustrating both in Vietnam and, increasingly, at home. In 1966 Johnson blurted out the problem: "Most people wish we weren't there; most people wish we didn't have a war; most people don't want to escalate it, and most people don't want to get out."

## VIETNAM IN THE WHITE HOUSE

Yet the President insisted on remaining in the war. Escalating troop strength to 485,000 by 1968, he committed the country to the longest and most tragic of all its wars. He did so for several reasons.

First, he believed that South Vietnam was the test of whether the United States could prevent communism—particularly the Chinese brand, which resulted from peasant revolution—from controlling all of Asia. After a fact-finding journey to Vietnam in 1961, Johnson reported to President Kennedy that since "there is no alternative to United States leadership in Southeast Asia," Americans must make a "fundamental decision whether we are to attempt to meet the challenge of Communist expansion now in Southeast Asia by a major effort . . . or throw in the towel." He never changed that view. Nor did he ever doubt that the civil war was caused not by Vietnamese nationalism but by Vietnamese who were part of a worldwide Communist movement inspired by China. The Chinese were his primary concern: "Communist China apparently desires the war to continue whatever the cost to their [*sic*] Allies," the President remarked on May 13, 1965. "Their target is not merely South Vietnam. It is Asia."

Second, Johnson believed that he was carrying on an essential American policy, for he was stopping communism in Asia just as President Truman had contained the Russians in Europe. He did not wish to repeat the mistake made at Munich in 1938, when Great Britain and France allowed Hitler to take Czechoslovakia and open the way for World War II. Johnson and Secretary Rusk directly compared Munich and Vietnam, a comparison that would have resulted in an instant "failure" for any college student who tried to make it in a history class. But neither Johnson nor any of his close advisors suggested that economic and political conditions in Asia differed fundamentally from those in Europe, or that the United States enjoyed strong allies in Europe (allies tied together by language, culture, and wealth) whereas no such friends existed in Asia. Instead, the President attacked critics who pointed out these vital differences by calling them "special pleaders who counsel retreat in Vietnam. . . . We cannot accept their logic . . . that subjugation by an armed minority in Asia is different from subjugation by an armed minority in Europe."

Third, he claimed that he was defending commitments in Vietnam made by Eisenhower and Kennedy. His relationship with Kennedy's ghost, however, involved both love and hate. He publicly pledged to carry out the late President's policies, but privately Johnson never forgave Kennedy for relegating him into the background between 1961 and 1963. He especially grew bitter as many of Kennedy's former aides quit the foundering Johnson administration to protest against the war they had helped begin. When once reminded of a Kennedy policy, Johnson barked, "The touch football crowd isn't making decisions around here anymore." But the Texan was equally determined not to give up where Kennedy had taken the stand. He would maintain the hallowed commitment and also show the Kennedyites.

Fourth, the President believed that the commitment was consistent with American interests at home as well as abroad. He emphasized "one overriding rule: . . . that our foreign policy must always be an extension of this nation's domestic policy." This "rule" had an ironic ring in the 1960s, for the fire, rioting, and violence that ripped American cities between 1965 and 1968 mirrored the much greater destruction inflicted on Vietnam. Johnson was not, of course, referring to *that* mirror, but was pointing to the New Deal tradition, which shaped his political outlook. The New Deal had used government action in an attempt to improve living conditions for poor Americans. As President, Johnson announced a "Great Society" program to modernize and complete the New Deal. He believed that in a world made smaller by technology, Americans had to help others if they hoped to improve their own society. He proposed an Asian Development Bank and a vast plan to enrich the Mekong Valley in Southeast Asia, much as the New Deal had built the Tennessee Valley Authority. Only the Communists stood in the way. To eliminate them, however, became so costly that by 1966 Johnson was forced to cut back his Great Society at home. "Because of Vietnam," he finally admitted, "we cannot do all that we should, or all that we would like to do" in the United States.

Fifth, economic bonds between the United States and Vietnam developed, but quite differently than the administration had planned. The money pumped into the military buildup brought a rosy glow to the American economy. One economic expert concluded that American defense expenditures supported 95 percent of the employment in aircraft and missile industries, 60 percent in shipbuilding, and 40 percent in radio and communications. Including 3 million in the armed services, nearly 7 million Americans were dependent on the Defense Department budget, and Vietnam expenditures constituted an increasingly larger proportion of that budget. When peace rumors circulated in 1965–66, the New York Stock Exchange was hit with heavy losses as investors rushed to cash in their securities before prices dropped. One broker believed that "a genuine peace offer" would "knock the market out of bed." After all, he observed, the government had scheduled a $60 billion defense budget on the assumption that the war would continue. In Vietnam itself, American oil companies and banks led the way, investing to benefit from the war and particularly from the gigantic reconstruction effort that would follow. The government encouraged such investment; its Agency for International Development provided a 100 percent guarantee against loss of money because of war or confiscation. The American business community did not turn against the war until after 1967, when the conflict began to erode rather than accelerate the economy.

Sixth, Johnson believed that he possessed the presidential power required to realize his objectives. By the mid-1960s the presidency dominated the nation in a manner undreamed of by the Founding Fathers. The Constitution's framers

# CHILD CARE: DR. SPOCK AND THE PEACE MOVEMENT

Benjamin Spock was born in 1903. He attended Yale University, cast his first vote for Calvin Coolidge in 1924 ("my father said he was the greatest president we've ever had"), attended Columbia University's medical school, and in 1929 began practicing pediatrics in New York City. At the time, the most popular child-raising manual was John Watson's *The Psychological Care of Infant and Child* (1928). Watson believed that every action was a response to a stimulus, that a person was "an organic machine that takes in food and lets out waste products." The chief danger facing children was that they would be smothered by parental love and, conse-

quently, become dependent rather than self-reliant. Warning against the "dangers lurking in the mother's kiss," Watson asserted that cuddling a child would lead to "invalidism," the inability to cope with the harsh realities of life. Children should be treated as though they were young adults. "If you must, kiss them once on the forehead when they say good night. Shake hands with them in the morning." Watson left a professorship at Johns Hopkins to become vice-president of an advertising agency, where he applied his theory to the task of finding the right stimuli to induce consumers to respond to his clients' products.

Dr. Benjamin Spock with nursery school children. *(Hella Hammid/Photo Researchers.)*

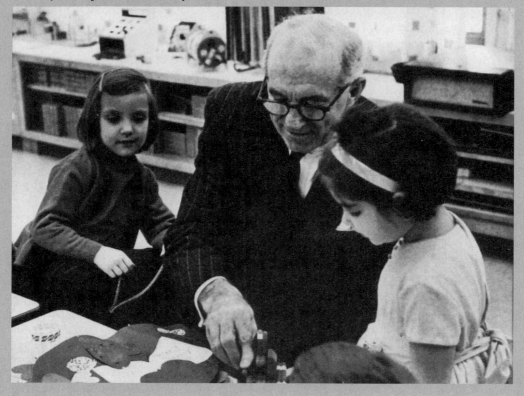

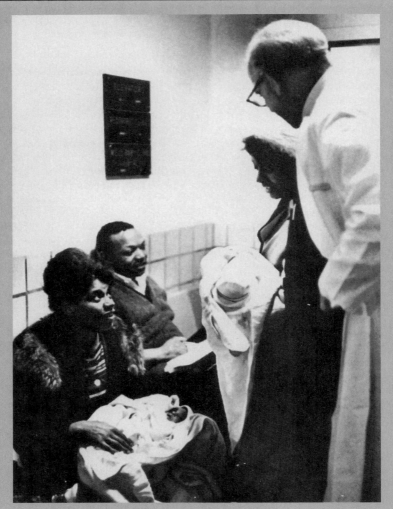

Dr. Spock conferring with parents. *(Hella Hammid/Photo Researchers.)*

In the 1930s and 1940s the study of child development was revolutionized by Dr. Arnold Gesell, who attempted to establish scientific norms for each stage of mental and physical growth. But it was Dr. Spock who popularized the new approach. His *Pocket Book of Baby and Child Care* (1946), written while he was serving in the U.S. Naval Reserve, contradicted Watson. Spock advised parents to relax, use their common sense, trust their own judgment, and "be flexible and adjust to the baby's needs and happiness." "Don't be afraid to love him and enjoy him. Every baby needs to be smiled at, talked to, played with, fondled—gently and lovingly—just as much as he needs vitamins and calories. That's what will make him a person who loves people and enjoys life." Spock, however, did not advocate total permissiveness. "Parents can't feel right toward their children in the long run unless they can make them behave reasonably, and children can't be happy unless they are behaving reasonably."

By 1963 Spock's book was selling about a million copies a year. Spock's career took him to the Mayo Clinic in Minnesota, the medical school at the University of Pittsburgh, and Western Reserve University in Cleveland. Gradually, he turned to political action. In 1960 he supported John F. Kennedy, and in 1962, when the President resumed nuclear testing in response to Russian tests, Spock joined the peace movement. In 1964 he campaigned for Lyndon Johnson, but then became a sharp critic of the war in Vietnam. In 1967 Spock and 28,000 other people signed "A Call to Resist Illegitimate Authority," which branded the war in Vietnam illegal and unconstitutional, supported those who opposed the draft, and called on others to join in "this confrontation with immoral authority." Early in 1968 Spock and four others were indicted for conspiring to counsel violation of the Selective Service Act.

The trial, which took place in Boston, lasted nearly a month. Spock took the witness stand to explain why he opposed the war in Vietnam. "I believed that we were destroying a country that had never intended us any harm. . . . What is the use of physicians like myself trying to help parents to bring up children, healthy and happy, to have them killed in such numbers for a cause that is ignoble?" Four of the defendants, including Spock, were

Dr. Spock at antiwar rally, 1967. *(Black Star. Reprinted with permission.)*

found guilty, fined, and sentenced to two-year prison terms. But in July 1969 a U.S. court of appeals reversed the convictions on the grounds that the judge's instructions to the jury were improper. The charges against Dr. Spock were dropped. He responded, "I shall redouble my efforts to free the hundreds of young men who are now serving time for resisting the war."

had feared unchecked power, and with Congress's abdication of responsibility in the Gulf of Tonkin Resolution, the President's power in foreign affairs had few limits. As journalist James Reston observed, "Something important has happened in America since Woodrow Wilson went to his grave" believing that a President's foreign policy could be paralyzed by Congress. Military efficiency as well as Congress's weakness had helped create that power. Johnson was the first president in the nation's history to enter war with a great army prepared to fight. Indeed, it was too easy to order this remarkable striking force halfway around the world.

Finally, the President had strong public support. In December 1965, as he rapidly escalated the conflict, public opinion polls indicated that 58 percent of the American people believed that increased bombing was the way to peace, and 82 percent agreed that U.S. troops would have to remain in Vietnam until the Communists agreed to terms. One-third of those having an opinion thought nuclear weapons should be used if they would shorten the war. (Such an opinion allowed Johnson, who opposed using nuclear weapons, to appear as a moderate as he escalated the conventional war.) Support came from all sectors. Some 477,000 students in 322 colleges gave their written commitment to the President's policies in 1966. The American Federation of Labor's national convention pledged "unstinting support" for all measures necessary "to halt Communist aggression" and bring peace to Vietnam. When antiwar spectators got in a shouting match with union delegates, union leader George Meany ordered that "those kookies" be thrown out of the hall. The president of the 250,000-member U.S. Jaycees—formerly the Junior Chamber of Commerce—announced a program to expose "leftists" and "peace advocates," adding that the Jaycees would work closely with the FBI. A critical newspaper suggested that the Jaycees might better sponsor discussions of the Bill of Rights.

Both the public and Congress were supporting an anti-Communist cold war policy that had existed since 1947. Neither was capable of questioning that policy. Nor was Johnson. "The President is still confusing popularity with policy," James Reston noted in late 1965. "And this could easily lead us deeper into the bog."

## VIETNAM AT HOME

By 1965 important segments of public opinion were beginning to change, and this change was partly inspired by intellectuals—historians, political scientists, and sociologists—who raised fundamental questions about the administration's war policy. Naturally, the questioning was loudest on college campuses, especially at "teach ins" which began at the University of Michigan in March 1965 and then had spectacular success at other universities. But the administration refused to take its critics seriously. Although many were specialists in Asian and international affairs, Rusk disparaged their credentials, remarking, "That a man knows everything there is to know about enzymes doesn't mean that he knows very much about Vietnam." Johnson simply recruited advisors from among like-minded scholars. One was Walt W. Rostow, a vocal advocate of "staying the course." Rostow, the President said, was "going to be *my* goddamned intellectual."

Yet as the war continued to escalate, so, too, did opposition to it. By 1967 and 1968 it began to seem as if society was on the edge of a breakdown. The President implored American troops to "hang the coonskin on the wall." In Vietnam, when an army chaplain was asked to pray for a victory, he is supposed to have pleaded: "Oh, Lord, give us the wisdom to find the bastards and the strength to pile it on." After troops devastated a village allegedly controlled by the NLF, an American officer blurted out, "It became necessary to destroy the town in order to save it." At home, protesters chanted, "Hey, hey, LBJ, how many kids did you kill today?" as they tried to disrupt draft boards and block troop trains. One person burned himself to death at the door of the Pentagon. Students publicly set fire to their draft cards even after Congress passed a law imposing a $10,000 fine or five years in jail for such an act. Colleges were disrupted as students occupied buildings and sometimes battled police summoned to evict them.

Soon the disenchantment approached the White House itself. Senator J. William Fulbright, Democrat of Arkansas and chairman of the powerful Senate Foreign Relations Committee, had long been a close friend of Johnson's, but turned against him after he discovered that the President had lied about the Gulf of Tonkin affair and the Santo Domingo intervention. Even more ominous, Secretary of Defense Robert McNamara began doubting. The President depended on him more than on any other man in the government. In August 1967, McNamara publicly called the bombing campaign a failure. Three months later Johnson sent him off to become president of the World Bank, a position that McNamara held with great distinction through the next decade as he multiplied the bank's resources for helping feed and develop newly emerging areas.

The closest American allies also fell away. Western Europeans enjoyed prosperity and new political cohesion from their European Economic Community (EEC). When it accepted Great Britain as a member in 1970, the EEC joined the United States, USSR, and Japan as the world's great economic powers. The Europeans viewed the Vietnam War as a terrible mistake, for it forced Johnson to neglect vital ties with the Atlantic nations and severely weakened the American economy, the EEC's main overseas customer. Not even the British would help in Vietnam. Frustrated and angered, Secretary of State Dean Rusk exploded to a British journalist, "All we needed [from you in Vietnam] was one

During the Tet Lunar New Year's 1968 crisis, South Vietnamese national police chief shoots suspected North Vietnamese terrorist. *(AP/WIDE WORLD PHOTOS.)*

regiment. . . . But you wouldn't. Well, don't expect us to save you again. They can invade Sussex and we wouldn't do a damned thing about it." With few friends at home and even fewer overseas, Johnson observed that he was "in the position of a jackrabbit in a hailstorm, hunkered up and taking it."

## THE NEW LEFT AND THE COUNTERCULTURE

The war in Vietnam inspired a broad indictment of American society by "new left" radicals and by those who considered themselves part of the "counterculture." The merging of the two streams of criticism—one chiefly political and the other cultural—meant that each tended to reinforce the other. Each also found its natural constituency among the nation's youths, particularly those attending college. By 1968, close to half of all young men and women between the ages of 18 and 21 were college students. The size of the student population, its mobility, leisure time, and sense of generational cohesion all contributed to the currents of political and cultural protest.

Those currents first appeared at the Berkeley campus of the University of California in the fall of 1964. When the university administration banned the setting up of tables at which political literature was distributed, students responded by creating the Free Speech Movement (FSM). Demanding an end to restrictions on political expression, students adopted new, confrontational tactics that would later make an appearance on many other campuses: sit-ins, building takeovers, and strikes. By 1965 the issue had broadened beyond the original one of free speech. Students began to talk about their sense of power-lessness, the way the university thwarted their creativity, and their desire to have a greater say in university governance. Their growing sense of genera-tional cohesion and revolt was captured by one FSM leader, Mario Savio, when he wrote: "I'm tired of reading history. Now I want to make it."

New left groups in the 1960s held disparate views and were often torn by bitter factional discord. Yet most radicals agreed with the findings of sociologist C. Wright Mills, who argued that American society was governed by a "power elite" made up of businessmen, military officials, and political leaders, "an elite whose power probably exceeds that of any small group of men in world his-tory." Moreover, radicals believed that domestic reforms only siphoned off dis-content and thereby propped up an immoral social system. Tom Hayden, a founder of Students for a Democratic Society (SDS), argued that many reforms were "illusory or token serving chiefly to sharpen the capacity of the system for manipulation and oppression." Finally, radicals argued that the responsibility for American involvement in Vietnam rested with liberals like John F. Kennedy and Lyndon Johnson. "Think of the men who now engineer that war—those who study the maps, give the commands, push the buttons, and tally the dead," said Carl Oglesby, another SDS leader: "They are not moral monsters. They are all honorable men. They are all liberals."

Members of the new left, centered in the universities, naturally focused much of their attention close to home. They criticized the impersonal quality of education in "multiversities," the restriction on political activity, the retention of outdated requirements, and the absence of relevant courses. Denouncing the alleged complicity of the universities in the development of weapons systems and counterinsurgency plans, radicals charged that institutions of higher learn-ing were not engaged in an objective search for truth but rather were molding students to fit appropriate slots in the worlds of business, politics, and the mil-itary. Since, in their view, existing scholarship was committed to preserving the status quo, radicals called for a new scholarship frankly committed to chang-ing things for the better.

The new left did not succeed in winning over large segments of the pub-lic, or even a majority of college students. As their frustration mounted, some radicals turned to violence. The career of SDS illustrated this transformation. At its founding in 1962, SDS asserted: "We find violence to be abhorrent because it requires generally the transformation of the target, be it a human being or a community of people, into a depersonalized object of hate." But by 1969, mem-bers of an SDS faction known as the "Weathermen" had concluded that it was necessary to disrupt American society. A few hundred young people descended on Chicago to "tear pig city apart." Dressed in "full street-fighting gear" and chanting "pick up, pick up, pick up the gun," they stormed through the city smashing windows. While only a few engaged in such activities or justified them, much of the public came to associate radicalism with social disorder.

The public also associated radicalism with a related development: the rise of a counterculture. The counterculture had a distinctive look—love beads, sandals, jeans, long hair—and an equally distinctive sound—"acid rock" as performed by Jimi Hendrix, the Grateful Dead, and the Jefferson Airplane. Even more than clothing or musical styles, the counterculture was defined by a freer code of sexual behavior, a use of hallucinogenic drugs, and an interest in mystical experiences. Theodore Roszak, whose *The Making of a Counter Culture* (1968) not only chronicled the new developments but also justified them, favored replacing an older "cerebral mode of consciousness" with "non-intellective consciousness." Roszak denied that reality consisted only of what objective consciousness could describe. He favored "a naive openness to experience" and a recognition that the warmly visionary could reveal as much as the coldly rational.

For all the differences between the new left and the counterculture, each, in its own way, represented a challenge to the supremacy of cherished assumptions. The new left denied that politics always required a willingness to compromise and that moral issues had no place in politics. Instead, radicals made "non-negotiable demands," and posed issues in stark, right-versus-wrong terms. Similarly, the counterculture rejected technological progress and personal achievement, offering as alternatives a return to the land or simply "dropping out." The two movements therefore intersected in important ways, and both political and cultural radicals believed that what was wrong with America was most clearly revealed by its waging of an immoral war in Vietnam.

## THE 1968 ELECTION

Throughout 1967, American military commanders confidently predicted victory in that war, but the bombing had not prevented the North Vietnamese from doubling their army in the south to 475,000 between 1965 and 1967. The buildup on both sides had changed a civil war within South Vietnam to a war between the United States and North Vietnam. In early February 1968, during the Tet Lunar New Year holiday, the Communists launched a devastating attack that resulted in the seizure of vital portions of the country; they even threatened the supposedly impregnable U.S. Embassy in Saigon. Because large numbers of Communists were killed in the offensive, the Johnson administration claimed victory. But the American generals then stunned Johnson by requesting another 206,000 more men to continue the war.

The President ordered an in-depth analysis of the war by experts in and out of government. They bluntly informed Johnson that he was "being led down the garden path" by the American military in Vietnam. This news was coupled with returns from the first Democratic presidential primary in New Hampshire, where Johnson barely defeated antiwar critic Senator Eugene McCarthy of Minnesota, who received a surprising 42 percent of the vote. In late March, the President dramatically announced on television that he was cutting back bombing in order to get North Vietnam to the peace table, and, so that he could concentrate on obtaining peace, he would not run for reelection in 1968.

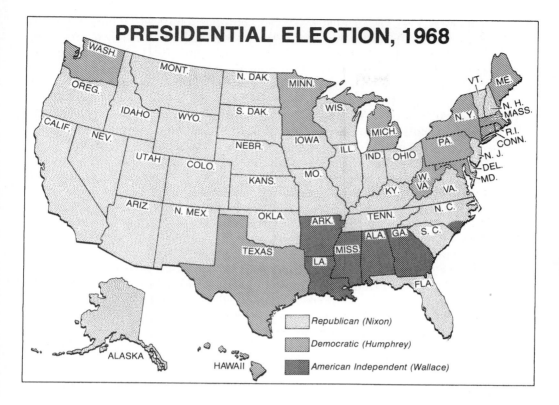

## PRESIDENTIAL ELECTION, 1968

Republican (Nixon)

Democratic (Humphrey)

American Independent (Wallace)

Lyndon Johnson had become a casualty of the war. Not only had the fighting gone badly, but because the administration had underestimated war expenses in 1966–67, the economy entered a sharp inflationary spiral. It was the beginning of the worst sustained inflationary period in twentieth-century America. In April 1968 Martin Luther King's assassination set off riots in many cities, including Washington, D.C., where smoke from burning buildings floated over the White House. Two months later, presidential candidate Robert Kennedy, Democratic senator from New York, was murdered in Los Angeles. A climax to the violence occurred with the Democratic convention in Chicago during August, when police and U.S. Army troops used tear gas to control antiwar demonstrators. Johnson could send a half-million men to Vietnam, but could not attend his own party's nominating convention. Through the smoke and the suffocatingly sweet smell of tear gas, Vice-President Hubert Humphrey was named as the Democratic nominee, and Senator Edmund Muskie of Maine the vice-presidential candidate.

The Republican ticket was headed by Richard Nixon and Spiro Agnew, governor of Maryland. Nixon had risen from the political dead after his loss in 1960 and then another defeat in the California governor's race in 1962. In the next six years he traveled widely to cement his ties with grass-roots Republicans and was in the forefront of those who attacked Johnson for not ending the

Vietnam War on American terms. Nixon, however, emphasized law-and-order themes during the campaign while deemphasizing the war by saying only that he had "a plan" for stopping it. Agnew was more direct, blasting Humphrey for being "soft on inflation, soft on communism, and soft on law and order."

The presence on the ballot of Governor George C. Wallace of Alabama did much to shape the outcome of the election. Formerly a Democrat, Wallace broke with the party in 1968 to run on the American Independent ticket. He adopted a hard-line anti-Communist foreign policy, even selecting retired General Curtis E. LeMay (who spoke of bombing North Vietnam "back to the Stone Age") as his running mate. Wallace appealed to normally Democratic voters, especially in the South, who were dismayed by the breakdown of law and order and by antiwar demonstrations but were not prepared to vote Republican. Wallace received 9.9 million votes, or 13.5 percent of the total. So Richard Nixon, with only 43.4 percent of the popular vote, eked out a victory over Hubert Humphrey by a 1 percent margin.

Although the war in Vietnam was not the only issue in 1968, it had nevertheless altered the course of American politics. In 1964 the voters had given Lyndon Johnson a dual mandate: for reform and for peace. Johnson had fulfilled the first part of the mandate, but not the second. By 1968 the war had made the return of the Republicans possible, and even the reforms so important to Johnson were placed in jeopardy.

## Suggested Reading

For political, social, and economic developments in the 1960s, consult David Steigerwald, *The Sixties and the End of Modern America* (1995); and Allen J. Matusow, *The Unraveling of America: A History of Liberalism in the 1960s* (1984). For analyses of the Great Society, see Irving Bernstein, *Guns or Butter? The Presidency of Lyndon Johnson* (1996); Vaughn Davis Bornet, *The Presidency of Lyndon B. Johnson* (1983); and Doris Kearns, *Lyndon Johnson and the American Dream* (1976). Political developments may also be followed in Arthur M. Schlesinger, Jr., *Robert Kennedy and His Times* (1978).

Appraisals of the Supreme Court are provided in two collections of essays: Mark Tushnet, ed., *The Warren Court in Historical and Political Perspective* (1993); and Bernard Schwartz, ed., *The Warren Court: A Retrospective* (1996). There are many informative judicial biographies, including: G. Edward White, *Earl Warren: A Public Life* (1982); Bernard Schwartz, *Super Chief: Earl Warren and His Supreme Court* (1983); Roger Goldman, *Thurgood Marshall: Justice for All* (1992); and two works by Howard Ball: *Of Power and Right: Hugo Black, William O. Douglas, and America's Constitutional Revolution* (1992), and *Hugo L. Black: Cold Steel Warrior* (1996).

The student protest movement is described in James Miller, *"Democracy Is in the Streets"—From Port Huron to the Seige of Chicago* (1987); David Farber, *Chicago '68* (1988); W. J. Rorabaugh, *Berkeley at War* (1989); and Terry H. Anderson, *The Movement and the Sixties* (1995). For a different sort of political protest, consult Dan T. Carter, *The Politics of Rage: George Wallace, the Origins of the New Conservatism, and the Transformation of American Politics* (1995).

For the resurgence of feminism in the 1960s, see Sara Evans, *Personal Politics: The Roots of Women's Liberation in the Civil Rights Movement and the New Left* (1979); Jo Freeman, *The Politics of Women's Liberation* (1979); Cynthia Harrison, *On Account of Sex: The*

*Politics of Women's Issues, 1945–1968* (1988); and Alice Echols, *Daring to Be Bad: Radical Feminism in America, 1967–1975* (1989). For the civil rights movement, black power, and the ghetto riots, consult David J. Garrow, *Protest at Selma: Martin Luther King, Jr. and the Voting Rights Act of 1965* (1978); Steven F. Lawson, *Black Ballots: Voting Rights in the South, 1944–1969* (1976); Clayborne Carson, *In Struggle: SNCC and the Black Awakening of the 1960s* (1981); Robert Fogelson, *Violence as Protest* (1971); and Kenneth O'Reilly, *"Racial Matters": The FBI's Secret File on Black America, 1960–1972* (1989).

On foreign policy, begin with the well-annotated bibliography in R. D. Burns, ed., *Guide to American Foreign Relations Since 1700* (1983); and relevant entries and bibliographies in Bruce Jentleson and Thomas Paterson, eds., *Encyclopedia of American Foreign Relations*, 4 vols. (1997). There is no comprehensive treatment of LBJ's foreign policies, but the following are useful: Warren Cohen, *Dean Rusk* (1980); George W. Ball, *The Past Has Another Pattern* (1982), a key insider who dissented; and W. W. Rostow, *Diffusion of Power, 1958–1972* (1972), another insider; as well as Johnson's own *Vantage Point* (1971). For Vietnam, begin with George Herring, *America's Longest War* (1996); Lloyd C. Gardner, *Pay Any Price* (1995); Michael Hunt, *Lyndon Johnson's War* (1996); Edwin E. Moise, *Tonkin Gulf and the Escalation of the Vietnam War* (1997); William Appleman Williams, et al., *America in Vietnam; A Documentary History* (1985); Larry Berman, *Planning a Tragedy* (1982), on the pivotal 1965 decisions; Marilyn Young, *The Vietnam Wars: 1945–1990* (1991); George McT. Kahin, *Intervention* (1986); Patrick J. Hearden, ed., *Vietnam: Four American Perspectives* (1990); Neil Sheehan, *A Bright Shining Lie: John Paul Vann and America in Vietnam* (1988); William M. Hammond, *Public Affairs: The Military and the Media, 1962–1968* (1988), crucial on the false charge that the American media lost the war for the military; William C. Berman, *William Fulbright and the Vietnam War* (1988); Randall Woods, *Fulbright* (1995), the standard biography; and Melvin Small, *Johnson, Nixon, and the Doves* (1988). A superb account is Louis Fisher, *Presidential War Power* (1995). For general overviews and recent bibliography, see Warren Cohen, *America in the Age of Soviet Power, 1945–1991* (1993), and Walter LaFeber, *America, Russia, and the Cold War, 1945–1996* (1997).

Both Jessica Mitford, *The Trial of Dr. Spock* (1969), and Lynn Z. Bloom, *Dr. Spock: Biography of a Conservative Radical* (1972), are informative.

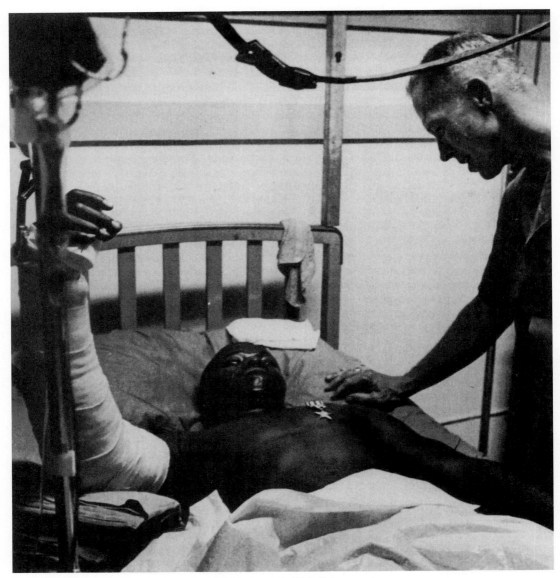

Wounded and decorated in Vietnam. *(Philip Jones Griffiths/Magnum.)*

# CHAPTER FIFTEEN

# 1969–1975

## The Imperial Presidency
## and Watergate

This chapter discusses:
- How Richard Nixon won two presidential elections but lost
  the presidency
- Why many Americans died in Vietnam while others walked on
  the moon
- Finally, a new ERA?
- A turn in the history of Native Americans

Richard Nixon narrowly won the 1968 election by promising to restore law and order and to end a frustrating and unpopular war. He did neither, but nevertheless managed to attract broad new political support by adopting policies he had spent a lifetime denouncing and by exploiting ugly social divisions. In the war, he reduced American casualties through "Vietnamization." By 1972 these tactics had been so successful that Nixon won reelection by an overwhelming margin. His victory promised still further enlargement of an already bloated executive authority; indeed, a cartoon appeared with the purple-robed figure of "King Richard." But even more swiftly than Nixon had donned the robes of the imperial presidency, they were stripped from his shoulders. The Watergate scandal erupted, leading not only to Nixon's own downfall but to a widespread crisis of confidence in government. As polls showed that more people than ever before believed "there is something deeply wrong with America," new restrictions on the imperial presidency were imposed by Congress and the courts.

## THE NIXON FOREIGN POLICIES

The new President appointed Henry Kissinger, a professor of international relations at Harvard, as his national security advisor. The two men privately formulated their own foreign policy, neglecting Congress and the State Department, and in some instances not even bothering to keep these two bodies informed. Kissinger believed such secrecy necessary in order to carry out plans quickly and effectively. Nixon agreed, for he cared relatively little about domestic affairs (once remarking that the nation did not need a President to handle internal matters), but deeply involved himself in foreign policies. He also harbored a strong desire to have a private, shielded presidency. Before some of his most momentous decisions, Nixon would isolate himself for long periods, talking with no one.

The President slowly changed the emphases of American foreign policy. He reduced the commitment in Vietnam (and showed less interest in newly emerging areas, such as Latin America and Africa), while opening new relationships with Russia and China. Nixon responded to the new post-1956 world by deemphasizing the Kennedy-Johnson policies in the more volatile southern half of the globe and working instead for a settlement with the two giant Communist powers. Nixon understood that the world contained not two great powers but, in his words, "five economic superpowers"—the United States, Russia, Japan, China, and the European Economic Community. Because the first two balanced each other militarily, these five powers "will determine the economic future, and because economic power will be the key to other kinds of power," they will determine "the future of the world in other ways in the last third of this century." Russia and China, moreover, were enemies. As Kissinger noted,

"The deepest international conflict in the world today is not between us and the Soviet Union but between the Soviet Union and Communist China."

All this was not new. It had been apparent since 1960, but Nixon was the first President to act upon it. He understood that this five-power world opened a marvelous opportunity for the United States to play the other four powers against one another. He could, for example, cooperate with both the Chinese and Soviets to control the threatening economic expansion of Japan and Europe. Nixon could use American technology (such as computers) and agricultural products, which both Communist nations badly needed, to strengthen political ties and gain access for American business executives to the vast Chinese and Russian markets. Finally, if such ties were made, the United States could trade its products for Russian and Chinese help in stopping the Vietnam War so that American troops could be withdrawn on honorable terms. In all, Nixon's plans were imaginative and sweeping.

He understood, above all, that the United States had overreached itself during the 1960s with commitments that had already led to violence, inflation, and the political demise of Johnson. Thus he began by announcing a "Nixon Doctrine" in 1969 that pledged continued economic aid to allies in Asia and elsewhere but added that these allies should no longer count on the presence of American troops. He also announced that he would end the draft within two years. American troop strength would be reduced systematically in Vietnam while the South Vietnamese received more military equipment so that they could fight their own wars. This policy became known as "Vietnamization."

## THE NIXON FAILURES: 1970–71

Vietnamization, however, was failing by early 1970. As American troops left, the South Vietnamese proved incapable of driving out Communist forces. Using bases in neighboring Cambodia, a supposedly neutral state, the North Vietnamese and the National Liberation Front of South Vietnam threatened to bring down the Saigon government. Nixon responded with heavy bombing of the Cambodian bases but kept the raids secret from everyone except a few top officials in Washington and, of course, the Cambodians and Vietnamese. On April 30, 1970, after a conservative, pro-U.S. government suddenly came to power in Cambodia, the President announced that American and South Vietnamese troops were temporarily invading Cambodia to destroy the Communist bases. Having promised to end the war, Nixon was now actually expanding it into neighboring areas. Worse, the American troops did not succeed in destroying the bases, for after they retreated, the Communists simply moved back in and then threatened to overthrow the Cambodian government itself.

The effect on the American people was electric. College campuses, including many that had remained quiet during the 1960s, erupted into antiwar violence. The nation was shaken when four students were shot to death by Ohio

National Guard forces during the antiwar demonstration at Kent State University. Polls showed that half the American people disbelieved Nixon's announcement that the invasion would shorten the war. A lack of confidence in the President's foreign policy seemed to be developing, a rare event in recent American history. Henry Kissinger privately shuddered at the possible consequences, for he believed that the antiwar demonstrations were not just against Vietnam policies, but

> against authority of any kind, not just the authority of this President, but the authority of any President. . . . If confidence in him and in all institutions is systematically destroyed, we will turn into a group that has nothing left but a physical test of strength and the only outcome of this is Caesarism. . . .
>
> The very people who shout "Power to the People" are not going to be the people who will take over this country if it turns into a test of strength. Upper middle-class college kids will not take this country over. Some more primitive and elemental forces will do that.

But demonstrations continued, and an angry Senate finally repealed the Gulf of Tonkin Resolution (see pages 442–443). The President, however, claimed that he could continue to fight in Southeast Asia, regardless of what Congress did, in order to protect American troops already in Vietnam.

Announcing that the Cambodian invasion had been successful in removing one threat to American troops, the President further widened the war in February 1971 by invading Communist bases in Laos. This time, however, South Vietnamese rather than American troops went in; it was to be a test of Vietnamization. South Vietnam flunked the test. Meeting tough resistance, its troops scattered and ran. The Communists retained their hold on strategic areas despite an intensification of American bombing that had been carried out secretly since 1964. By mid-1971 the Communists controlled more of Laos than ever before.

The failure of Vietnamization was one of two early crises to confront Nixon. The other was a baffling economy—baffling in that, on the one hand, it was by far the world's greatest; in 1970 it had passed the trillion-dollar level in annual gross national product (that is, the total product of all goods and services produced in the nation). On the other hand, it also suffered from inflation that made American goods more expensive and hence less competitive on the international market. American products lost ground to such cheaply produced Japanese and German products as the Datsun and Volkswagen automobiles.

In 1971, for the first time since 1893, the United States suffered an overall deficit trade balance. It paid out more money to satisfy its international debts ($45.5 billion) than it received from exports and services abroad ($42.8 billion). The world's greatest economy was sick. In August 1971 President Nixon attempted to supply a remedy by devaluing the dollar, that is, reducing each dollar's worth in gold, which is the leading international exchange standard. This act cheapened the dollar and thus made American goods cheaper and easier to purchase internationally. By early 1973 the inflation and deficits continued, so the President again devalued the dollar. American exports picked up, but inflation was not halted.

# RACING TO THE MOON

Amid the gloom caused by Vietnam and the economy, the human race realized an age-old dream by sending astronauts safely to the moon and back in July 1969. That venture, the "great leap for mankind" as Neil Armstrong announced when he made the first human imprint on the moon's surface, will doubtless be remembered longer, and be of greater historical importance, than the crises that vexed the earthbound that year.

In a strict sense, space flight developed during the American Century but was the child of both Russian and American scientific breakthroughs. In 1903 a Russian, K. E. Tsiolkovsky, began making basic discoveries (including the idea for a multistage rocket, in which one stage propelled the vehicle and was then discarded as another stage took over to boost the rocket). Between 1919 and 1943, a scientist at Clark University in Massachusetts, R. H. Goddard, improved Tsiolkovsky's findings and made many of his own, especially in fuels. Goddard worked virtually alone and received little long-term support. Not even the U.S. military supported him during the 1930s because his small rockets seemed unable to carry payloads (such as explosives) of more than several pounds. Goddard, quietly experimenting at Clark or in the

Dr. Robert Goddard with early space rocket. *(National Aeronautics and Space Administration.)*

New Mexico desert, nevertheless developed automatic steering systems, self-cooling combustion chambers, and other discoveries that led to over two hundred patents in his name.

In the 1930s and 1940s the lone figure making basic findings on bare-bones budgets suddenly gave way to a mammoth wartime rocket project in Germany that employed twenty thousand people. By 1944–45 that program produced V-2 rockets that killed thousands in Great Britain. It also produced scientists who were secretly spirited out of Germany by the victors to shape the American and Russian space programs. By 1957 the Soviets had moved ahead by launching *Sputnik,* the first artificial satellite to spin into space. They also sent the first human in a rocket beyond the earth's atmosphere. The cold war now replaced Goddard's personal curiosity as the driving force in the discovery of space. In 1961 the United States began to catch up as Alan Shepard became the first American to travel into space. The following year John Glenn became a national hero by becoming the first American to orbit the earth. President John Kennedy committed the nation to be the first to land on the moon. The $24 billion Apollo project climaxed in 1969 when Armstrong planted the Stars and Stripes on the lunar surface, an event whose miraculousness was matched by the magic of the cameras that televised the event on earth. The Soviets meanwhile suffered fatal accidents in 1967 and 1971, then gave up their race to the moon to concentrate on learning how to live in space for long periods. Tsiolkovsky and Goddard had anticipated traveling into the new frontier of space, but not the incredible cost and deadly military competition that now resulted from their pioneering research.

## THE NIXON SUCCESSES: 1971–72

A year before the 1972 presidential election, Nixon's misfortunes in Vietnam and with the economy hurt his chances for reelection. Any President, however, can use his control of foreign policy to make dramatic headlines and some political gains if he has made adequate preparation and has a sense of timing. No one knew this better than Nixon.

In August 1971 he announced that he would become the first President to travel to China. Chairman Mao Tse-tung in Beijing had happily cooperated, for he hoped to use his new friendship with the United States as a weapon against his major enemy, Russia, which was massing troops along the Sino-Russian border. In an instant, twenty-two years of Sino-American enmity began to dissolve. Americans who had vocally denounced Red China for years could say little, for Richard Nixon had long been among the most vocal. Nor was there an outcry when, over U.S. objections, the People's Republic of China replaced Chiang Kai-shek's Taiwan government as the representative of China in the United Nations. In February 1972 Nixon dominated the television screens as he exchanged toasts with Chinese leaders. Americans overwhelmingly applauded his effort to ease tensions.

Henry Kissinger, Richard Nixon, and Chou En-lai in Peking, 1972. *(AP/WIDE WORLD PHOTOS.)*

But he parlayed the journey into an even greater gain. By pitting the two enemies, Russia and China, against one another for American favors, and by sending badly needed American wheat to both, Nixon freed his hand to deal with North Vietnam without fear that the two great Communist powers might intervene. Since 1969 he had searched for an agreement with the North Vietnamese and hoped to reach one before the 1972 election, but none had been concluded. In April 1972 the North Vietnamese launched an offensive against the weakened American–South Vietnamese forces. The President responded with the heaviest bombing of the war, the bombing of Hanoi, and then mined North Vietnamese harbors. The mining endangered Russian ships using the harbors and was such a threatening move that Lyndon Johnson had flatly refused to do it. But now the Russians and Chinese made no active response.

Indeed, as the mines were being sown, the Russians welcomed Nixon in Moscow as the first American President to make the journey to the Soviet Union. In SALT I (Strategic Arms Limitation Talks), U.S. and Soviet leaders signed an important pact limiting the number of defensive missiles each nation could possess. They also agreed to a five-year freeze on testing and the deployment of intercontinental missiles. Putting multiple warheads (Multiple Independent Reentry Vehicles, or MIRVs) on the missiles, however, was not prohibited. Both nations promised that SALT I was only the first of several treaties that would reduce the number of nuclear weapons. The treaties would come none too soon, for the nuclear stockpile in the world amounted to the equivalent of fifteen tons of TNT for every man, woman, and child on earth, and the stockpile was growing steadily.

In early 1972 a majority of Americans had disliked Nixon's Vietnam policies. After he mined and bombed North Vietnam, however, and then flew to China and Russia, the nation approved his policies by a ratio of 2 to 1. The President had used foreign policy much as a director uses music to build emotions to a pitch during a movie. "A lot of things are coming together at a point," said Nixon's right-hand man John Ehrlichman with a smile just before the 1972 election. "And it is a point, frankly, which we selected as a target time as a matter of enlightened self-interest."

## RICHARD NIXON AND THE NEW MAJORITY

Shortly after the 1968 election Kevin Phillips, a Nixon campaign aide, published *The Emerging Republican Majority.* The book attempted to explain why Nixon had won and how he could consolidate his position. Phillips believed that the Democrats' electoral base was shriveling while the Republicans' was expanding. The Republicans had a magnificent opportunity to make further inroads among ethnic voters (particularly Irish, Polish, and Italian Catholics), the working classes, and Southern whites. George Wallace's supporters were central to this effort, for Phillips thought that they were mainly conservative Democrats in the process of abandoning their traditional allegiances and preparing to support the Republicans. They represented large numbers of people who were fed up with judicial activism, moral permissiveness, forced integration, and massive welfare spending. Phillips suggested that the Republicans could safely ignore urban blacks, youthful dissenters, and liberal intellectuals. "From space-center Florida across the booming Texas plains to the Los Angeles–San Diego suburban corridor, the nation's fastest-growing areas are strongly Republican and conservative."

Nixon's first administration, in many respects, faithfully followed Phillips's blueprint. Nixon recognized that the 1968 election left him in a precarious political position. His 43.4 percent of the vote was the smallest winning share since 1912. For the first time since Zachary Taylor's election in 1848, a first-term President failed to carry a majority in either house of Congress. The Democrats retained an edge of 58 to 42 in the Senate and 243 to 192 in the House. To ensure his reelection, Nixon, without alienating the Republican faithful, had to do several things: reassure blue-collar workers that Republicans would not dismantle the welfare state or create economic hardship; exploit social issues that could appeal to ethnic voters; and demonstrate to whites, in the South and in the suburbs, that he opposed forced integration.

In the realm of economics, the search for a new majority required considerable ideological flexibility. Nixon, an economic conservative who had always advocated a balanced budget, soon approached the problem of unemployment as if he were a liberal Democrat. Unemployment stood at 3.5 percent in December 1969, but it rose sharply to 6.2 percent in the next year. That represented the highest level of joblessness in a decade. To deal with it, the President resorted to planned budget deficits, which, he hoped, would create new jobs by pumping money into the economy. Early in 1971 he presented a "full-employment budget," one that would be balanced if the economy were operating at full tilt but that under existing circumstances would produce a $23 billion deficit. In January Nixon asserted: "I am now a Keynesian in economics." This, one observer noted, was "a little like a Christian crusader saying, 'All things considered, I think Mohammed was right.'"

Similarly, Nixon moved to an acceptance of economic controls to curb inflation. In 1969, recalling the World War II experience, he remarked: "Controls, oh my God, no! . . . They mean rationing, black markets, inequitable

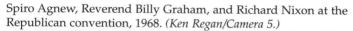
Spiro Agnew, Reverend Billy Graham, and Richard Nixon at the Republican convention, 1968. *(Ken Regan/Camera 5.)*

administration. We'll never go for controls." But by 1971, as the rate of inflation rose to 5 percent, the nation experienced a trade deficit, and the stock market tumbled, Nixon reversed fields. In August he imposed a ninety-day freeze on wages, prices, and rents. In November he established a Price Commission and Cost of Living Council to restrain both wage boosts and rent increases. The President later experimented with mandatory wage and price controls but then abandoned them in favor of voluntary compliance. Nixon always approached controls hesitantly, emphasizing the need for cooperation from business and labor. But the controls, however cautious, helped restrain inflation during 1972 and temporarily defused it as a political issue.

Nixon campaigned in 1968 against the Great Society's "welfare mess," claiming that it was "time to quit pouring billions of dollars into programs that have failed." Yet his own welfare proposals looked toward reform of the system. The Family Assistance Plan, which he proposed in 1969, would have provided a minimum income of $1,600 a year for a family of four, which, together with food stamps, would have meant an income of $2,460. This was more than welfare systems provided in twenty states. The plan also offered income supplements for the working poor in order to reduce welfare rolls by making it more profitable to hold a job than to receive public assistance. To qualify, however, heads of households (except for the infirm and mothers with small children) would have to register for job training and accept "suitable jobs." This, Nixon said, would restore the incentive to work and identify welfare chiselers. The House enacted a version of the measure, but it died in the Senate Finance Committee. In 1970, however, the administration succeeded in federalizing the food-stamp program. National criteria for eligibility were established, based on the cost of a nutritionally adequate diet, and benefits were adjusted automatically to take account of inflation.

## THE "SOCIAL ISSUE" AND THE SUPREME COURT

Nixon's economic policies were not entirely successful in checking inflation or reducing unemployment, but they preserved a level of prosperity through 1972 that enabled him to attract blue-collar support. Beyond this, however, the administration brilliantly exploited the "social issue"—fears that stemmed from a rising crime rate, the widespread use of drugs, increasingly permissive attitudes toward sex, and growing disdain for patriotic values. The President played on these fears, which cut across usual party lines, in everything from wearing an American flag in his lapel to denouncing the "Spock-marked" generation. Vice-President Spiro Agnew did the same in his attack on student protesters (an "impudent corps of snobs") and their "effete . . . hand-wringing, sniveling" apologists.

Three issues particularly aided Nixon among working-class Catholics. The President firmly endorsed federal aid to parochial schools, informing a Catholic audience that new ways should be discovered to provide direct assistance to nonpublic schools. Nixon also entered an explosive controversy over liberalization of the New York State abortion law, which the Catholic church bitterly opposed. He told Terence Cardinal Cooke in May 1972, "I would personally like to associate myself with the convictions you deeply feel and eloquently express." In 1970 the Commission on Obscenity and Pornography, all but one of whose members had been appointed by Lyndon Johnson, recommended that all laws "prohibiting the sale, exhibition, or distribution of sexual materials to consenting adults should be repealed." The President repudiated the commission, and Agnew thundered, "As long as Richard Nixon is President, Main Street is not going to turn into Smut Alley."

The social issue also encompassed racial fears. The President, who had received no more than 5 percent of the black vote in 1968, had a mixed civil rights record. The administration supported the "Philadelphia plan" to eliminate discrimination on federal construction projects by establishing a quota system under which trade unions had to accept a certain number of black youths as apprentices and guarantee them union membership at the end of a training period. The plan was upheld in the courts, but implementing school desegregation was a different story. The Justice Department favored the postponement of desegregation plans in communities where strong local opposition existed. In October 1969, however, the Supreme Court upset the administration's strategy. In *Alexander* v. *Holmes County Board of Education* the Court declared unanimously that "deliberate speed" no longer sufficed; school desegregation must begin "at once."

Given existing patterns of residential segregation, this decision merely raised a more difficult question: Should children be bused to achieve racial balance in the schools? There was no more highly charged issue in the early 1970s. Public opinion polls indicated that 78 percent of the people opposed the idea of busing. In some places, attempts to introduce such plans led to violence, disorder, and school boycotts. Maintenance of the "neighborhood school" became a central concern, particularly in the South, in the suburbs, and in ethnic enclaves in the large cities. Many people had moved to the suburbs to be in better school districts. Now they faced the prospect of sending their children back into the inner cities every morning. Yet busing plans met with the approval of the Supreme Court in April 1971. In *Swann* v. *Charlotte-Mecklenburg Board of Education* the justices found that busing, even if awkward or inconvenient, was an acceptable means of integrating "schools that are substantially disproportionate in their racial composition."

The issue was tailor-made for a President intent on currying favor with Southern whites, suburbanites, and uneasy ethnic groups. Nixon at the same time reflected the nation's mood and contributed to its intransigence. In March 1970 he called for an "open society" that "does not have to be homogeneous, or even fully integrated. There is room in it for communities. . . . It is natural and right that we have Italian or Negro or Norwegian neighborhoods." He disagreed with those who said that "the only way to bring about social justice is to integrate all schools now, everywhere, no matter what the cost in the disruption of education." The President reiterated his stand during the next two years. In January 1972 a federal district judge in Richmond, Virginia, ordered school boards to use busing to eradicate racial distinctions between schools. In March, with Congress considering a constitutional amendment to forbid busing, Nixon urged the legislators to impose a moratorium on the issuance of busing orders by federal courts while a measure could be devised looking toward a permanent solution. Congress then barred the implementation of such orders until all legal appeals had been exhausted. Although the bill did not go far enough to suit him, the President signed it in the summer of 1972.

Nixon also sought to use Supreme Court appointments as part of a broader political strategy. Having pledged in 1968 to appoint strict constructionists as a way of reversing the Court's activism, Nixon had the unusual opportunity of choosing four members in his first term. Late in 1969 he nominated Clement Haynsworth of South Carolina. Many considered this a way of paying a debt to Senator J. Strom Thurmond, a staunch conservative from South Carolina. Opposition to Haynsworth quickly developed when the Senate discovered that he had once acted as a judge in a case that could possibly have served his own interests. The Senate rejected the nomination by a vote of 55 to 45, with seventeen Republicans deserting the President. Nixon next submitted the name of G. Harrold Carswell of Florida. A new storm arose, primarily because an extraordinarily high number of Carswell's decisions had been reversed by higher courts. He appeared to lack any intellectual distinction, as even a supporter, Senator Roman Hruska of Nebraska, conceded: "Even if he were mediocre, there are lots of mediocre judges and people and lawyers. They are entitled to a little representation aren't they? . . . We can't have all Brandeises and Frankfurters and Cardozos and stuff like that there." The legal profession, regarding the appointment as an insult, lobbied against it, and in April 1970 the Senate turned it down. Seeking to squeeze the last ounce of political advantage from the situation, Nixon said that the issue involved "the Constitutional responsibility of the President to appoint members of the Court." Carswell's rejection, he asserted, was an act of "regional discrimination" against the South.

Ultimately Nixon appointed Harry Blackmun of Minnesota to the vacancy. The three other appointees were Lewis F. Powell, William Rehnquist, and Chief Justice Warren E. Burger. In many respects the Court veered in a more conservative direction. It ruled more frequently in behalf of the prosecution in criminal trials, declaring that a defendant who disrupted a trial by disorderly behavior could, after a warning, be removed from the courtroom or even bound and gagged. It also held that a confession extracted by unconstitutional means did not automatically invalidate a conviction if other evidence of guilt existed. The Court also made it easier for prosecutors to establish the admissibility of contested confessions. In *Miller* v. *California* (1973) the Court widened the grounds for ruling books and films obscene and expanded communities' power to ban offensive material. With respect to reapportionment, the Court softened the one-person, one-vote rule to widen somewhat the permissible disparity between voting-district populations. In 1973 the Court found that schools could be financed by property taxes even though disparities resulted, for, as Justice Powell said, "at least where wealth is involved, the equal protection clause does not require absolute equality or precisely equal advantages."

Yet the Court by no means pursued a course entirely to the President's liking. In the cases involving school desegregation and busing, even some of Nixon's appointees disappointed him. In *Furman* v. *Georgia* (1972) the Court held, by a vote of 5 to 4, that the death penalty as then prescribed was imposed unfairly. It fell more heavily on the poor and violated the constitutional injunction against cruel and unusual punishment. Many states then attempted to make the death penalty mandatory for certain offenses, but the Court had greatly aided opponents of capital punishment. In 1970, in *Welsh* v. *United States,* the Court ruled that a man whose opposition to military service was rooted in a deeply held moral or ethical conviction, rather than in religious belief, could qualify for conscientious objector status. Finally, the Court upheld civil liberties in two landmark decisions. In 1971 it ruled that the government could not prevent the publication of the "Pentagon Papers," a secret, multivolume collection of key U.S. government documents on the war that covered the years 1945 to 1968. On June 19, 1972, the Court rejected the attorney general's claim that the government had the right to use wiretapping against alleged subversives or domestic radicals without first obtaining a court order. Justice Powell said: "The price of lawful public dissent must not be a dread of subjection to an unchecked surveillance power." The decision, ironically, was handed down two days after burglars working for the President's reelection were arrested as they tried to place wiretaps in Democratic national headquarters.

## THE IMPACT OF THE WOMEN'S MOVEMENT

On August 26, 1970, thousands of women across the nation celebrated the fiftieth anniversary of the ratification of woman suffrage with parades, demonstrations, and a triumphal march down New York's Fifth Avenue. The celebration marked a peak in feminist mobilization; the start of the 1970s was an era of women's coalitions, collectives, and caucuses. Every national television network and major publication devoted time and space to the women's movement, calling on spokespersons such as Gloria Steinem, who had just started *Ms.* magazine, or the National Organization for Women's Betty Friedan, or any of a shifting galaxy of women's liberationists. An outpouring of feminist literature was also much in evidence. "What goes largely unexamined in our social order . . . is the birthright priority whereby males rule females," charged Kate Millett in *Sexual Politics* (1969). "Every avenue of power . . . is entirely in male hands." In *The Dialectic of Sex* (1970), Shulamith Firestone depicted a world of the future where adults might apply for licenses to live in "reproductive social structures," where childbirth would be "so diffused as to be practically eliminated," and where "humanity could finally revert to its naturally 'polymorphously perverse' sexuality."

But even the most far-fetched of liberationist visions served a political purpose: they made simple equity demands seem more acceptable by comparison. Or, as a suffragist once told Charlotte Perkins Gilman early in the century, "What you ask is so much worse than what we ask, that they will grant our demands in order to escape yours." Rapid acceptance of more moderate proposals, in fact, constituted the feminist "revolution" of the early 1970s.

The symbol of feminist success was congressional adoption of the Equal Rights Amendment (ERA), which stated that "equality of rights under the law shall not be abridged by the United States or by any state on account of sex." (The amendment prohibited sex discrimination by the government, its agencies and officers, and all institutions closely tied to the government, such as federal contractors.) An ERA had been favorably reported by the Senate Judiciary Committee since 1964, but it had then been opposed by the labor movement, the Women's Bureau, and major women's organizations, such as the League of Women Voters, all of which viewed it as a threat to protective laws. By 1970, federal courts were invalidating such laws as discriminatory to women, and the ERA's long time opponents changed their minds. The amendment was approved by the House in 1971 and by the Senate in 1972, and it was ratified by twenty-eight states within a year. Feminists now had every hope that it would be ratified by thirty-eight states within seven years. "Our reward," Betty Friedan told a National Organization for Women convention in 1971, "is the absolute passionate excitement . . . of making history ourselves."

Not only did Congress endorse the ERA by wide margins but it seemed to make many efforts to satisfy feminist demands. Between 1971 and 1974, Congress enacted an unparalleled number of laws promoting sex equity. (The only precedent, in fact, was the Equal Pay Act of 1963, enacted before the resurgence of feminism.) During the early 1970s, for instance, Congress prohibited sex discrimination in medical training programs, enabled middle-class families to claim tax deductions for child care if both spouses worked, and extended the benefits of married women in federal service jobs. It prohibited creditors from discriminating on the basis of sex, extended the Equal Pay Act by an Educational Amendments Act, and passed a Women's Educational Equity Act, which supported training and counseling for women. The only major setback came in 1972, when President Nixon vetoed the Comprehensive Child Development bill, which would have provided a national network of day care centers—and also would have required far more federal funding than any other equity measure. The President denounced the bill's "family-weakening implications."

Congressional efforts were complemented by a series of executive orders and labor department directives that supported feminist demands. In some cases, civil rights measures were extended to include women. In 1967, for instance, President Johnson had extended an executive order prohibiting racial discrimination by federal contractors to prevent sex discrimination as well. The order had far-flung ramifications. By 1970, the Labor Department issued affirmative action guidelines to all federal contractors (such as universities) to ensure nondiscriminatory hiring. The same year, after a class-action suit by the Women's Equity Action League, colleges and universities had to turn personnel files over to the government so that their efforts at nondiscrimination could be validated. Feminist demands for equal opportunity rapidly had a widespread impact.

Federal court decisions, meanwhile, imposed equity in other ways. Lower courts voided protective laws, challenged sex labeling of jobs (such as "stewardess"), and reaffirmed the principle of equal pay for equal work. Even the avoidance of court decisions had results. In 1972, a sex discrimination suit against American Telephone and Telegraph was settled out of court with a multi-million-dollar payment to women workers (such as operators who had been kept out of better paying jobs as linemen). The settlement suggested that the average working woman, who was usually underrepresented in feminist organizations, might have much to gain from the women's movement.

The Supreme Court did its part as well. During the early 1970s, the Court invalidated a state law giving preference to men as executors, banned references to sex in want ads, and equalized benefits for members of the armed services. But the Supreme Court's major decision was on the controversial issue of abortion. State abortion laws had been in effect since the late nineteenth century, prohibiting abortion in all cases except to preserve a mother's life. During the 1960s a movement grew to liberalize abortion laws by permitting abortion in other cases, such as rape and incest. By 1972, sixteen states had liberalized their laws. But feminists demanded repeal of all abortion laws, making abortion available to all women. In 1973, in *Roe* v. *Wade*, the Supreme Court declared state abortion laws unconstitutional on the grounds that they invaded the right of privacy. As legal abortion became available, maternal deaths from illegal abortions dwindled. The Supreme Court's decision had a more far-reaching effect than any other item on the feminist agenda.

While Congress, the courts, and the executive branch transformed feminist demands into federal policy, the women's movement caused other changes as well. Public opinion polls reported significant shifts in attitudes among women and men, from disapproval of the movement to increase women's rights in the late 1960s to support for feminist planks in the early 1970s. Educational changes were widespread. Publishers revised textbooks to eliminate sexual stereotypes; schoolboards revised curricula so boys and girls would not be segregated in shop and cooking classes; women's studies programs multiplied, reaching five hundred colleges by 1974; and all-male colleges rushed to welcome women (though often for financial, not feminist, reasons). Meanwhile, a vocational revolution seemed to have begun, as all-male or mostly male job classifications broke down. Women were becoming real estate agents, insurance adjusters, bus drivers, and bartenders; their numbers were rising as lawyers, judges, physicians, engineers, executives, ministers, and television anchorpersons. Most significantly, they were moving into the labor force at unprecedented rates. The new entrants were mainly married women, especially those with young children at home, who seemed to be abandoning the feminist mystique with alacrity.

The widespread impact of the women's movement in the early 1970s sparked a bitter debate. A conservative backlash against women's liberation erupted. "For women to announce that their very womanliness results from a bad and meretricious culture is the expression of deep self-hatred," Midge Decter charged in *The New Chastity* (1972). Working-class women and black women seemed to have little enthusiasm for feminist ideology, which in their view reflected white middle-class biases. A grass-roots middle-class aversion was visible as well, along with concern about whether women were acting in their own interest. "Most just trade the drudgery of housewifery for the drudgery of an office job," one woman wrote to *Time* in 1970. "Already women have more legal freedom than they know what to do with," wrote another. The most well-organized antifeminist movement, however, consisted of newly mobilized opponents of abortion rights and the ERA, who would, by the end of the 1970s, make their voices heard in public debates.

## NATIVE AMERICANS AND WOUNDED KNEE II

Of all American minorities, Native Americans suffered most during the 1960s and 1970s. Their population grew at four times the national rate, reaching 792,000 in 1970, but life expectancy was only 46 years (compared with the national average of 69), infant mortality rates were the nation's highest, and the suicide rate was double the country's average. Reservations lacked industry and good schools. Unemployment rates above 50 percent were not uncommon. A startling 50 percent of Native Americans on reservations, and even 20 percent of those in cities, lived below the poverty level in the late 1970s.

Indian leaders tried to deal with this tragedy, but they were divided between young and old, between those living in urban areas and on reservations, and between tribes. The Kennedy, Johnson, and Nixon administrations attempted to return policy to Indian officials. However, this did little to dampen the anger of the many Native Americans who joined militant youth groups (patterned on the black organizations of the 1960s) and, in 1968, formed the urban-based American Indian Movement (AIM). Until 1973, few whites seemed to care.

Then came the second episode of Wounded Knee (for the first, see Chapter 1). Wounded Knee is a town in the Oglala Sioux Reservation of South Dakota. The reservation, twice the size of Delaware, contained 3 million acres of which one-third was owned by whites, one-third leased by the Sioux to white cattlemen, and one-third used by the Sioux themselves. Seventy percent of the teachers on the reservation were white. Pine Ridge, the capital, was "a motley collection of shacks and houses of varying degrees of decrepitude," according to one reporter, with "a fine, tan, gritty dust . . . coating everything and getting into mouths and lungs, contributing to the hacking cough that people seem to develop rapidly here."

The reservation contained some of the nation's worst poverty: Half the families were on welfare and a moccasin factory served as the main industry. Most of the employed were mixbloods (Native Americans having both Native American and white blood), who controlled the reservation and worked in patronage jobs handed out by Washington officials. Full-blooded Native Americans lived in rural shacks where they tried to save themselves and their culture. The school dropout rate was 81 percent. Alcoholism was rampant among adult males. Considerable tension divided whites and Native Americans. When Raymond Yellow Thunder visited nearby Gordon, Nebraska, in 1972, he

Native Americans standing guard near a church in Wounded Knee, South Dakota, 1973. *(BETTMANN.)*

was beaten and murdered. Two white attackers were released without bail and charged only with second-degree manslaughter. Not wanting to cause further problems with the whites, neither Bureau of Indian Affairs officials nor the Sioux mixbloods controlling the reservation pushed for an investigation of the murder.

But, led by women, an angry group of Sioux repudiated their leaders, whom they considered corrupt and the puppets of white government officials, and asked for help from AIM. In February 1973 two hundred AIM members and their supporters occupied Wounded Knee. They demanded that the government honor some 371 treaties it had broken and also insisted that the reservation's regime be radically changed. U.S. forces encircled the area, partly to keep the two Native American factions from attacking each other, but also to block the entry of food into the town. The siege lasted 71 days. When AIM tried to move in reinforcements, government gunfire killed one Native American and wounded another. AIM and the Washington officials finally agreed to lift the siege and reexamine treaty obligations. The government, however, finally did little except bring suit against AIM leaders and sympathizers.

"Wounded Knee II" symbolized the tragedy of the Native American. Indeed, a white backlash erupted in the late 1970s. The backlash was notable in Congress, which had obtained almost dictatorial power over Native American affairs. White congressmen, many from Western states, proposed bills based on a ruthless policy of "termination"—that is, ending federal protection, revoking treaties, and opening Native American lands to the highest bidders. One embittered Native American spokesperson believed that "it all has to do with natural resources," for Congress wanted to "open up Indian lands to energy development interests, ranchers, and commercial fishermen." Tragically, little changed at Wounded Knee itself. One frustrated government official cried, "Damn it, there are no winners." But there were. Elsewhere new, younger Indian leaders, inspired by the confrontation, became more active. They successfully exerted pressure to obtain a new self-governing act that empowered Native Americans themselves. They also instituted lawsuits to obtain economic rights, not least the rights in some states to build enormously profitable gambling casinos. Wounded Knee II, like its 1890 predecessor, marked a turning-point in Native American–white relations.

## THE ELECTION OF 1972

By 1972 the President had taken great strides toward constructing what he called a "new majority." The Democrats tried to counter by nominating George McGovern of South Dakota. After the upheaval at the 1968 Chicago convention, the Democrats had thoroughly revised their delegate selection procedures. In an attempt to open the party to groups that had been excluded, those procedures were democratized and rules were adopted requiring that delegations "reasonably" reflect the proportion of women, blacks, and other minorities in the population. The result was a convention unlike any seen before. Those groups with ample time, energy, and ideological fervor—such as upper-middle-class activists in the antiwar, women's liberation, and civil rights movements—enjoyed greater representation than ever before. By contrast, the traditional power brokers—trade-union leaders, big-city mayors, and Southern bosses—enjoyed less.

McGovern's difficulties were compounded when it was learned that his running mate, Thomas Eagleton of Missouri, had some history of mental illness. After days of hesitation, which apparently convinced some voters that he lacked decisiveness, McGovern replaced Eagleton with Sargent Shriver, who had formerly headed the war on poverty. But McGovern's chief problem was that the Republicans succeeded in centering attention on the "social issue" and branding him a radical who favored "the far-out goals of the far left." The code words in 1972 were amnesty, acid, and abortion, and it made little difference that McGovern, who was a much-decorated bomber pilot in World War II, favored only the first, and then only with reservations. Condemning American involvement in the Vietnam War as immoral, he urged amnesty when the war ended for those who had fled the country to avoid the draft. McGovern did not favor legalized abortion or the use of drugs, but many Americans believed that he did or that, in any event, his supporters did. McGovern did not help his cause by stating, "Quite frankly, I am not a 'centrist' candidate." Nixon's margin of victory was decisive: 47 million votes (to McGovern's 29 million), 61.3 percent of the total vote, and a 520-to-17 electoral college majority. One Democratic campaign worker sighed, "I felt like the recreation director on the *Titanic.*"

## WATERGATE AND THE PRESIDENCY

Since the era of Franklin Roosevelt, Americans had looked to the President for leadership in solving the nation's social and economic problems. When Americans were asked in the 1970s which famous people, living or dead, they would like as visitors to their homes, Lincoln was named first, four other presidents followed, and Jesus Christ came in eleventh, just behind Harry Truman.

Such presidential popularity occurred in part because an increasingly complex society seemed to require centralized direction. More important, presidential authority was pumped up by thirty years of international crises. Throughout the cold war, presidents exercised powers once reserved for use in full-scale war, for many believed the executive needed a free hand to respond quickly and energetically to foreign threats. Richard Nixon carried the strong presidency to its furthest point in peacetime. Senate Democratic leader Mike Mansfeld admitted that Congress had handed much of its foreign policy power to the President "on a silver platter." Too late, Americans were learning a lesson taught more than 140 years earlier by Alexis de Tocqueville, a perceptive French visitor, in *Democracy in America:*

> No protracted war can fail to endanger the freedom of a democratic country. . . . War does not always give over democratic communities to military government, but it must invariably and immeasurably increase the powers of civil government; it must almost compulsorily concentrate the direction of all men and the management of all things in the hands of the administration. If it leads not to despotism by sudden violence, it prepares men for it more gently by their habits. All those who seek to destroy the liberties of a democratic nation ought to know that war is the surest and shortest means to accomplish it.

Tocqueville emphasized a point that Americans often failed to understand: foreign and domestic policies intertwine and shape one another.

The President and the nation learned this the hard way. In June 1972 five men connected to the Committee to Re-elect the President were caught trying to burglarize Democratic party headquarters in Washington's Watergate Apartments. Dismissing the break-in as a "bizarre incident," the President insisted that the White House was not involved. But in May 1973 a Senate investigation of Watergate uncovered a cesspool of illegal administration activities. Key White House aides were implicated in an attempt to cover up the burglary, and several admitted their guilt. Other revelations indicated that Nixon's campaign staff had illegally accepted large donations from corporations and individuals. In some instances the administration had apparently given the contributors political favors in return. In October 1973, with evidence accumulating that he had accepted payoffs from building contractors, Spiro Agnew resigned as vice-president. The Justice Department permitted him to plead guilty to a charge of tax evasion. He was fined and sentenced to three years of unsupervised probation. The President named Gerald Ford, a leader of the House of Representatives from Michigan, to replace Agnew.

Nixon desperately tried to halt the rising tide of criticism, but his efforts were complicated by the discovery that an intricate recording system had for years been tape-recording almost all his White House conversations. Nixon refused to surrender these tapes. He claimed that to do so would cripple the President's authority and violate the constitutional principle of separation of powers. When subpoenas were issued, he released a few tapes. But investigators found that several contained gaps at crucial points, gaps that could not, despite the President's claims, have been caused by accident. To prove that he was, in his words, "not a crook," Nixon authorized publication of his personal tax returns. These showed that in 1970 and 1971, claiming deductions of dubious legality, he had paid a federal tax of about $800 annually on a salary of $200,000. Nixon had, moreover, paid no state income taxes since 1969 although he was a legal resident of California.

Charges were also leveled that expensive improvements on the President's oceanside residences at San Clemente, California, and Key Biscayne, Florida, had been made at the taxpayers' expense without justification. In one instance, the Secret Service claimed it had installed a $621 ice-making machine "to insure that the President was not using poisoned ice." The White House mess chief put it more directly: "The President does not like ice cubes with holes in them." An audit of his tax returns by a congressional committee added to Nixon's difficulties. The committee found that the President had improperly taken a $428,000 charitable deduction for donating his vice-presidential papers to the National Archives, had failed to report a capital gain on the sale of property, had incorrectly written off business expenses, and had failed to declare $92,298 worth of improvements made at San Clemente and Key Biscayne that were "undertaken primarily for the President's personal benefit." In April 1974, Nixon agreed to pay $444,000 in back taxes and $32,000 in interest.

The effect of these disclosures on the presidency was stunning. For years Congress had endured insults from the Nixon administration. When some members of Congress protested the continued bombing of Cambodia and North Vietnam, for example, a State Department official cynically told them that the "justification" was "the reelection of President Nixon." One newspaper observed that "by that theory he could level Boston." But the Nixon administration's arrogance, Watergate cover-up, and other illegal activities soon led the Senate and House to strike back.

They passed a landmark measure that limited presidential power to make war without Congress's assent. The War Powers Act of 1973 provided that (1) "in every possible instance" the President must consult with Congress before ordering U.S. troops into any hostilities overseas; (2) whenever the President dispatched troops to foreign lands, he must, within forty-eight hours, send a full explanation to Congress; and (3) the President must begin to

# FOOTBALL (AND POLITICS)

The game began in eleventh-century England, when players representing towns pushed animal skulls, and later cow bladders, between towns that stood for "goals." King Henry II outlawed the sport in the twelfth century because its popularity interfered with archery practice needed to defend the kingdom. Reborn four hundred years later on playing fields, it became the British sport of rugby and then caught on in the United States. The first college football game was won by Rutgers' six goals to Princeton's four in 1869.

Within twenty years coaches were selecting the best players on "All America" lists. Through the mid-1890s only one non-British name was on such lists, but Irish, Jewish, and finally Polish and Hungarian players were honored after 1900 as the new immigration from Europe created an increasingly pluralistic society. The ethnic divisions led to rules that all could understand. Thus instead of having wild scrambles (as in rugby), the game of football was controlled by having fixed scrimmage lines. The new rules also allowed growing numbers of spectators to learn and follow the sport. Football was nevertheless brutal. The bloody Stanford–California game of 1904 was followed by riots in San Francisco. Even Theodore Roosevelt, who prided himself on the "strenuous life," finally ordered that football be civilized or, he thundered, it would be ended by presidential proclamation.

So the forward pass was legalized in 1906 to open and speed up the game. This weapon was used by an unknown Notre

The Four Horsemen of Notre Dame: the famous backfield of 1924. *(Library of Congress.)*

Dame team to upset mighty Army in 1913. Thus began the Notre Dame tradition, for the school soon attracted the athletic sons of Roman Catholic immigrants. Colleges began recruiting players in 1915, so some immigrants and other poor Americans suddenly found higher education available simply by playing football in the autumn. The sport entered glory days in the 1920s and professional teams appeared. The most renowned coach was Notre Dame's Knute Rockne, who believed that "After the Church, football is the best thing we have." His backfields moved in precise formations like the mass production assembly lines that Americans so admired. And like industry, football became a game for specialty teams of defense, offense, and even kicking. But Americans who preached the virtues of rugged individualism could proudly point to the exploits of Red Grange ("the Galloping Ghost") of Illinois teams in the 1920s, Charlie ("Choo-Choo") Justice of North Carolina squads in the 1940s, and, in the 1960s, Joe Willie ("Broadway Joe") Namath of Alabama.

Football's popularity peaked in the 1970s. Its quick action and pageantry suited color television screens. Television in turn provided immense wealth ($13.5 million in 1973 for college games alone) for football teams and such $250,000-a-year quarterbacks as Namath. (By the 1990s, quarterback Joe Mon-

Knute Rockne. *(Culver Pictures.)*

Red Grange, 1925. *(Culver Pictures.)*

tana of San Francisco earned more than $3 million a year.) In the 1970s George Allen of the Washington Redskins symbolized the tough, disciplined life with his eighteen-hour-a-day attention to detail and his remark, "Losing is like death. If you don't win you're dead and you don't know it." Allen's good friend, President Richard Nixon, was the nation's leading fan. "The President thinks football is a way of life," Allen observed. "He is a competitor." The game provided the language for politics and diplomacy. The American bombing of North Vietnam in late 1972 was codenamed "Operation Linebacker," and Nixon's code name was "Quarterback." Conversely, such metaphors of war as the "blitz" and the "bomb" were applied to the gridiron.

A University of Oklahoma athletic director declared, "We teach a philosophy, we teach a skill, and we danged sure also teach a little bit of religion. And we teach discipline. This is one of the last areas where true discipline is taught, where love for the American flag and respect for the American President is taught, through discipline." Others, however, deplored football's commercialism and its use as an example for fighting the cold war. Former star Dave Meggysey quit the game, claiming that he had illegally received money for playing in college and had been treated as an animal by professional coaches and owners. "Politics and pro football," Meggysey declared, "are the most grotesque extremes in the theatric of a dying empire." In the 1970s football nevertheless seemed to have replaced baseball as the so-called national pastime.

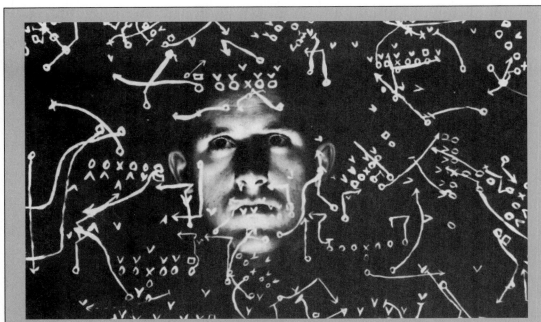

Fran Tarkenton of the Minnesota Vikings studies offensive plays, 1961. (*Myron Davis*, Life *Magazine* © *Time Inc.*)

withdraw the troops within sixty days unless Congress had given him specific authority to maintain them abroad.

To no one's surprise, Nixon vetoed the act. He argued that such a bill would have dangerously tied the President's hands during the Berlin confrontation of 1961 and the Cuban missile crisis of 1962. Others opposed the bill for opposite reasons. They claimed it gave the President power to wage war on his own for sixty days without having to obtain congressional approval. Congress, however, believed it had found a useful middle ground, and that the measure would at least prevent future Vietnam-type interventions. The necessary two-thirds of the House and Senate voted to override Nixon's veto. That vote marked an important reversal in the thirty-year enlargement of presidential power.

Watergate not only weakened Nixon's standing with Congress, but also destroyed his ability to lead the Republican party. By 1974 even those who had stood by Nixon were shocked by each fresh disclosure. One Senator said that it was like waiting for the other shoe to drop, except "I don't know how many shoes there are to fall. I feel like I've been dealing with a centipede this past year." One poll found that only 24 percent of the voters classified themselves as Republicans, the smallest percentage identified with any major party in the twentieth century. The Democrats virtually swept the 1974 congressional elections, including such traditional Republican seats as one in Michigan that the Democrats had not held since 1932.

Watergate altered the American political landscape and undermined presidential power. In the late 1960s a majority of Americans had identified the groups dangerous to society as atheists, black militants, student demonstrators, prostitutes, and homosexuals. In 1968 and 1972, Nixon, by running on the social issue, had successfully exploited those fears. But by late 1973, pollster Louis Harris reported, none of these groups was considered harmful by a majority of people. Instead, the groups considered dangerous were people who hired political spies, generals who conducted secret bombing raids, politicians who engaged in wiretapping, business executives who made illegal campaign contributions, and politicians who attempted to use federal investigatory agencies for partisan purposes.

## THE LOSS OF CIVIL LIBERTIES

While the Watergate scandal was unfolding, the American people learned that the federal government had, for more than a decade, systematically violated their constitutional rights. First exposed by the *New York Times* in 1974, and then confirmed over the next two years in the reports of a House committee chaired by Democrat Otis Pike from New York, a Senate committee headed by Democrat Frank Church from Idaho, and a special committee under Vice-President Nelson Rockefeller, those violations had begun even before the United States entered the war in Vietnam. But that war, and especially the turmoil and dissent accompanying it, led the Central Intelligence Agency, the Federal Bureau of Investigation (FBI), and other agencies to mount their most aggressive campaigns against civil liberties, and to do all they could to conceal their actions from Congress, the courts, and the people.

Nothing better illustrated the government's behavior than the Central Intelligence Agency (CIA) program known as "Operation CHAOS." Although the CIA was prohibited by law from spying on American citizens, the agency had begun to do so in the 1950s. In the summer of 1967, with antiwar demonstrations reaching a crescendo and with President Johnson convinced that the demonstrators were being funded by foreign powers, the CIA stepped up its activities. Although it discovered no foreign involvement, the agency nevertheless accelerated its campaign at President Nixon's behest in 1969. By 1974 the CIA had compiled dossiers on 7,200 American citizens, stored the names of 300,000 individuals and groups in a computerized index file, opened 215,000 first-class letters, placed wiretaps on telephones, installed bugging devices in people's homes, and burglarized the offices of dissident groups. Speaking of the mail-opening program, one CIA official admitted, "This thing is illegal as hell." Not to be outdone by the CIA, the FBI remodeled its own counterintelligence program, COINTELPRO, and began to shift its attention to black militants, the new left, and the antiwar movement. A House committee summarized some of the results of the FBI program:

"Careers were ruined, friendships severed, reputations sullied, businesses bankrupted and, in some cases, lives endangered."

Two actions demonstrated Richard Nixon's own cavalier disregard for civil liberties. In May 1969, furious that news of the "secret" bombing of Cambodia had leaked to the press, the Nixon administration placed wiretaps on a number of government officials and newspaper reporters. For nearly two years the Justice Department monitored their phone calls although, as the President later conceded privately, the transcripts produced no evidence of subversion, but "just gobs and gobs of material: gossip and bullshitting." In July 1970 Tom C. Huston, a presidential aide, concocted a plan designed at once to expand and centralize the government's counterintelligence operations. Proposing that surreptitious entry be used to obtain information, Huston admitted: "Use of this technique is clearly illegal: it amounts to burglary." But he explained further: "It is also the most fruitful tool and can produce the type of intelligence which cannot be obtained in any other fashion." The President approved these recommendations, but when FBI Director J. Edgar Hoover objected (primarily, it seems, because he feared their implementation would reduce the FBI's role), Nixon rescinded his approval.

The administration's contempt for civil liberties was again evident a year later. In June 1971 Dr. Daniel Ellsberg, a former Pentagon expert on Vietnam, made public the secret "Pentagon Papers," which documented American policy in Indochina between 1945 and 1968. The administration first attempted to block their publication in newspapers, but the Supreme Court ruled against prior restraint by a 6-to-3 vote. A majority of the justices found that the government had failed to prove that release of the documents would "inevitably, directly and immediately" injure the nation. Indeed, Nixon never believed that the documents jeopardized the nation's security, although he did fear their release might set a dangerous precedent. Ellsberg was then indicted for stealing government property.

At the same time the White House created a "plumbers" group of secret agents to "stop security leaks and to investigate other sensitive security matters." One of the group's first tasks was to discredit Ellsberg, and this, in turn, seemed to require a covert operation. The plumbers believed that damning evidence might be found in the office files of a Los Angeles psychiatrist whom Ellsberg had been consulting. The President's chief domestic advisor, John Ehrlichman, approved a burglary of the office as long as "it is not traceable." In September 1971 the plumbers broke into the psychiatrist's office, but failed to turn up evidence that would, in their words, "nail the guy cold." Documents released in the 1990s revealed Nixon to be so obsessed with what he considered to be a conspiracy that he was willing to commit crimes to obtain evidence: "All evidence we find with regard to the conspiracy," he told his closest aides, "is going to be leaked, to columnists and the rest. And we'll kill these sons of bitches."

Daniel Ellsberg's trial for espionage and the theft of government property was held in 1973. The government's behavior during the trial was consistent with its previous behavior. While the trial was in progress, John Ehrlichman offered the directorship of the FBI to the presiding judge, Matthew Byrne. The offer, if not actually improper, was surely irregular. The administration only grudgingly confessed that it had masterminded a burglary of Ellsberg's psychiatrist's office, and then urged Judge Byrne—unsuccessfully—not to make the information public. Finally, the government did not reveal, until ordered to do so by the judge, that the wiretaps it had installed in 1969 had inadvertently picked up some of Ellsberg's conversations. Furious at this behavior, Judge Byrne declared a mistrial and dismissed the charges against Ellsberg. He noted that the circumstances in the case offended "a sense of justice." That judgment was equally applicable to CHAOS, to COINTELPRO, to wiretapping, to the Huston plan, and, as the Watergate investigation had already begun to reveal, to a much broader range of White House activities.

## IMPEACHMENT: THE PRESIDENCY FROM NIXON TO FORD

In late 1973 the House of Representatives ordered its Judiciary Committee to determine whether Nixon had committed impeachable offenses, defined by the Constitution as "Treason, Bribery, or other high Crimes and Misdemeanors." During nine months of study, the committee wavered in its view of whether the President should be impeached. Nixon's headline-making trips abroad, Americans' veneration of their President, and the memory of Nixon's triumph in the 1972 elections raised dangerous political problems for Congress. The dilemma was especially acute in an election year. By July 1974, however, the Judiciary Committee had assembled a massive amount of evidence that seemed damning to the President's case. Nor did Nixon help his cause by withholding more than one hundred tapes of private conversations on the grounds of "executive privilege," asserting that they must remain secret or otherwise the President's ability to protect the national interest would be endangered.

Three weeks in the summer of 1974 marked a turning point in American history. On July 24 the Supreme Court unanimously ordered the President to surrender sixty-four tapes to John Sirica, judge of the district court in the District of Columbia where the Watergate trial was held. After listening to the tapes, Sirica could give all relevant portions to special Watergate prosecutor Leon Jaworski, who could then turn them over to Congress. The President thus had to retreat from his claim of executive privilege for all his documents. For the first time, however, the Supreme Court also ruled that the President had the right to withhold information on the grounds of executive privilege when the information concerned military or diplomatic matters. Since the tapes in dispute did not cover such national security issues, Nixon had to surrender them so the courts could base their decisions on all possible evidence.

One week later, John Ehrlichman, who as the President's chief domestic affairs advisor had held great power, was found guilty of directing the break-in at the office of Daniel Ellsberg's psychiatrist. Ehrlichman was also found guilty of lying to investigators about his role in the crime. He received a sentence of twenty months to five years in prison. Four of Nixon's Cabinet officials, his two top White House assistants, and former Vice-President Agnew had now been named in criminal cases. In all, thirty-eight officials associated with the Nixon administration had either pleaded guilty to or been indicted for crimes. American history offered no parallel.

On July 30 the House Judiciary Committee completed six days of public debate by recommending that the full House of Representatives approve three Articles of Impeachment. The first article accused the President of lying about, and trying to conceal, the role of his White House staff in the Watergate break-in. The second article alleged that Nixon had violated the constitutional rights of citizens by placing unlawful wiretaps on telephones and by using the FBI, CIA, and Internal Revenue Service to harass his political opponents. The third article declared the President had refused to comply with congressional subpoenas for documents and taped conversations. Two other articles, one condemning Nixon's secret bombing of Cambodia during 1969–70 and another accusing him of income tax evasion and of using government monies for private gain, were rejected by the committee as inadequate reasons for impeachment.

The Judiciary Committee reached its decision after long, bitter debate and intense soul searching. Republicans and Southern Democrats were especially uncomfortable as evidence against the President accumulated. But as a leading conservative from Alabama commented: "And . . . what if we fail to impeach? Do we ingrain forever in the very fabric of our Constitution a standard of conduct in our highest office that at the least is deplorable and at the worst is impeachable?" In the end, as many as seven Republicans and all twenty-one Democrats on the Judiciary Committee voted for at least one of the articles. The committee's debate, which attracted a huge television and radio audience, had an immense political impact. Congressmen effectively used a medium that, until 1974, had been so manipulated by the White House that it had been called "Presidential television."

No one any longer doubted that the House would vote to impeach the President by a wide margin. Nixon's last hope lay in the Senate, but that hope quickly died. On August 5 he released the transcripts of three conversations he had held with his chief White House assistant, H. R. Haldeman, a few days after the June 1972 Watergate break-in. These tapes showed that Nixon had raised the possibility of getting the CIA to order the FBI to halt its investigation of the burglary. "Don't go any further into this case period!" was the language the President proposed. The President also conceded that he had kept this information from his own lawyers and from the impeachment inquiry. Granting that he had committed a "serious act of omission," and that impeachment in the House was "virtually a foregone conclusion," Nixon insisted that his behavior did not warrant a conviction in the Senate.

But the disclosure that he had obstructed justice and withheld the truth provided the "smoking pistol" for which many congressmen were searching. And the fingerprints were unmistakably clear. Support for the President evaporated overnight. Republicans began a stampede for resignation or impeachment. The situation in the White House became tense. According to investigative reporters, Nixon began to roam the mansion at night, communing with the

Senator Sam Ervin swears in John Dean, facing the camera, at the Watergate hearings. *(BETTMANN.)*

portraits of past presidents, and at one point summoning Henry Kissinger to kneel with him in prayer. White House aides feared that if they pressured him to quit, Nixon might respond irrationally. All orders from the President to the military were carefully monitored by top civilian officials in the Pentagon.

Finally, on the night of August 7, Nixon met with two conservative Arizona Republicans, Senator Barry Goldwater and Representative John Rhodes, the House minority leader. They reported that the Senate would surely vote to impeach. Even the ten Republican members of the Judiciary Committee who had defended the President a few days earlier had reversed their positions. One member reportedly asked if the committee could reconvene so he could change his vote, but he was informed that "the train had left the station." Its destination became known on August 9, 1974, when for the first time in history an American President was forced to resign his office. Vice-President Gerald Ford, whom Nixon had appointed to replace Agnew, became chief executive.

The presidency, which had increasingly dominated foreign and domestic policies in the American Century, had finally been curbed by Congress and the Supreme Court. Yet Nixon's resignation occurred primarily because he had tape-recorded incriminating conversations and then refused advice from close friends to destroy the tapes. A disturbing question remained: whether the unconstitutional acts described in the Articles of Impeachment could have been uncovered if Nixon had not made the recordings, or if he had destroyed them before Congress learned of their existence.

Gerald Ford, moreover, unilaterally used his new power to protect Nixon from criminal prosecution. On September 8, 1974, the President said that he was pardoning Nixon for all federal crimes he "committed or may have committed" during his years in the White House. Ford's announcement set off a storm of protest since it precluded a trial and thereby undercut proper legal processes. Two years later, the pardon returned to haunt Ford. It was an important reason why many Americans preferred Jimmy Carter instead of Ford in the presidential election. The ghost of Richard Nixon continued to stalk the corridors of American politics.

## HENRY KISSINGER: FOREIGN POLICY FROM NIXON TO FORD

One official, however, emerged from the morass of Watergate with an enhanced reputation. In 1973, after having served as the President's national security advisor, Henry Kissinger became secretary of state. That same year he finally succeeded in negotiating a Vietnam cease-fire with his North Vietnamese counterpart, Le Duc Tho. The two men were rewarded with the 1973 Nobel Peace Prize. Tho refused his share, correctly asserting that war between North and South Vietnam continued. The American troops left, however, and Kissinger accepted his share of the prize. "Half a prize for half a peace seems just about right," one journalist observed.

Kissinger followed with equally successful (from his and Nixon's view), if less publicized, diplomacy in Chile. Since 1970 President Salvador Allende had turned Chile toward a more nationalist, independent course, and attempted to gain his nation's economic independence—and distribute its wealth more equitably—by seizing property owned by North American corporations and wealthy Chileans. Kissinger and Nixon secretly moved to undermine the new regime. By 1973 Allende's government suffered severely not only from its own economic errors but also from a cutoff of the U.S. aid on which Chile had long depended. Kissinger meanwhile strengthened Washington's ties with the Chilean army. In September 1973 the army struck. It overthrew Allende, who died in the struggle, ended all attempts at reform, established a military regime, and then tortured and murdered thousands of political prisoners. Both North and South Americans were saddened by Chile's new course, but Kissinger and Nixon were pleased that they had played a major part in overthrowing a government they had always mistrusted and feared. They believed the United States had proved that it could still guide the fortunes of third-world nations, at least those in Latin America.

Turning from Chile with satisfaction—and from Vietnam with obvious relief—Kissinger pledged his full attention to renewing frayed ties with Western Europe. This important relationship had deteriorated politically and eco-

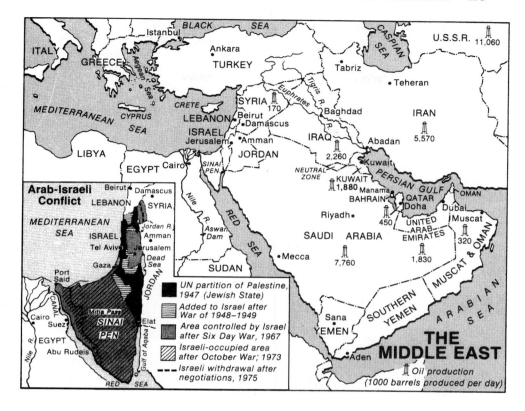

THE MIDDLE EAST

Oil production
(1000 barrels produced per day)

Arab-Israeli Conflict

UN partition of Palestine, 1947 (Jewish State)
Added to Israel after War of 1948–1949
Area controlled by Israel after Six Day War, 1967
Israeli-occupied area after October War; 1973
Israeli withdrawal after negotiations, 1975

nomically. The Nixon administration placed first priority on détente with Russia and China. The policy worked well (Soviet Premier Brezhnev was so pleased that he embarrassed Kissinger by kissing him full on the mouth when they met), but relations with the Atlantic partners suffered, for they feared the superpowers might be making deals that did not consider Europeans' interests.

Before Kissinger could move to repair the Atlantic alliance, however, war in the Middle East wrecked his plans. The roots of the conflict went back to 1967 when the Egyptians blockaded several ports that were crucial for Israel's security. On June 5, 1967, the Israelis suddenly retaliated. In the "Six-Day War," they humiliated the Egyptians and their Arab allies by seizing the prized city of Jerusalem (the world home of three great religious faiths—Islam, Judaism, and Christianity), sweeping across the Sinai Desert to the Suez Canal, and wiping out large portions of the Egyptian and Syrian armies. The Arabs refused to discuss peace until Israel returned the conquered areas. The Israelis rejected this demand, claiming that the new boundaries were necessary for their security.

Re-equipped with massive Soviet aid, the Egyptians and Syrians suddenly attacked Israel in October 1973. The Egyptian army redeemed itself. Israel staved off a major setback only with a brilliant crossing of the Suez that enveloped large numbers of Egyptian troops and placed Israeli forces in Egypt itself. Kissinger flew to the Middle East five times in six months, and with cooperation from the Soviets (who feared a prolonged war would result in Egyptian defeat), brought about direct Egyptian-Israeli talks, the first since Israel was founded in 1948. A temporary settlement provided for mutual troop withdrawal and creation of a buffer zone in the Sinai Peninsula.

Although key problems remained unresolved in the Middle East, the Egyptian-Israeli disengagement gave Kissinger cause for satisfaction. The same could not be said for developments in Southeast Asia. After pulling out its combat troops, the United States cut aid to the Saigon government in 1974. During the spring of 1975, the North Vietnamese Communists launched an all-out offensive. The beleaguered Saigon regime, riddled with corruption and deserted slowly by Washington, asked desperately for American help. Investigation revealed that two years before, Nixon had secretly assured the South Vietnamese that in such a situation the United States would use its great power to protect the South: "You can count on us," he had told them. But in April 1975, Nixon was in disgrace at San Clemente, California. Across the Pacific television cameras recorded the sordid details of U.S. officials shoving aside former Vietnamese allies so the Americans could escape by helicopter moments before the Communists seized Saigon. The long U.S. war in Southeast Asia was finally over.

## Suggested Reading

For Richard Nixon and his administration, see Joan Hoff, *Nixon Reconsidered* (1994); Tom Wicker, *One of Us: Richard Nixon and the American Dream* (1991); and the second and third volumes of Stephen E. Ambrose, *Nixon* (1987, 1991). An exceedingly informative work is Kathryn Olmsted, *Challenging the Secret Government: The Post-Watergate Investigations of the CIA and FBI* (1996). The Supreme Court is evaluated in Bernard Schwartz, *Ascent of Pragmatism: The Burger Court in Action* (1991); and Charles H. Lamb and Stephen C. Halpern eds., *The Burger Court: Political and Judicial Profiles* (1991). For Nixon's successor, consult John Robert Greene, *The Presidency of Gerald R. Ford* (1995).

On the impact of the women's movement, see Janet Giele, *Women and the Future: Changing Sex Roles in Modern America* (1978); and William H. Chafe, *Women and Equality: Changing Patterns in American Culture* (1977). For the 1973 abortion ruling, see Marian Faux, *Roe v. Wade: The Untold Story of the Landmark Supreme Court Decision that Made Abortion Legal* (1988); and David J. Garrow, *Liberty and Sexuality: The Right to Privacy and the Making of Roe v. Wade* (1994). For Native Americans, consult Vine DeLoria, Jr., *Behind the Trail of Broken Treaties* (1974); Russell Means, *Where White Men Fear to Tread* (1995), for the AIM leader's story; and Stanley David Lyman, *Wounded Knee 1973* (1991), for a governmental view. A good overall view is Richard Lowitt, ed., *Politics in the Postwar American West* (1995). The erosion of civil liberties is documented in Athan Theoharis, *Spying on Americans* (1979); Morton H. Halperin, et al., *The Lawless State* (1976); David Wise, *The American Police State* (1976); David J. Garrow, *The FBI and Martin Luther King, Jr.* (1981); and Peter Schrag, *Test of Loyalty* (1974), an account of the Daniel Ellsberg case.

The literature on Watergate is extensive. Some of the more important works are J. Anthony Lukacs, *Nightmare: The Underside of the Nixon Years* (1976); Theodore H. White, *Breach of Faith: The Fall of Richard Nixon* (1975); Jim Hougan, *Secret Agenda: Watergate, Deep Throat and the CIA* (1984); and Stanley I. Kutler, *The Wars of Watergate* (1990).

On foreign policy, the key sources for further research are R. D. Burns, ed., *Guide to American Foreign Policy Since 1700* (1983); and Bruce Jentleson and Thomas Paterson, eds., *Encyclopedia of U.S. Foreign Relations*, 4 vols. (1997), which has useful bibliographies. The standard account is Louis Fisher, *Presidential War Powers* (1995). The historical context is well presented in Burton Kaufman, *The Arab Middle East and the United States* (1996). The most detailed biography is Walter Isaacson, *Kissinger* (1992). On antiwar protest, note Jeane Ziedler's essay on Jane Fonda in Edward P. Crapol, ed., *Women and American Foreign Policy* (1992). Indispensable are the two-volume (and massive) memoirs by Henry Kissinger, *The White House Years* (1979) on 1969–72, and *Years of Upheaval* (1982) on 1972–73. Compare these with Nixon's own memoirs, *RN* (1978), and especially with Seymour Hersh, *The Price of Power* (1983), as well as with Lloyd Gardner, "The Burden of Richard Nixon," in *A Covenant with Power* (1984). John Newhouse, *Cold Dawn* (1973), covers the SALT I agreement. A good assessment on Vietnam, especially on the military side, is Timothy J. Lomperis, *The War Everyone Lost—and Won* (1984). The Soviet side is analyzed in Joseph G. Whelen, *Soviet Diplomacy and Negotiating Behavior* (1982). Fine case studies of the oil crisis are Stephen G. Rabe, *The Road to OPEC: U.S. Relations with Venezuela, 1919–1976* (1982); and Bennett H. Wall, *Growth in a Changing Environment* (1988), on Exxon. A superb critique of the international economic policies is David Calleo, *Imperious Economy* (1982). Overviews and recent bibliography can be found in Warren Cohen, *America in the Age of Soviet Power, 1945–1991* (1993); and Walter LaFeber, *America, Russia, and the Cold War, 1945–1996* (1997).

A place to begin in understanding football in American life is David Riesman and Reuel Denney, "Football in America," *American Quarterly* (1951), pp. 309–25; also see Michael Oriard, *Reading Football; How the Popular Press Created an American Spectacle* (1993). On the development of space technology, see Barton C. Hacker, "Robert H. Goddard and the Origins of Space Flight," in Carroll W. Pursell, Jr., ed., *Technology in America: A History of Individuals and Ideas* (1981).

Young urban professionals, New York City, 1984. *(Melchior DiGiacomo/The Image Bank.)*

# CHAPTER SIXTEEN

# 1976–1984
## New Directions

This chapter discusses:
- Why Jimmy Carter's hopes were followed by Ronald Reagan's realities
- New religious fundamentalists, in both the United States and Iran
- Yuppies amidst poverty
- How Reaganites battled "evil empires," Central American reforms, and the villains in "Star Wars"

Vietnam and Watergate continued to influence American life long after the last soldier had returned home and the last conspirator had gone to jail. It was only logical, in the aftermath of Watergate, that successful politicians would be those who had no connection with the Washington establishment. Neither Jimmy Carter nor Ronald Reagan had held federal office, elective or appointive, before being elected President. Politics became the art of running against the government. Winning elections became the art of selling a candidate's personal integrity to the voters. It was equally logical, in the aftermath of Vietnam, that an assertive foreign policy, a promise to make America strong again, would exert a strong appeal. Although the policies that Carter and Reagan adopted differed in important respects, the differences concerned the speed at which the nation was moving more than the direction in which it was going: toward a dousing of social reform at home and a rekindling of cold war hostilities abroad.

## JIMMY CARTER AND THE "NEW REALITIES"

In 1971, when he became governor of Georgia, Jimmy Carter regarded the presidency with "reverence." Then he had an opportunity to meet the men—Nixon and McGovern, Humphrey and Muskie, Reagan and Rockefeller—who had been contesting for the office over the years and, as Carter recalled, "I lost my feeling of awe about presidents." In early 1973, undaunted by the label applied to him by journalists—"Jimmy Who?"—Carter set out to win the Democratic nomination. By 1976, with his only political experience one term in the Georgia Senate and one term as the state's governor, Carter recognized that the Watergate backlash might do wonders for his candidacy.

He portrayed himself as an "outsider" who never had been involved in corrupt Washington politics. To voters fed up with deception in high places, he promised, "I will never lie to you." Gambling that his status as a Southerner, his image as an unknown newcomer without Washington connections, and his emphasis on personal integrity would strike responsive chords in the electorate, Carter collected Democratic delegates as a gambler gathers chips. "We figured the odds as best we could," he explained, "and then we rolled the dice."

In his speech accepting the Democratic nomination in June 1976, Carter placed himself squarely within the party's reform tradition. Calling for "an end to discrimination because of race and sex," he said: "Too many have had to suffer at the hands of a political and economic elite who have shaped decisions and never had to account for mistakes or suffer from injustice." Pledging support for a revamping of the income tax structure, Carter lashed out at "unholy, self-perpetuating alliances . . . between money and politics." Urging enactment of new welfare programs, including a "nationwide comprehensive health program for all our people," Carter stated: "The poor, the weak, the aged, the afflicted must be treated with respect and compassion and with love."

Although Carter also warned that government could not solve every problem, most of his listeners detected strong populist overtones in the speech.

Many things helped Carter in the campaign, not the least President Gerald Ford's reputation as a bumbler. Ford tripped down some steps on a state occasion, cut himself diving into the White House swimming pool, and bumped his head boarding a helicopter. Newsmen adapted Lyndon Johnson's cruel remark that Ford had played too much football without a helmet, and made it crueler still: "He can't even play President without a helmet." Nor did Ford's choice of Senator Robert Dole of Kansas as his running mate help the Republicans. In a televised debate with his Democratic counterpart, Senator Walter Mondale of Minnesota, Dole charged that World War I, World War II, and Korea were "all Democrat wars." Such remarks angered Democratic moderates whom the Republicans badly needed on election day. Finally, Ford's own statement during a debate with Carter that, partly due to Republican policies, "There is no Soviet domination of Eastern Europe," cost the President crucial support from Poles, Czechs, and other Americans of Eastern European origin.

Yet the electorate, or at least the 54 percent that bothered to vote, responded to more than mishaps, mudslinging, and miscues. Ford did best among the affluent and the comfortable; Carter, among the poor and disadvantaged. The vote, pollsters found, "fractured to a marked degree along the fault line separating the haves and the have-nots." Carter won about 55 percent of the Catholic and Jewish vote, but more than 90 percent of the black vote. The Georgian carried ten of the eleven Southern states (all except Virginia); in seven of the ten, black voters provided his margin of victory. With a total of 40.8 million votes to Ford's 39.1 million, Carter emerged with a 297-to-241 victory in the electoral college.

Expectations that Jimmy Carter would preside over a new era of reform were short-lived. Within one hundred days of his taking office, many people thought that Carter had begun "shifting to the right." Within a year disgruntled liberals believed that Carter was the most conservative Democratic President since Grover Cleveland. Within eighteen months, critics charged that Carter "is a Democrat who often talks and thinks like a Republican." And within two years, they claimed that Carter, "a counterfeit populist," was in truth "as Republican as Gerald Ford."

Liberals centered their fire on three aspects of the President's legislative program. They claimed that his energy bill, enacted in 1978 after a fierce congressional struggle, benefited the oil companies by deregulating natural gas prices; that his tax reform measure, approved in 1977, failed to close loopholes enjoyed by the wealthy and offered little relief to middle-income individuals; and that his medical care proposals fell far short of the comprehensive health programs supported by Senator Edward Kennedy, Democrat from Massachusetts. By 1978 Kennedy had begun to complain that the administration was sacrificing the needs of "the poor, the black, the sick, the young, the cities and the unemployed."

Carter's policies undoubtedly reflected his own managerial outlook, his tendency to convert social problems into engineering problems and to seek technical solutions for them. Moreover, Carter found it necessary to placate members of Congress, especially the chairs of powerful committees. Demanding modifications in the energy and tax proposals, these Democratic leaders forced Carter to retreat or even surrender. The President could no longer invoke party discipline against Democrats who increasingly divided along geographic ("sun belt" versus "snow belt") and ideological lines. As the party system fragmented, congressional defiance of the White House became more common. In the late 1970s power shifted dramatically up Pennsylvania Avenue to Capitol Hill.

As presidential influence over—and party discipline in—Congress declined, pressure groups rushed to fill the vacuum. Carter had promised to attack the "unholy" alliance "between money and politics," but these groups, representing virtually every important economic interest in the country, nevertheless gained tremendous influence in Congress. They multiplied "like rabbits," Senator Edward Kennedy warned, "and are doing their best to buy every senator, every representative, and every issue in sight." The groups included trade associations (such as the American Medical Association and the National Education Association), corporations, labor, and single-issue interests (anti-abortion and anti-gun-control advocates, for example). They cemented their power by giving lavishly to congressional campaigns. Not surprisingly, Congress passed laws encouraging such gifts. Labor unions had long been allowed to contribute to campaigns, but corporations had not—until, that is, new laws in the 1970s permitted them to set up political action committees (PACs) to support sympathetic politicians. The PACs transformed political fund-raising, especially since the unions' political power seemed to be fading. By 1978 a top advisor to Carter mourned, "We have a fragmented, Balkanized society," with each special economic group "interested in only one domestic program"—its own.

More than anything else, however, the nagging problem of inflation limited Carter's freedom of action. To fight inflation, he believed, it was essential to reduce the federal budget deficit. But since the President also wanted to increase spending for national defense, he recommended a moderate reduction in social welfare expenditures. Carter's proposed budget for 1980, therefore, elicited anger from liberals and cautious approval from conservatives. The Black Congressional Caucus termed the budget "immoral and unjust," while a Bank of America spokesperson thought "it catches the right mood."

In January 1979 Carter's chief domestic policy advisor, Stuart E. Eizenstat, explained that the President's scaled-down domestic agenda reflected the "new realities" of the late 1970s. Those "unhappier realities" included "high inflation coupled with high unemployment, and widespread public cynicism toward the government." Such realities—combined with Carter's own managerial disposition, the erosion of presidential power, and the growing influence of interest groups—constituted the legacy of the 1970s, a legacy that would shape politics in the 1980s.

# CARTER'S FOREIGN POLICY: CONFUSION . . .

Americans had to deal not only with a fragmented society at home, but also with a fragmented world abroad. They faced complex problems in the newly emerging nations that had little to do with Soviet communism. Dealing with these problems frustrated Americans, who prefer their foreign relations to resemble a baseball game—to be of short duration with clearly identified opponents and a definite winner. Foreign policy refuses to be so simple.

Jimmy Carter came to power with little knowledge of foreign policy. His colorful younger brother, Billy, was astonished at Jimmy's ambition to lead the world's greatest power: "My mother joined the Peace Corps when she was 70, my sister Gloria is a motorcycle racer, my other sister, Ruth, is a Holy Roller preacher, and my brother thinks he is going to be President of the United States! I'm the only normal one in the family."

The new President tried to make up for his inexperience by appointing Cyrus Vance (a New York lawyer) as secretary of state, and Zbigniew Brzezinski (a Columbia University expert on Eastern Europe) as National Security Council advisor. Both had extensive experience in foreign policy. But they offered Carter conflicting advice. Vance hoped to be patient and conciliatory in strengthening relations with Russia. He wanted to deal with crises in the newly emerging nations not by blaming them on the Soviets, but by treating them as problems of new, ambitious nationalisms. Vance received support from Andrew Young, Carter's ambassador to the United Nations. A well-known black leader, Young believed that African problems, for example, should be dealt with by Africans; neither of the two superpowers had the understanding or power to control such affairs. (Young's approach helped resolve several African crises, especially in removing obstacles so the former British colony of Rhodesia could become the black-governed nation of Zimbabwe.) Brzezinski, on the other hand, viewed the world largely in terms of the U.S.-Soviet conflict. He saw a grim Russian face behind upheavals in third world countries, and increasingly urged a tough military line toward the Soviets.

Carter had to choose between the Vance-Young and Brzezinski views. The President was not well equipped for the task. Trained as an engineer at the U.S. Naval Academy, he remained, in the words of close observers, "an engineer, a manager," and a "problem-solving President" who might know "how every single engine or pump works," but had little sense of the larger structure within which machinery had to function. He had no consistent larger view of world affairs. In 1973 Brzezinski had brought Carter into the new Trilateral Commission for an education in foreign policy. Brzezinski and New York banker David Rockefeller had formed the commission to coordinate policies among Japan, the United States, and Western Europe so these industrial powers could deal with the sudden economic and third world crises of the 1970s. But the trilateral approach proved disappointing. Even Brzezinski disgustedly wrote in 1976 that "neither Europe nor Japan is prepared to play a major role" in solving the crises. By 1980, indeed, the Western alliance would be in its worst shape since 1945.

The United States thus moved more and more on its own. Carter determined to restore its authority abroad (and reinvigorate Americans' faith in their own values at home) by sharply cutting the Vietnam-inflated military budget and emphasizing his support of human rights. Those rights were to include personal freedom from torture and imprisonment for political reasons. They also included access to food, shelter, medical care, and education, and the right to enjoy such liberties as free speech and assembly. Such rights, Carter declared, were "the soul of our foreign policy." He soon learned, however, that he could not practice what he preached. Some of the world's worst violators of human rights (South Korea, Argentina, Guatemala, Nicaragua, Iran) were also important allies of the United States. He therefore did little to pressure the Korean or Iranian governments. When he criticized Argentina and Guatemala, they refused to cooperate any longer with U.S. military programs. The President's policy was both needed and decent (and helped return Argentina to democratic government in 1984), but even his advisors admitted that the policy had never been thought through, never reconciled with the major security needs of U.S. foreign policy.

Carter's relations with the Soviets meanwhile steadily declined. When he publicly attacked Moscow's human rights violations and welcomed Soviet dissidents to the White House (a welcome that Nixon and Kissinger had refused to give), Brezhnev delivered an icy political blast. Talks aimed at slowing the runaway arms race nearly collapsed. In October 1977 one breakthrough did occur when the two superpowers agreed to work for peace in the explosive Middle East. But the possibility of a larger Russian presence frightened both Egyptians and Israelis. A firestorm of objection from U.S. friends of Israel forced Carter (in Brzezinski's words) to "walk away" from the deal. Brezhnev was outraged, but Carter managed to score a major victory in 1979 when he mediated the Camp David accords between Egypt's leader, Anwar Sadat, and Israeli Prime Minister Menachem Begin. The agreement, reached at the presidential retreat in the Maryland mountains, marked the first peace treaty between Egypt and Israel after three decades of war. Begin also pledged to return the large Sinai area to Egypt that Israel had seized in 1967. No deal, however, could be reached on the festering question of other areas claimed by both Israeli settlers and hundreds of thousands of Palestinians.

The Soviets perhaps became most disturbed when the United States announced in 1978 that it would begin formal diplomatic relations with China. The Chinese needed U.S. arms to protect the long border they shared with the Soviet Union and claimed they wanted $100 billion of outside investment to develop their economy in the 1980s. Carter was happy to open China to U.S. investors, but he severely limited any military aid out of fear of possible Russian reaction. Superpower relations further soured during 1978–79 when Soviet officials and thirteen thousand Cuban troops appeared in Ethiopia to help that East African nation in a war begun by neighboring Somalia. The region was strategically located along the oil shipping lanes of the Middle East (see map, page 493). The United States consequently quickly sent aid to the Somalis.

Against this ominous background, Carter and Brezhnev met in Vienna in 1979 to negotiate SALT II (the second Strategic Arms Limitations Talks). Under the agreement, each side was to have no more than 2,400 nuclear missile launchers (with that number reduced to 2,250 in eighteen months). Not more than 1,320 of the launchers were to be "MIRVed"—that is, have as many as ten Multiple-Independent-Reentry-Vehicle nuclear bombs that could be separated in midflight and hit individual targets. U.S. critics claimed that SALT II favored the Russians, whose nuclear force was comprised of large, single-head missiles, and hurt the U.S. force, which depended more on MIRVs and other new-technology weapons. These critics vowed to kill the treaty when it came before the Senate for ratification.

Carter had not been effective in dealing with Congress. Since the early 1970s, moreover, the two legislative bodies had become fragmented. House and Senate leaders could no longer deliver votes for Carter as, for example, Senator Lyndon Johnson had delivered support for Eisenhower's policies in the 1950s. The Georgian had also spent much of his political capital in pushing through two treaties in 1978 that would give the Panama Canal to the Panamanians in the year 2000. The Panamanians had often rioted against the U.S.-built and -controlled Canal Zone, which had split their country since 1903. U.S. military officials worried that the waterway could not be protected against future rioting. The final treaties gave the North Americans special privileges (including the right to intervene militarily to keep the canal open). But led by conservative senators and former California Governor Ronald Reagan, opponents fought the pacts until the treaties were ratified with only a single extra vote needed for ratification in the Senate.

## . . . TO COLD WAR

As SALT II came before the Senate, a series of events suddenly erupted and—like machine guns—destroyed both Carter's presidency and his hope of thawing the cold war. The blasts occurred in Iran, Central America, and Afghanistan.

In late 1978 a revolution led by Moslem religious leaders undermined the Iranian government of Shah Riza Pahlevi. The shah was Washington's closest military ally in the Middle East. He had used his immense oil wealth to purchase billions of dollars in U.S. arms. But he had also tried to modernize his nation too rapidly. When conservative opposition appeared, especially among college-age Iranians as well as the Moslem leaders, the shah imprisoned and killed many of his critics. As the crisis grew, Carter's advisors again split: Vance wanted to talk with the shah's opposition, but Brzezinski considered even the use of U.S. troops to keep the shah in power. While Americans debated, the shah was toppled from his famous Peacock Throne in early 1979. Ayatollah Ruhollah Khomeini, the 80-year-old Moslem leader, took control.

More shocks quickly followed. The disruption of Iranian oil exports gave the Organization of Petroleum Exporting Countries (OPEC) (the organization of Arab and other oil producers) a chance to raise their prices by 50 percent. The price rise drove up inflation in the United States until it skyrocketed from the 7 percent annual increase of 1974–78 to more than 13 percent in 1979. Alarmed Americans watched 30 billion of their dollars flow to oil producers instead of being used to pay for higher food and housing costs. (A second cause of the disastrous U.S. trade balance was the $7 billion Americans illegally spent to import cocaine.)

Nor could Carter prevent the overthrow of another U.S. friend, Anastasio Somoza, the dictator of Nicaragua. The revolutionary Sandinista Front had been fighting Somoza since the early 1960s. Named after Augusto Sandino, the guerrilla fighter who forced U.S. Marines to stop occupying Nicaragua in 1933, the Sandinistas disliked and feared the United States. Carter (as had many Presidents before him) supported Somoza, but also pushed the dictator to pursue human rights principles. That policy undercut Somoza, whose authority increasingly depended on brutality. Carter finally tried to intervene so the Sandinistas could not gain power. When not a single Latin American nation would join Carter, his efforts failed and the Sandinistas marched into the capital, Managua, in July 1979. By 1980 the new government carried on most of its trade with the United States, but increasingly dealt with Castro's Cuba to obtain educational, medical, and military help. The revolution, moreover, threatened to spread to help left-wing forces in neighboring El Salvador, but the rebels' "final offensive" was turned back by the U.S.-supplied Salvadoran army in January 1981.

The setbacks in Iran and Nicaragua were disasters for Carter. Worse, however, lay ahead. In October 1979 he decided to allow the shah, suffering from cancer, to enter the United States for treatment. Infuriated Iranian mobs, encouraged by Khomeini, stormed the U.S. Embassy in Teheran on November 4 and seized sixty-nine American diplomats. Fifty-three of them were finally held as hostages; the rest were freed. The crisis dominated American television screens (the popular American Broadcasting Company's late-night news show "Nightline" was born during the crisis). Unable to deal with Khomeini, Carter watched his own popularity sink to new lows. In April 1980, as the presidential election campaign intensified, Carter ordered a secret rescue mission. But several of the U.S. helicopters crashed in an Iranian desert and killed eight American soldiers. Vance resigned after the President overruled his opposition to the mission. (Only after months of secret talks and U.S. economic pressure were the hostages released in January 1981.)

As Americans were preoccupied with the Iranian crisis, the Soviet Union invaded its southern neighbor Afghanistan in late December 1979. It marked the first time in the post-1945 era that Russian troops had launched an invasion outside their East European bloc. Afghanistan was a strategic gateway for both the Soviets' southern borders and the Middle East oilfields. During 1978–79 the pro-Russian Afghan government had become wobbly. Moscow officials also feared that Khomeini's Moslem fanaticism (in which communism was hated as much as U.S. capitalism) would spread over Afghanistan. They therefore dispatched eighty thousand troops to take control. Poorly armed Afghan guerrillas fought back with surprising effectiveness and tied down the Soviets in a long, bloody struggle. A stunned Carter, who in 1977 had declared his policies would not be shaped by "the inordinate fear of Communism," had become consumed by the fear. He sent arms to the Afghan rebels and then stopped shipment of 17 million tons of U.S. wheat promised to the Soviets. The Russians badly needed the grain because of their own failed agricultural system, but they quickly obtained supplies elsewhere, especially from Argentina and Canada. American farmers bitterly attacked Carter for the loss of the Russian market, and George Shultz (Nixon's former secretary of the treasury) condemned the President for turning vital trade "on and off like a light switch."

The President then dramatically announced a "Carter Doctrine": the United States would, if necessary, unilaterally use force to prevent any further Russian encroachment in the Middle East–Southwest Asia region. He backed up his doctrine with a military budget (which he had promised in 1976 to cut by $5 billion) that now rose $20 billion to a record peacetime high of $106 billion. Carter thus helped prepare the way for Ronald Reagan's massive military buildup. But the Georgian also prepared the way for Reagan's 1980 election triumph with his ineffectual responses to the crisis of SALT II (which died without a vote in the Senate), economic problems, the overthrow of Somoza and the shah, and the Soviet invasion of Afghanistan. *Business Week* caught the nation's mood: "The country is entering the decade of the 1980s as a wounded, demoralized colossus."

## POLITICAL EVANGELICALISM AND THE MORAL MAJORITY

American politics in the 1980s were influenced not only by these reversals but also by the impact of evangelical Christianity. The word *evangelical* derives from the Greek for "good news," and evangelicals devoted themselves to spreading the good news that Jesus had come into the world to save sinners and make them whole. Evangelicals emphasized the responsibility of each person, believing an individual could be redeemed only by being "born again"—that is, confessing one's sins, accepting a resurrected Jesus as a "personal savior," and leading a new life. Jimmy Carter was born again after listening to a sermon titled "If you were arrested for being a Christian, would there be any evidence to convict you?" Although he was already a Sunday school teacher and deacon in his church, Carter decided that "if arrested and charged with being a committed follower of God, I could probably talk my way out of it! It was a sobering thought." Carter then began to search "for a closer relationship with God," to devote himself to religious concerns, and to witness publicly. His election gave born-again Christianity wider visibility and recognition.

George Gallup, Jr., termed 1976 "the year of the evangelical," and the late 1970s and early 1980s saw a burgeoning of the movement. Books by evangelical authors became best-sellers. Billy Graham's *How To Be Born Again* (1977) had an initial printing of eight hundred thousand copies, the largest for any hardcover

Jimmy Carter with a gift from the
American Bible Society, 1977.
*(BETTMANN.)*

book ever published, and another five hundred thousand copies were soon
needed. Widely sold in supermarkets and drugstores, evangelical books
became so successful that, as one critic noted, "customers could find books on
Christian weight loss and Christian money management." In many large cities,
there were "Christian Yellow Pages," directories that would sell space only to
an advertiser who "accepts Jesus Christ as . . . personal Lord and Savior and
acknowledges Jesus as the Son of God." One million schoolchildren were soon
attending five thousand Christian elementary and high schools where subjects
were taught from an evangelical perspective. In Christian nightclubs patrons
could order grape juice cocktails and listen to gospel songs. By 1978 1,300 radio
stations—one out of every seven in the country—were Christian owned and
operated, and one new such station was being added every week.

But television, not radio, became the chief medium for spreading the new
message. Pat Robertson's "700 Club," aired on his Christian Broadcasting
Network from Virginia Beach, Virginia, was a pioneering venture. Viewers
could phone an operator who would take a pledge and then pray with the
caller. One of the regulars on the show, Jim Bakker, eventually decided to create his own program—the PTL, or Praise the Lord, Club. Bakker's program,
televised from Charlotte, North Carolina, combined sermons, inspirational
conversation, faith healing, speaking in tongues, and entertainment. Bakker

made the PTL Club the most-viewed daily television program in the world, one observer noted, by adopting a format used on secular nighttime talk shows: "the major star with an opening monologue, a co-host to feed the star straight lines, guest celebrities giving brief but fervent testimonials, guest singers, or instrumentalists." The new "electronic church" and the "televangelists" had many critics in the mainstream religious community, but by 1978 Robertson was receiving $30 million a year in contributions, and Bakker, at $25 million, was not far behind.

The new evangelicalism was characterized by social conservatism and political activism. Born-again Christians attacked "secular humanism," by which they meant the view that all truths are relative, all moral values situational, and all ethical judgments tentative. They supported the "right to life" movement and condemned legalized abortion. They opposed the Equal Rights Amendment (ERA) and other feminist demands. They attacked court decisions that they claimed legalized pornography. They blasted the gay rights movement on the grounds that homosexuality is sinful. Just as many of their demands focused on the family and sex roles, so others focused on the public schools. Evangelicals favored reintroducing prayer, teaching "scientific creationism" as an alternative to the theory of evolution, and imposing stricter discipline on students. To a considerable extent, they attributed permissiveness and moral decay to the behavior of politicians who were insensitive to family values.

It was, then, only a short step to full-fledged political action. Many recognized the truly awesome potential of the movement, with its captive television audience and appealingly simple message, but none more clearly than the Reverend Jerry Falwell. Minister for many years of the Thomas Road Baptist Church in Lynchburg, Virginia, Falwell had taken a congregation of thirty-five souls (who met "in the former plant of the Donald Duck Bottling Company") and built it into one of seventeen thousand. He had his own television program, "The Old Time Gospel Hour," which raised more money each year than Robertson's or Bakker's. In July 1979 Falwell founded the "Moral Majority" and within two years was claiming 4 million members. Combining old-time religion with the most sophisticated computer technology, Falwell not only targeted potential contributors but also evaluated candidates for office on the basis of their votes on such issues as the ERA, federal funding for abortions, and school prayer. In 1980, after developing a "hit list" of liberal senators and congressmen, the Moral Majority mailed more than one billion pieces of literature to selected voters. "What can you do from the pulpit?" Falwell asked. "You can register people to vote. You can explain the issues to them. And you can endorse candidates, right there in church on Sunday morning."

In 1980 there was never any doubt which presidential candidate Falwell or most other evangelicals would endorse. Democrat Jimmy Carter, Republican Ronald Reagan, and independent John Anderson were all born-again Christians (as was one voter in every three), but Carter's brand of evangelicalism, and Anderson's, was distinctly too liberal for the Moral Majority. Richard Viguerie, one of the new breed of conservative fund raisers, wrote in *The New*

Reverend Jerry Falwell, 1984. *(Art Stein/Photo Researchers.)*

*Right: We're Ready to Lead* (1980): "Not only has the Carter administration ignored the born-again Christians, it has actively and aggressively sought to hurt the Christian movement in America." Ronald Reagan said that he deplored the "wave of humanism and hedonism in the land. I think there is a hunger in this land for a spiritual revival, a return to a belief in moral absolutes." He was talking Jerry Falwell's language. As the Republicans looked for a vice-presidential candidate in 1980 Falwell let it be known he would support Reagan "even if he has the devil running with him." To consolidate his hold on the religious right, Reagan appointed Reverend Bob Billings, the first executive director of the Moral Majority, as his campaign's religious advisor.

Evangelicals were fond of quoting a verse from the Book of Proverbs: "Righteousness exalteth a nation; but sin is a reproach to any people." Righteousness and sin, however, could be defined in different ways. Evangelicalism could be, and for a minority of believers was, hospitable to ideals of reform, social justice, and disarmament. There were born-again Christians who asserted that Scripture "is clearly and emphatically on the side of the poor, the exploited and the victimized," who spoke out against nuclear proliferation and pledged themselves "to non-cooperation with our country's preparation for nuclear war. On all levels—research, development, testing, production, deployment, and actual use of nuclear weapons—we commit ourselves to resist in the name of Jesus Christ." Yet as the Reagan era dawned, the majority of evangelicals had lined up solidly behind a conservative social agenda and a President committed to cutting social welfare expenditures and building up the military. In the 1980 election, Ronald Reagan received 51 percent of the popular vote, but 63 percent of the votes of white born-again Christians.

## THE REAGAN REDIRECTION

The contours of Reagan's victory were also shaped by the large number of eligible voters who did not bother to vote. The turnout—52 percent—was the lowest in a presidential election since 1948. As a group, those who actually voted were older, whiter, and wealthier than the eligible voters, since young, black, and poor people have the lowest turnout rates. This worked to Reagan's advantage. He was supported by 55 percent of voters who were 45 years or older, by 55 percent of voters who were white, and by 63 percent of voters earning over $50,000 a year. Carter did well but not as well as necessary among traditional Democrats. Trade-union households, for example, gave him only a 3-point margin over Reagan compared with a 20-point margin over Ford four years earlier. Although polling experts noted that the election represented "a strong call for moderate change," the outcome was widely construed as a mandate for conservatism because of Reagan's electoral college margin (489 to 49) and his party's congressional gains. Republicans took control of the Senate for the first time since 1954.

An avowed conservative, Ronald Reagan for much of his life had been a staunch liberal. In 1932, at the age of 21, he had supported Franklin D. Roosevelt, and he remained a Democrat, actively involved in liberal causes, through the 1940s. Reagan described himself then as a "very emotional New Dealer" and a "near hopeless, hemophilic liberal." But by 1947 he feared that Communists were attempting to infiltrate the motion picture industry and that liberals were ignoring the danger. "Light was dawning in some obscure region of my head," Reagan wrote in his autobiography, *Where's The Rest of Me?* (1965). He began to move to the right, a move sharply accelerated by his marriage in 1952 to Nancy Davis, herself a dedicated conservative. During the 1950s and 1960s, as a popular speaker for General Electric, Reagan asserted that the welfare state was "the most dangerous enemy ever known to man," the progressive income tax was an invention of Karl Marx, and unemployment insurance often amounted to "a prepaid vacation plan for freeloaders." In 1962 he formally changed his party affiliation, and in 1964 endorsed the candidacy of Barry

Ronald Reagan in *Law and Order,* 1953. *(Courtesy of Ludlow Sales Corporation.)*

Goldwater who, he later said, "was possibly a little ahead of his time." Elected governor of California in 1966 and then reelected in a landslide, he sought the Republican presidential nomination in 1968 and 1976, and finally obtained it in 1980.

Reagan's critics, before his election and after, disparaged his abilities by poking fun at his alleged shallowness, superficiality, and inattention to detail. "You can wade through Ronald Reagan's deepest thoughts and not get your ankles wet," said one pundit; Reagan was "the President with the seven-minute attention span," said another. Indeed, Reagan was known on occasion to confuse Afghanistan with Pakistan, to forget the name of a Cabinet member, or to watch movies instead of reading briefing papers. Yet it was all too easy to underrate his political ability. Reagan understood that the public cared less whether a President had all the facts at his fingertips than whether an administration had an overall sense of direction. He used television more successfully than any of his predecessors to convey his message to the public. He recognized the importance of finding talented administrators and of delegating authority to them. He knew which voters had elected him, and what he had to do (and what he did not have to do) to be reelected.

In 1980 the presidency was widely thought to have entered its "postimperial" phase: Gerald Ford claimed it was "imperiled, not imperial," and Walter Mondale called it "the fire hydrant of the nation." Ronald Reagan set out to refurbish executive authority, and to a considerable extent he succeeded by reasserting influence over Congress, centralizing the budget-making process, bringing the bureaucracy to heel, and, according to pollsters, persuading most Americans that he had "strong qualities of leadership." The expansion of executive authority, however, was designed to curtail rather than expand the scope of government. Federal programs to combat poverty, to advance civil rights, to protect the environment, and to safeguard consumers were so well entrenched after years of steady growth that it would take an activist in the White House to trim them back. As an Urban Institute study put it, "Reagan found it necessary to adopt the approach of Wilson and Roosevelt in order to pursue the objectives of Coolidge and Harding."

In truth, Reagan endeavored to reverse the direction social policy had taken ever since the New Deal, but especially since the Great Society. Liberals, who thought they had been unhappy with Jimmy Carter as President, discovered in 1981 the true meaning of the word "unhappiness." The Reagan administration announced that it was prepared to slice federal welfare spending and adopt "supply-side economics." Supply siders held that the government could stimulate business growth, create new jobs, and ensure widespread prosperity by giving everyone greater incentives—by rewarding entrepreneurial risk taking, by increasing opportunities for profit making, by enlarging take-home pay—in short, by expanding the supply of goods, which would then create a greater demand for them. The centerpiece of supply-side economics was, from a political standpoint, almost too good to be true: a whopping tax cut.

In 1981 the administration won Congressional approval for just such a massive tax cut, providing for across-the-board reductions of 5 percent the first year and an additional 10 percent in each of the succeeding two years. The measure was undeniably popular. In a nationwide television address, Reagan asked viewers: "Are you entitled to the fruits of your own labor or does government have some presumptive right to spend and spend and spend?" Public pressure on Congress became irresistible, and as it appeared a bill would, in fact, pass, a multitude of interests clamored for special breaks: accelerated depreciation, lucrative write-offs, near-elimination of the estate tax. An exasperated

Democrat finally announced, "the auction is over." But Reagan's own budget chief, David Stockman, offered the most candid description of what had happened: "Do you realize the greed that came to the forefront? The hogs were really feeding. The greed level, the level of opportunism, just got out of control."

Tax reduction benefited all taxpayers, but not equally. The Treasury Department's estimates showed that, over the three years, 9 percent of the total relief would go to those earning under $15,000, and 36 percent to those earning more than $50,000. There were 162,000 families with incomes of $200,000 or more; their taxes were cut by $3.6 billion. There were 31,700,000 families who earned $15,000 or less; they realized a saving of $2.9 billion. The administration's overall policies reflected a similar distribution of benefits. Real disposable family income (adjusted for taxes and inflation) fell in 1981 and 1982, then rose in 1983 and 1984 until it was, on the average, 3.5 percent higher than in 1980. But averages could be deceiving. Over the four-year period, the real disposable income of the poorest fifth of American families declined by nearly 8 percent, while that of the middle fifth rose by about 1 percent and that of the wealthiest fifth jumped by almost 9 percent. The Reagan administration presided over a major redistribution of income away from the poor and toward the rich.

Many economists had predicted that a tax cut coupled with increased outlays for defense would produce record deficits. The predictions soon came true. As military spending soared (from $133 billion to $246 billion) and annual budget deficits approached $200 billion, the total national debt, which stood at $800 billion in fiscal year 1981, grew to $1.5 trillion in fiscal year 1985. Nearly as much debt accumulated in Reagan's first administration as in the nation's entire history prior to his election. As the administration understood, such deficits threatened to produce sky-high interest rates and eventually retard economic growth. As some scholars pointed out, however, those deficits were also "a means of advancing the Reagan revolution." A colossal national debt—by 1985 one dollar in every seven spent by the federal government went to pay interest on that debt—created permanent pressure to reduce federal spending for social programs.

One of Reagan's purposes was to cut taxes even if it meant creating deficits; a second was to curb inflation even if it meant temporarily increasing unemployment. The inflation rate in 1980, more than 12 percent, had proven politically fatal for Jimmy Carter. Like Carter, Reagan knew that the surest way to reduce inflation was to permit unemployment to rise, but unlike his predecessor he was willing to do it. The unemployment rate was about 7 percent in November 1980; two years later it was 10.8 percent, the highest level since the late 1930s. Not only were 12 million people jobless, but 1.6 million were too discouraged to look for work and 6.5 million were working fewer hours a week than they wanted. "The current recession," Reagan's top economic advisor at the time commented, "is an unavoidable cost of slowing inflation." The inflation rate indeed fell to about 4 percent in 1983 and 1984, and as the recession ended the unemployment rate returned to about the level it had been under Carter.

A third objective of the Reagan administration was to cut welfare spending even if it increased the number of people who lived in poverty. The President proposed reducing social programs by a considerably larger margin than Congress would approve. He asked Congress to appropriate $75 billion less for these purposes over a four-year period than would have been spent at prevailing levels; this would have amounted to a 17 percent reduction. Congress grudgingly granted a little more than half of what the President wanted, agreeing to a cutback of $38 billion, or 9 percent. Significantly, the administration requested the most draconian reductions—totaling 28 percent—in programs that directly benefited the poor, such as food stamps, Aid to Families with Dependent Children, school lunches, housing assistance, and Medicaid. The administration sought only an 11 percent reduction in social security, Medicare, and unemployment insurance, many of whose beneficiaries were not poor. When Ronald Reagan took office, 11.7 percent of Americans had incomes that placed them below the poverty level. The figure had remained steady for about a decade, but by 1982 it had risen to 15 percent, the highest since Lyndon Johnson had launched the war on poverty.

## THE POOR AND THE YUPPIES

The antipoverty crusade had been inspired, in part, by the appearance of Michael Harrington's *The Other America* in 1962. Harrington's *The New American Poverty*, published in 1984, met a chillier response. Harrington pointed out that government social programs primarily aided those who were not poor rather than those who were. The chief beneficiaries were not welfare recipients but rather the aged, who were entitled to Medicare and social security. "The welfare state in the United States is primarily for people over sixty-five," he wrote, "most of whom are not now, and for a long time have not been, poor." Harrington described the new poor—the "uprooted" and the "superfluous," the homeless men and women sleeping in doorways, the deinstitutionalized mental patients roaming the streets aimlessly, the black teenagers facing unemployment, the illegal aliens toiling in sweatshops, and the Native Americans, "the poorest of the poor in a land that was once their own." Harrington called for expanded welfare services, for a full-employment program, and for "a new campaign for social decency."

Harrington also said that it was the young in particular who "need a vision that transcends the mindless hedonism of so much of contemporary life." But according to *Newsweek* magazine, which dubbed 1984 "the year of the Yuppie," a new class of young urban professionals could not get enough of hedonism, mindless or otherwise. Yuppies were characterized by their age (which ranged from the early twenties to late thirties), their income (which began at $40,000 but seemed not to have an upper limit), and their occupations (which cut across the professional and managerial worlds), but especially by their concern with "lives, careers, apartments and dinners," by their willingness to "define themselves by what they own." They joined expensive fitness

Homeless woman, New York City, 1979. *(John Veltri/Photo Researchers.)*

clubs, exchanged business cards at "networking" parties, shopped at gourmet food stores, wore designer-label clothing, and lived, when they could, in newly "gentrified" districts. *Newsweek* concluded that millions of Yuppies, who were generally conservative on economic issues but liberal on social issues, voted for Ronald Reagan in 1984. One who did not, a 25-year-old woman who was an advertising executive, liked Reagan "for financial reasons" but disliked his stand on abortion. "I knew Reagan would win easily anyway," she explained. "I had the best of both worlds. I could vote my conscience and still come out ahead financially."

In 1984 Reagan not only captured a large share of the Yuppie vote but also consolidated his hold on a very different constituency: evangelical Christians.

The President, who effected virtually all of his economic policies, instituted virtually none of the Moral Majority's social program. Reagan first deferred congressional consideration of antiabortion and school prayer proposals so his tax and budget policies could be enacted. By 1983, when the administration got around to supporting the measures, it could not muster the necessary support in Congress. In March 1984 the Senate turned down a constitutional amendment permitting voluntary individual or group prayer in the public schools. The vote, fifty-six in favor and forty-four opposed, fell eleven short of the needed two-thirds majority; of the opponents, twenty-six were Democrats and eighteen were Republicans. One Reagan aide, asked what the administration planned to give the Moral Majority, replied "symbolism." The President granted a White House audience to right-to-life marchers, supported tax-exempt status for Christian schools that barred blacks, pronounced 1983 "the year of the Bible," and endorsed the entire evangelical platform. He told the National Religious Broadcasters early in 1984 that "the spectacular growth of C.B.N. and P.T.L." proved that "so many millions hunger for your product: God's good news." In the election, exit polls indicated, Reagan was the choice of 80 percent of white born-again Christians.

## AFFIRMATIVE ACTION AND UNDOCUMENTED ALIENS: DILEMMAS OF RACE AND ETHNICITY

The problems of "affirmative action" and "undocumented aliens," which plagued Ronald Reagan's administration as they had Jimmy Carter's, were in a sense legacies of the 1960s. The Civil Rights Act of 1964 had barred discrimination on the basis of race or sex, and the Equal Employment Opportunity Commission thereafter instituted policies to ensure that all federal contractors, city and state governments, and colleges and universities established goals or timetables for the hiring and promotion of members of minority groups. The purpose was to remedy years of discrimination by acting affirmatively in behalf of blacks, women, Hispanics, Native Americans, and Asian Americans, but the method sparked bitter controversy. Similarly, the Immigration Reform Act of 1965 had abolished the discriminatory policy of admitting people on the basis of their national origins, but established, for the first time, numerical limits on immigration from nations in the Western Hemisphere. As population pressures mounted in Mexico, Central America, and South America, millions of illegal or undocumented aliens entered the United States. Their presence posed a dilemma that was as much political as it was legal.

Carter approached the problem of affirmative action cautiously because the issue was one on which Democrats sharply disagreed. Civil rights organizations viewed all-out support for affirmative action, including the setting of "quotas," as a litmus-paper test of an administration's commitment to racial justice, but such quotas offended other important elements in the Democratic coalition, especially labor unions, whose members felt threatened, and Jews, who historically had been victimized by quotas. These differences were evident

Developed Nations in the 1990s

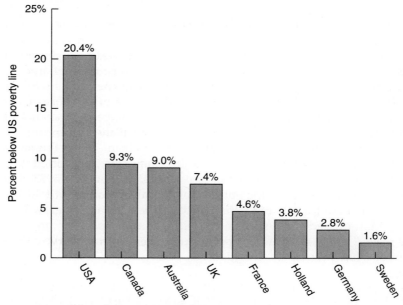

Children are those under 18 years of age.

Children in poverty. *(Urie Bronfenbrenner, et al.,* The State of Americans *[New York: Free Press, 1996], p. 148.)*

in 1977 when the administration decided to file a brief in the case of Allan Bakke, who was challenging "race conscious" admissions policies at the medical school of the University of California at Davis. The Department of Justice first circulated a brief which defended the principle of affirmative action but opposed actual quotas. When civil rights leaders and the Black Congressional Caucus protested strongly, Carter came to believe that submitting the brief would be politically disastrous. So the department prepared a new statement which omitted any condemnation of quotas, thereby mollifying some groups while antagonizing others.

In June 1978 the Supreme Court handed down its ruling in the Bakke case. Bakke, having twice been turned down by the medical school at Davis, in 1973 and 1974, had appealed to the courts to gain admission. The school then reserved sixteen of one hundred places in its entering class for "disadvantaged students"—blacks, Chicanos, Native Americans, and Asian Americans. Bakke had a better academic record than those admitted under this minority quota, and so he claimed he had been denied the equal protection of the law. By a 5-to-4 margin the Supreme Court ruled in his favor: The use of an "explicit racial classification," in situations where no former discriminatory behavior had been demonstrated, violated the Fourteenth Amendment. At the same time, however, the Court approved, by another 5-to-4 vote, programs that used race as "simply one element in the admissions process." Justifying such "race-conscious programs," Justice Harry A. Blackmun said: "In order to get beyond racism, we must first take account of race."

The Reagan administration took a much dimmer view of affirmative action programs than had the Carter administration. Reagan called quotas "reverse discrimination," a "federal distortion of the principle of equal rights." The assistant attorney general for civil rights in the Department of Justice, William Bradford Reynolds, echoed these sentiments. The government would not "in any respect support the use of quotas or any other numerical or statistical formulas," Reynolds said, for they subverted "the color-blind ideal of equal opportunity for all." When the Detroit and the New Orleans police departments established quotas for promoting blacks, the administration interceded to overturn the agreements, which had been entered into voluntarily. This opposition to affirmative action had much to do with the widespread perception among blacks that the Reagan administration was hostile to their best interests. Blacks, who had given Reagan only 11 percent of their votes in 1980, gave him a minuscule 9 percent in 1984.

The Supreme Court also began to edge away even from its very limited endorsement of affirmative action in the Bakke case. In 1980 the Memphis fire department had agreed to fill one-half of all new vacancies with blacks (and upgrade many black employees), but in 1981, city agencies, facing financial difficulties, were forced to cut back. To preserve seniority rights, the fire department began laying off the recently hired blacks. Black firefighters obtained an injunction to stop the department from implementing this policy, the union fought back, and the Supreme Court, in June 1984, ruled that the injunction had been improperly granted. A six-member majority declared that it was not permissible to give preferential treatment to black firefighters who had not themselves been discriminated against. The Court declared that Congress had not intended, in passing the Civil Rights Act of 1964, to fix racial quotas. The majority included President Reagan's appointee, Sandra Day O'Connor. The prospect of additional Supreme Court appointments in the President's second term gave little comfort to those who supported what the minority in the Memphis case called "race-conscious remedies to correct patterns of discrimination."

Patterns of discrimination—less familiar, perhaps, but no easier to erase—also affected millions of undocumented aliens. Calculations of the number of people who were, by the mid-1980s, living and working in the United States illegally varied widely, but the lowest figure anyone cited was 4 million, and some observers thought 6 million or 8 million was a better estimate. The Census Bureau indicated that 45 percent of the undocumented aliens came from Mexico, 17 percent from countries of Central and South America, and the remainder from Asia, Africa, and Europe. Most of the illegal aliens worked at hot, dirty jobs for minimum, or below-minimum wages, doing the kind of work for the kind of pay that American citizens would not do. The states with large numbers of illegal aliens—California, Texas, Florida—were those with low rates of unemployment. Although undocumented aliens paid social security taxes, income taxes, and sales taxes, they were not eligible for food stamps, Aid

Surveillance of the Mexican border through an infrared sighting device, 1983.
*(J. P. Laffont/Sygma.)*

to Families with Dependent Children, Medicaid, or school lunch programs. They often did not make use of social services for which they were eligible for fear of being discovered and deported.

As public awareness of the problem increased, Carter and Reagan appointed special commissions to devise a solution. The commissions made three recommendations: "amnesty" for illegal aliens who had resided continuously in the United States for a certain period; stiff sanctions for employers who knowingly hired illegal aliens; and a system of national identification to permit employers to distinguish between citizens and others. These proposals formed the basis of the Simpson-Mazzoli bill, a bipartisan measure, which was passed by the Senate in 1982 and 1983, and then by the House in 1984. The bill then went to a conference committee, but the conferees were unable to agree on an acceptable version. The measure died a silent death, deserted by conservatives who feared it was too costly and liberals who feared it would constitute a "major step toward a police state."

Not until 1986 would Congress enact a modified version of Simpson-Mazzoli which provided amnesty to undocumented aliens who could prove they had entered the United States before 1982, and penalized employers who hired illegal aliens. In the meantime, one of the most crucial rights enjoyed by illegal aliens—the right of their children to attend the public schools—was preserved by the narrowest of margins. In June 1982, by a vote of 5 to 4, the Supreme Court declared that a Texas ordinance that denied funding for the education of children who had entered the country illegally violated the equal protection clause of the Fourteenth Amendment. To deny these children a public education, the majority said, deprived them of "the ability to live within the structure of our civic institutions" and "does not comport with fundamental conceptions of justice." Chief Justice Warren Burger wrote the minority opinion

# THE COMPUTER REVOLUTION—AFTER FOUR CENTURIES OF EVOLUTION

*Time* magazine annually chooses a "Man of the Year" or "Woman of the Year." Churchill, Hitler, Queen Elizabeth II of England, and the astronauts have been acclaimed. In 1983, however, an object—the computer—won for the first time. As *Time* explained, the computer had revolutionized American life for it "can send letters at the speed of light, diagnose a sick poodle . . . , test recipes for beer," and be used by the rock group Earth, Wind, and Fire to explode smoke bombs at precise moments in concert. A California high school programmed a computer that at 5:15 P.M. each day phoned the parents of absent students. The truancy rate in the school dropped 64 percent in one year.

The machine's effect on the exchange of information—especially the printing of newspapers, the publishing of books, and the writing of college term papers and laboratory reports—had no parallel since Gutenberg first used movable type in Germany during the 1450s. More than half of all employed Ameri-

cans in the 1980s made their living not by making products but by exchanging information. This rapidly growing part of the work force depended on computers whose disk memory was small enough to be carried in a handbag but contained the equivalent of more than one thousand books. With lightning speed, the machine carried out its two basic functions: computing numbers and storing and retrieving information.

Most Americans encountered the computer in the 1970s and 1980s, but some of its basic principles date back to the seventeenth century when the great French philosopher Pascal devised the first machine that could multiply as well as add. At about the same time a mathematician, John Napier, invented logarithms that allowed complex figures to be adapted easily to computing machines. The next key step occurred two centuries later when an eccentric British inventor, Charles Babbage (who also devised the speedometer) spent forty years building a huge, incredibly

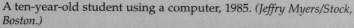

A ten-year-old student using a computer, 1985. *(Jeffry Myers/Stock, Boston.)*

complex machine that contained nearly all the main features of the modern computer. It could even be programmed.

Americans then stepped in to make the Pascal-Babbage inventions more practical. Herman Hollerith was an engineer working with the U.S. census of 1880 when he borrowed Babbage's device of putting information on punched cards and then retrieving it with spring-loaded pins that corresponded to the holes of the cards holding the information wanted. The 1890 census results were consequently tabulated in one-third the time spent on the 1880 survey. Hollerith quit government to build a fortune with his now-famous punch-card system. In this first great era of American corporate development and mergers (the 1890s through the 1920s), Hollerith's Tabulating Machine Company became in 1924 International Business Machines (IBM).

Within a decade, IBM dominated the business machine industry. Over the next sixty years it became the most glamorous and successful of American corporations. But IBM's initial successes came from fast-talking salesmen, not technical breakthroughs. Important

scientific innovations began in the 1940s and were spurred on by U.S. military needs in the early cold war years. Scientists at the University of Pennsylvania built the ENIAC, whose thirty tons, 18,000 vacuum tubes, and 6,000 switches performed 5,000 computations a second to target artillery fire. Sperry-Rand Corporation's UNIVAC of 1951 first used modern programming, including magnetic tapes instead of punched cards. UNIVAC helped make computers famous by accurately predicting Dwight Eisenhower's triumph in the 1952 presidential elections.

American scientists were now making breathtaking discoveries. In 1947 researchers at Bell Telephone Laboratories had developed the transistor. This device used semiconducting materials (silicon, for example) to control electrical currents, and it did so more rapidly, cheaply, and with cooler temperatures than could vacuum tubes. Within a decade transistors were being printed on silicon pieces to become "microchips," or integrated circuits for computers. In the early 1970s engineers succeeded in putting the machine's entire processing unit on a single silicon chip. The chip

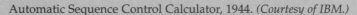

Automatic Sequence Control Calculator, 1944. *(Courtesy of IBM.)*

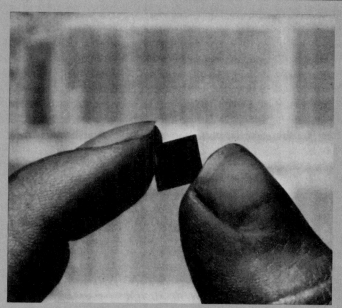

Microchip. *(Charles Feil/Stock, Boston.)*

thus became a "microprocessor." As one observer summarized the change in computer technology by the 1980s, "if the automobile business had developed like the computer business, a Rolls-Royce would now cost $2.75 and run 3 million miles on a gallon of gas."

In the early 1980s small, pioneering businesses, led by Apple and Hewlett-Packard—and joined later by IBM—developed desk-top-size computers that cost under $1,000 and could be used in the home or office. The American industrial revolution had thus come full circle. The single craftsman in his eighteenth-century cottage had become the centralized giant corporation producing iron, steel, and automobiles in the early 1900s. But now, as the twentieth century came to a close, the "electronic cottage," as futurist Alvin Toffler called it, created new possibilities for decentralization and individual enterprise.

and was joined by Justice O'Connor. Burger conceded that the Texas statute was wrongheaded, even harmful. But he warned: "The Constitution does not provide a cure for every social ill, nor does it bestow judges with a mandate to try to remedy every social problem."

## FEMINIZATION OF POVERTY, THE ERA, AND THE GENDER GAP

In the fifteen years since the rebirth of feminism, many changes had reshaped women's lives. In 1960, 35 percent of American women were in the labor force;

by 1980, over half were wage earners. In the past, only a minority of married women worked outside the home, and they tended to enter the job market after their children were grown. By 1980, three out of every five married women with school-age children had joined the work force, as had half of married women with children under six. Women's private lives had also changed. In 1960, under one-third of women aged 20 to 24 were unmarried; by 1980, half were unmarried. Prospects for motherhood shifted too. In 1960, just after the peak of the baby boom, a woman might expect to have 3.61 children; by 1980, she was having only 1.86, less than the number needed for a no-growth population rate. Finally, family life became less stable. Between 1960 and 1980, the divorce rate doubled. During the 1970s, the number of families headed by women steadily rose, as did the number of women living alone.

Whether women were finally "free to become themselves," as Betty Friedan had hoped, remained uncertain. Clearly, women's roles were in a state of flux. Some statistics suggested indisputable advances. By 1980, for instance, women constituted a majority of the college population; they entered prestigious professions and profitable vocations. Record numbers ran for public office, and many won, especially on the state and local levels. But other developments were less auspicious, such as the rapid rise of the female-headed family and the consequent "feminization of poverty." By 1980, two out of three female-headed families received child welfare, and two-thirds of the long-term poor were women. In some instances, the mounting rate of marital breakdown contributed to a drop in female living standards. According to one study of the early 1980s, divorce could mean "financial catastrophe" for women: it caused a 75 percent drop in ex-wives' income, while that of ex-husbands rose 42 percent. A massive rise in births to never-married mothers led even more directly to the feminization of poverty. During the 1970s, the number of families headed by unwed mothers increased more than 400 percent. Half of all illegitimate births were to teenagers.

Although the illegitimacy rate rose most rapidly among whites, it was highest among blacks. At the start of the 1980s, over half of all black children were born to unwed mothers. Almost half of black families with children were headed by women, compared with 21 percent of such families in 1960. The vast majority of black teenage mothers were unmarried. In 1983, the National Association for the Advancement of Colored People (NAACP) warned that "deterioration of the black family" threatened to negate all the social and economic advances blacks had made since 1960. The National Urban League blamed the deterioration on "steady attrition" in the numbers of black men who could support families. In 1984, almost 30 percent of black men 20 to 60 years old were unemployed or not seeking work. Since 1960, the league pointed out, the black divorce rate had increased by 400 percent, and by 1984, the rate at which black couples separated was five times as great as that among white couples.

The major issues of the women's movement reflected concern over women's family roles. During the late 1970s, an antifeminist backlash gained momentum. The "Stop ERA" campaign, led by Phyllis Schlafly, lobbied in state legislatures to prevent ERA ratification; the deadline had been extended by

Congress until June 1982. Schlafly argued that the ERA would cause "radical loosening of the legal bonds that keep the family together." The National Organization for Women (NOW) contended that the ratification battle was a referendum over sex discrimination. When the amendment failed, three votes short of ratification, Schlafly claimed that feminists had "shot themselves in the foot"; NOW vowed to continue the campaign. One factor that abetted the ERA's failure was the very difficulty of the amending process. Another was a high degree of ambivalence among women. Even among sympathizers, some doubted that the ERA would have a significant impact, or could not judge what that impact might be. A third factor was the voluble conflict between polarized, politicized groups of women. Opponents believed that supporters disparaged women's traditional roles and felt that the ERA devalued their lives. Advocates never paid heed to such objections, nor did they assuage their opponents' suspicion that legal equality might exact a price. Despite the ERA's widespread support, conflict among women had an impact on state legislators, who controlled the ratification procedure.

The ERA was not the sole source of controversy. The "right to life" movement that began in the 1970s advocated a constitutional amendment that would reverse federal policy and prohibit all abortions. Life, it contended, began at conception. In June 1983 the Senate defeated the antiabortion amendment and the Supreme Court confirmed women's constitutional right to abortion by upsetting city ordinances that limited access to it. But right-to-life advocates mobilized to continue their campaign. Like the conflict over the ERA, the abortion controversy evoked strong sentiments. Feminist issues had become a controversial and permanent part of the political agenda.

According to opinion polls of the early 1980s, a majority of both men and women supported the ERA and abortion rights. But a "gender gap" had developed on other issues. It first appeared in the 1980 presidential election, where women provided a far larger proportion of the Carter vote (58 percent) than the Reagan vote (49 percent). Subsequent opinion polls and the 1982 congressional vote suggested that more women than men favored Democratic candidates and Democratic policies on employment, inflation control, and staying out of war. Pollsters also discovered that the greatest contributors to the gender gap were wage-earning women and women under 45, two categories of voters that were expected to grow. As the election of 1984 approached, Democratic presidential candidates tried to capitalize on the new trends in voting behavior, while Republicans either denied that a gender gap existed or declared that it was based on a misreading of Republican policies.

## NEW DIRECTIONS IN U.S. FOREIGN POLICY? (OR: THE GREAT DEBATE OVER THE USE OF FORCE)

"When we move from domestic affairs . . ." Reagan proclaimed to the roaring 1980 Republican party convention that nominated him, "we see an equally sorry chapter in the record" of Jimmy Carter. The Californian then ticked off

Carter's failures: a Soviet military presence in Cuba; the Soviet Union's invasion of Afghanistan; American defense strength "at its lowest ebb in a generation, while the Soviet Union is vastly outspending us"; and the holding of "more than 50" American hostages by "a dictatorial foreign power that holds us up to ridicule before the world." On his inauguration day Reagan was able to welcome home the hostages. They had been freed by Carter's last-minute diplomacy. But the other problems remained. None was more important to Reagan than building up tremendous military strength and then demonstrating that the "Vietnam syndrome"—American reluctance to use military force because of the Vietnam debacle—no longer existed.

The new President used his communication skills honed as a movie actor to convince Americans to follow his foreign policies. "The White House always seemed like a set," Reagan's speechwriter, Peggy Noonan, recalled. "I wasn't surprised when I heard what Reagan said twenty years earlier, when he was asked, 'What kind of governor will you be?' He answered, 'I don't know, I've never played a governor.'" Reagan did know the kind of President he wanted to be in foreign affairs and successfully talked Congress into "rearming America" (as he misleadingly called it) by raising defense spending until it would amount to $1.5 trillion over the next five years (1981–86). Unlike earlier Presidents (especially Eisenhower), Reagan had little experience with the military. He had spent World War II living in Hollywood making Army training films. From then until 1980 he had shown little interest in military affairs. He nevertheless decided that spending on arms was to be the cornerstone of his foreign policy. In early 1982, he signed a directive, National Security Decision Directive 32 (NSDD 32), instructing military leaders to build forces so they could prevail either in a prolonged global conflict with conventional weapons or in a nuclear war. The officials warned Reagan that such plans could cost as much as $625 billion more than the planned $1.5 trillion. He told them to go ahead on the basis of NSDD 32.

The President's plans quickly ran into obstacles. His advisors could not come up with a coherent foreign policy that could justify and wisely use such huge amounts of money. For example, the President pledged to fight for freedom everywhere, but no one (including Reagan) argued that U.S. troops should actually fight in Communist Vietnam again, or in Afghanistan. Another obstacle was that as many as 70 percent of Americans who were asked disagreed with the President's belief that Vietnam was "a noble cause." They wanted no more Vietnams but, instead, wanted what one public opinion expert described as "win quickly or get out." Any kind of protracted war (as suggested in NSDD 32) would not sit well with most Americans. That sentiment soon combined with another problem for Reagan. Huge government deficits by 1984–85, caused in part by the military spending, led many in Congress to question the arms budgets. By the mid-1980s Congress had cut Reagan's defense-budget growth rate to the level proposed by Jimmy Carter in 1980 when he actually began the arms buildup.

Reagan and Carter also had something else in common: each President's closest advisors bitterly differed with each other over policy. Reagan's secretary of defense, Caspar ("Cap") Weinberger, led the drive for huge military budgets. Much of the money was spent on overpriced items which enriched defense contractors. Weinberger soon "became a captive of his generals and admirals," recalled Larry Speakes, the White House press secretary, "and it was while Weinberger was in charge that we had . . . $640 toilet seats and $7,400 coffee brewers for air force planes." But the secretary of defense was reluctant to use the military force he created. In late 1984 Weinberger delivered a remarkable speech that declared U.S. troops would not be sent to war unless certain conditions existed. It was the first time in history that a Washington official publicly told potential enemies the exact conditions that had to be met before Americans would fight. Two of his conditions were shaped by the Vietnam experience: strong support from the U.S. public for any fighting; and assurance that military commanders in the field would be allowed to "win" wars.

On the other hand, Reagan's two secretaries of state, Alexander Haig (1981–June 1982) and George Shultz (1982–1989), were more willing to use force. Shultz, a tough ex-Marine and seasoned government in-fighter, even publicly answered Weinberger with a speech of his own in 1984. The secretary of state declared that "power and diplomacy" were inseparable. He believed that successful diplomacy could not be conducted without using force, or at least threatening to use it.

Shultz's first experience in the use of force, however, had been a disaster. In 1982 Israel's armies struck at their leading enemy, the Palestinian Liberation Front (PLO), which had bases in neighboring Lebanon. Lebanese groups armed by Syria (which was supplied by the Soviets) struck back and bogged down the Israeli troops. Shultz proposed a peace plan and sent 1,500 U.S. troops as part of a multination force to pacify the area. The Israelis left Lebanon, but U.S. forces then tried to separate warring Christian and Moslem armies. Encamped in an indefensible position in the Lebanese capital of Beirut, the troops became the target of snipers and terrorists. In late 1983, a Moslem terrorist drove a truck full of explosives into a U.S. Army barracks and killed 241 American soldiers. Reagan quickly declared that the troops would remain because pulling them out would amount to a "surrender" to the pro-Soviet, Syrian-Lebanese groups. But as more Americans died, the policy became unpopular, the 1984 election approached, and Reagan reversed himself. The troops came home.

The President had learned a lesson about American public opinion. In October 1983, within days after the tragic American deaths in Lebanon, Reagan and Shultz decided to invade the tiny Caribbean island of Grenada. The island was controlled by a pro-Cuban government whose radical wing had executed its opponents. Reagan announced that he invaded to protect the safety of American citizens on the island and at the request of worried neighboring states. Weinberger's Pentagon had opposed the hurried invasion, and the operation nearly turned into a disaster. Forty-five Grenadans, 18 Americans, and 24 Cuban technicians were killed in the fighting before the tiny island (the size of the District of Columbia) was pacified after nearly ten days of shooting. Reagan, however, scored a major political victory at home. He demonstrated he was not afraid to use force, and he kept the public happy by observing the rule "win quickly and get out." The question became whether the President could win such victories so easily elsewhere.

## CENTRAL AMERICA

Reagan and Shultz learned from their quite different experiences in Lebanon and Grenada. Determined to fight revolutionaries, the two officials understood that the fight had to be waged cheaply, especially in terms of U.S. lives and money. Believing that pro-Soviet revolutionaries controlled Nicaragua and threatened to control El Salvador, Reagan and Shultz tried to reimpose U.S. power over Central America by using proxy armies, that is, native troops supplied and trained by the United States. This approach, however, inflamed North American opinion in a way unmatched since the intense Vietnam debate a decade earlier.

Reagan had bitterly attacked the Sandinista government in Nicaragua for its Cuban ties, aid to Salvadoran leftists, and reluctance to hold elections. In 1981 Secretary of State Haig had even declared that it might be necessary to "go to the source" (that is, Cuba) to destroy the threat. Unwilling to accept a political settlement, and refusing to work with democratic nations in the region that criticized his military approach, Reagan chose to try to overthrow the Sandinistas with force. Working through the Central Intelligence Agency (CIA), he armed a force of anti-Sandinista Nicaraguans (soon known as "Contras"), that by 1985 numbered ten thousand troops. This force used U.S.-created camps in Florida for training (an act that was illegal under U.S. law), and bases in Honduras for attacks on Nicaragua.

The Contras, however, were so ineffective that the CIA decided to take direct charge. It led attacks deep into Nicaragua, flew air missions, then aided in mining Nicaraguan harbors. The mining proved to be a mistake. Neutral ships suffered damages, and in 1984 an outraged U.S. Congress, following vocal groups in public opinion, stopped all government aid to the Contras. The aid, however, was replaced by more than $5 million of supplies sent by private American groups. The CIA also continued to be active in the region. The Sandinistas meanwhile conducted an election in late 1984 that consolidated their hold on the country, although it also brought a strong opposition minority group into the government.

Perhaps more important, Reagan's military policies produced results opposite from those he intended. To meet the U.S. pressure, the Sandinistas doubled their army to fifty thousand regular troops, armed over one hundred thousand civilians to fight invaders, tightened their control over the country, and moved closer to Cuba and the Communist bloc for help. The President responded with maneuvers of up to thirty thousand troops in Honduras that threatened the Sandinistas, and permanently stationed U.S. warships off Nicaraguan coasts. The Contra attacks meanwhile destroyed millions of dollars of property and further worsened an already desperate economic situation in Nicaragua. More than four thousand lives were lost in the fighting. As the war intensified, so did the U.S. debate over Reagan's policy, especially as the President suddenly shut off U.S. trade with Nicaragua in 1985 in an effort to bring down that nation's economy.

Washington officials claimed greater success in El Salvador, but that claim was also challenged. The smallest country in the region, El Salvador suffered one of the widest gaps between the few rich (the so-called forty families) and the millions of poor. In 1979 some army officers tried to stop a spreading revolution by seizing power and promising reforms. But little happened. Instead the army split between right-wing leaders, who frequently murdered civilians whom they suspected of "liberal" tendencies, and the moderates, who became politically isolated. By 1984 the right-wing "death squads" had killed forty thousand civilians. But the terror only strengthened the revolutionaries who controlled much of the eastern part of El Salvador, and it sickened U.S. public opinion.

To check the revolution, Washington officials began a massive training program for Salvadoran troops (including instruction on treating civilians more humanely). Reagan also picked José Napoleón Duarte, a U.S.-educated politician, to create a government that could effectively wage war but also impress North Americans with its moderation. In 1984 Duarte won the presidency in an election heavily influenced by millions of dollars sent into El Salvador by the Reagan administration. U.S. officials and key Salvadoran army officers accelerated the war in the belief that total military victory was possible.

Many critics disagreed with that policy. They claimed (correctly, as it turned out) no military victory was in sight and that the Reagan administration, in both Nicaragua and El Salvador, was willing to "fight to the last Central American" while understanding that U.S. troops could not be directly used. The wars meanwhile devastated the already poor countries. El Salvador was completely dependent on U.S. aid for its survival. One of every seven Salvadorans fled to the United States, and the overwhelming majority did so illegally. When the Reagan administration cracked down and tried to return some of these Salvadorans to their own country, U.S. church leaders began a "sanctuary movement" that defied Reagan on the grounds that the Salvadorans' return to their homeland meant their death. Washington officials responded with a number of arrests, including the arrest of priests and nuns. But the sanctuary movement nevertheless spread—along with the instability, poverty, terror, and revolution in Central America.

# NEGOTIATING WITH THE "EVIL EMPIRE"

Reagan had a simple explanation for his Central American, and indeed global, problems. "The Soviet Union underlies all the unrest that is going on," he declared in 1980. By 1983 he was denouncing the Soviets as "the evil empire" with which diplomatic talks were of little use. Moscow officials, he claimed, "reserve unto themselves the right to commit any crime, to lie, to cheat." The Soviets responded in kind. Their policies, moreover, became more unpredictable, even threatening, when death struck their aged leadership. Three different men headed the Soviet government within just the 1982–84 years. The leadership and indeed the entire system of the Soviet Union became less stable as Reagan became more aggressive. In September 1983, the Soviets shot down a civilian South Korean airliner that had wandered 350 miles off its route and over highly sensitive Russian strategic bases. One U.S. congressman was among the 269 people who perished. Relations between the two superpowers sank to the lowest level since the worst days of the cold war in the early 1950s.

As Reagan accelerated his military buildup, he also moved to quiet his critics by agreeing to talk with the Soviets about limiting the number of nuclear missiles. The talks continued until 1983, when the Russians walked out because the United States began placing new intermediate-range missiles in Western Europe. This emplacement was a U.S. response, begun by Jimmy Carter, to similar missiles installed by the Soviets after 1977 in Eastern Europe. The talks had actually been of little use. In Washington, officials split between Pentagon leaders, who wanted no arms agreements that might limit their military buildup, and State Department officers, who hoped that a treaty could make U.S.-Soviet relations less explosive and more manageable.

President Reagan had to choose between the Pentagon and State Department positions, but he was remarkably ignorant of basic facts about the arms race. (He wrongly believed, for example, that the Soviet SS-19 missile was larger than the SS-18 because, as he pointed out, 19 is larger than 18.) In truth, he cared less about an arms treaty than his military buildup which, he hoped, would force the Soviets to accept his terms. But as he approached his reelection campaign in 1984, polls revealed that Reagan's popularity was  weakest on arms issues. Voters' fear that the President might be trigger-happy was reinforced when word leaked that he had signed NSDD 32 to win, supposedly, a protracted nuclear war. Democratic party leaders joined a "nuclear freeze" movement that aimed at freezing the present number of missiles of both the superpowers until a treaty could be negotiated. To undercut these threats to both his arms buildup and his reelection plans, Reagan suddenly  softened his anti-Soviet rhetoric and pledged new arms talks.

Most dramatically, he announced on national television in mid-1983 that more military spending could lead to scientific breakthroughs that might produce a foolproof defense against a missile attack. He urged Congress to begin a multi-billion-dollar program to develop this Strategic Defense Initiative (SDI), or "Star Wars," as his critics quickly labeled it. Reagan's plans called for technology that, one expert predicted, would require new discoveries equal to those of eight of the projects that first sent astronauts to the moon. (The moon, moreover, had not put up any resistance; the Soviets would certainly try to counter each American discovery with new weapons of their own.) Even if these problems were solved, SDI would be so complicated that it could be operated only by computers that were a thousand times faster—and, one hoped, many more times more dependable—than present systems, which had triggered a number of false nuclear alerts. SDI, moreover, even if developed, could not protect Americans against new Soviet "Cruise" missiles that delivered nuclear bombs in the atmosphere—that is, below the proposed "SDI" system. Reagan, it was discovered, had not consulted closely with his top military and scientific advisors before making his speech. He had been heavily influenced instead by Edward Teller, a superhawk among scientists, who had helped develop the hydrogen bomb in the early 1950s and was a model for the war-crazed central character in the popular 1960s movie, *Dr. Strangelove.*

The President and his advisors worked to neutralize the importance of foreign policy in the 1984 election campaign. As the electioneering began, Reagan withdrew U.S. forces from Lebanon. He also moved the explosive Central American question off the front pages of newspapers by temporarily pulling some U.S. military advisors and CIA agents out of the region. In dealing with the Soviets, he continued his arms buildup, but also promised talks and the ultimate security blanket of the SDI. Aside from the invasion of Grenada, the President could claim no major foreign policy victories. But American voters did not notice or did not care. As usual, they voted on the bases of their pocketbooks and their personal liking of the President. Reagan scored heavily on both counts. Helping to open the 1984 Summer Olympic Games in Los Angeles, he became a glamorous television image as hundreds of thousands of spectators waved American flags and proclaimed "We're Number One." Perhaps the former actor had not known how to play a governor in the 1960s, but he certainly knew how to play the President in the 1980s.

## THE 1984 ELECTION

Hoping to counter the President's popularity, the Democrats nominated former Vice-President Walter Mondale, and he chose New York representative Geraldine Ferraro as his running mate at the 1984 Democratic convention. Describing herself as a "housewife from Queens," Ferraro had spent three terms in the House and served as head of the 1984 Democratic Platform Committee. A combination of circumstances led to her candidacy. First, there were no self-evident competing choices for the vice-presidential spot, especially since the runner-up in the primaries, Gary Hart, seemed to be incompatible with nominee Mondale. In addition, Mondale was under pressure from NOW, which had given him its support early on (and some of whose members briefly threatened to withdraw their support were a woman not chosen). More effective was Betty Friedan's argument that selecting a woman would represent a commitment to expansion of opportunity for all, a theme Mondale wished to stress. Among women candidates, Ferraro appeared to be the most promising because of her potential appeal to an ethnic vote—Catholic, Italian American, and working-class—as well as to other traditional Democrats. The daughter of immigrants, she had worked her way up in the world as teacher, lawyer, and public prosecutor. Ferraro also had much support from important politicians such as New York's Governor Mario Cuomo and House Speaker Thomas ("Tip") O'Neill, who found her "spunky and game." Finally, the Mondale camp

Geraldine Ferraro, 1984.
*(D. Goldberg/Sygma.)*

felt that a bold, unconventional step was needed, both to energize the campaign and to prove that the candidate could take strong, decisive action.

Ferraro's historic nomination generated widespread enthusiasm, drew an outpouring of volunteers, and represented a triumph to feminists. Republicans criticized the nomination as tokenism. "I would like it better if she were a candidate, and not a woman candidate," said former Maine Senator Margaret Chase Smith, when interviewed in retirement. "Now, I was never a woman candidate." No sooner had the campaign started than a furor erupted over whether Ferraro would reveal the entirety of her family finances beyond the income tax statements required by law. To do so, as the press demanded, meant a public airing of her husband's finances, a possible source of irregularities, as well as her own. No comparable concern over a spouse's finances had arisen before a woman candidate ran for vice-president. That Ferraro finally released the information demanded by the press and handled the situation with aplomb won her acclaim. But the controversy hurt the Democratic campaign.

When votes were counted, the gender gap seemed to have all but vanished. President Reagan won 57 percent of the women's vote, as opposed to 42 percent for Mondale. (The male vote was 61 percent to 37 percent.) All nine women challengers for Senate seats lost, as did thirty-nine of forty-one women challengers for House seats. Recriminations about the women's vote were rampant in the Democratic camp. "The party got a gun put to its head . . . to choose a woman for Vice President," a Mondale staff member told the press.

"They didn't bring in anything. Women vote for President just like men do." Feminists were "remote from the women's vote," a top Democratic consultant charged. "These people can't deliver their sisters." With an 18-point gap between the candidates, Democratic women pointed out, the gender gap could not be expected to have had much impact. "We didn't invent defeat," said Ann Lewis, political director of the Democratic National Committee. "White men have been losing elections for years."

The extent to which Ronald Reagan had succeeded in altering the political agenda was evident in the kind of campaign waged by the Democrats. Walter Mondale represented a traditional brand of Democratic liberalism, but his speech accepting the nomination called for a well-managed, not merely a well-meaning, government, a president who could say no to special-interest groups, a strong military posture with no major cuts in defense spending, policies to ensure private-, not public-sector, economic growth, and the maintenance of family values. "I will cut the deficit by two-thirds," the liberal Democrat promised; "we must cut spending and pay as we go." Mondale did attack Reagan for pandering to the rich and powerful, but the Democrat said little or nothing about social welfare, racial justice, or immigration reform. In November, Reagan captured 59 percent of the popular vote and carried forty-nine of fifty states. Ronald Reagan had established the terms of political debate for the 1980s as surely as Franklin Roosevelt had for the 1930s.

## Suggested Reading

For Jimmy Carter's political career and presidency, see James Wooten, *Dasher: The Roots and the Rising of Jimmy Carter* (1976); Charles O. Jones, *The Trusteeship Presidency: Jimmy Carter and the United States Congress* (1988); Burton Ira Kaufman, *The Presidency of James Earl Carter, Jr.* (1993); and M. Glenn Abernathy et al., eds., *The Carter Years: The President and Policy Making* (1984). On the evangelicals, consult Erling Jorstad, *Evangelicals in the White House* (1981); Robert C. Liebman and Robert Wuthnow, eds., *The New Christian Right* (1983); and Hunter James, *Smile Pretty and Say Jesus: The Last Great Days of PTL* (1993). The Reagan administration is discussed in Robert Dallek, *Ronald Reagan: The Politics of Symbolism* (1984); Garry Wills, *Reagan's America* (1987); Lou Cannon, *President Reagan: The Role of a Lifetime* (1991); and Michael Schaller, *Reckoning with Reagan: America and Its President in the 1980s* (1992).

The controversy over affirmative action is discussed in Allan P. Sindler, *Bakke, DeFunis, and Minority Admissions* (1978); and Joel Dreyfuss and Charles Lawrence III, *The Bakke Case: The Politics of Inequality* (1979). For the background of the controversy over undocumented aliens, see Richard Polenberg, *One Nation Divisible: Class, Race, and Ethnicity in the United States since 1938* (1980). The feminization of poverty is discussed in Ruth Sidell, *Women and Children Last: The Plight of Poor Women in Affluent America* (1986); and Leonore J. Weitzman, *The Divorce Revolution* (1985). For women's political activism, see Jane J. Mansbridge, *Why We Lost the ERA* (1986); Kristin Luker, *Abortion and the Politics of Motherhood* (1984); and Susan M. Hartmann, *From Margin to Mainstream: American Women and Politics Since 1960* (1989).

On foreign policy, begin with the relevant entries in Bruce Jentleson and Thomas Paterson, eds., *Encyclopedia of U.S. Foreign Relations*, 4 vols. (1997), with succinct bibliographies. Also see Gaddis Smith, *Morality, Reason and Power* (1986). Books on Carter's diplomacy include three "inside" accounts: Carter's own *Keeping Faith* (1982); Cyrus Vance, *Hard Choices* (1983); and the most revealing, Zbigniew Brzezinski, *Power and Principle* (1983). Human rights policies are analyzed in Lars Schoultz, *Human Rights and U.S. Policy Towards Latin America* (1981). A useful account of the Iranian crisis is James A. Bill, *The Eagle and Lion* (1988). On Reagan, the Cannon, Barrett, and Dallek biographies listed above are useful, but most important is George Shultz's memoir of 1982–1989, *Turmoil and Triumph* (1993). Two indispensable books on the Reagan administration's view of the Soviets, and especially arms negotiations, are Strobe Talbott, *Deadly Gambits* (1984); and Robert Scheer, *With Enough Shovels* (1982). Defense policy is critiqued in Ronald V. Dellums, R. H. Miller, and H. Lee Halterman, *Defense Sense* (1983). Central American policy for both the Carter and Reagan years is analyzed in Robert S. Leiken, ed., *Central America: Anatomy of Conflict* (1984); the readings in Marvin Gettleman et al., *El Salvador* (1982); and the expanded edition of Walter LaFeber, *Inevitable Revolutions* (1984, 1993) while Americans' opposition to the policy is analyzed in Christian Smith, *Resisting Reagan* (1996). The Reagan view is in *The Report of the President's National Bipartisan Commission on Central America* (1984), which was chaired by Henry Kissinger. On the Middle East, see Itamar Rabinovich, *The War for Lebanon, 1970–1983* (1984); and William B. Quandt, *Camp David* (1986). On the Panama Canal debate, see Michael J. Hogan, *The Panama Canal in American Politics* (1986); and Walter LaFeber, *The Panama Canal* (1989).

The following are useful for understanding the historical meaning of the computer's development: Martin Campbell-Kelly and William Aspray, *Computer* (1996); Robert Sobel, *IBM* (1981); and David F. Noble, *Forces of Production: A Social History of Industrial Automation* (1984).

A veteran of the Persian Gulf war being welcomed home by his daughter, March 1991. *(MICHAEL OKONIEWSKI/NYT PERMISSIONS.)*

# CHAPTER SEVENTEEN

# 1985–1992

## The End of the Cold War Era?

This chapter discusses:
- What some Americans do, and watch, when they feel rich
- How Robert Bork and Clarence Thomas became symbols of debates over the Constitution
- Women in a transformed workplace
- The scourge of drugs, the tragedy of AIDS
- Americans marking the end of the cold war against the Soviets with a hot war against Iraq

After Ronald Reagan's sweeping victory in 1984, one of his most vigorous critics, House Speaker Thomas ("Tip") O'Neill, told him, "I've never seen a man more popular than you are with the American people." Reagan maintained that popularity throughout his second term, even though he failed to effect promised changes in social, judicial, and environmental policies, and failed to find solutions for growing budget deficits, declining American productivity, and a widening gap between rich and poor. The President even managed to emerge largely unscathed from "Irangate" and a savings-and-loan scandal. But as domestic difficulties mounted, relationships with the Soviet Union dramatically improved. It was left to Reagan's successor, George Bush, to discover that the end of the cold war did not mean an end to foreign policy difficulties, or even an end to the threat of war—or war itself.

## THE ROARING '80s

Having triumphed in one of the largest political landslides in the nation's history, Ronald Reagan began his second term as "Ronald II"—a smiling monarch who watched contentedly as his country seemed to grow richer amid the greatest economic boom of the post–World War II years. A combination of massive tax cuts and growing government deficits fueled the boom. In 1980 his political opponent, George Bush, had ridiculed Reagan's promise to cut taxes (and thus reduce government income) while boosting military spending and at the same time balancing the budget. Bush called this "voodoo economics." He nevertheless gladly joined up as Reagan's vice-president and shared the glory of the "Reaganomics" boom. The U.S. gross national product (GNP) mushroomed to $5 trillion, nearly twice the size of the Soviet and Japanese economies.

Some Americans grew very rich. In 1982 there were thirteen billionaires; by 1988, at least fifty-one. New long-distance telephone area codes had to be devised for the Atlantic and Pacific oceans because of the many phone-equipped private yachts. New cultural heroes included multimillionaire basketball, football, and baseball players (some baseball pitchers averaged a $10,000 income for each inning they worked); New York real estate tycoon Donald Trump; and Wall Street wizards Michael Milken and Ivan Boesky. The world's most widely watched television program was "Dallas," which told lurid stories about superrich and superdevious Texas oil families. "Falcon Crest," starring Reagan's ex-wife Jane Wyman, did the same for the California superrich. New law school graduates worked long hours but enjoyed $50,000 to $75,000 or more in annual income at Wall Street firms. As the New York Stock Exchange's equities soared to all-time high prices in early 1987, one broker was stupefied: "It's unbelievable the amount of money that is out there."

For various reasons, however, the economy's health was less rosy than it appeared. First, Reaganomics, especially the tax laws of 1981 and 1986, badly skewed income distribution. In 1979, the average corporation's top executive made twenty-nine times the income of the average manufacturing worker; by

By Age, 1960–1993

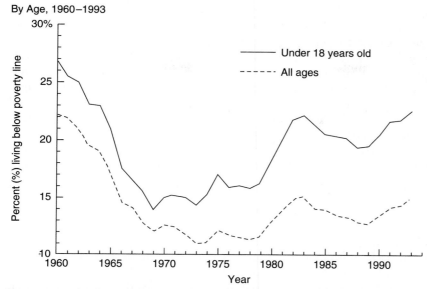

Percentage of Americans living in poverty. *(Urie Bronfenbrenner, et al.,* The State of Americans *[New York: Free Press, 1996], p. 66.)*

1988 it was ninety-three times. Or, to put it more broadly, the share of the nation's total after-tax wealth enjoyed by the top 10 percent of the nation's families rose from 67 percent in 1979 to 73 percent in 1988. By 1990 the richest 2.5 million Americans had enjoyed a spectacular 75 percent income increase during the 1980s. They now had nearly as much income as the 100 million Americans who had the lowest incomes.

By the end of the Reagan years, 31.5 million people, or about 12 percent of the population, lived at the poverty level. (The U.S. government defined that level as below a $9,885 annual income for a family of three.) The figure was higher than at any time in the 1970s. Blacks and other minorities especially suffered. Over 9 million black people, or 2 million more than in 1978, lived at or below poverty levels despite the economic boom. Unemployment among blacks hovered around 15 percent, twice that of unemployment among whites. Among inner-city young black adults, the rate soared to 50 percent. American children also suffered amid the boom. By 1990 almost 20 percent of them lived in poverty, but for black children the figure skyrocketed to 45 percent. It was the worst record among industrialized Western nations. Critics doubted whether many of these children could escape poverty through education. Many inner-city schools were battlegrounds. In the drug-soaked schools of Washington, D.C., and within sight of the nation's Capitol, 13-year-olds came to class armed with automatic weapons. The United States meanwhile ranked fourteenth out of sixteen industrialized nations in spending on elementary and secondary school students. As the poor became relatively poorer, the nation became more violent and less educated.

A second problem with Reaganomics also appeared. The President argued that his tax cuts would leave wealthier Americans with money that they could invest in productive enterprises. Instead, these Americans spent their money on personal goods. Investment in the nation's factories and service sectors remained relatively flat. Between 1972 and 1989, Americans spent about 12 percent of their GNP on plant and equipment—the goods that produced new jobs and higher real income. Japan spent an average of 17 percent of its GNP on investment, and in 1989 that figure rose to 23 percent. The difference between American and Japanese investment figures helped explain why the Japanese were replacing Americans as the richest and most productive people in the world.

A third problem was that Americans demanded more from their government than they were willing to pay in taxes. Reagan had promised to cut government spending, but, bowing to voters' demands, he and Congress instead increased it. Such "entitlement" programs as social security and Medicaid benefits nearly doubled in the 1980s. Government subsidies for American farmers in 1979 amounted to nearly $5 billion; by the late 1980s the subsidies reached $26 billion. Military spending doubled to $300 billion during the decade. The overall government budget, which Reagan had pledged to balance, was in the red by $100 billion or more every year by the end of his presidency. The U.S. national debt doubled to nearly $3 trillion.

In 1986 alone, Americans spent $150 billion more than they produced. Private borrowing and indebtedness approached $9 trillion, or twice the level of 1980. Much of that spending, moreover, went to foreign producers. Americans bought shiploads of Toyotas, Walkmans, BMWs, and machine tools from abroad. In 1981 Americans had a favorable balance in their overall foreign trade. But between 1984 and 1989 they bought from $100 billion to $150 billion more each year from overseas than they sold.

Such spending led to the fourth problem: to cover the gap between what they spent and produced, Americans borrowed from foreigners—especially the British, Canadians, Japanese, and Germans. In 1981 the United States had been the world's largest creditor, the globe's main source of money. By 1986 the United States had suddenly become the world's largest debtor. Because of its spending spree, it owed others a half-trillion dollars by the end of the 1980s. It was the first time in seventy-five years that Americans had owed money to foreigners. It would be "our children," as one economist wrote, who would have to pay off the 1980s debts, or else sell off U.S. properties "our kids would otherwise have inherited." Many such properties still existed, he noted with sarcasm: "There's Fifth Avenue in New York, and the whole state of Oregon. Why not liquidate some of those assets and live it up a little longer?" It was not entirely a joke. British capitalists, who led the foreign investment in U.S. properties, bought up American factories and real estate. Japanese investors stunned Americans by purchasing a controlling interest in Rockefeller Center in New York City.

Democratic Senator Daniel Patrick Moynihan from New York feared that the 1980s would be remembered as the decade when Americans "borrowed a trillion dollars from the Japanese and threw a party." Congress tried to discipline its spending by passing a bill sponsored by Republican Senators Phil Gramm from Texas and Warren Rudman from New Hampshire. The Gramm-Rudman measure aimed to cut the government's deficit from $172 billion in 1986 to zero in 1993 by setting ever-lower deficits as targets for the years in between. If Congress could not meet the target amounts, Gramm-Rudman required automatic cuts from domestic and military spending. Social security was exempted from the cuts. Congress had little difficulty making the required reductions until 1990, when no agreement could be reached before the new fiscal year began on October 1. Automatic cuts began and for several days the government was in near-chaos until a deal could be struck.

Americans received other jolts. On the single day of October 19, 1987, the New York Stock Exchange's main economic indicator, the Dow-Jones average of 30 industrial stocks, dropped a historic 508 points. A half-trillion dollars of wealth disappeared in a matter of hours. As the market sank, Wall Street firms fired 15,000 employees, including many newly hired recent college graduates. Fraud and corruption through stock-rigging was discovered. Former cultural heroes such as Ivan Boesky and Michael Milken were sentenced to jail, while Donald Trump lost much of his financial empire. Stocks rose to all-time highs in 1990, then fell sharply again.

During 1988–89, Americans began to learn of the single greatest economic failure in their history. More than a thousand savings-and-loan banks (S&Ls), in which millions of Americans had deposited their savings—and from which millions more had borrowed to buy property—went bankrupt. The disaster began in the early 1980s when many government regulations (some dating from the New Deal) were lifted by Reagan's deregulation program. S&L owners raised interest rates to attract depositors, then put the money in risky, get-rich-quick real estate ventures. When real estate slumped in the Southwest in the mid-1980s, and then in the Northeast, the banks lost billions of dollars. Individual depositors, luckily, were insured by the U.S. government for up to $100,000 per savings account. But that insurance had to be paid by taxpayers who would have to give $500 billion (or $5,000 per household) over the next 40 years to bail out the S&L industry. By 1991, key commercial banks, also weakened by dropping real estate prices, threatened to follow S&Ls into bankruptcy.

By 1990, Americans had less control over their own economic future than at any time in the twentieth century. Foreigners controlled one-third of all U.S. savings and investments. In addition, Americans' dependence on imported foreign oil, after dropping in 1981–82, rose to historic highs in 1990. Americans were the most energy-guzzling people in the world. The Japanese, who had begun radical energy-saving measures after the 1973 oil crisis, were two-and-one-half times more energy-efficient than Americans. This meant that the Japanese could produce two-and-one-half times more goods per unit of energy than could Americans. The business executive who chaired the U.S. Presidential

Council on Competitiveness concluded, "America is losing its ability to compete in world markets."

## AMERICANS AND THE EMERGING WORLD: THE REAGAN DOCTRINE TO IRANAMOK

The nation's economic difficulties meant not only increasing problems at home, but they also meant that U.S. officials had less power to control problems abroad. The days when America enjoyed a large superiority in nuclear weapons, the economic strength to rebuild and control key regions of the world, and the ability to land troops, or Central Intelligence Agency (CIA) agents, to prop up or overthrow governments against little opposition—all that seemed to be about over. Ronald Reagan, however, refused to believe it.

Having run in 1984 on the sunny campaign slogan that "It's Morning in America," the President announced in his 1985 State of the Union Address that freedom "is the universal right of all God's children." Therefore, "we must stand by all our democratic allies. And we must not break faith with those who are risking their lives—on every continent, from Afghanistan to Nicaragua—to defy Soviet-supported aggression and secure rights which have been ours from birth." This "Reagan Doctrine," as observers called it, came under attack for implying that Americans actually had the power to "secure" such rights as democracy in, say, the Middle East or poverty-stricken parts of Africa. The President nevertheless increased aid to the Afghan resistance that had fought a bloody war since 1979 against the Soviet invaders. By 1986 the aid included ground-to-air missiles that destroyed Red Army helicopters. In 1988, as 100,000 Russian troops bogged down and took heavy casualties, Moscow officials announced their forces would be withdrawn. But a pro-Soviet regime remained in power as the resistance forces fell to bitter fighting among themselves over who would lead their movement.

In two other areas, the Reagan Doctrine worked even better—but, oddly, not as Reagan himself liked. In South Africa, 5.5 million whites dominated 23 million blacks through the policy of segregation and military control known as *apartheid*. Because the white government seemed stable, was the economic powerhouse for most of Africa, and shipped valuable minerals (including uranium used in nuclear weapons) to the United States, the Reagan administration followed a policy called "constructive engagement." This policy tried to reform apartheid in a slow, friendly fashion. During 1984–86, however, black towns exploded against the South African police. As the police killed 6,000 protesters, Reagan did little. But over his opposition the U.S. Congress passed a bill to cut most American–South African economic ties. This measure was helped along when opponents of apartheid forced some U.S. colleges and state legislatures to pull their profitable investments out of South Africa. By 1989 the South African economy was badly hurt. A new white government began repealing apartheid policies and released from jail the black community's most powerful leader, Nelson Mandela.

In the Philippines, meanwhile, Ferdinand Marcos, who had reigned as dictator since 1972, was overthrown and was replaced through elections by Corazón Aquino (wife of the murdered opposition leader Benigno Aquino). She came to power with the help of pressure from the U.S. Department of State (who feared that instability could increase Communist rebels' power in the Philippines), and despite Reagan's support for his good friend Marcos. The Reagan Doctrine was working, but not always with the help of Reagan.

It turned out that he was somewhat more involved in making Middle East policy, but it erupted into his gravest crisis. Since his 1980 campaign, Reagan had promised he would never negotiate with terrorists who held American hostages. He took an especially tough public line against the fundamentalist Islamic regime in Iran that had overthrown the pro-U.S. shah in 1979. By 1985–86, Iran was fighting neighboring Iraq in one of the bloodiest and most brutal of twentieth-century wars. The Iranians needed military help. Pro-Iranian groups in the Middle East had seized American hostages, including at least one CIA agent. Pressured both by his close friend William Casey (the CIA director), and by Israel (which greatly feared Iraq's military capacity), Reagan secretly agreed to send weapons to Iran in return for the release of hostages. He made the decision over the strong objections of Secretary of State George Shultz and Defense Secretary Caspar Weinberger. After several hostages were freed, the White House lied by asserting that "no deal was made and that our position on no concessions to terrorists has not changed."

Casey had used a White House military aide, Lieutenant Colonel Oliver North, to help arrange the secret deal. A superpatriot who believed the Reagan Doctrine must be carried out at all costs, North had fought in Vietnam and swore that Americans must never again lose such a conflict. He was obsessed with the fear, however, that the Vietnam disaster was being rerun in Central America. There the Sandinistas controlled Nicaragua with help from Cuba and the Soviet Union (as well as from many West European democracies). The Sandinistas had consolidated their power in 1984 by winning a national election—which Reagan refused to recognize as valid—and by militarily defeating the U.S.-supported Contra rebels. In Washington, Congress viewed the Contras not only as losers, but as gross violators of human rights. Congress made illegal further U.S. government aid to the Contras. North then led an effort that obtained funds, from private U.S. citizens, for more than $22 million worth of military supplies for the rebels. In late 1986, however, the Justice Department discovered that North, with the approval of his superiors in the National Security Council and of Casey, had broken the law by selling weapons to Iran and then sending the proceeds to the Contras.

Reagan denied any crimes and applauded North as "a national hero." But special investigations revealed that the laws no doubt had been broken, especially as North tried to cover up by lying to congressional committees and destroying and falsifying government documents. The President apparently knew little about the deals. Investigations showed the 75-year-old chief executive to be an uninvolved, not very knowledgeable President who devoted most of his time to speeches and television appearances. As the true story of

Lieutenant Colonel Oliver North being sworn in at the Iran-Contra hearings. *(Terry Ashe/*Time *Magazine.)*

"Iranamok" (as the scandal was soon tagged) emerged, Reagan admitted mistakes had been made, but denied he knew of the illegal diversion of funds to the Contras. Several of North's associates were indicted for the crimes, but although he was convicted for obstructing Congress and destroying documents, his convictions were reversed in 1990 on technical legal grounds. The Iran-Contra episode dragged Reagan into the lowest point of his presidency in 1987, just as the nation was celebrating its two-hundredth anniversary of constitutional government.

## THE COURT AND THE CONSTITUTION: BORK AND THE BICENTENNIAL

In 1987, the celebration of the Constitution's bicentennial coincided with a bitter debate over President Reagan's nomination of Robert H. Bork as an associate justice of the Supreme Court. Relatively little controversy had surrounded Reagan's earlier appointments of Justices Sandra Day O'Connor and Antonin Scalia, or the choice of William Rehnquist to replace retiring Warren Burger as Chief Justice in 1986. But the circumstances of the Bork nomination were unusual. As the replacement for Justice Lewis Powell, a moderate who had often cast the deciding vote in crucial 5-to-4 decisions, Bork could swing the Court in a new direction. No one doubted what direction that would be.

Robert H. Bork at Senate Judiciary Committee hearings. *(Terry Ashe/Gamma-Liaison.)*

Throughout a distinguished career as a law professor at Yale, as U.S. solicitor general, and as a circuit court judge, Bork had attacked the Supreme Court's liberal rulings. He had argued that, in weighing a statute's constitutionality, judges merely had to decide whether it accorded with the "original intent" of the Founding Fathers, a view that perfectly suited Attorney General Edwin Meese and other conservatives.

During much of the 1980s, the Burger Court, with some notable exceptions, had handed down liberal rulings that frustrated the Reagan administration's "social" agenda. For example, the Court ruled in *City of Akron* v. *Akron Center for Reproductive Health* (1983) that local ordinances making it difficult for women to obtain first- and second-trimester abortions were unconstitutional. Speaking for a majority of six, Justice Powell affirmed the *Roe* v. *Wade* precedent and described the right of privacy as a "long-recognized and essential element of personal liberty." In 1985, in *Wallace* v. *Jaffree,* the Court struck down an Alabama statute providing for a minute of silence in the public schools "for meditation or voluntary prayer." In a concurring opinion, Justice O'Connor declared that the Constitution prohibited "making adherence to a religion relevant in any way to a person's standing in the political community." In other decisions, the Court ruled that a Louisiana statute which required teachers to give "creation science" equal time with the theory of evolution was an improper attempt to inject religion into the public schools, maintained the "exclusionary rule" (a ban on introducing illegally seized material into evidence), and supported an increasingly strict equal protection standard for women.

Those who supported Robert Bork, and those who opposed him, recognized that his confirmation could move the Court sharply to the right. The nominee had condemned provisions in the Civil Rights Act of 1964 which outlawed discrimination in places of public accommodation on the grounds that legislating morality was a "principle of unsurpassed ugliness." Bork had written that the First Amendment did not protect literary or artistic expression, but only political speech, and only when it did not advocate violating the law. He considered the Court's one-person, one-vote reapportionment rulings misguided. He condemned the case which helped establish the right of privacy as "an unprincipled decision," and added that *Roe* v. *Wade* was "an unconstitutional decision." To hold, as the Court had, that women as well as blacks deserved equal protection reflected, in Bork's view, "current fads in sentimentality." Terming himself an "originalist" judge, who would always be guided by "the intentions of those who framed and ratified our Constitution," Bork said he would have no difficulty overturning a "non-originalist precedent."

So it is not surprising that his nomination sparked a vitriolic debate. From the standpoint of one conservative evangelical organization, Bork's elevation to the Court was "our last chance . . . to ensure future decades will bring morality, godliness and justice back into focus." Liberal Democrats like Senator Edward M. Kennedy of Massachusetts countered that "Bork's America is a land where women would be forced into back-alley abortions, [and] blacks would sit at segregated lunch counters." In September, when the Senate Judiciary Committee considered the nomination, both sides organized extensive lobbying campaigns which included dramatic, and sometimes misleading, newspaper and television advertisements. Bork's supporters argued that he had impeccable personal and intellectual credentials, and that senators should not refuse to confirm such a nominee simply because they disagreed with his judicial philosophy. The anti-Bork coalition—consisting of civil rights, labor, women's, and consumer's groups—held that his outlook was so extreme as to place him outside the judicial "mainstream."

Eventually, the Judiciary Committee recommended against approval, and although it was apparent that the Senate would vote against confirmation, Bork refused to ask the President to withdraw his nomination. In October the Senate defeated the nomination by a vote of 58 to 42. Attorney General Meese thundered that Bork was a victim of "gutter politics"; the President blamed the defeat on a "lynch mob"; and Bork himself said he was "tarred, feathered, and ridden out of town on a rail." But while political considerations certainly played a role in the defeat, many senators, including conservative Democrats and moderate Republicans, had concluded that Bork's brand of conservatism

Opponents and supporters of abortion rights demonstrating outside the U.S. Supreme Court building, July 1989. (*ANDREA MOHIN/NYT PERMISSIONS.*)

did, indeed, place him outside the mainstream. Eventually, President Reagan nominated Anthony Kennedy, an outspoken but less abrasive conservative, who soothed Senate sensibilities by speaking of a Constitution with a capacity for growth, and of framers who had "made a covenant with the future." The Senate quickly confirmed the new nominee.

By 1988, therefore, the Supreme Court had begun to take on a more conservative cast. Nothing more clearly illustrated this than its attitude toward abortion. In *Webster* v. *Reproductive Health Care Services*, decided in July 1989, a five-member majority upheld a Missouri statute containing twenty provisions designed to curb a woman's right to choice. Physicians, before consenting to abortions, were supposed to perform tests (of weight, size, and lung capacity) to determine whether a fetus they thought was more than twenty weeks old was "viable"; no viable fetus was to be aborted except to preserve the pregnant woman's life or health. In addition, the statute prohibited the use of public facilities or employees to perform abortions, except, again, if the woman's life or health were at risk. Four justices indicated they were prepared to overturn *Roe* v. *Wade;* but Justice O'Connor, although voting with the majority, did not believe the Missouri statute required the Court to reconsider that precedent. Speaking for the majority, Chief Justice Rehnquist held that the various state legislatures should set policies on abortion. The Supreme Court's goal, he said, "is not to remove inexorably 'politically divisive' issues from the ambit of the legislative process." In a scathing dissent, Justice Harry Blackmun charged that the decision would precipitate "a constitutional crisis," foment "disregard for the law," and dangerously enhance "the coercive and brooding influence of the state."

In other areas, however, even this more conservative Court adhered to liberal precedents. Perhaps the most controversial case concerned flag burning. In 1989, in *Texas* v. *Johnson,* Justices Scalia and Kennedy joined three liberal colleagues in holding that flag burning conveyed an "overtly political" message and therefore merited constitutional protection. The "bedrock principle" underlying the First Amendment, Justice William Brennan declared, was that government could not "prohibit the expression of an idea simply because society finds the idea itself offensive or disagreeable." Congress, seeking to get around the decision, passed a Flag Protection Act in 1989, but it too was ruled unconstitutional in 1990 in *U.S.* v. *Eichman.*

With Justice Brennan's retirement in 1990 and his replacement by President George Bush's first nominee, Justice David Souter, it seemed that the Court might move in a more conservative direction. Yet the justices' inclination to adhere to precedent, and the existence of a consensus in behalf of certain rights, worked against any dramatic turnabout. Prior decisions protecting freedom of speech and religion and outlawing racial and sexual discrimination enjoyed support across the judicial spectrum. Moreover, the Court had begun to consider a new range of problems—the right to die, for example, and surrogate parenthood—which did not easily fit the liberal-conservative categorization. Still another new issue was the environment. As concern with environmental health and safety grew in the 1980s, so did the number of cases brought before the courts by environmental activists.

## EARTH DAY AND THE ENVIRONMENT

When Ronald Reagan was first elected president, a National Broadcasting Company news analyst predicted "the end of the environmental movement." Given Reagan's views, the prediction did not seem unreasonable. As governor of California, he had opposed the expansion of Redwood National Park with the comment, "a tree is a tree. How many more do you need to look at?" He also remarked that a study had shown "that 80 percent of air pollution comes not from chimneys and auto exhaust pipes, but from plants and trees." Convinced that environmentalists were "radical extremists," the Reagan administration, according to one historian, "launched a massive assault on two decades of environmental programs."

In the course of those two decades, the environmental movement had done much to alter the American landscape. Rachel Carson's 1962 best-seller, *Silent Spring,* showed how the massive aerial spraying of toxic pesticides, such as DDT, damaged plants, animals, and people. "For the first time in the history of the world," she wrote, "every human being is now subjected to contact with dangerous chemicals, from the moment of conception until death." The book, one scholar has written, "indicted government and research scientists who were lobbied and bought by the pesticide industry for collusion in the chemical assault on nature. . . . It summoned government to regulate the manufacture and use of synthetic chemicals and to enforce environmental laws."

The first "Earth Day," observed on college campuses in 1970, launched an annual campaign to educate people about threats to the land, air, and water. Responding to a growing public awareness, Congress, in 1970, passed the National Environmental Policy Act, and then a series of laws designed to limit environmental hazards, protect wilderness areas, and preserve endangered species. Supported by such organizations as the Sierra Club and the Wilderness Society, most of the legislation won broad, bipartisan approval. Moreover, the Supreme Court generally granted conservationists "standing," thereby enabling them to bring suits against business concerns responsible for pollution and against government agencies which failed to enforce the new laws. "Ecology," commented a California Democrat, "has become the political substitute for the word 'mother.'"

Public concern focused first on the need to maintain forests, parks, wildlife refuges, and open spaces, then on the dangers of air and water pollution, and, by the mid-1970s, on the importance of energy conservation and the cleaning up of hazardous wastes. Widespread publicity surrounding tragic incidents stimulated that concern. In 1978, for example, it was discovered that residents near the Love Canal in Erie County, New York, an area used as a chemical junkyard, were experiencing abnormally high rates of cancer, miscarriages, and birth defects. President Carter designated the Love Canal an emergency area, but an Environmental Protection Agency official admitted, "We just don't know how many potential Love Canals there are." In 1979, an accident at the Three Mile Island power plant in Pennsylvania revealed the danger posed by radioactive material in nuclear reactors. By 1980, many Americans recognized the crucial importance of energy conservation, pollution control, and recycling. Barry Commoner, a leading environmentalist, warned that the continuation of older, wasteful policies "will destroy the capability of the environment to support a reasonably civilized human society."

But programs to protect the environment conflicted with the incoming Reagan administration's determination to cut federal spending, reduce federal control, and promote private enterprise. With these goals in mind, Reagan sought to eliminate the Council on Environmental Quality, slashed funding for the Environmental Protection Agency, and placed such crucial agencies as the Bureau of Land Management, the Occupational Safety and Health Administration, and the National Park Service in the hands of administrators who had little sympathy for environmental concerns. James Watt, the new secretary of the interior, had championed the "Sagebrush Rebellion," an attempt to turn acreage in the national forests over to the states and permit private development. Anne Gorsuch, who headed the Environmental Protection Agency, favored permissive policies in policing pollution. By 1982, Congressman Morris Udall, an Arizona Democrat, could comment that Watt and Gorsuch "have done for the environment what Bonnie and Clyde did for banks."

# THE FITNESS CRAZE

"Energy is like sex," *Esquire* magazine announced in 1988. "You either use it or lose it." As an illustration, *Esquire* told the story of a 41-year-old Seattle venture capitalist who had "never made a sustained effort to keep himself in shape." Recently separated from his wife and facing "some tough business challenges," he suffered from high blood pressure and could "barely summon up the energy to get through the day." But his situation soon changed, for the venture capitalist began an eight-week program to increase energy that had been developed by a local consulting firm. Walking with weights, pursuing a course of aerobic exercise, doing push-ups and stretches, and changing his diet, he lost body fat, increased his lean body mass, lowered his cholesterol, and boosted his strength and flexibility. At the end of the program, the people with whom he worked reported "a startling shift in his ability to come up with innovative ideas" and "to follow through on his commitments."

The experience of the Seattle investor was part of a physical fitness vogue that exploded during the Reagan years. The vogue gained momentum in the 1970s, when joggers and runners became visible. Running, its advocates claimed, increased longevity, prolonged youthfulness, staved off heart disease, built up endurance, reduced minor ills, and induced exhilaration, or at least gave practitioners a sense of being "in control." Doubters cited a list of hazards, such as strained knees, stress fractures, bone bruises, and inflamed tendons; but the benefits of running, enthusiasts contended, outweighed the liabilities. By 1977, the Road Runners Club, a national runners' organization, boasted 125 local chapters. Big-city marathons attracted hundreds of thousands of competitors. Of a dozen runners' magazines, the leader, *Runner's World*, claimed a circulation of 165,000.

By the 1980s, the passion for fitness had generated a new institution, the health club. A descendent of the neighborhood gym, the

The New York City marathon, 1990. (*SARA KRULWICH/NYT PERMISSIONS.*)

one-time hangout of weight lifters and body builders, the health club catered to a larger and more upscale clientele. In 1980, there were about 10,000 such clubs and a decade later, twice as many. Full-fledged health clubs provided squash and racketball courts, jogging tracks, lap pools, whirlpools, steam rooms, saunas, scuba classes, weight training, and nutrition counseling. They contained an array of fitness machinery, such as treadmills, Lifecycles, Stairmasters, Versaclimbers, and the Nautilus, a weight-lifting machine that provided a complete workout. Health clubs also offered classes in physical conditioning—calisthenics, yoga, stretching, self-defense, and aerobics. Following the commands of energetic instructors, students of aerobics leapt and gyrated to tapes of disco and rock music, played at high volume and sped up to 150 beats a minute. The health club doctrine of "no pain, no gain" could cause problems. A California survey of 1,200 participants in aerobic classes reported that 43 percent had suffered minor injuries, as had 76 percent of their instructors. *Newsweek* advised readers to avoid cut-rate chain clubs and seek instructors with degrees in exercise physiology, or join deluxe establishments, where members received electrocardiograms, cholesterol analyses, and personal programs prescribed by cardiologists. By the end of the decade, sophisticated clubs offered courses in self-esteem and stress management. Health facilities now appeared in luxury apartment

An aerobics class. (*David Madison.*)

buildings and hotels, and business magazines advised fitness-minded travelers on how to keep in shape on the road.

The fitness craze also invaded the home, via the videocassette recorder and fitness tapes. "After you bring a tape home, don't abandon your club," counseled an article in a women's sports magazine. But many enthusiasts preferred their living rooms to live classes. Between 1983 and 1986, Jane Fonda's videotapes sold over 900,000 copies worldwide. The profits of home exercise extended to the makers of exercise machinery. According to the National Sporting Goods Association, consumers spent $1.58 billion on home-workout equipment in the single year 1987. Retailers had sold more than a million stationary bikes and as many rowers; hundreds of thousands of treadmills, stair climbers, cross-country trainers, and weight benches; and 586,000 home gyms—machines that provide complete workouts and ranged in price from $1,300 to $2,495.

By the start of the 1990s, the big spender had replaced the humble jogger. Physical fitness was not merely a craze but a major industry. No facet of the industry had made more impressive progress than athletic footwear: the simple sneaker had developed into a wardrobe of "athletic shoes" for specialized purposes. By 1990, the nation had a $5 billion athletic footwear business. As the attributes and prices of the shoes increased, so did the profits of their producers. Between 1984 and 1990, the revenues of Reebok International, the largest manufacturer of athletic footwear after Nike, increased 2,760 percent. The company's chairperson became the best-compensated chief executive, in terms of salary and bonus, of any publicly owned American corporation. His annual income skyrocketed from $1.2 million in 1984 to $14.6 million five years later, before he took a voluntary pay cut.

As the cold war thawed and opportunities arose for business ventures in the Soviet Union, athletic footwear gained access to new markets. In 1990, a Long Island corporation signed an agreement with a Soviet firm for the manufacture of equipment and the training of six hundred Russian workers, who would then produce 50 million pairs of shoes over a ten-year period. The major item on the production list, not surprisingly, was an inexpensive "canvas-and-leather jogger shoe."

In time, however, Reagan's "antienvironmental revolution" failed. Membership in national environmental groups soared from 4 million to 7 million in the 1980s—the Sierra Club alone grew from 180,000 to 480,000 members—and so did the organizations' political effectiveness. Congress frequently blocked efforts to undermine protective policies. Many states created their own, highly effective enforcement programs. Some of the most ardent antienvironmentalists were forced to resign and were replaced by administrators who more nearly reflected the national consensus. Reagan reluctantly approved environmental laws that added more acreage to the National Wilderness Preservation System in the forty-eight contiguous states than had been added under any previous president. Twenty-nine new wildlife refuges were established, and two hundred plants and animals were added to the nation's list of endangered species. Measurable progress was also made in removing hazardous wastes from landfills, eliminating lead from gasoline, and protecting the ozone layer by reducing the use of chlorofluorocarbons.

Environmentalists had turned back a frontal assault. As Carl Pope, a Sierra Club official, noted: "By the middle of Reagan's second term his administration's new initiatives were far closer to the mainstream than to the privatized, deregulated world the President's pre-inauguration team had laid out." But Pope also offered an equally important, and less comforting, observation: "We should not forget that on mountaintops and beaches, in small woodlands and majestic rainforests, in cities and playgrounds, in the oceans and the atmosphere itself, reminders of the Reagan Era will linger for decades. . . . Eight precious years have been lost."

## WOMEN, THE WORKPLACE, AND THE FAMILY

"The long, ill-fated battle for the Equal Rights Amendment means nothing to young women who already assume they will be treated as equals," *Time* magazine declared in 1989. For women wage earners of the 1980s, however, the campaign for equality continued in the workplace. By mid-decade, 55 percent of women had joined the labor force, where they held about 45 percent of the jobs. Since 1980, notably, women had filled four out of five new jobs. Major concerns included wage inequities, prospects for advancement, and the integration of paid work with family life.

Some issues reflected the rapid increase in the number of working mothers. By the end of the 1980s, 68 percent of women with children were employed. Most working parents of preschoolers left them with relatives or private caretakers, or in informal, unlicensed child care arrangements. One-quarter of young children attended day care centers. Still, day care remained a minimum-wage industry, with low-paid personnel and high turnover, that usually offered only custodial care. "Quality care" entailed considerable expense. Surveys reported that working women's major goals were "helping balance work and family" and "getting government funding for programs such as child-care and maternity leave."

Pregnant workers faced special problems. The Federal Disability law of 1978 barred discrimination against prospective mothers, and a California law went further. It required unpaid leave of several months for pregnant women, who would be guaranteed their original jobs on return. In 1987, the Supreme Court upheld the California measure in *California Savings and Loan Association v. Guerra*. But the case evoked a furor about "preferential treatment." The National Organization for Women (NOW), for instance, criticized the California law. To regard women under law as a different class of workers, NOW contended, would foster sexist stereotypes and increase discrimination against women. One solution seemed to be "parental" leave, available to either parent. By the end of the 1980s, seven states had passed parental leave laws. In 1990, President Bush vetoed a "family leave" bill that would have offered unpaid leave to workers with family obligations. Although he favored the policy, the President claimed, it should be voluntary and not obligatory on the part of employers.

Other issues involved wage differentials between male and female workers. By the end of the 1980s, the average earnings of full-time women workers

Construction workers, Chicago, 1990. (*STEVE KAGAN/NYT PERMISSIONS.*)

were 70 percent those of men, and young women earned yet higher proportions of male wages. "Women are entering the kinds of occupations traditionally dominated by men—professional, managerial, and technical positions—and the male-female wage gap within those occupations is narrowing," a federal spokesman explained. Still, discrepancies remained and experts offered many possible explanations: women were predominant among new entrants to the job market; they had more interruptions in their work careers; they were less likely to work in unionized sectors; if they had families, they may have preferred convenient or flexible work to higher pay; or they may have met discriminatory treatment. A lobbyist for the Women's Equity Action League blamed wage differentials on "sex discrimination, the old boys' network, and massive stereotyping of women's work." Despite the female invasion of higher-paid occupations, most women of the 1980s faced a segregated job market. Three out of five held pink-collar jobs, and as a Census Bureau official explained, "Working in an occupation that has a high proportion of women has a negative effect on earnings."

The segregated job market fostered the demand for "pay equity" or "comparable worth"—an effort to raise pay levels in occupations in which women predominated. A clerical worker, pay equity advocates contended, should receive the same pay as a truck driver working for the same employer. The premise of pay equity was that the "worth" of a job could be rationally determined, based on such factors as skill, training, effort, and responsibility. Critics contended that the concept took no notice of "market forces," or the demand for certain types of workers. Supporters, too, voiced qualifications. A study published in the *Harvard Law Review* contended that comparable worth, though desirable, defied implementation by the courts and would have only a negligible impact on women's wages. A study of pay equity among public employees in Minnesota, which adopted the policy in the mid-1980s, suggested that it remedied low wages but increased managerial power. Yet for feminists, pay equity retained appeal. It would affect large numbers of ordinary wage earners rather than those professionals who had thus far been the main beneficiaries of feminist breakthroughs.

A third issue concerned opportunities for advancement. Attention centered on the business world. By the mid-1980s, 30 percent of managerial personnel were women. A slew of advice books on "the right moves" and "feminine leadership" presented strategies for success in business circles, and counsel on such matters as "corporate romance" and "corporate manners." But studies of women executives revealed "ambivalence," "business burnout," and a feeling that "something's missing." Success in the higher ranks of business or the professions seemed to exact a high price in personal life. In 1989, Felice Schwartz, president of a research group that focused on women in business, urged in the *Harvard Business Review* that women who chose to fulfill family obligations might join a slower work track that peaked at middle management. The "mommy track" evoked a storm of protest. One critic charged that it would "perpetuate a cycle in which generations of women have been depreciated, divided, and weakened." Schwartz replied that she was urging employers to "create policies that help mothers balance career and family responsibilities" and "eliminate barriers to productivity and advancement."

The changing structure of the economy itself posed problems for women workers. Since 1970, the rise of service industries and the impact of advanced technology had created many jobs for women. But new options entailed new liabilities. Computers, for instance, had both increased female employment and transformed the nature of office work. They may have also devalued the labor of clerical employees, to whom repetitive data-processing tasks resembled piecework. "Automation is producing the sweatshops of the 1980s," an official of a secretarial union declared. Part-time work presented problems, too. As women surged into the labor market, employers relied increasingly on temporary or part-time workers. At mid-decade, over half of women wage earners worked part-time or for only part of the year. Less costly to employers, such "contingent" workers lacked the benefits guaranteed to full-time employees. Women's need for flexible jobs could create a class of second-class workers.

Although married women constituted the majority of new employees, another group of women workers had steadily grown. While politicians endorsed "family values," family life had undergone a transformation. Between 1970 and the mid-1980s, the numbers of women living alone increased by 73 percent, the rate of separation and divorce increased by 80 percent, and the number of women heading households increased by 84 percent. In 1986, 45 percent of women workers were single or formerly married, and many were heads of households with families to maintain. The decline of the "traditional" family increased women workers' need for a "family wage." Advocates of equity for women workers therefore faced a variety of considerations. Any acceptance in law or custom of gender distinctions might foster discrimination against women workers and leave them at a competitive disadvantage. On the other hand, insistence on absolute equality could limit the options for "flexible work" and "balance" that many women wage earners demanded. The concerns of the growing female labor force seemed destined to continue into the 1990s.

## AIDS, DRUGS, AND PRIVACY

Concern with two more immediate problems—the AIDS (acquired immune deficiency syndrome) epidemic and the growing use of crack cocaine—also came to shape public policy in the 1980s. The two problems resembled each others in certain ways: both were unknown in 1980 but had become focal points of public attention by the early 1990s; both involved issues of personal conduct that gave rise to moral judgments; both had a racial dimension; and both led to a debate over testing that posed profound questions about freedom, privacy, and social control. Moreover, women who contracted AIDS and those who used crack often gave birth to children who suffered from severe disorders or who were doomed.

Homicide death rates across time. (*Urie Bronfenbrenner, et al.,* The State of Americans *[New York: Free Press, 1996], p. 31.*)

Males Aged 15–24, in Canada, the United States, the Federal Republic of Germany, England and Wales, and Japan

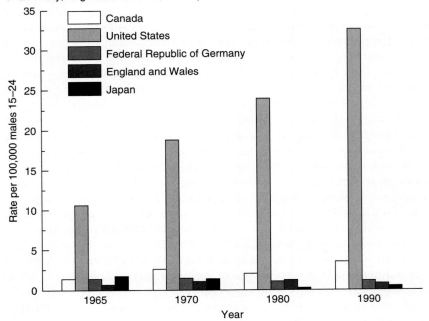

In 1981, the first cases of AIDS were diagnosed among gay men. Caused by a slow-acting virus, the disease was spread through contaminated blood or semen. Since transmission usually occurred through anal intercourse or the use of shared hypodermic needles, AIDS chiefly affected homosexual males and intravenous drug users. But the disease also claimed other victims: heterosexuals who had unprotected sexual relations with carriers of the virus; patients who received transfusions of contaminated blood; newborns who were infected with the virus through their mothers' placentas; and, in a very few instances, physicians, nurses, and other health care workers who were exposed accidentally.

By 1983, 1,000 cases of AIDS had been diagnosed in the United States; by 1985, 9,000 cases; by 1990, 150,000 cases; and by 1996, nearly 515,000 cases. By then the disease had claimed the lives of 320,000 Americans. Males accounted for approximately 85 percent of those who contracted the disease, women for approximately 13 percent, and children under the age of thirteen for less than 2 percent. AIDS exacted a disproportionate toll among racial and ethnic minorities: 50 percent of the victims were whites, but 33 percent were African-Americans, and 17 percent were Hispanics. Since persons infected with HIV (human immunodeficiency virus) usually remain asymptomatic for many years, many thousands more were certain to develop AIDS.

Because the illness could not be discussed without frankly mentioning sexual practices that had always been regarded as taboo, it took several years for AIDS to enter the public's consciousness. By the mid-1980s, however, the subject had become ubiquitous. In July 1985, *Life* magazine ran a cover story titled "Now No One Is Safe from AIDS"; in 1986, Surgeon General C. Everett Koop called for AIDS education "at the earliest grade possible"; in 1987, half a million people marched on Washington to demand gay rights and increased AIDS funding; in 1988, President Reagan signed a bill designating October as AIDS Awareness/Prevention Month.

Eventually, Surgeon General Koop unveiled a national advertising campaign designed to promote the use of condoms to fight AIDS. Angry conservatives denounced Koop's approach, grumbling that it would encourage young people to have illicit sex, and that it "tacitly endorses the moral position of those who consider homosexuality an acceptable alternative life-style." Despite such complaints, by 1990 the nation experienced what one writer dubbed "condomania": "safe sex" Valentine's Day cards, with enclosed condoms, soon appeared on the shelves of greeting card stores, a major university hosted a "Condom Olympics," and sales of prophylactics skyrocketed.

One of the most controversial issues associated with the disease was that of testing for HIV. The advantages of testing were obvious: people who were infected with the virus but still asymptomatic would be able to conduct their lives, inform their partners, and plan their futures accordingly. Yet, as gay rights activists pointed out, testing could invade individuals' privacy and make it easier to enforce discriminatory measures. "Will test results be used to identify the sexual orientation of millions of Americans?" one gay newspaper asked. "Will a list of names be made? How can such information be kept confidential? Who will be able to keep this list out of the hands of insurance companies, employers, landlords, and the government itself?" Nevertheless, public opinion polls revealed high levels of support for mandatory testing, and by 1987 the government had introduced such programs for all military personnel, reservists, and new recruits; for immigrants and illegal aliens applying for amnesty; for patients seeking admission to Veterans Administration hospitals; for inmates in federal prisons; and for applicants to the Peace Corps, Job Corps, and Foreign Service programs.

By 1989, one newspaper opinion poll showed that Americans ranked AIDS ahead of crime, taxes, education, and the budget deficit on their list of national problems. That concern reflected the publicity surrounding the illness, the fear it would spread generally among heterosexuals, and the recognition that AIDS exacted a heavy financial toll not only on individuals but also on government agencies. After spending relatively little to combat AIDS early in the 1980s, the federal government began to increase its expenditures. By 1989, the Public Health Service spent $1.3 billion for education and research, and President Bush proposed an allocation of $1.6 billion for fiscal 1990, a larger sum than that proposed to fight cancer or heart disease, each of which claimed many more lives than AIDS.

One of the few problems Americans ranked in importance even above AIDS was drugs. The two were linked, of course, since intravenous drug use was one way of spreading the deadly virus. But concern with drugs soon focused on a new form of cocaine, crack, that began to be sold in 1985. Soaking cocaine and baking soda in water, then applying heat, produced crystals. Called "crack," the crystals could then be crushed and smoked. Crack was relatively cheap (selling for $5 or $10 a vial) and therefore readily available. As one expert explained, the onset of the drug's impact is "a matter of six to eight seconds, and the intense, orgasmlike high or rush lasts for perhaps two minutes, followed by a kind of afterglow that lasts ten to twenty minutes." Crack users experience a physical addiction, as well as an overpowering psychological dependence.

While cocaine use was widespread in the 1980s—22 million Americans said they had tried the drug, and 6 million used it regularly—crack, more than any other form of the drug, created chronic, compulsive users. To obtain money to support their habit, many users committed violent crimes: in 1989, for example, one-quarter of all convicted prison and jail inmates had used crack or cocaine in the month before their offense. Crack addicts were also prone not only to hurting others but also themselves: cocaine-related hospital emergency admissions jumped from 4,300 in 1982 to 46,000 in 1988. Some urban communities were ravaged by wars between rival drug gangs. It was estimated that from 30,000 to 50,000 "crack babies" were born each year, 7,000 in New York City alone. Writing in the *New York Times* in 1990, Anna Quindlen described a neo-natal intensive care unit: "Babies born months too soon; babies born weighing little more than a hardcover book; babies that look like wizened old men in the last stages of a terminal illness, wrinkled skin clinging to chicken bones; babies who do not cry because their mouths and noses are full of tubes."

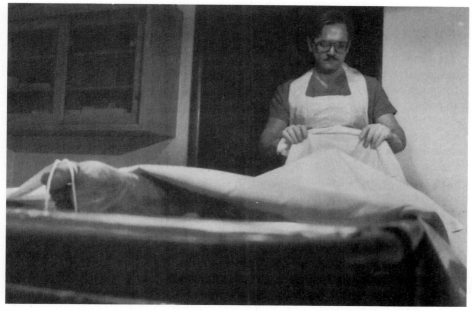

Detroit morgue: the body of a 14-year-old crack dealer. *(Eugene Richards/Magnum.)*

Politicians outdid each other in taking a tough stand on drugs. President Reagan pledged "to do what is necessary to end the drug menace" and "to cripple the power of the mob in America." In 1988, Congress passed a harsh Anti-Drug Abuse Act, which imposed stiff fines for the possession of illegal drugs, even if only for personal use; sanctioned pretrial detention and mandatory life sentences for some offenders; authorized urine testing of civil service and other workers; and provided for bus boardings, roadblocks, and other dragnet enforcement techniques. The war on drugs required an enormous increase in law enforcement personnel and, therefore, in expenditures. Federal spending on drug enforcement rose accordingly: from $1.5 billion in 1981, to $6.7 billion in 1989, to $11.9 billion in 1992.

Because crack was relatively cheap and widely available in the inner cities, it had an especially ravaging effect on African-Americans. This racial aspect led to a heated debate when Congress imposed harsher penalties for crack than for powder cocaine offenders. The government argued that such penalties were warranted because of crack's "greater abuse and dependency potential, its marketing in inexpensive quantities that makes it accessible to youth and those in a lower socioeconomic status, its association with violent crime, and its contribution to the deterioration of neighborhoods and communities." But Reverend Jesse L. Jackson, citing statistics to show that while most crack users were white, most of those incarcerated in federal prisons for crack use were black, condemned the disparity in penalties. Echoing his view, the

American Civil Liberties Union claimed that sentencing differentials "are highly inequitable against African-Americans, and represent a national drug policy tinged with racism."

The war on drugs scored some important victories, which could be measured by arrests and convictions of drug dealers, seizures of their supplies, and forfeitures of their assets. From 1984 to 1992, arrests by state and local police for the sale or manufacture of drugs doubled, while arrests for possession increased by 40 percent. The public favored stiff penalties for drug dealers and the testing of workers in dangerous or sensitive jobs. But all the punitive measures did not make much of a dent in the problem, as one crucial set of statistics revealed: in 1981, 25 tons of cocaine entered the United States; in 1985, 85 tons; and in 1988, 120 tons. Moreover, as the number of drug-related convictions rose, judges imposed longer sentences and parole became more difficult to obtain, the prisons filled to the bursting point, and the cost of maintaining them became burdensome. President Reagan's goal of a "drug-free America" remained elusive.

## BUSH VERSUS DUKAKIS, 1988

As the 1988 election approached, the nation faced a backlog of problems. The budget deficit and trade deficit, the epidemics of drugs and AIDS, the S&L debacle, the neglect of the environment, and the long-term decline of American industry—all seemed to play into the Democrats' hands. So did the "sleaze factor" that had characterized the Reagan years. Scores of administration officials had been convicted of misconduct in office or awaited trial, as did the leading figures in the Iran-Contra scandal. Astoundingly, none of these issues dominated the 1988 presidential race. Instead, the campaign itself took precedence. The "sound bite" on the nightly television news, the political commercial with a startling "visual," and "negative campaigning" became the most prominent features of the election.

At the Democratic convention in Atlanta, Massachusetts Governor Michael Dukakis captured the nomination. His major rival in the primaries had been Jesse Jackson, who won both the black vote and a larger share of white votes than he had in his 1984 campaign. Dukakis chose as his running mate Texas Senator Lloyd Bentsen, a conservative Democrat who had once defeated George Bush in a Texas Senate race. Bentsen, it was expected, would appeal to Southerners and to party members who found Dukakis too liberal. The Democrats launched their attack on Bush with a rush of enthusiasm. Keynote speaker Ann Richards, the state treasurer of Texas, mocked the vice-president's upper-class upbringing and proclivity for inept remarks. "Poor George," she declared. "He was born with a silver foot in his mouth." When the convention ended, public opinion polls gave the Democrats an overwhelming seventeen-point lead.

Republican nominee George Bush had to overcome a liability called the "wimp factor," or a tendency to seem weak and ineffective. He also had to shed

George Bush, 1988. (*GEORGE TAMES/NYT PERMISSIONS.*)

his eight-year record as Reagan's shadow and establish an independent identity. His acceptance speech, composed by former Reagan speechwriter Peggy Noonan, suggested that he might do both. To sever himself from his predecessor, Bush urged a "kinder, gentler America." Borrowing a popular phrase from a Clint Eastwood movie—"Read my lips"—he promised "no new taxes." Expressing interest in the young, he vowed to become the "education president." Ignoring the economic crises that the Reagan years had precipitated, Bush urged Americans to develop private agencies of voluntary benevolence, "a thousand points of light." Peggy Noonan's phrases and the vice-president's effective delivery were undercut only by the nominee's choice of running mate. Bush selected Senator Dan Quayle of Indiana, who seemed likely to be a docile henchman, as Bush had been for Reagan, and whose youthful looks, Republicans hoped, would sway the women's vote. Quayle at once proved a liability. Unprepared and inarticulate, he was unable to field reporters' questions. Moreover, the press reported that he had probably used family connections to gain admission to his state's National Guard in 1969 and thereby avoid combat service in Vietnam. For the rest of the campaign, the Republicans surrounded Quayle with an entourage of advisors, separated him from Bush, and kept him out of the limelight.

George Bush quickly proved an effective and professional campaigner. Ignoring the budget crisis and the Iran-Contra scandal, he capitalized on the positive: the nation enjoyed a period of peace, low inflation, and better relations with the Soviet Union. Simultaneously, his campaign team seized the offensive. Dukakis, the Republicans charged, was weak on crime, defense, and patriotism. Bush attacked Dukakis for vetoing a bill requiring Massachusetts schoolchildren to recite the Pledge of Allegiance. The Supreme Court had declared such laws unconstitutional, the Democratic nominee explained, but his "negative" ratings rose. As a follow-up, Bush visited a flag factory. He then assaulted Dukakis as soft on criminals. Republicans ran television commercials about a black man who had committed rape and murder while on release from a Massachusetts prison on a furlough program. Negative campaigning was under way and affected state races as well. New Jersey voters viewed television spots that depicted the rival gubernatorial candidates as liars: each was shown with a nose that grew like Pinocchio's.

Spurning the very notion of negative campaigning, Michael Dukakis refused to reply to the Bush assaults. Instead, he posed in a tank to indicate his interest in a strong defense, promised "good jobs at good wages," stressed his managerial know-how, and pointed to the "Massachusetts Miracle." Nor did he attack the failures or philosophy of the Reagan administration. The election was not about "ideology," Dukakis claimed, but about "competence." Running-mate Lloyd Bentsen, an experienced and astute campaigner, presented a reassuring image. But the nominee himself seemed moody, awkward, defensive, and unable to find an effective campaign theme. Only in the last few weeks of the contest did he mobilize a counterattack, refute the Republican negative charges as "lies" and "garbage," and defend his role as a "liberal," a word that the Republicans had used as a term of opprobrium. But this effort came too late. The Democrats had been forced to wage a defensive fight and had never controlled the campaign agenda.

On election day, the Republicans won 54 percent of the popular vote for president to the Democrats' 46 percent, and an electoral college victory of 426 to 112. The Bush-Quayle ticket had carried forty states, including the entire South and almost all of the western half of the nation. The Democrats fared better in the contest for president than they had in their four losing races since 1968. They also retained control of the House and the Senate, gained seats in both, and won majorities in most state legislatures. Still, in presidential races, the Democratic party apparently faced an uphill road. Democrats had won 88 percent of black votes for president, but only 4 out of 10 white votes. They had not regained the once-solid South, now solidly Republican, nor the support of blue-collar voters, who had defected to the Republicans in the Reagan years. The traditional Democratic coalition seemed to have vanished. Most troubling was the impact of negative campaigning. As an Ohio pollster for a Democratic candidate commented, "The issues mean less and less, and the ads mean more and more." And in 1988, campaign ads had conveyed distorted messages that played on voters' fears.

# CULTURE WARS AND THE BUSH ADMINISTRATION

In 1991, midway through the Bush administration, sociologist James Davison Hunter published a book entitled "Culture Wars." The American people, Hunter maintained, were divided between those with an "impulse toward authority" and those with an "impulse toward progressivism," between those who regarded morality as fixed and definable, and those who considered it changeable and subjective. Battles over issues relating to the family, art, education, and the law, he asserted, resulted from "political and social hostility rooted in different systems of moral understanding." To a remarkable degree, public attention in the late 1980s and early 1990s focused on just these kinds of disputes.

Some of the conflicts were of long-standing duration, such as those between pro-choice and right-to-life groups, between supporters and opponents of prayer in the public schools and between advocates of teaching "creation science" to school-children and critics who claimed the subject was not a science at all but rather religion masquerading as science. But a host of new issues arose which revealed deeply rooted cultural divisions just as clearly. In 1988, for example, Universal Studios released "The Last Temptation of Christ," directed by Martin Scorsese, a film depicting Jesus as afflicted by doubt, and subject to lust, pride, anger, and the fear of death. While a sympathetic reviewer termed it "one of the most serious, literate, complex, and deeply felt religious films ever made," conservative Catholics and Evangelicals, such as Reverend Jerry Falwell, denounced the film as "utter blasphemy of the worst degree."

In this contentious atmosphere, it was not surprising that the National Endowment for the Arts, which with taxpayers' money funded a wide range of cultural activities, became a lightning rod for criticism. In 1989, the Endowment came under fire for indirectly funding the work of photographers Andres Serrano and Robert Mapplethorpe. Serrano had photographed a crucifix in a jar of urine and entitled the work, "Piss Christ." Some of Mapplethorpe's photographs were explicitly homoerotic, and another one turned the image of the Virgin Mary into a tie rack. To admirers of the avant-garde, these works fulfilled an artist's responsibility to explore "the forbidden frontiers of human experience." But to critics, they were simply "morally reprehensible trash." Senator Jesse Helms of North Carolina led a drive to prohibit any federal funding for "obscene or indecent" art, and while Congress did not go as far as Helms wanted, it slashed the NEA's budget and made it clear to the agency that certain kinds of art should not be funded.

Although George Bush had successfully exploited these kinds of cultural divisions in his 1988 election campaign, he showed little inclination, once ensconced in the White House, to exploit them any further. An instinctively cautious politician, with a risk-averse temperament, Bush, unlike Ronald Reagan, distrusted change and disliked domestic crusades. Nor did he enjoy his predecessor's ardent support among conservative ideologues in the Republican Party. Much better informed about government than Reagan ever was, and therefore more willing to speak to the press, Bush nevertheless sought a relatively low profile, at least in domestic affairs. As his director of communications once said, "The President does not see himself at the center of national attention."

His personal style shaped the way Bush dealt with a Congress which remained under Democratic control throughout his administration. The President seldom proposed bold domestic programs. Instead, he relied on his veto power to check congressional initiatives. By May 1992, he had vetoed 28 bills, and the Democrats had never been able to muster the two-thirds vote in both houses necessary to override. But Bush's strategy paid few political dividends. When, in the summer of 1990, he accepted a tax increase in order to induce Congress to pass an acceptable budget, he was blamed for going back on a campaign promise even though he succeeded in implementing spending controls. When he vetoed a highly popular family and medical leave bill, he alienated a large number of voters who thought the measure made good sense, and this time his veto was overridden. Moreover, he received virtually no credit for the significant Americans with Disabilities Act of 1990, which prohibited discrimination against people with disabilities in employment, public services, transportation, and public accommodations. It required employers to make reasonable accommodations for workers who had a physical or mental impairment, who had a record of such impairment, or who were regarded by others as having such an impairment (for example, a disfiguring scar). The act covered all private firms, local and state governments, and trade unions with fifteen or more employees.

As President, however, George Bush presided over a dramatically expanded federal establishment. The average annual growth in domestic spending during his years in office was $29 billion, five times the rate under Ronald Reagan. In part, the increased expenditures were simply a legacy of the Reagan years: interest on the national debt amounted to $286 billion a year by 1992, and the bailout of savings and loan institutions cost $300 billion from 1989 to 1991. But the spending also reflected the President's support for programs like Head Start, AIDS research, and environmental protection, including proposals to reduce acid rain, halt the destruction of the wetlands, end the contamination of ground water, and ban the ocean dumping of medical wastes.

Recognizing that some of his policies had alienated conservative Republicans, the President sought to regain their favor by appointing a conservative ideologue to the Supreme Court. His selection of David Souter in 1990 had not served that purpose, but in 1991, when Justice Thurgood Marshall resigned, Bush sought to mend his political fences. He nominated 43-year-old Judge Clarence Thomas, an African-American who, although lacking in significant judicial experience, was a darling of the far right. As chairman of the Equal Employment Opportunity Commission during the Reagan years, Thomas had come out against affirmative action. But his nomination proved unexpectedly controversial when law professor Anita Hill, a former employee of Thomas's at the EEOC, claimed that he had sexually harassed her. During televised hearings of the Senate Judiciary Committee, Hill said Thomas had pressured her for dates, and had described sexually explicit acts he had viewed on pornographic films. "On various occasions," she reported, "Thomas told me graphically of his own sexual prowess." Thomas denied her allegations and denounced the proceedings as "a high-tech lynching for uppity blacks." In October, the Senate finally voted to confirm Thomas by a vote of 52-48, the fewest number of votes any successful nominee to the Court had ever received.

The hearings went far toward solidifying a gender gap that was destined to have far-reaching political implications. Polls revealed that women were far more likely to believe Hill's story than were men, and Senators (and the EEOC) were inundated with letters from women who said they had experienced similar types of harassment. Coinciding, as they did, with the so-called "Tailhook scandal," in which navy officers were found to have behaved improperly toward women at a convention, and with evidence that Senator Robert Packwood of Oregon had for many years harassed women who worked for him, the Thomas hearings helped raise the nation's consciousness about an issue that had too often been hushed up, minimized, or ignored.

In domestic affairs, George Bush had sought, with only partial success, to preserve the status quo. The President's view of Congress had been expressed by John Sununu, his chief domestic aide, in November 1990. Speaking to a conservative group in Washington, D.C., Sununu said that the administration had already obtained what it wanted from Congress and nothing more was needed: "In fact, if Congress wants to come together, adjourn, and leave, it's all right with us. We don't need them." It was in foreign affairs that George Bush—resembling no one so much as Richard Nixon—wished to leave his mark. And it was in foreign policy that he became the beneficiary of an unanticipated windfall: the sudden termination of the cold war.

## THE END OF THE "EVIL EMPIRE"— AND OF THE COLD WAR ERA?

As George Bush entered the White House, the cold war was changing more radically than it had in forty-five years. No change was more important than the surprising crumbling of Communist party control inside the Soviet Union and the rapid collapse of the Communist bloc abroad. The Soviet revolution, which had spanned, and shaped, so much of the twentieth century, seemed to be ending.

The person who presided over this change, Mikhail Gorbachev, had led the Soviet Union since 1985. A devout Communist and brilliant politician who became the youngest leader of the nation since Stalin rose to power in the 1920s, Gorbachev was also well educated, having studied agriculture and the law, and had traveled in the West. He realized that the Soviet economic system had slowed to the point of stagnation in the 1970s, lagged a generation behind the West's technology (especially in computers), and was increasingly unable to put food on the table or up-to-date weapons in the field. He proclaimed a policy of *perestroika* (economic restructuring), that was to be pushed ahead by *glasnost* (political openness). Russians found themselves freer than at any time since 1917. But the economy continued to rot away. Gorbachev blamed Communist

*Glasnost:* Soviet leader Mikhail Gorbachev and President
Ronald Reagan in Red Square, Moscow. *(AP/WIDE WORLD
PHOTOS.)*

party bureaucrats who clung to "the old ways." He moved to replace them with
a new government based on a Congress of People's Deputies, many of whom
were chosen in open elections in which Communist party members suffered
embarrassing defeats. Gorbachev headed both the new government and the
Communist party.

When these measures did not help the economy, he took the next step
during 1989–90. He refused to spend more resources on controlling a sullen,
unproductive Eastern Europe. Without full support from Moscow, the governments crumbled, first in Poland and Czechoslovakia, then in East Germany, Bulgaria, and Romania. Most dramatically, on November 9, 1989, a
hated symbol of the cold war, the cement and barbed-wire wall that had separated West and East Berlin since 1961, was dismantled by the Communists.
East and West Germans flooded across the former barrier as two Germanies
began to become one.

In an about-face that seemed nearly as remarkable as Gorbachev's, Ronald Reagan held four major summit conferences with the Soviet leader in just three years. The two leaders signed agreements which opened scientific and cultural exchanges, promised to reduce strategic arms and conventional forces, and pledged cooperation to clean up the environment. They even signed a treaty to destroy, for the first time, an entire family of nuclear missiles each had placed in Europe. Visiting and enjoying Moscow in the springtime of 1988, Reagan was asked about his earlier remark that the Soviets were an "evil empire." He replied, "I was talking about another empire." After taking power in early 1989, President George Bush held two summits with Gorbachev in which they agreed to speed up arms reductions and the opening of U.S.-Soviet trade.

Many U.S. corporations were already moving into the Soviet Union, despite such obstacles as the lack of a Russian banking system and a badly trained labor force. McDonald's opened a huge outlet close to Red Square in Moscow, H. J. Heinz sold baby food, Philip Morris shipped billions of cigarettes, Pepsi-Cola sold more than 9 million bottles of soft drink annually, and Coca-Cola prepared to challenge Pepsi for the entire former Communist bloc by building a bottling operation in France that produced three-and-a-half cases of cola each second. It was the West Germans, however, who led the drive into the East European market. They eased the way for Gorbachev's agreement for a unification of East and West Germany in 1990 by agreeing to send nearly $15 billion to help revive the Soviet economy.

Gorbachev's "new thinking," as he termed it, set off not merely ripples but political tidal waves outside Europe. Communist-supported regimes in Africa, Southeast Asia, and the Middle East undertook major policy changes to find replacements for lost Soviet support. Even Cuba, where Fidel Castro had won his own revolution in 1959 with little Russian help, suffered badly when Gorbachev threatened to reduce his $5 billion annual aid, then criticized Castro for clinging to old ways of thinking. The Sandinista government of Nicaragua also felt the waves. During the middle 1980s the Sandinistas received more than $500 million in aid each year from the Soviets, primarily to fight the U.S.-supported Contras. In 1987, however, the president of neighboring Costa Rica, Oscar Arias Sanchez, proposed a plan to bring peace and elections to Central American battlefields. Arias won the Nobel Peace Prize for his efforts, although U.S. officials greeted the plan with open hostility; they believed the Sandinistas understood direct military force only. Nicaragua nevertheless went along with much of the Arias plan and held elections in early 1990. To the Sandinistas' (and nearly everyone else's) surprise, a loose anti-Sandinista coalition led by Violetta Chamorro won. Gorbachev told the Sandinistas to abide by the results. Chamorro became president. Unfortunately, the Arias plan was less successful in El Salvador, where another Central American revolution had taken 75,000 lives since 1979. Some 700,000 Salvadorans, or about one in every seven, sought safety by emigrating, usually illegally, to the United States. Although the United States had spent more than $4 billion in the 1980s to defeat the revolutionaries, neither the war nor the Salvadoran army's brutalities against civilians stopped.

## THE PERSIAN GULF WAR

With the Soviet military withdrawing from Latin America and Eastern Europe, Bush found himself heading the world's only remaining superpower. Not reluctant to use force, he used it twice within eight months. In December 1989, he sent 27,000 troops into Panama to capture dictator Manuel Antonio Noriega and install a pro-U.S. regime. Noriega, whose power had been created through his work with the CIA and other U.S. agencies, had after 1984 refused to help the United States fight the Sandinistas. He also had enriched himself through the drug trade. U.S. forces finally captured Noriega, but did so at the cost of at least 500 (mostly civilian) lives. The drug trade through Panama, moreover, continued to flourish. In August 1990, Iraq's dictator, Saddam Hussein, invaded the neighboring, oil-rich kingdom of Kuwait and threatened to strike at Saudi Arabia, whose desert sands covered one-quarter of the world's known oil and which had long been a close U.S. friend. Bush moved more than 400,000 military personnel into the region to prevent an invasion of Saudi Arabia and to pressure Saddam Hussein to leave Kuwait. Unlike the case in Panama, where he acted without regard to the United Nations or world opinion, the President obtained support from the United Nations, from a cooperative Gorbachev, and from several Islamic nations in the Middle East who feared Iraq's power and ambitions.

On January 16, 1991, Americans entered their largest war since the Vietnam conflict when President Bush ordered U.S. and allied planes to attack Baghdad and other targets in Iraq. Seeking first to destroy nuclear and chemical production plants, the planes also began round-the-clock bombing of Iraqi troops who occupied Kuwait. The assault was led by guided missiles and by hundreds of B-52 aircraft, each of which carried 40 to 50 tons of explosives. Some 550,000 U.S. and allied troops prepared for a bloody ground war against dug-in Iraqi forces.

The war was important historically for a number of reasons. First, after an intensive debate, Congress narrowly passed a resolution in January 1991 that authorized Bush to use military force against Iraq. It marked the first time since 1941, a half-century earlier, that the presidency followed a semblance of constitutional procedures by seeking the equivalent of a congressional declaration of war. Second, the United States relied extensively on new, high-technology weapons. Most notable was the Patriot anti-missile weapon that destroyed low-flying Iraqi missiles. A number of the Iraqi projectiles nevertheless evaded the Patriots and killed civilians in Israel and Saudi Arabia. Third, Americans were able to follow much of the war on a twenty-four-hour basis, especially on the CNN cable-news network that became famous for its live, on-the-spot coverage. Even Saddam Hussein watched CNN. But television and newspaper reporters were tightly controlled by the U.S. military, which heavily censored the news Americans received. Military officials continued to believe—quite mistakenly—that biased, anti-U.S. media coverage had led to the defeat in Vietnam. This time Americans were to see only what U.S. officials wanted them to see. Throughout the conflict, even after scores of American lives had been lost, few bodies and little bloodshed from the war were shown on television—a

Soldiers of the U.S. Eighty-second Airborne wearing gas masks, Saudi Arabia, 1990. *(Dennis Brack/*Time *Magazine.)*

medium that otherwise displayed considerable killing and gore in its regular, prime-time programs.

U.S. foreign policy was not primarily motivated by a concern for "democracy," although most Americans liked to assume it was. Freeing Kuwait of Iraqi troops would mean restoring a feudal, nondemocratic regime to power in that small kingdom; and because of the heavy censorship, the American people were not well informed about the realities of war. In early 1991, the United States was spending upwards of $1 billion a day and sending its forces into battle for two main objectives: to keep Middle Eastern oil in friendly hands and to destroy Saddam Hussein's military power before the dictator could control much of the region's affairs through force—perhaps, in the not distant future, through nuclear weapons.

On February 23, 1991, Bush sent the 700,000 ground troops of the U.S.-directed coalition into action. Within 100 hours they overwhelmed the Iraqis and a truce was arranged. The President's supporters reveled in the triumph. Bush's approval ratings of over 90 percent were unmatched in the history of the polls. Grateful Americans, having covered front yards with yellow ribbons to remember their soldiers, welcomed them home with festivities unmatched since 1945. Pundits again discussed "the unipolar world" of a *pax Americana.* The President proclaimed that Americans had finally "kicked" the "Vietnam syndrome"—that is, they were no longer reluctant to trust their military to use massive force. Only 120 Americans died in action after fears had spread that thousands would be killed. The U.S. commander, General Norman Schwarzkopf, became a hero admired for his public concern for his soldiers' well being and for his quick military triumph.

Critics, however, were not silenced. Their four main charges had as much to do with the deeper history of the twentieth century as with the hours of

# THE MIDDLE EAST AND THE WAR AGAINST IRAQ, 1991

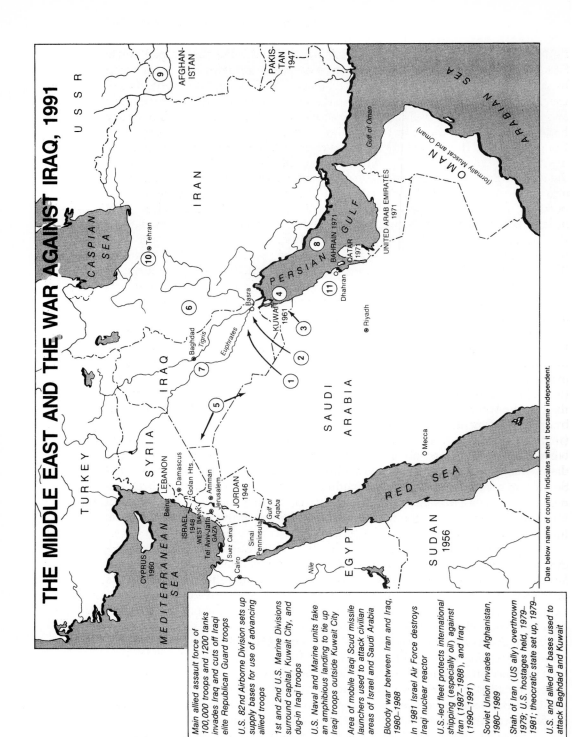

1. Main allied assault force of 100,000 troops and 1200 tanks invades Iraq and cuts off Iraqi elite Republican Guard troops

2. U.S. 82nd Airborne Division sets up supply bases for use of advancing allied troops

3. 1st and 2nd U.S. Marine Divisions surround capital, Kuwait City, and dug-in Iraqi troops

4. U.S. Naval and Marine units fake an amphibious landing to tie up Iraqi troops outside Kuwait City

5. Area of mobile Iraqi Scud missile launchers used to attack civilian areas of Israel and Saudi Arabia

6. Bloody war between Iran and Iraq, 1980–1988

7. In 1981 Israeli Air Force destroys Iraqi nuclear reactor

8. U.S.-led fleet protects international shipping (especially oil) against Iran (1987–1988), and Iraq (1990–1991)

9. Soviet Union invades Afghanistan, 1980–1989

10. Shah of Iran (US ally) overthrown 1979; U.S. hostages held, 1979–1981; theocratic state set up, 1979–

11. U.S. and allied air bases used to attack Baghdad and Kuwait

Date below name of country indicates when it became independent.

fighting in 1991. First, they charged that Reagan and Bush had helped create Saddam Hussein's power by selling him weapons throughout the 1980s when he was at war with the Americans' archenemy, Iran. The two Presidents, moreover, even secretly tolerated Saddam Hussein's terrorism against Americans and Israelis so that the anti-Iran policy could be continued. Foolish U.S. policy had helped bring about the war, critics charged. Second, they downplayed Congress's role. They noted that in November 1990 Bush used his Commander-in-Chief powers under the Constitution to double the number of U.S. troops in the Middle East. This move suddenly put the forces into an offensive alignment and made it impossible for the coalition to await the slow pressure of more peaceful economic sanctions on Iraq. Bush did not consult Congress about this; indeed, some congressmen charged that he misled them about his intentions. By January 1992, he, like many of his twentieth-century predecessors who found themselves in crisis, had given Congress little alternative but to follow the President's wishes for war. Third, critics charged that Bush did not obtain his goal of destroying Saddam Hussein but, instead, used such an enormous amount of firepower to obtain a quick victory that the President caused "near-apocolyptic" damage (to use the United Nations' phrase) and possibly the death of 50,000 people in Iraq. Smoke from Kuwait's oil wells, set afire by the Iraqis, turned day to night, and that cataclysm, combined with the incredible military destruction, turned the region into a gigantic ecological disaster. Later evaluations, moreover, concluded that probably 70 percent of U.S. bombs (including so-called "smart bombs" that could be guided to targets) missed their objectives. Finally, the critics believed the war did not bring peace and stability. When Bush asked Iraqis to overthrow Saddam Hussein, the ethnic Kurds (who had long suffered at the dictator's hands) rose up, only to be brutally beaten down by the Iraqis. Thousands of Kurds died of starvation, cold, and disease despite a too-late U.S. relief effort. Two long-time foes of the United States, Iran and Syria, both of which had sponsored international terrorism, rose to dominance in the region as Iraq lay destroyed. Oil prices did drop, and U.S. oil companies prospered (Exxon enjoyed its most profitable year since John D. Rockefeller had formed the parent company in 1882), but the American economy remained mired in recession. Critics concluded that Bush lacked the strategy and economic resources to control these foreign policy dilemmas. Despite his claim to the contrary, he could not use military power to solve the problems that had limited U.S. diplomatic options since the Vietnam conflict.

## TO THE END OF THE CENTURY—AND HISTORY?

Amid the threats of such dangerous disorder, debates erupted over the question of what shape the 1990s and the early twenty-first century would take. Heated discussion focused on Francis Fukuyama's essay "The End of History," published in the summer 1989 issue of *The National Interest*. A member of Bush's State Department at the time, Fukuyama argued that communism's failure and liberal capitalist democracy's triumph meant an end to the ideological wars that had torn apart the twentieth century. He admitted that sharp conflicts could occur over religion and environmental issues, especially in the less industrialized areas. For the industrialized world that Fukuyama cared about, however, a new—although not necessarily better—era was dawning. People, he feared, would now spend time wallowing in consumer goods and gulping down fast foods rather than fighting for great causes. "The end of history will be a very sad time," Fukuyama concluded.

A year after his essay appeared, the beginning of the new decade lacked neither excitement nor great causes. Economically, American trade and government deficits threatened to cripple the economy. A root cause of the economic problem was the falling productivity of each American worker—that is, the rate at which a worker increased his or her production of goods. The 1970s and 1980s were the worst decades for productivity in the century. As a result, the average U.S. worker had not enjoyed a gain in real take-home pay for twenty years. The number of poor grew rapidly, especially among minority groups. There seemed to be much left to do to make the nation's economic system function sufficiently, let alone well.

Nor did communism's collapse necessarily create a safer world. In trying to restructure, Mikhail Gorbachev lifted sixty-year-long Stalinist controls off the Soviet people. Divided among one hundred nationalities and impoverished by the breakdown of the economic system, the Soviets fell to fighting one another. Major battles erupted between ethnic groups; homeless and starving people were evident for the first time since World War II; and Russia, the largest by far of the fifteen Soviet republics, threatened to leave the Soviet Union and become an independent nation despite Gorbachev's heated opposition. If the Soviet Union spun out of control, all of world affairs would become dangerously unpredictable, not least because the fate of the Red Army's 30,000 nuclear warheads would be at stake. Gorbachev won the 1990 Nobel Peace Prize for allowing the East European peoples to vote democratic governments into power. But by 1991 the Soviet Union was disintegrating economically and politically, and Gorbachev was cooperating more with the military and secret police to maintain order.

The power vacuums created by the American and Soviet dilemmas were quickly being filled. Twelve European nations pledged they would form a European community without internal tariffs or other obstacles to the movement of trade, people, or money. By the year 2000, the 350 million people in the community could form the West's richest market. It would be a Europe that could act more independently of Washington and also exclude American goods. In the middle of the new Europe lay a united Germany whose economic power could, by the year 2000, dominate the entire Eurasian landmass. Gorbachev, who now talked about "our common European home," sought to join the new Europe. The American relationship to this Europe was not clear. Since 1949 the key U.S. tie to Western Europe had been the North Atlantic Treaty Organization. With the Soviet military threat disappearing, economics, not NATO, could shape the future.

On the other side of the world, Japan was becoming the world's richest nation. It was also becoming the center of an East Asian region that, as a top

U.S. official declared in 1988, "could become the world's largest source of credit" and "the world's technological leader." By the late 1970s, for the first time in its history, the United States had more trade with the Pacific rim countries than with Europe. How the United States could compete for these rich markets, or even maintain control of its own home market in the face of Asian competition, promised to be pivotal questions for Americans in the twenty-first century. In the meantime, tensions between the United States and Japan rose to dangerous levels. Dislike of Japan had become "a tidal wave and you have to run very fast to be in front of it," a Bush administration official declared in 1990. The Japanese, for their part, increasingly saw Americans as wasteful, less competitive than the Japanese, and undisciplined.

Reagan and Bush had an answer, indeed an historic answer, to these economic threats posed by the Europeans and Japanese. In 1988 Reagan signed a pact with Canada providing that in ten years the two nations would create a giant free-trade community. Already the leading American trade partner ($200 billion annually), Canada now saw its trade jump with its southern neighbor another $12 billion in 1989–1990. Investment capital moved rapidly in both directions. In 1990 Mexico reversed its historic opposition and declared it wanted to form a common market with the United States. Despite bitter opposition from American labor unions, textile manufacturers, and environmentalists (who feared low-wage Mexican competition that had relatively little concern for environmental standards), Bush pledged to build this U.S.–Canada–Mexico free-trade community by the mid-1990s.

Some experts feared that given its rapid population increase and growing environmental problems, the globe was a ticking time bomb. Between World War II and the 1990s world population shot up from 2.5 billion to 4.5 billion, with a projected 8 billion to 9 billion in the early twenty-first century. (It had taken 1 million years to produce the first billion, but only 120 years for the second, 32 years for the third, and 15 years for the fourth.) In Africa and the Middle East especially, growing populations, economic inequality, and political frustrations produced a surge of religious Islamic fundamentalism that posed new questions for Americans. They first had faced that challenge during the 1979 Iranian revolution. By the 1990s, Islam, which compares with Christianity as an expansive, proselytizing religion, had in its more radical form become a force in a half-dozen other nations. Its radical members fueled terrorist acts and support for Iraq's invasion of Kuwait in 1990.

Surging populations wiped out huge chunks of the earth's resources, especially rain forests necessary to cool and purify the globe. Scientific knowledge existed to meet this challenge, although science also offered problems of its own, especially in the field of biotechnology—the new industry that by combining discoveries in biology and technology gave scientists almost godlike power over human life. For three centuries researchers had known that cells form the foundation blocks of life, but not until 1951 did California researchers discover the spiral shape of the protein molecules that make up most of a cell. Two British scientists then took the crucial step of finding the specific molecules in the cell that carry genetic information (hair and eye color, height, and so on) from one generation to the next. Once it was understood how genes were made up (that is, in long chains of DNA, or deoxyribonucleic acid), and how the long chains worked, the genes could be manipulated. "Gene machines" could even synthesize different parts of the chain.

Within thirty years, this international scientific effort produced "genetic engineering" that could, for example, transplant genes into a patient's cells to make the patient immune to certain diseases. Such research developed new medicines, seeds, foods, even animals. New species of grain were formed that miraculously gathered nitrogen from the air (thus making fertilizers unnecessary), were immune to insect pests, and needed little water. But playing with nature's basic tool posed great, even unknown, dangers. One laboratory used genetic engineering to produce a bacterium that could prevent a potato crop from being destroyed by frost. A judge, however, refused to allow the bacteria to be spread because no one knew what else the bacterium might do once it was released into the air. An uproar ensued when a biotechnological report noted the possibility of creating a disease-resistant person "which has only in part human attributes." Leading Protestant, Jewish, and Roman Catholic leaders warned that unless such work was closely controlled, biotechnology could lead to the horrors glimpsed in Nazi Germany:

> History has shown us that there will always be those who believe it appropriate to "correct" our mental and social structures by genetic means, so as to fit their vision of humanity. . . . Those who would play God will be tempted as never before.

Eventually, the National Institutes of Health (NIH) issued national guidelines for the splicing of genes.

Whether Americans looked at their own overstretched economy, the crisis in the Middle East, the growing inequality of their society, the new challenges of a united Europe and a rising Japan, or the explosive secrets of science and technology, it was clear they confronted some of the greatest challenges of their two-hundred-year history as an independent people. The question was not whether history, as twentieth-century Americans had known it, had come to an "end" (for in crucial areas it was clearly only beginning). The question was whether Americans could learn from their history to deal with the awesome challenges of the twenty-first century. Bill Clinton now entered the White House to lead Americans as they tried to answer that question.

## Suggested Reading

On judicial appointments during the Reagan years, see Herman Schwartz, *Packing the Courts: The Conservative Campaign to Rewrite the Constitution* (1988); and on the controversy over Robert Bork's Supreme Court nomination, see Michael Pertschuk and Wendy Schaetzel, *The People Rising: The Campaign Against the Bork Nomination* (1989). For the environment, see Samuel P. Hays, *Beauty, Health, and Permanence: Environmental Politics in the United States, 1955–1985* (1987); Peter Borrelli, ed., *Crossroads: Environmental Priorities for the Future* (1988); and H. Patricia Hynes's brilliant analysis of Rachel Carson's work, *The Recurring Silent Spring* (1989).

On pay equity, see Sara M. Evans and Barbara J. Nelson, *Wage Justice: Comparable Worth and the Paradox of Technocratic Reform* (1990). For feminist problems of the 1980s, see Susan Faludi, *Backlash: The Undeclared War Against American Women* (1991). A first-rate study of legal issues is Lise Vogel, *Mothers on the Job: Maternity Policy in the U.S. Workplace* (1993). Kevin Phillips, *The Politics of Rich and Poor* (1990), is key.

The literature on AIDS is extensive, but some of the most important books are Randy Shilts, *And the Band Played On: Politics, People, and the AIDS Epidemic* (1987); Susan Sontag, *AIDS and Its Metaphors* (1989); James Kinsella, *Covering the Plague: AIDS and the American Media* (1989); Martin Gunderson et al., *AIDS: Testing and Privacy* (1989); Ronald Bayer, *Private Acts, Social Consequences: AIDS and the Politics of Public Health* (1989); and Michael Fumento, *The Myth of Heterosexual AIDS* (1990). On drugs, two useful studies are Erich Goode, *Drugs in American Society* (1989); and Steven Wisotsky, *Beyond the War on Drugs* (1990).

On the Bush-Dukakis contest, Sidney Blumenthal, *Pledging Allegiance* (1990), has the historical context; Gerald M. Pomper et al., *The Election of 1988* (1989), is a good overview. For accounts of the Bush years, see Colin Campbell and Burt A. Rockman, eds., *The Bush Presidency: First Appraisals* (1991); Michael Duffy and Dan Goodgame, *Marching in Place: The Status Quo Presidency of George Bush* (1992); and David Mervin, *George Bush and the Guardianship Presidency* (1996). Jane Mayer and Jill Abramson, *Strange Justice* (1994) is a good account of the controversy over the nomination of Clarence Thomas.

On foreign affairs, begin with relevant entries and bibliographies in Bruce Jentleson and Thomas Paterson, ed., *Encyclopedia of American Foreign Relations*, 4 vols. (1997). James Baker III, *The Politics of Diplomacy* (1993), drawn from newly declassified documents, is the detailed account of Bush's Secretary of State. On changes in U.S.-Soviet/Russian relations, start with Ambassador Jack Matlock's excellent *Autopsy on an Empire* (1995); and Michael Beschloss and Strobe Talbott, *At the Highest Levels* (1993). Philip Zelikow and Condoleezza Rice, *Germany United and Europe Transformed* (1995), is a pro-Bush perspective but draws on still-classified material. Bruce Jentleson, *With Friends Like These* (1994) is the indispensable starting place for understanding the Persian Gulf War; and note Bob Woodward, *The Commanders* (1991), an inside account of the war; Lawrence Freedman and Efraim Karsh, *The Gulf Conflict* (1993), best on the war itself; Burton Kaufman, *The Arab Middle East and the United States* (1996); Thomas L. Friedman, *From Beirut to Jerusalem* (1989), on the Israeli-Arab conflict; and Daniel Yergin's massive *The Prize* (1991) on oil's importance since 1860. Akira Iriye and Warren I. Cohen, eds., *The United States and Japan in the Postwar World* (1989) provides both U.S. and Japanese perspectives. On the central American wars, consult John A. Booth and Thomas W. Walker, *Understanding Central America* (1993); Kenneth Coleman and George Herring, eds., *Understanding the Central American Crisis* (1991); Christian Smith, *Resisting Reagan* (1996), on anti-war opposition; and Dennis Gilbert's superb *Sandinistas* (1988). Raymond Bonner, *Waltzing with a Dictator* (1987) analyzes the Philippine crisis. Leonard Thompson, *A History of South Africa* (1990), is a starting point. Iran-Contra and the dangers of presidential powers are well examined in Harold Hongju Koh, *The National Security Constitution* (1990); and Louis Fisher's definitive *Presidential War Power* (1995), also important on the Persian Gulf War.

The Global Village of the 1990s. *(AFP CORBIS-BETTMANN.)*

# CHAPTER EIGHTEEN

# The 1990s: Who Will Control the Bridge to the Twenty-First Century?

This chapter discusses:
- Bill and Hillary Clinton coming to power
- The new post-industrial age of technology and its effects on Americans
- A changing society and how an explosive new wave of immigrants is reshaping it
- Clinton's conservative domestic policies and how they thwarted the Republican "revolution"
- Clinton's changeable foreign policies and the "Clinton Doctrine"

Americans in the twentieth century witnessed three eras of social reform: Woodrow Wilson's New Freedom, Franklin D. Roosevelt's New Deal, and Lyndon Baines Johnson's Great Society. To many, it seemed that Bill Clinton's election, following twelve years of Republican rule, would inaugurate a fourth such era. But after the new administration failed to win popular backing for its chief initiative—health care reform—and after the Republicans swept the midterm elections, Clinton moved rapidly toward the political center and even adopted policies, such as a balanced budget, that had long been a staple of conservative thought. At century's end, however, American life was being shaped not only by partisan politics, but also, and even more crucially, by ongoing changes in the world economy, by rapid technological innovation, by new patterns of immigration, by women's influence in the public sphere, and by the nature of the nation's commitments abroad.

## "A DIFFERENT KIND OF DEMOCRAT": THE MEDIA AND THE ELECTION OF 1992

When Bill Clinton entered the Democratic primaries in 1992, many assumed that he sought merely to lay the groundwork for some future run for the presidency. But the 45-year-old governor of Arkansas had more ambitious plans. Clinton presented himself as a "different kind of Democrat." A member of the Democratic Leadership Council, formed to support moderate policies, Clinton sought to shift the party's image away from traditional liberal concerns, such as aid to the poor. He appealed to the middle class. His campaign planks included higher taxes for the richest Americans, more funds for infrastructure (roads and bridges), a national health care system, and welfare reform. He promised new jobs, supported protection of the environment, and urged voters to "have the courage to vote for change." Above all, the Democratic nominee recognized the voters' concern with economic issues. At Clinton headquarters in Little Rock, the staff posted reminders of campaign themes: "Change vs. More of the Same," "Don't Forget Health Care," and "It's the Economy, Stupid."

George Bush began his bid for reelection with apparent advantages, especially since the most powerful of his potential Democratic opponents failed to enter the race. The President strove to regain the great popularity he had enjoyed in the immediate wake of the Gulf War, to reenact his 1988 victory, and to capitalize on his experience in foreign affairs, an area in which Clinton seemed weak. Both nominees, however, faced unexpected problems.

First, the presidential race drew a third candidate: billionaire executive Ross Perot, founder of a data-processing firm. Unhindered by campaign finance law, which limited contributions from wealthy supporters, Perot spent $60 million of his own money and became omnipresent on radio and television. Reiterating the need to reduce the national deficit, the Texas businessman and his "Reform Party" reached out to voters disaffected from both major parties.

576

While Perot rallied supporters nationwide, the difficulties of the Bush and Clinton campaigns mounted. The Republicans' focus on foreign affairs backfired: voters resented that Bush had broken his pledge not to raise taxes ("Read my lips: No new taxes"). Strident and divisive speeches at the Republican convention, which centered on "family values," alienated suburban women who had previously voted Republican. In addition, the President seemed unable to communicate effectively with the electorate. Clinton ran into obstacles, too. Rumors of marital difficulties had plagued him since the primaries, when a former girlfriend, Gennifer Flowers, revealed a long-term relationship. Moreover, concern arose over how the Democratic nominee had managed to avoid military service during the Vietnam War. Finally, reporters raised questions about Whitewater, a failed investment made by Clinton and his wife, lawyer Hillary Rodham Clinton, in Arkansas real estate. All of these issues fueled doubts about Clinton's ethics and character.

The election results reflected the candidates' liabilities. Perot, who struck many observers as increasingly eccentric, still captured a hefty 19 percent of the popular vote, the largest third party showing since 1912, when Theodore Roosevelt won 27 percent. Clinton won a huge electoral college triumph (370 to 188) but only 43 percent of the popular vote, to Bush's 38 percent. The Clinton plurality represented the smallest winning percentage since that of Woodrow Wilson in 1912 (almost 42 percent). The Democrats, however, held both houses of Congress, where African-Americans, Hispanics, and women almost doubled their numbers. In the wake of the Thomas-Hill hearings, where Anita Hill faced an all-male judiciary committee, many women had mobilized to support women candidates. The new Congress found six women in the Senate and 47 in the house, up from 28. The press dubbed 1992 "The Year of the Women."

In the election's wake, analysts reviewed the Republican defeat. Why had Bush lost? First, the Clinton team had forced the Republicans to run a negative campaign. The Bush campaign staff had failed to read the electorate's mood, to recognize the public's concern with economic issues, or to heed a steady stream of polls that suggested objections to the way the President handled the economy. Consequently, the Republicans had never articulated a domestic agenda. Second, Bush had proved a less effective candidate than Republicans anticipated. He made many gaffes, such as voicing unfamiliarity with a supermarket cash register, or calling Clinton and his popular running-mate, Albert Gore, "crazies" or "bozos." Third, although Perot made incursions among both Democrats and Republicans, it was likely, as exit polls suggested, that he took more votes from Bush than from Clinton. Fourth, a mood of anti-incumbency had injured the Republicans. Finally, the Democratic candidate had shown unusual political skill, or what one columnist called a "virtual ability to see around corners."

But perhaps the most distinctive feature of the campaign, and one that abetted the Republican loss, was the new role that the media played. The presidential race of 1992 was the most media-driven campaign in American history. Perot, for instance, had announced his candidacy on a popular cable television program, had appeared on many talk shows, and had run "infomercials," thirty-minute television advertisements for himself. Clinton, too, had proved an adept television personality. He had played his saxophone on a late night comedian's show, appealed to younger voters on music television, performed with aplomb at televised "town meetings" in targeted states, and excelled in three televised debates that reached 88 million people. The Clinton campaign, analysts agreed, had used the media in effective ways. Its focus on pop culture served to deflect attention from mainstream press coverage, which tended to dwell on Clinton's problems—that is, on unflattering controversies about his character or patriotism. The innovative Clinton campaign also shunned expensive network television advertising in favor of purchases of local media time in states where it was most needed. Finally, the Clinton team launched challenges in states where the Republicans usually prevailed, thus making the Bush campaign use up time and money.

Clinton's triumph was a turning point. The new chief executive was the first member of the baby boom generation to become President. His victory, however, as the press observed, embodied a paradox. According to the conventional wisdom, voters held politicians and "politics as usual" in contempt. Still, they had elected a man distinguished by political savvy, skilled in political tactics, and driven by political ambition. As he entered office, without a ringing mandate, Bill Clinton faced the task of leading a nation drastically transformed by a global economic revolution.

## THE WORLD OF MULTINATIONALS—AND MILITIAS

The 1989–91 years marked the end of the superpower rivalry between the United States and the Soviet Union, but the Cold War era had actually begun to end in the early 1970s. It was then that the Soviet economy and political system became notably bankrupt and that the American economy and society, driven by a technological revolution, entered a different historic era.

Beginning in the 1970s, a giant wave of capital and trade began to wash over the world. The sources of this trade and capital were chiefly the United States and Japan. This marked the third such wave of movement abroad by U.S. multinational corporations (that is, corporations headquartered in the United States, but producing goods, and often having subsidiary units, in many foreign nations). The first wave had begun after the Civil War when new, highly competitive manufacturers such as Standard Oil set up overseas operations. The second occurred in the 1950s when a rebuilt Europe attracted many United States companies that dominated such basic industries as autos (where General Motors reigned) and chemicals (led by DuPont).

The third wave, however, differed from the first two. To begin with, it was formed less by manufacturing or raw material companies than by new technology (as computers), services (insurance or accounting), and retailing (McDonald's, Wal-Mart). The 1970s thus began a post-industrial era. Moreover, the new wave was moved less by goods (such as oil or autos), than by capital—that is, by enormous flows of money searching for profitable investment in nearly every corner of the globe. By the 1990s, some $1.3 trillion moved through the world's financial center, New York City, each *day*. That incredible sum revealed another characteristic of the new wave: it was so huge and moved across global computer systems so rapidly that governments had little control over it. Indeed, in 1992, fast-moving speculators nearly brought Great Britain's financial system to its knees when they believed the British pound was overvalued, then drove its value down in a matter of hours with overwhelming amounts of money.

This crisis revealed how the world had changed since 1900. At that time, the British government's treasury controlled world investment. Now it was nearly forced into surrender by individual speculators, most of whom operated out of the United States or Switzerland. The modern nation-state had dominated world affairs since it first appeared in the seventeenth century, but now increasingly found itself at the mercy of wealthy capitalists who moved across nations' borders with the ease and speed of the fastest computers.

Although the third wave emphasized capital, not the exchange of products, the trade in goods remained significant. By the 1990s, U.S. foreign trade amounted to more than one-third of a trillion dollars each year. Americans were the world's greatest traders. They were so integrated into the global economy that tens of millions of their jobs depended on world markets—and the foreign policies that shaped those markets. But more than three times that amount of money moved each day in the form of capital, money that built plants in such distant, vast markets as Russia and China. Some U.S. corporations (such as producers of sneakers and other sports goods) invested abroad to take advantage of cheap labor. But most companies moved overseas to ensure they could enjoy access to national markets and not have their goods shut out by tariffs. As great as American trade had become by the 1990s, it was dwarfed by the movement of money.

This movement meant that U.S. jobs were sometimes lost to the new plants and investments abroad. By the mid-1990s, American firms employed 5.5 million people overseas, 80 percent of them in manufacturing plants. This loss was offset to a degree by British, Dutch, and Japanese capitalists who invested in the United States. The state of North Carolina, for example, alone had sixty Japanese companies. Japanese auto plants in Tennessee, Indiana, and elsewhere employed tens of thousands of Americans. Good manufacturing jobs were nevertheless lost in the United States, especially to Latin American and Asian countries—regions which increasingly replaced Europe as the target for investors. After all, these were the regions most needing the new technology. "Half the world's population has never made a phone call," one investor observed. So U.S. firms led by AT&T rushed into China, Mexico, and elsewhere to obtain rich contracts for developing communication systems. That giants such as AT&T, Microsoft, or Japan's Toshiba shaped the third wave was not surprising. They had the necessary amounts of money. Except in a few fields, small firms could not compete for the richest prizes. The world's largest 100 multinationals controlled about one-third of the globe's direct foreign investment.

Aside from those who lost their jobs, other losers appeared as well in the post-1970s era. Africa was largely by-passed by the third wave. That continent was too poor, too torn by violence, too lacking in infrastructure (highways, dependable government) to attract desperately needed capital. Except for mineral-rich South Africa (where the black majority finally obtained power after 1991), and parts of northern Africa, poverty only led to more poverty over the vast continent. Losers also included law-abiding citizens. Global crime, made possible by fast-moving mobs linked by technology, took a shocking $750 billion annually from the world economy. About two-thirds of that amount came from the illegal drug trade. Americans with out-of-control drug habits handed as much as $100 billion annually to these criminals. New technology made possible mind-boggling crime little dreamed of a generation before. For example, a young man working alone out of Baring Brothers banking offices in Singapore and Hong Kong used his computer to play the volatile Tokyo stock exchange, lose billions of dollars, and thus in 1995 bankrupt Baring Brothers— a nearly 300-year-old British bank that had seemed as solid as a mountain.

Political leaders tried to keep up with this revolution by forming new regional organizations. These regional blocs were designed to attract investment and trade, but also—the designers hoped—to provide ground rules and regulations to protect the public. The European Common Market of the 1950s was the model. By the 1990s, it had evolved into the European Union (EU). The EU aimed at what it called a "single internal market" throughout much of Europe, but also worked to lessen the political hostility between France and Germany that had led to two world wars. In the Far East, the Asia Pacific Economic Cooperation (APEC) group brought together Asians and Americans to work out economic ties and, as well, to lower the risk of conflict. After all, since 1941, Americans had fought in three wars in Asia. Latin Americans also formed several common markets while aiming at the formation of a thirty-four-nation free-trade area of the Americas by 2005.

Perhaps the most important of these groups was the North American Free Trade Association (NAFTA). Its origins went back to dreams in the 1850s and the 1910s of uniting the U.S. and Canadian markets, although Americans were usually far more enthusiastic than were wary Canadians who feared the power of their southern neighbor. In 1988, the two countries had signed a treaty triggering a 10-year transition period to complete free trade. Mexico, under severe economic pressures, then asked to enter NAFTA. In 1993–94, a treaty was worked out. The U.S. Senate approved the pact only after an all-out fight. American labor opposed the treaty out of fear that jobs would move to cheaper Mexican plants. Environmentalists worried that strong U.S. laws to protect the environment would give way to weaker Mexican standards. President Bill Clinton, with solid Republican support, nevertheless pushed the NAFTA pact through the Senate. The result was the world's largest common market in terms of population (420 million) and production (more than $8 trillion each year.)

The first years of NAFTA did not produce massive movements of jobs in either direction. Unfortunately, neither did NAFTA improve labor and environmental standards significantly. As industrial and power plants grew in northern Mexico, they spewed smoke and chemicals into Texas and elsewhere along the common border. Many Canadians meanwhile rebelled against

**THE INCOME GAP . . .**
Increase or decrease in family income from 1979 to 1995.

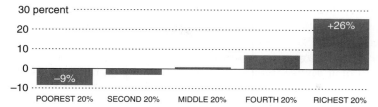

Share of the nation's income received by the richest 5 percent and the poorest 40 percent of families.

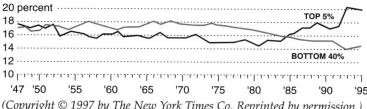

*(Copyright © 1997 by The New York Times Co. Reprinted by permission.)*

NAFTA. They believed Canada was being flooded with U.S. goods and—worse—with such cultural products as banal television programs made in Hollywood. Canadians also noted that some of their firms moved across the border where U.S. taxes and governmental regulations were sometimes not as burdensome. But NAFTA nevertheless seemed firmly cemented in place.

Such drastic economic and political change can disorient, frustrate, and anger the people involved. Americans were no exception, despite their proud claim that they have always been on the cutting edge of supposed progress. In the 1890s, for example, when the powerful new corporations (such as Carnegie steel or Armour meats) transformed the economy, beat down labor movements, and ruined smaller competitors, many Americans blamed the government, attacked immigrants who competed for jobs, and tried to form new political parties to protect themselves. The 1990s repeated this process. As the post-industrial technology changed the economic landscape, and as the end of the cold war removed many jobs in defense industries, a growing number of Americans were put out of work.

From 1979, when the new technology was taking hold, to 1995 more than 43 million jobs were lost in the United States. The peak occurred in 1992, when 3.4 million disappeared. Between 1991 and 1994, just five companies (IBM, AT&T, GM, Sears, and GTE) laid off 325,000 workers. These firms claimed that only such drastic cuts could allow them to compete in the heated global marketplace. The firings became especially difficult to explain, however, when it was revealed that the average chief executive in a U.S. corporation took home $224 for every $1 taken home by an average factory worker. (In Germany, the ratio was $14 to $1.) The rich were getting richer, the poor poorer, in relative terms. And not only were less-skilled workers hit hard. In the 1980s and 1990s, the rate of layoffs doubled for college-educated workers. The number of jobs did increase from 90 million in 1979 to 117 million in 1995, but many were low paying. In the early 1990s, the median pay for a worker who had lost a full-time job fell $85 a week—from $507 in the old job to $422 in the new.

Some Americans said, as the popular film *Network* noted, "we're mad as hell and we're not going to take it anymore." Organized labor, however, could do little to help. Representing 30 percent of U.S. workers in the early 1970s, labor unions in the 1990s had less than 18 percent of the work force. Many frustrated Americans turned to third-party movements, especially businessman Ross Perot's Reform Party. Others blamed government, either for not protecting them or, more often, for taxing and spending on programs and people (such as welfare and inner-city needs) they believed to be unfair.

When compared with other industrial societies, U.S. culture is notoriously violent. That violence can intensify when the society is beset by economic change of global dimensions. At the extremes, so-called militias appeared, especially in the Midwest and Rocky Mountain states. These groups were prepared to use force if necessary to defend their own culture, which was often racist and authoritarian. A small militia group apparently bombed the Oklahoma City federal building in 1995. The crime killed 169 people. One suspect, Timothy McVeigh, had earlier publicly written, "We have no proverbial tea to dump [as in the 1770s]; should we instead sink a ship full of Japanese imports?"

Such rebellion, resembling the economic change itself, broke out on a worldwide stage. In the Middle East, Africa, and South Asia, for example, religious fundamentalists used violence as they attempted to keep out Western culture and politics. In Mexico, the indigenous people of the Chiapas region rose up against their government. Their cause was considerably more justified than the cause of the U.S. militias. For generations, the Mexican government had systematically oppressed the Chiapas population. The rebels now proclaimed that NAFTA and the resulting flow of U.S. agricultural products into their country signed "the death certificate for the indigenous people of Mexico. We rose up in arms to respond." The rebels successfully used computer links to rally international support and to pressure Mexico City officials to compromise.

In the United States, those who developed the new technology and headed the multinational corporations that sold it grew wealthy. Bill Gates, the young head of Microsoft, was among the globe's richest persons with a net worth of over $20 billion. Many of Gates's associates in technology-related firms were the Rockefellers and Carnegies of their generation. Those who suffered from the new technology lost out and at times even turned to violence. Whatever the response, the post-1970s post-industrial revolution was a fact of life for all Americans who, whether they liked it or not, were figures on a global stage.

## THE NEW IMMIGRATION AND ITS IMPACT

Even as the United States felt the effects of this far-reaching economic change, the nation was being reshaped by new patterns of immigration. The Immigration

Reform Act of 1965 abolished quotas based on race or national origins that had favored northern Europeans but imposed the first limits on immigration from the western hemisphere. According to the law, 170,000 immigrants could enter annually from the eastern hemisphere and 120,000 from the western hemisphere. Close relatives of immigrants already here would be exempt from quotas. Over the next three decades, the new policy transformed immigration to the United States, sometimes in unexpected ways. First, legal immigration exceeded the limits Congress had imposed. Second, immigrants from Asia and Latin America quickly surpassed in number those who came from Europe. Third, illegal immigration soared. By the mid-1980s, at least 4 million undocumented aliens had arrived in the United States (see Chapter 16).

Subsequent immigration statutes modified the 1965 law but left the basic pattern of the new immigration intact. In 1986, the Immigration Reform and Control Act (the Simpson-Rodino Act) outlawed the hiring of illegal aliens, penalized employers who did so, strengthened immigration controls on the southern border, and offered amnesty to aliens who could prove that they had lived in the United States since January 1, 1982. About 3 million illegal aliens won amnesty under the law. A 1990 law, the most generous of the post–World War II era, made it possible for over 800,000 immigrants to enter the United States each year. Combined with other provisions, such as those that granted asylum, this meant that legal immigration to the United States in the 1990s would probably exceed 10 million, plus an estimated 320,000 illegal entrants each year.

Who were the new immigrants? Since 1960, about 45 percent came from the western hemisphere and 30 percent from Asia. Some fled repression or political turmoil in their lands of origin. Most sought economic opportunity and higher living standards. Since 1975, Asians—from China, Taiwan, Hong Kong, Vietnam, Cambodia, Japan, the Philippines, and South Korea—accounted for over 40 percent of total immigration. In the 1980s alone, the Asian American population grew by 80 percent. Hispanic immigrants, the fastest growing group of newcomers, arrived in yet greater numbers. Between 1970 and 1990, the number of Hispanics in the United States leapt from 9 million to 26 million. Much Hispanic immigration, especially in the Southwest, reflected poor conditions in Mexico, where unemployment was high and per capita income low. Collapse of world oil prices in the 1980s made Mexico's chronic poverty worse. Then, between late 1994 and early 1995, when the Mexican government vastly devalued the currency, more jobs vanished and motives for immigration increased. Mexico's economic woes also fueled illegal immigration. The largest numbers of undocumented aliens in the 1990s came from Mexico, El Salvador, Guatemala, and Haiti, as well as from Canada, Poland, China, and Ireland. Illegal immigrants often worked without protection of law under harsh conditions, in manual labor, in garment sweatshops, or as agricultural or household workers.

New immigrants had the greatest impact in places where they congregated. In the 1990s, over 70 percent of immigrants, legal and illegal, lived in six states: California, Texas, Florida, Illinois, New York, and New Jersey. In 1993, the foreign born accounted for 27 percent of New York City dwellers, 45 percent of Miami area residents, and one out of every three residents of the

Los Angeles–Long Beach metropolitan area. California's growth alone suggests the impact of the new immigration. The population of the state leapt by 6 million in the 1980s, 37 percent due to immigration, mainly from Mexico, Central America, and Asia. In the early 1990s, over a third of total immigrants to the United States went to California. Over half the 3 million illegal aliens who claimed amnesty in 1986 settled in the state, three-quarters of them from Mexico. By 1996, California was home to half of the nation's foreign born.

When protests against the new immigration emerged in the 1990s, states with the largest concentrations of newcomers led the way. In 1994, California passed Proposition 187, which cut off all education and non-emergency health benefits to illegal immigrants and their children. Legal challenges prevented the law's immediate implementation. The same year, California's governor, Pete Wilson, demanded that the United States government reimburse the state for $2.4 billion it spent on undocumented aliens. Similarly, in Florida, Governor Lawton Chiles sued the federal government for its alleged failure "to enforce or rationally administer its own immigration laws." In 1996, the Welfare Reform Act prevented noncitizens from receiving public assistance, causing a rush to naturalization.

Official protests mirrored widespread ambivalence about or hostility to the new immigration. Public opinion polls in the early 1990s, for instance, suggested that over 60 percent of respondents wanted immigration decreased. The Civil Rights Commission reported growing numbers of bias episodes, such as black boycotts of Korean-owned grocery stores in New York in the 1980s and an inter-ethnic riot in Los Angeles in 1992. Organizations opposed to immigration included the Federation for American Immigration Reform (1979) and American Immigration Control Foundation (1983). Other pressure groups promoted laws to make English the official language, a measure adopted in twenty-two states, including California. In 1993 and 1994, when tens of thousands of Haitian and Cuban refugees fled their homelands to seek asylum in the United States, concern about immigration mounted further.

The debate that arose over the new immigration in the 1990s echoed past debates. Defenders of liberal immigration policies argued variously that America had always been a nation of immigrants, that immigration revitalized the economy, that the taxes immigrants paid exceeded the costs that they incurred, that newcomers took jobs that others disparaged, that they contributed their education and skills to American enterprise, and that they had become scapegoats for other causes of economic distress, such as foreign competition and technological change. Critics of immigration policy contended that legislators since the 1960s had underestimated the size and consequences of the new immigration, that its hazards outweighed its benefits, and that cultural and economic considerations made continuing current immigration policy unwise.

According to the cultural argument, high rates of immigration would erode America's common culture. Foes of immigration voiced concern that large numbers of third world immigrants, language differences, and cultural diversity would divide Americans and slow assimilation. The economic argument involved two facets of immigration's impact. According to one part of the economic argument, high rates of immigration increased competition for jobs,

OLDER AMERICANS WILL SOON OUTNUMBER
CHILDREN UNDER 18, 1940–2080

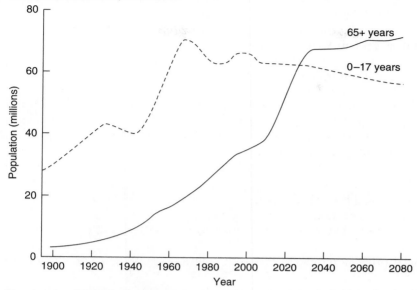

*(Reprinted with permission of The Free Press, a Division of Simon & Schuster from* The State
of Americans: This Generation and The Next *by Urie Bronfenbrenner, Peter McClelland,
Phyllis Moen, Elaine Wethington, Stephen J. Ceci. Copyright © 1996 by Urie Bronfenbrenner,
Peter McClelland, Elaine Wethington, Phyllis Moen, and Stephen J. Ceci)*

caused unemployment, depressed wages, curbed the power of labor, widened
the gap between rich and poor, and especially harmed those with low rank in
the labor market. "The continued enlargement of the low-wage labor pool in
the United States by immigration since the sixties is probably one of the reasons
that wages have stagnated or decreased at the bottom of the American class
system," contended *New Republic* editor Michael Lind, for instance. Since 1965,
Lind argued, the black working poor, in particular, had suffered from high rates
of immigration. He also claimed that current immigration policy served the
"American overclass," which appreciated a large labor supply, competition for
jobs, and low wages. "From the point of view of business class conservatives,"
Lind wrote, "the labor supply can never be too large and wages never too low."

Another facet of the economic argument involved suspected abuse by
immigrants of social and economic services. Critics claimed that immigrants,
especially illegal aliens, received more in benefits (welfare, food stamps,
schools, medical care, social security) than they paid in taxes. Consequently, as
Governor Wilson of California argued in 1994, state and local governments had
to assume the burden of these costs. Overall, factors that fostered the critical
response to immigration in the 1980s and 1990s included the unforeseen consequences of federal immigration laws since 1965; recent episodes of economic
hardship, such as in California in the early 1990s; and incidents that evoked
fear of foreign criminals, such as the ties of illegal aliens to the bombing of the

# BASKETBALL: FROM NAISMITH TO NIKE

It began with one man and eighteen overactive students in a Massachusetts gymnasium and ended with millions of customers around the world.

In 1891, as Americans turned sports crazy, 31-year-old James Naismith single-handedly invented the game of basketball. His superior at Springfield College, Massa-chusetts, begged him to find something for the bored YMCA students to play between football and baseball seasons. Naismith, borrowing from games played in his Canadian childhood, came up with the idea of throwing a soccer-type ball through a peach basket (handy from a nearby orchard) set ten feet high. That was the height of the college's gym-

Notre Dame vs. the City College of New York. (*UPI/CORBIS-BETTMANN.*)

nasium balconies to which the basket could be most easily attached. As befitted a YMCA teacher, Naismith insisted on no violence. There was to be no tackling, little contact (or "fouling"), no hard throwing of the ball (hence the ten-feet-high baskets requiring a lob).

Within a week, Naismith's gym class was playing before fascinated crowds. In 1892, women first played the game at nearby Smith College. By 1901, the *Basketball Guide for Women* observed that females took to the game at "a time of great unrest in regard to the status of women." Contrary to Naismith's hope, however, the nonstop action and a rule that players could chase a ball out-of-bounds quickly made it a rough sport—so rough that high wire cages were built to confine the players and protect the spectators (hence the "cage game").

As early as 1896, professional basketball appeared when Trenton, New Jersey, players received $15. But the game grew most popular in city gyms and playgrounds where the YMCA promoted it. Jane Addams's Hull House had one of Chicago's most popular teams. The dribbling of the ball was probably first used to score points on a Philadelphia playground. Before that, only passing had been used. After 1920, an annual national championship was held, as small colleges (e.g., Wabash College of Indiana), and larger schools (e.g., the Big Ten and City College of New York) became famous for their hardwood skills. Pro teams, especially the all-white New York Celtics and the all–African-American New York Renaissance Five and Harlem Globetrotters, played before large crowds as they barnstormed across the country. In 1940, television first covered a college game from New York City's Madison Square Garden. That year, *Time* magazine believed basketball, with its 70,000 teams, was followed by more Americans than any other sport.

The game, linked to the new media, was poised for even greater popularity. The appearance of talented giants, such as DePaul University's 6'10" George Mikan (voted the player of the 1891–1950 era); the introduction of the twenty-four-second clock (forcing teams to shoot in twenty-four seconds instead of just holding the ball); and the breaking of the racial barrier in 1951, when African-Americans began playing more regularly in the pros—all these changes drew increased numbers of fans. The University of Kentucky dominated the postwar era until the white-only-players philosophy of its coach, Adolph Rupp, made the team less competitive than the University of Cincinnati or—above all—UCLA, where John Wooden coached such legendary black players as Lew Alcindor (Kareem Abdul-Jabbar) and Sidney Wicks. In 1968, UCLA and Houston played before 53,000 fans and the then largest television audience in sports history, 30 million.

The U.S. Congress played a central role. In 1972, it passed Title IX of the Education Act that required colleges to provide similar resources for men's and women's sports. Women's basketball became popular as rule changes speeded up the game and stars such as Carol Blazejowski ("Blaze") of Montclair State College of New Jersey and Cheryl Miller of the University of Southern California (and later a noted television announcer) appeared. The U.S. Women's team took the Olympic gold medal in 1984.

Professional basketball, however, was in trouble by the early 1980s—the victim of sliding attendance, too much violence, high ticket prices, and competing sports attractions. The National Basketball Association (NBA), however, turned the corner and developed into one of the best-known sports organizations in the world when it began using television, including global media made possible by new space satellites, to promote its players and products.

This new media was ready made for Michael Jordan, who in 1983 moved from the University of North Carolina team to the professional Chicago Bulls. He became perhaps the world's most popular (and many said basketball's best ever) athlete. In the early 1990s, Chinese school children voted one of their political leaders the greatest person of the twentieth-century—and ranked Jordan second. They knew Jordan because of his worldwide

Michael Jordan, Chicago's most-popular athlete. (*AP/WIDE WORLD PHOTOS.*)

The U.S. women's basketball team won olympic gold in 1984. (*AP/WIDE WORLD PHOTOS.*)

advertisements for Nike shoes and the global marketing of the NBA.

In 1996, *Time* named Nike's founder, Phil Knight, one of "America's 25 most influential people." In 1964, Knight's new company had made $3,240. In 1996, Nike's revenue hit $6.5 billion. The company controlled one-quarter of the globe's sports-shoe sales. A turning point came in 1984 when Jordan endorsed Nike products. Advertising, it has been said, has been the leading art form of the American Century. Knight and Jordan took it to new heights as Nike's swoosh symbol and Jordan's personality and championship seasons with the Bulls became basketball's best-known products. In 1996, Jordan signed a contract with the Bulls that paid him $30 million a year, but he was probably earning even more from his endorsements.

Critics, however, condemned Nike's advertising (such as the slogan, "Just Do It")

that, they claimed, led children to attack each other to steal sports shoes and jackets. The critics also noted that Knight moved Nike production into Southeast Asia to exploit some of the world's cheapest labor and worst working conditions. He responded that production was often done with subcontractors over whom Nike had little supervision, and that, in any case, "Our business practices are no different from those of our competitors."

A century after James Naismith invented basketball, the game, like the United States itself, was a global happening, a worldwide money-making machine. In the post–cold war world of the 1990s, the U.S. power that affected billions of people's lives each day was less military than it was the culture of sports and the economics of sports marketing.

New York World Trade Center in 1993. Other factors were concerns about fraudulent asylum claims, border problems, illegal entrants, and the ethnic diversity of the new immigration.

Proposals to curb immigration in the 1990s included limiting the number of immigrants to as few as 200,000 a year, more severe clamps on illegal immigration, restriction of legal immigration to those with skills, discarding the family reunification policy, and a five-year moratorium, followed by cuts in admissions. Former Texas representative Barbara Jordan, chair of the bipartisan Federal Commission on Immigration Reform, called in a 1995 report for limiting family reunification to the nuclear family, eliminating 10,000 visas a year to unskilled workers, deterring illegal immigration by a national identity card, and capping legal immigration at 550,000 a year. President Clinton nominally endorsed the commission's recommendations, and, in 1996 with bipartisan support, the Clinton administration increased the budget of the Immigration and Naturalization Service, the number of agents in the border patrol, and the rate of deportation of illegal immigrants. Still, immigration policy seemed resistant to more drastic change. The debate continued over the impact of new immigration and over whether current immigration rates should be maintained, modified, or ended.

## BILL CLINTON AND THE END OF LIBERALISM

As Bill Clinton entered the White House in January 1993, one columnist observed that the new President offered an "ambitious, expansive, romantic vision . . . a national rebirth, a revival of hope." Clinton had encouraged such expectations when he told the Democratic Convention in July 1992 that "a President ought to be a powerful force for progress," and again, in his first address to Congress, when he asserted: "Tonight I want to talk to you about what government can do because I believe government must do more." But as a self-styled "New Democrat," Clinton was always more concerned with "renewal" than "reform," and his personal style was more naturally suited to conciliation than to conflict. After a number of initiatives failed during his first two years in office, and after the Republicans chalked up massive gains in the midterm elections of 1994, the President rapidly moved to occupy the political middle-ground. By January 1996, he could proclaim that "the era of big government is over."

For the most part, Clinton's successes in 1993 and 1994 came when he received bipartisan support, as in the case of the North American Free Trade Association pact. Gun control was another area in which Republican votes proved essential. The Brady Bill—named for Ronald Reagan's press secretary, James Brady, who had been severely wounded in an assassination attempt on the President in 1981 and had then with his wife Sara spearheaded a crusade for effective gun control—was finally enacted in 1993. It provided for a five-day waiting period to allow a background check before anyone purchasing a handgun could take possession of the weapon. Clinton's two Supreme Court nominees, Ruth Bader Ginsburg and Steven Breyer, also had impeccable credentials and received overwhelming support from Senators of both parties. But two other proposals of the new administration triggered angry opposition, chiefly from Republicans, but also from members of the President's own party.

The first concerned the issue of whether gay men and women should have a right to serve in the military. During the 1992 campaign, Clinton had promised to issue an executive order to remove the longstanding ban on the grounds that "patriotic Americans should have the right to serve the country as a member of the armed forces, without regard to sexual or affectional orientation." But the President's proposal was doomed from the start: conservative religious groups opposed any policy that legitimized or sanctioned homosexuality, and the Joint Chiefs of Staff defended the ban as necessary to preserve discipline and morale. Senator Sam Nunn of Georgia, who headed the Armed Services Committee, threw his considerable prestige against the President's plan and scheduled hearings in the spring of 1993 which provided a platform for opponents. The issue remained a thorn in Clinton's side until September, when he finally agreed to a compromise. Under the so-called "don't ask, don't tell" policy, gays could serve in the military so long as they did not reveal their sexual orientation or engage in sexual conduct or behave in ways that would indicate they were homosexuals, such as reading gay magazines, frequenting gay bars, or participating in gay pride marches. The nine-month-long controversy cost the President public support, and the outcome angered gay-rights groups which felt he had turned his back on a campaign pledge.

No sooner had this issue been resolved than Clinton produced his ill-fated plan to reform the nation's health care system. He had made health care a central theme of his campaign, tapping into a widespread feeling that the nation faced a crisis. Health care accounted for one in every seven dollars spent in the United States. Costs were rising rapidly each year, much more rapidly than the rate of inflation; many people had no health coverage at all; and many others had inadequate coverage. In September 1993, the President offered a proposal based on a report of a task force which had been headed by his wife, Hillary Rodham Clinton.

Health care, he maintained, like Social Security, should be safe and available to all, a "comprehensive package of benefits over the course of an entire lifetime." His plan was designed to ensure "health care that can never be taken away," he added, and was based on six key principles: security, simplicity, savings, choice, quality, and responsibility. More concretely, Clinton endorsed the idea of "managed competition within a budget": employers would have to offer managed care insurance plans to employees; a nonprofit health alliance would serve as a clearinghouse for all the plans in a given region and would negotiate rates with all health care providers, thereby helping to control costs.

Fully 60 percent of the American people approved Clinton's plan, leading the *Congressional Quarterly* to report that "for the first time in years, it seemed as if Congress was filled with a sense of the possibility of enacting a piece of sweeping social legislation." But public and legislative support began to erode almost immediately. The plan was inordinately complex—the bill Clinton sent to Congress was 1,342 pages in length—and it involved more government control than its sponsors were prepared to admit. The Health Insurance Association of America, representing many small and mid-sized insurance companies, launched an advertising campaign, revolving around the homey characters, "Harry and Louise," designed to show that Clinton's plan would not only be costly but would also deny patients their choice of physicians. Republicans in Congress had a field day portraying the plan as an example of big, intrusive government, while Democrats, who had not been consulted in drafting the measure, had little incentive to support it. Thomas Foley of Washington, the Democratic Speaker of the House, dubbed it a policy "Godzilla."

The hostile response to Clinton's health care proposal bore out the fears of some of his advisors. Donna Shalala, the Secretary of Health and Human Services, had warned that the administration's program "will turn off liberals and conservatives; no one will be enthusiastic. All the interest groups will be mad—the doctors, the hospitals, the labs. You're building on all the negatives." By September 1994, a year after its unveiling, Clinton's program was, by common consent, dead in the water. The President's inability to mobilize a constituency in behalf of the measure or to sell it to Democratic members of Congress contributed to a sense that the administration was inept. Even worse, Clinton had given his Republican opponents exactly the kind of ammunition they wanted for the midterm elections.

In 1994, Newt Gingrich of Georgia, who had served in the House of Representatives since 1978, emerged as the master Republican strategist. Gingrich once said that "The Sands of Iwo Jima" was "the formative movie of my life"; he sought to emulate the film's hero, John Wayne, a tough drill officer who shaped his troops into a successful fighting force. Gingrich attempted to do as much for Republican congressional candidates. He proposed that they sign a "Contract with America," consisting of ten items which could be enacted within 100 days if the party carried Congress and published it in *TV Guide* in order to reach the broadest possible audience. The stated goal of the contract was to bring an end to "government that is too big, too intrusive, and too easy with the public's money." Most of the proposals were traditional conservative fare—a balanced budget amendment, tougher anticrime laws, a diversion of funds from summer youth employment programs to prison construction, cuts in welfare, including a "tough two-years-and-out provision with work require-ments to promote individual responsibility," a capital gains tax break, and incentives for small business. The measures were given such benign titles as a "Fiscal Responsibility Act," a "Personal Responsibility Act," a "Family Reinforcement Act," and an "American Dream Restoration Act."

What the contract omitted was as significant as what it included. There was no mention at all of two controversial issues that had been part of the con-servative agenda since the Reagan years: prayer in the public schools and abor-tion. To take a stand on those issues, one Republican strategist said, would "cloud the clarity of our message." To appease the Christian Coalition, the authors of the contract spoke generally of electing a Congress "that respects the values and shares the faith of the American family" and supported a $500 per-child tax credit. Although fewer than one-third of voters said they had even heard of the contract with America by election day, Gingrich had largely suc-ceeded in nationalizing the midterm elections and making them a referendum on Clinton's first two years.

The Republicans' efforts received a substantial boost from sympathetic talk-radio hosts, who reached millions of listeners every day. The popularity of call-in radio shows had grown dramatically during the 1980s. By 1994, nearly 1,200 radio stations were carrying such programs, twice as many as in 1988, and one in every six Americans tuned in daily. Many of the most popular hosts were conservative in outlook, and none was more popular than Rush Limbaugh. He first aired his nationally syndicated program in 1988; eventually he was carried on 660 stations and was reaching an audience of more than 20 million a week. Limbaugh denounced liberal intellectuals as "pointy headed academic think-tank types," branded feminists "femi-nazis," and termed environmentalists "tree-hugging wackos." He called Vice-President Al Gore "a man with a room temperature IQ." Limbaugh, an aide to Republican Congressman Richard Armey of Texas marvelled, "is an independent power."

The results of the 1994 elections exceeded Gingrich's, and perhaps even Limbaugh's, expectations. The Republicans swept Congress, winning fifty-two seats in House and eight in Senate. They picked up still another Senate seat when an Alabama Democrat switched parties, resulting in a 53–47 majority in that chamber. They controlled the House by a comfortable 230–204 margin (there was one Independent) and quickly moved to elect Newt Gingrich as Speaker. The Republicans also elected eleven new governors, giving them con-trol of governors' mansions in thirty states, including eight of the nine largest states. In 1994, not a single incumbent Republican governor, senator, or member of the House was beaten. The Democrats, on the other hand, saw such prominent figures as governors Ann Richards in Texas and Mario Cuomo in New York go down to defeat.

It did not take President Clinton long to read the handwriting on the wall. He quickly recruited a new political advisor, Richard Morris, who had assisted him in Arkansas many years before and who had helped run Texas Republican Trent Lott's successful Senate campaign in 1994. Clinton had to "coopt the more popular parts of the G.O.P. agenda," Morris said, and thereby "return to traditional Democratic issues of a kind that have strong middle-class appeal, such as education and the environment." Morris thought that the President had to position himself between ultra-liberal congressional Democrats and ultra-conservative congressional Republicans. He proposed that Clinton follow a policy of "triangulation," as he called it, allying himself with Democrats on some issues and Republicans on others, but never allowing himself to become hostage to either. For a President badly shaken by the 1994 elections—so shaken indeed that in April 1995 he was saying, somewhat plaintively, that "the President is relevant here"—the strategy Morris proposed was highly attractive.

The policies Clinton embraced faithfully reflected Morris's advice. The President proposed a "Middle-Class Bill of Rights," for example, which would allow tax deductions for education and training after high school and permit tax-free withdrawals from individual retirement accounts for education, medical costs, the purchase of a first home, or caring for a parent. Clinton came out for a balanced budget. He proposed tough new laws to fight crime. He denounced excessive television violence and endorsed a v-chip which would enable parents to control what their children could watch. He called for finding more room for religion (although not prayer) in the public schools. He condemned cigarette companies which attracted minors through cleverly designed advertising campaigns. In July 1995, the President emphasized the value of civility and the need to "move beyond division and resentment to common ground."

The issue of affirmative action, however, was potentially far more explosive and far less amenable to the new White House strategy. Ever since 1978, when the Supreme Court had accepted its constitutionality in the Bakke case, a debate had raged over the effectiveness and fairness of affirmative action. Clinton enjoyed overwhelming backing from African-Americans, but Morris's strategy clearly implied that he would have to attract the support of whites who felt victimized by "goals," "quotas," "minority set-asides," and the like. Then, on June 12, 1995, the Supreme Court handed down a landmark decision which permitted the continuation of federal affirmative action programs but only under tough, new guidelines. *Adarand Construction* v. *Pena* involved a construction company which lost a federal contract to a minority-owned "disadvantaged" business even though it had submitted a low bid. The Supreme Court, in an opinion by Justice Sandra Day O'Connor, accepted the racial classifications underlying affirmative action programs but allowed courts to review them under a "strict scrutiny" standard. This was too harsh a standard for the four dissenting Justices, the most liberal members of the Court, but the decision nevertheless went far toward resolving the President's dilemma. In

## VIOLENT CRIME VICTIMIZATION RATES

By Race, Income, and Place of Residence, Persons Aged 12 and Over,
United States, 1993

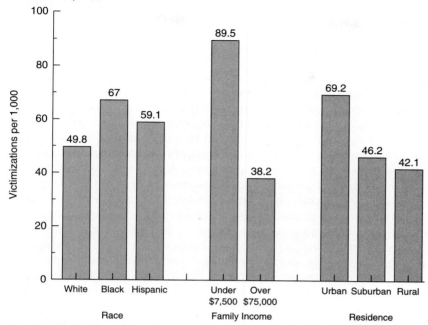

Violent crime is defined as rape/sexual assault, robbery, aggravated
assault, and simple assault. Victimization rate includes crimes not
reported to the police.

*(Reprinted with permission of The Free Press, a Division of Simon & Schuster from The State
of Americans: This Generation and The Next, by Urie Bronfenbrenner, Peter McClelland,
Phyllis Moen, Elaine Wethington, Stephen J. Ceci. Copyright © 1996 by Urie Bronfenbrenner,
Peter McClelland, Elaine Wethington, Phyllis Moen, and Stephen J. Ceci.)*

July 1995, Clinton announced that he was ordering a review of all federal affirmative action programs to see if they conformed to the Court's new standard. In general, he said, such programs had worked well and remained "a moral imperative, a Constitutional mandate, and a legal necessity." With respect to affirmative action, he said, his goal was "mend it; don't end it."

The crucial test of the new White House strategy occurred in 1996 when Congress passed a bill that revamped the nation's welfare system. At the time, direct federal welfare expenditures amounted to only $12.5 billion a year, about 1 percent of federal spending; a majority of welfare families were headed by women and most of the funding went to support children. Nevertheless, politicians in both parties were determined to cut welfare costs, although Republicans favored more drastic cuts than Democrats. The bill that finally emerged from Congress cut benefits more sharply than Clinton had wanted. Proponents of welfare reform said the measure would reduce the welfare rolls, end long-term dependence, move people into jobs, and save $60 billion over six years. Opponents predicted an increase in poverty, homelessness, and hunger. The Urban Institute thought the measure was "a Trojan horse designed to dismantle the welfare state that has existed for the past sixty years."

Clinton, following the advice of Richard Morris and others, decided to sign the measure, largely to deprive Republicans of a 1996 campaign issue. The Welfare Reform Act of 1996 reversed sixty years of federal policy. The existing program, Aid to Families with Dependent Children, was eliminated and replaced by block grants to the states: annual lump sum payments, known as Temporary Assistance for Needy Families, were to be made, but those payments would be capped rather than being adjusted to meet the need. The states would be permitted to establish their own requirements for recipients. Welfare payments would not be made to unmarried teenage mothers. Families could receive aid for a maximum of five years (although states could exempt up to 20 percent of the poor to account for emergencies). Adults who received welfare could be required to work in exchange. No aid was to be given to aliens, even to legal aliens. Unemployed adults could receive food stamps for only three months in any three-year period, unless they had children under the age of 18.

As the President became more conservative, Republicans grew more frustrated. In November 1995, a budget impasse between the White House and the House Republican majority, chiefly involving a dispute over how deeply to cut Medicare and Medicaid benefits, led to a six-day shutdown of the federal government. Many people who were hurt and inconvenienced by the closing blamed Newt Gingrich and his followers for the fiasco. Clinton suddenly saw his public opinion ratings improve. Even after Clinton accepted a compromise in which he agreed to pursue policies leading to a balanced budget by the year 2002, he could plausibly maintain that he had protected popular entitlement programs from a Republican onslaught.

"There will never be a time when government can do anything for people they won't do for themselves," President Clinton told the Democratic National Committee in 1995. The role of government, he added, was not to introduce bold new social programs, or even maintain those already in existence, but rather "to help people make the most of their own lives." He restated this theme in his 1996 State of the Union message when he declared the era of big government was over: "We know big government does not have all the answers. We know there's not a program for every problem." What was needed instead, he asserted, was "a relentless search for common ground."

So far, that search had led Clinton in a conservative direction, and the search was still in its early stages. The President would further improve his standing with the public before the 1996 election by supporting the right of schools to require students to wear uniforms as a means of insuring discipline, by signing an executive order denying federal contracts to businesses which hired illegal aliens, and by inducing the television networks to agree to expand educational programming for children. The Clinton administration's pattern in domestic policy—early reverses and a consequent decline in popularity, followed by later victories and an accompanying rise in the polls—would be replicated in foreign policy.

Newt Gingrich and Bill Clinton at odds. *(AP/WIDE WORLD PHOTOS.)*

## CLINTON'S FOREIGN POLICIES: REVERSES . . .

In the 1992 elections, Americans had viewed foreign-policy issues as important but not decisive. Bill Clinton, nevertheless, went out of his way to attack George Bush on these issues, in part because Bush's strength was his long experience and several successes (such as the Persian Gulf War) in the global arena. So Clinton effectively leveled a barrage of charges against the President: (1) the Persian Gulf War was not a great success because Iraq's dictator, Saddam Hussein, remained entrenched in power; (2) Bush coddled Chinese Communist leaders for the sake of keeping China open to U.S. goods, even as those leaders brutalized political dissenters; (3) U.S. policy toward Haiti, where the army had driven out an elected president, Jean-Bertrand Aristide, in 1991, had favored the military thugs, mistreated Aristide, and immorally sent back home Haitians who tried to find refuge in the United States; (4) Bush paid too little attention to the United Nations which, Clinton claimed, Americans would increasingly have to work with in the complex post–cold war world.

In the early months of his presidency, however, Clinton failed to reverse Bush's policies. He surprisingly even seemed to adopt them as his own. For example, when U.S.-Iraqi relations again boiled up in 1994–95, Clinton's response was so limited that his critics loudly claimed he had allowed Saddam Hussein to tighten his hold on key parts of Iraq. In regard to the Chinese, Clinton threatened to restrict trade unless the Communists better treated their dissenters. When Beijing officials nevertheless continued to crack down, Clinton backed down. By 1995, he no longer linked trade and human rights in his China policies. The bottomless market of 1.5 billion Chinese was too important, in his view, to sacrifice it to human-rights principles, especially as Japanese, Europeans, and others rushed to beat American business into that market. In Haiti, Clinton not only failed to restore President Aristide to power in 1993–early 1994, but an even more embarrassing event occurred. Clinton sent the warship, *Harlan County*, to warn the Haitian military to behave. A small mob appeared on the Haitian dock, threatening to fight anyone who landed from the *Harlan County*, and the ship retreated in disgrace. Finally, in dealing with the United Nations, officials at first did try to work with the international organization. By late 1993, however, they were backing away as critics blasted the United Nations (UN) for being inefficient or, in the eyes of some, a world government that threatened American liberties. The charge that the UN threatened to impose world government was empty. In truth, the UN was threatened with bankruptcy—in part because the United States owed it over a billion dollars, and neither Clinton nor the Congress showed much interest in paying this debt which, by solemn treaty, they were obligated to pay.

Why had Clinton so reversed himself and thrown U.S. foreign policy into such confusion? One reason was that he had little experience or interest in overseas affairs. He spent the overwhelming part of his time on domestic economic problems. A second reason stemmed from the President's and his advisors' inability to find a coherent foreign policy strategy. During the cold war, the strategy had been simple and direct: contain communism. Now, after the cold war, U.S. officials tried to use several strategies to replace containment, but none worked. Thus, Clinton, whose political antennae were extraordinarily sensitive and far-reaching, was too often left at the mercy of television and other media that blew American public opinion back and forth—with the President in pursuit.

An example was his approach to Somalia. During the cold war, this impoverished but strategically located East African nation had been fought over by Americans and Russians. Both superpowers pumped in money and arms to gain influence. When the cold war ended, both quickly lost interest in Somalia. (Indeed, U.S. officials and investors found little of interest in many parts of the continent other than South Africa.) Washington's view of Somalia changed, however, in late 1992 when television showed starvation and terrorism sweeping over the country as rival clans fought bitterly. With Clinton's support, in December 1992, Bush sent in 25,000 troops to feed the starving. The troops' night landing was spectacularly covered by Cable News Network and other television networks. Americans were on a mission of compassion. But in mid-1993, Clinton changed the mission. He decided Somalians could be helped only when one uncooperative clan leader, Mohammed Farah Aideed, was captured. Farah Aideed, however, proved elusive. In the autumn of 1993, his forces killed eighteen Americans, then dragged several of the bodies through the dust—again as television cameras rolled. By early 1994, Clinton had pulled out the troops. He had tried not merely to feed, but to change, Somalia. Neither U.S. power nor, especially, American public opinion was up to that task.

As the 1994 congressional elections approached, the President's foreign policies were in disarray. Perhaps the most dangerous stumble came in Yugoslavia. In 1991–92, that nation came apart as Croatia and Bosnia tried to separate from the dominant Serbian state. Serbians responded with force. Both sides, especially the Serbians, began "ethnic cleansing"—that is, killing masses of civilians (often after brutally raping the women) on the other side. Most Americans wanted no part of this conflict. Of special importance, the military wanted to keep its distance. A "Powell Doctrine," named after Chairman of the military Joint Chiefs, General Colin Powell, promised "no more Vietnams." According to this doctrine, U.S. troops would intervene abroad only when they knew that American interests were at stake; when the President assured them they could use their full conventional force to fight, if necessary; when the military was given a date not just for entering, but exiting, a conflict; and when the American people fully supported the operation. None of these preconditions existed in Yugoslavia. When Powell had allowed the troops to enter Somalia without these preconditions, tragedy resulted. So Clinton told Europeans they were responsible for defusing the Yugoslav conflict. The Europeans, however, turned out to be even more divided and reluctant than were the Americans. The war threatened to spread.

## . . . TO VICTORIES

Then, in 1994–95, Clinton's policies began to enjoy some successes. He even scored overseas triumphs that removed the growing hope of Republicans that they could use foreign-policy issues to humiliate him in the 1996 election. Three major reasons helped explain this turnaround. First, Clinton, understanding his political weakness, gave more personal attention to overseas crises. That attention grew after the Republican triumph in the 1994 congressional elections. Many Americans knew too little about foreign affairs, but they wanted their President to be an effective world leader, and Clinton could no longer afford to flunk this test. Second, General Colin Powell retired. The new military leaders were less haunted by Vietnam. They were willing to deploy troops in limited, open-ended operations—although they continued to insist that, if necessary, the troops could use all conventional power necessary to protect themselves from future Farah Aideeds or terrorists. Third, Clinton brought in new advisors who seized opportunities in several crisis areas to move quickly and successfully.

An initial success occurred in Haiti. Aristide, the president thrown out by the military, was a former Roman Catholic priest who condemned the exploitation of Haitians by the military and their rich civilian supporters. He wanted to end the nation's ranking as the poorest country in the entire hemisphere. But first, Aristide had to regain power. He received crucial help from African-American leaders, especially Randall Robinson of the Trans-Africa organization in Washington, D.C., who went on a widely publicized hunger strike aimed at forcing Clinton to restore Aristide's authority. Finally, in September 1994, Clinton moved U.S. forces toward Haiti and threatened to destroy the military thugs unless they left the country. They did so, taking, unfortunately, millions of dollars with them. As U.S. troops moved into the country, Aristide returned to power, the threat of Haitian refugees flooding into the United States stopped, and little was to be heard of the issue in the 1996 election campaign.

Another success followed in Yugoslavia. Here Clinton was helped in 1994–95 by Croatian military victories that checked Serbian forces. The President seized the advantage by committing U.S. air forces belonging to the NATO command in Europe to ensure that the Serbs would not regain the initiative. In truth, both sides were exhausted by three years of bloodsoaked war. Clinton dispatched Richard Holbrooke, his new assistant secretary of state for Europe, to broker a peace. Holbrooke did so, first with a truce in Yugoslavia, then at a late 1995 meeting in Dayton, Ohio, where tentative territorial settlements were worked out. Clinton then committed 20,000 U.S. troops as part of a NATO and UN force to oversee the Dayton Accords. Critics warned that the Somalia tragedy would be repeated. But Yugoslavia remained calm into 1997. The peace largely held, the President paraded American power (as Europeans followed along), and again the issue did not haunt Clinton in the 1996 campaign.

He also profited politically, perhaps unfairly so, from historic peace accords hammered out between long-time enemies Israel and the Palestinians. Indeed, the Middle East peace process moved along farther and faster in 1993–96 than at any time during the previous decade. The Palestinian Liberation Organization (PLO) obtained from Israeli Prime Minister Itzhak Rabin an agreement giving it a promise of self-rule on the West Bank of the Jordan River and on the Gaza Strip—both areas long bitterly fought over. In return, Rabin received important security guarantees from the PLO. Clinton officiated at a spectacular White House signing in September 1993 and again when the peace process moved forward in September 1995. But Rabin was assassinated in November 1995. The opposition party, Likud, came to power after condemning parts of the peace process as a sellout of Israeli security. Palestinians and Israelis lost their lives in renewed violence. In 1996, Clinton sent emissaries to try to pump life back into the peace talks. Since the bulk of U.S. foreign aid went to Israel and to Egypt (an ally of the PLO), the President had considerable leverage. By early 1997, parts of the agreement were restored. The Israeli-PLO conflict continued, sometimes violently, but Clinton benefited from the perception that his officials played a vital role in keeping the peace process alive.

One of the President's most important (if less visible) successes came in dealing with the other, former, superpower. In 1993–94, Boris Yeltsin continued

**THE BOSNIAN CRISIS, 1995–1996**

*(From Walter LaFeber,* America, Russia, and the Cold War, *1945–1996, 8/e. Copyright © 1997. Reproduced with permission of The McGraw-Hill Companies.)*

to lead Russia. But he suffered from heart disease, growing political opposition, and an economy riddled with out-of-control inflation and corruption. Yeltsin, moreover, tragically involved Russia in its own Vietnam when in 1994 he tried to use military force to prevent the Moslem enclave of Chechnya from leaving the Russian Federation. As they had for 1,000 years, the Chechens fought back violently and now did so against a bankrupt, dispirited Russian army that was falling apart. As Yeltsin's public-opinion support fell to 5 percent, observers speculated whether the Communists or reactionary nationalists would replace him in the 1996 presidential election. Clinton, however, continued supporting Yeltsin. He had little choice, given the unacceptable alternatives of communism or anti-Western nationalism. The United States funnelled millions of dollars to help Yeltsin, then shaped the International Monetary Fund's decision to give a $10 billion credit line to prop up Russia's economy. In 1996, Yeltsin won

Russia's first-ever democratic presidential election. His health continued to deteriorate, but the Communists and nationalists had been stopped, while Clinton's policies seemed vindicated.

Another policy toward the former Soviet Union also seemed to be working: patiently pressuring, and even paying, Ukraine, Belarus, and Russia itself to dismantle nuclear weapons. Ukraine and Belarus gave up their nuclear weapons, while Russia cut back more than half to about 20,000. Negotiations began in 1997 to reduce further the U.S. and Russian nuclear arsenals. The Clinton administration (with help from China) also successfully pressured Communist North Korea to freeze its nuclear-weapons program in return for badly needed economic aid. Washington led the effort to stop Iraqi, Iranian, Indian, and Pakistani nuclear programs, although it received little help from some Europeans who profited from assisting those programs.

An irony appeared: even as Clinton worked to reduce nuclear forces, his administration cooperated with arms producers to make the United States the world's greatest dealer in conventional weapons. U.S. officials were even willing to reverse their long-held view that up-to-date arms should not be sold to Latin American armies that had brutalized their own people and fought wars with neighbors. After all, as top Clinton advisors noted in 1997, since defense industries had to be kept busy, they might as well sell to Latin America (and the many other arms markets) before European, South African, or Asian competitors did so.

Clinton, indeed, had promised in 1992 to cut $60 billion over five years from the nearly $300 billion defense budget. Instead, he kept it about the $260 billion-a-year level, far higher than many experts had thought it would be after the end of the cold war. Both the President and Congress (which added billions of dollars to Pentagon budget requests) declared that a flourishing arms industry was necessary to keep thousands of Americans employed. By 1995–96, moreover, Clinton depended on the military not only for economic benefits, but to carry out his diplomacy. In Bosnia, the Middle East, Japan (where 47,000 U.S. military personnel were stationed to maintain security for the most important U.S. ally in Asia), and in the Taiwan Straits (where Clinton mobilized a war fleet in 1996 to warn China to stay away from Taiwan), the President deployed U.S. forces. A "Clinton Doctrine" had evolved. He defined this doctrine in mid-1996: "We cannot and should not be the world's policeman; but where our interests and values are clearly at stake and where we can make a difference, we must act and lead."

Since 1994, he had acted, often without the United Nations but with military force. In 1997, Clinton prepared for an historic extension of this military power: expanding the most successful alliance, NATO, into Eastern Europe. The nearly 50-year-old alliance (see p. 342) was widely credited with containing Soviet power in Europe. Now with Eastern Europe free of Russian forces, the inclusion of Poland, Hungary, and the Czech Republic in NATO would tie those nations into the West, while blunting any future Russian expansion. The expansion would also allow the United States, which dominated NATO, to have more political influence and arms sales in Eastern Europe. Critics, however, warned with compelling evidence that Russia would not look kindly on this military powerhouse moving so close to its borders. Critics also wondered

## Casualty Count: Number of U.S. Soldiers Who Died in Missions

| Mission | | Dead* | Wounded |
|---|---|---|---|
| 1941–1945: | World War II | 405,399 | 671,846 |
| 1950–1953: | Korean War | 36,914 | 103,284 |
| 1964–1973: | Vietnam War | 58,174 | 153,303 |
| 1983: | Grenada invasion | 19 | 119 |
| 1983: | Beirut bombing | 241 | 79 |
| 1989–1990: | Panama invasion | 23 | 320 |
| 1991: | Persian Gulf War | 146[†] | 465 |
| 1992–1993: | Somalia mission | 29 | 153 |
| 1994: | Haiti intervention | 4[‡] | 3 |
| 1996: | Bosnia[§] | 1 | 3 |

*Combat-related and noncombat-related deaths.
[†]Thirty-five were the result of friendly fire.
[‡]Three were suicides.
[§]As of February 1996.

*(From Walter LaFeber,* America, Russia, and the Cold War, 1945–1996, 8/e. *Copyright*
© 1997. *Reproduced with permission of The McGraw-Hill Companies.)*

whether Americans would, in a crisis, want their sons and daughters to die for, say, interests in Hungary. The NATO charter did declare that an attack on one member was to be considered as an attack on all. Americans were discovering that the end of the cold war did not mean the end of foreign policies that could threaten their vital interests, even their lives.

The drive to expand NATO was led by Madeleine Albright, whom Clinton named secretary of state in 1997. She became the first woman to hold the cabinet's premier position. Born in Czechoslovakia, Albright fully backed NATO expansion. While ambassador to the United Nations (1993–96), she also became more critical of that organization and supported unilateral uses of U.S. forces. Thus her views embodied the Clinton Doctrine and the new military commitments that formed a major theme of U.S. foreign policy in the 1990s.

A second central theme of that policy, as noted above, was Clinton's determination to open global markets to U.S. products. He had no choice: in the trading of goods (wheat, paper products, computer software) and the investment of money (Exxon, Pizza Hut, Pepsico), Americans led the world and depended on world markets for their prosperity. The Clinton administration signed more than 200 agreements between 1993 and 1997 to force open these markets. The President, over fierce opposition from labor unions in his own Democratic Party, pushed through legislation to meld the United States, Mexico, and Canada into a vast free-trade area. U.S. officials downplayed China's horrible record on human rights so American firms would not be shut out of the Chinese market which, experts believed, could overtake the United States and become the world's largest economy by the year 2020. Whether Western and Japanese goods and money would lead to a more just and less brutal Chinese political system remained a hotly debated question.

The Clinton foreign policies thus finally came to revolve around the unilateral use of U.S. military force and intense pressure to open global markets for the benefit of U.S. business. Both policies had deep, if not always blood-free, roots in the American Century.

## GENDER, LAW, AND POLITICS

By the end of the 1980s, the women's movement had shifted its focus to workplace issues, such as affirmative action and pay equity and to persistent questions about women and public policy. Could legislation insure equality, for instance, if structural equality persisted in the family and work force? Were policies that addressed sexual difference needed to provide equal opportunity? Or would any consideration of difference by courts or legislatures impose more problems than it solved? Three issues of the early 1990s—family leave, sexual harassment, and the gender gap in voting patterns—evoked these questions and suggested women's impact on law and politics.

Family leave policy developed out of the Pregnancy Disability Act of 1978 and controversy that arose over *California Savings & Loan* v. *Guerra* (1987), which upheld a state law providing unpaid leave and job security for pregnant workers. But to regard women as a different class of workers, some feminists had argued, would only perpetuate sex discrimination. The solution was a broader, gender-neutral policy, one not limited to pregnant workers, such as parental leave or family leave. In 1990, President Bush had vetoed a family leave bill that would have offered unpaid leave to workers with family obligations. President Clinton, however, signed a similar bill as soon as he took office in 1993. The new law enabled workers to take four months' leave for their own disabilities or to care for family members, such as new infants, sick spouses, or aged parents. Demands for maternity leave combined with feminist pressure for equal treatment, in short, had spurred a new broad-based policy that affected all workers. Of course, the new law provided only meager benefits to recipients, far less than the paid maternity leaves available to pregnant workers in European states.

Sexual harassment policy had also taken root in the 1980s, after a campaign by lawyer Catharine MacKinnon to make sexual harassment a form of sex discrimination, and thus prohibited by Title VII of the 1964 Civil Rights Act. According to the Equal Economic Opportunities Commission in 1980, sexual harassment meant "unwelcome verbal or physical conduct" that (1) made sex a precondition of advancement, (2) interfered with an individual's job performance, or (3) created an "intimidating, hostile, or offensive working environment." The Supreme Court endorsed both the concept of harassment as sex discrimination and the "hostile environment" test in *Meritor Savings Bank* v. *Vinson* (1986), a landmark case brought by a bank employee against a supervisor. A barrage of studies concurrently revealed the nature of sexual harassment, which had more to do with power than with sex. It was an abuse of power, a way to threaten women employees, and a tactic to devalue their role in the workplace. Some research suggested that office employees were most often victimized by sexual harassment. Other studies, however, contended that sexual harassment was most common in workplaces where women were new or in a minority such as blue-collar jobs, the military, or stockbrokers' firms.

Anita Hill's allegations in 1991 unleashed a torrent of complaints. By September 1992, the EEOC reported a 50 percent surge in harassment complaints since the Clarence Thomas hearings. Reported incidents of harassment abounded. Assaults on women at a convention of the Tailgate Association, a group of naval aviators, led to the resignation of the secretary of the Navy and other upheavals. Sexual harassment charges fell upon public officials, including two senators. In 1996, charges of harassment of women recruits at many army bases led to widespread investigations. In early 1997, the Supreme Court considered the question of whether harassment charges against the President could be pressed in court while he was still in office. Employers, meanwhile, made new efforts to sensitize workers to the nature of harassment and its consequences. According to the Civil Rights law of 1991, employers were now liable for up to $300,000 to victims of job discrimination, including sexual harassment.

The criteria for sexual harassment, however, especially the "hostile environment" provision, proved controversial because, in practice, the crime was defined neither by the perpetrator's intent nor by the conduct in question but by the victim's response to it. In 1991, in *Ellison* v. *Brady,* a federal appeals court set a slightly broader standard: harassment was what a "reasonable woman" found offensive. This definition seemed to recognize objections to the common legal standard "reasonable person," which, some feminists contended, did not reflect women's sense of vulnerability in the workplace and encouraged (male) judges to use mere intuition to reach decisions in harassment cases. But feminist objections to "reasonable woman" also developed. A standard that accepted female difference in any form, some feminists argued, imposed a false unity on all women. The issue came to a head in a 1993 sexual harassment case, *Harris* v. *Forklift Systems*, in which the Supreme Court endorsed the gender-neutral standard. A "hostile environment," said the Court, was one that a "reasonable person" would find hostile, abusive, or detrimental to job performance. The distinction between the two legal definitions, both of which mustered feminist support and critiques, represented a quandary.

The gender gap in voting behavior, meanwhile, elicited yet other questions about difference. Early in the century, suffragists had implied that, once enfranchised, women would vote as a bloc to support reform—such as good government, peace, temperance, and protection of children and families. But the bloc did not materialize; women seemed to vote independently, just as men did. Around 1980, however, pollsters found a 5 to 9 percentage point difference between men and women in the candidates that they supported for President. What issues caused the difference? Analysts agreed on only one facet of the gender gap: women voters (more than men) believed in activist government and the social safety net. They liked candidates who would protect Medicare, Social Security, and a system of provision for those in need. Beyond that, various hypotheses emerged. Did women share an economic perspective that differed from that of men? Were they more likely to support Democratic candidates because of their precarious vocational status and concentration in lower-income jobs? Did the care that they assumed for homes, children, and the aged affect their political vision? Or was the gender gap, in fact, caused by men, who, as writer Barbara Ehrenreich charged, lived "in a state of radical disconnection" from women and children?

Overall, research suggested mainly what the gender gap was *not*. It was not, for instance, determined by positions on abortion rights—although swing voters often turned out to be pro-choice women. It did not reflect higher standards of character, because women voters seemed to be more concerned with policy issues than with personality. Nor did the gender gap necessarily determine the outcome of elections: voters of both parties, pollsters noted, shrank from perceived "losers," as they had in the Republican landslide of 1988. Still, voting behavior consistently suggested that women had greater confidence than men in the state's capacity to help people and more concern about reduction in services for the young, old, or poor. And this could have an important effect, as was the case in 1996.

## THE ELECTION OF 1996

In 1992, a flagging economy and a wave of discontent had fueled a Democratic victory. Four years later, the major parties' roles were reversed. Cast as challengers, the Republicans nominated Bob Dole, long-time Kansas senator, majority leader of the Senate, and a decorated World War II veteran. Dole began the campaign weighted with liabilities. He had been sabotaged by fellow Republicans in the primaries; he was saddled with Newt Gingrich's decisions to shut down the government, which had alienated voters; plagued by the Democratic minority in the Senate, he had resigned to become "citizen" Dole, thus losing his major source of power and prestige. To compound Dole's problems, Republican strategists imposed a new campaign theme—tax cuts—a promise that contradicted the candidate's previous assertions and deficit reduction goals. Finally, Dole was handicapped by a gloomy persona, a staccato speaking style, and his age, 72. To younger voters, he seemed a relic of a bygone era.

Clinton started his fight for reelection with serious handicaps, too. His major initiative for health reform had drastically failed; he had suffered a crushing defeat in 1994; and he faced a long string of charges. As the campaign began, four independent counsels were examining the Clintons' role in Whitewater, efforts to influence the former secretary of agriculture, the business dealings of the former commerce secretary, and the honesty of the housing secretary. The Clintons also faced questions about gathering FBI files on prominent Republicans, missing records, the travel office dismissals, and withholding of documents. Hillary Rodham Clinton, subdued since the demise of health care reform, was at the center of most of the charges and investigations. Days before the election, a new issue arose: whether the White House condoned or aided the solicitation of questionable political contributions by a long-time Clinton friend and ally of Indonesian business interests.

Despite these handicaps, the Clinton campaign seized the initiative. Presidential advisor Richard Morris was forced by a sex scandal to resign on the day that the Democratic party nominated Clinton, but the strategy he had set in place succeeded. Defending the strong economy, Clinton sponsored an anti-terrorism bill and a defense of marriage act, as well as the Welfare Reform Act of 1996. An aggressive Democratic campaign, meanwhile, forced the Republicans to endorse popular middle-class entitlement programs, such as Social Security, Medicare, and veterans' benefits.

The Democrats turned apparent disaster into political capital: Clinton became the first Democratic president since FDR to win reelection. Third candidate Ross Perot drew half the percentage of votes that he had in 1992. Clinton won 49 percent of the popular vote to Dole's 41 percent and another electoral landslide. "You have to give the President credit," said his Republican opponent. "He's a very smooth talker. He hits the right buttons. He'll adopt things, things the Republican Congress has passed."

Why did Clinton win? First, voters were unlikely to unseat a President in times of peace and prosperity. Second, the President had developed a masterful ability to elude his problems. Shocked by the 1994 defeat, he had been forced to return to his "New Democrat" roots; he had been able to appropriate Republican issues, to make inroads among suburbanites and Perot voters, and to carve out a position that appealed to independents. "He was stealing the center, creating the center," said campaign aide George Stephanopolous. Third, Clinton ran against the now unpopular Gingrich, whom voters held responsible for bringing government to a halt. "The Republicans have given us great gifts," said a White House staffer. "Whether it's shutting down the government or the revolutionary rhetoric of Newt Gingrich or Bob Dole's inability to articulate a message, they all combined to create a much more favorable environment for Bill Clinton." Dole was especially injured by his tax reduction plank, which seven out of ten voters found unbelievable. Clinton, in contrast, was able to defuse his opponents' charges about "character" by redefining the term. "I think you can demonstrate character most effectively by what you fight for and for whom you fight," he told a television interviewer.

And finally, there was the gender gap. A colossal twenty-point gender gap in early campaign polls had simmered down to a more modest but still stunning 11 percent gap in the popular vote. The women's vote put Clinton over the top. The President won 54 percent of women's votes to Dole's 38 percent and only 43 percent of men's votes to Dole's 44 percent. If only men had voted, in short, Dole might well have eked out a narrow victory. According to the exit polls, significantly, six out of ten women who worked supported Clinton. So did younger women; the gender gap in the Clinton vote was 17 percent among voters under 30.

Clinton assumed office as the twentieth century's last President with several challenges ahead. He faced a divided Congress, since Republicans retained

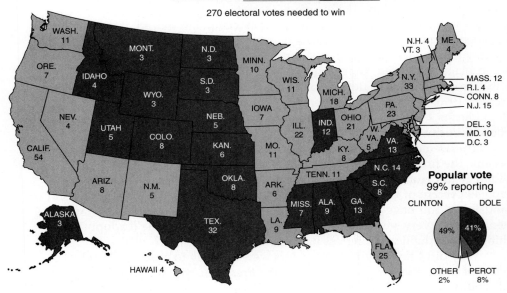

**The Presidency**

Electoral vote   CLINTON 379   DOLE 159

270 electoral votes needed to win

**Popular vote**
99% reporting

CLINTON    DOLE

49%   41%

OTHER   PEROT
2%    8%

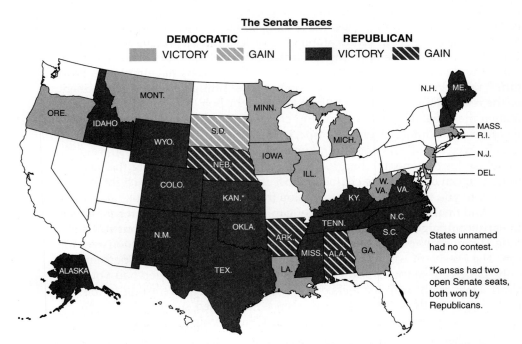

**The Senate Races**

DEMOCRATIC    REPUBLICAN

VICTORY   GAIN    VICTORY   GAIN

States unnamed
had no contest.

*Kansas had two
open Senate seats,
both won by
Republicans.

The 1996 presidential and senate races—Americans again vote for divided government.
*(Copyright © 1996 by The New York Times Co. Reprinted by permission.)*

**608**

control of both houses. He had to keep Medicare and Social Security solvent, to overhaul campaign finance law, and to establish a foreign policy record. He also had to eliminate the deficit, balance the budget, and subdue divisive issues, such as those over immigration and affirmative action. Finally, he would have to confront ongoing investigations, including Whitewater, the travel office, the FBI files, and the Democratic party's fund-raising relationship with foreign donors. It remained to be seen whether, and how, Bill Clinton would reshape American politics as the nation approached the twenty-first century.

## Suggested Reading

For the 1992 election, see Tom Rosenstiel, *Strange Bedfellows: How Television and the Presidential Candidates Changed American Politics, 1992* (1993).

On the Clinton administration generally, David Maraniss, *First in His Class* (1995), is a good biography of the President; Roger Morris, *Partners in Power: The Clintons and Their America (1996)* is useful on both Bill and Hillary Rodham Clinton; Mary Matalin and James Carville, *All's Fair: Love, War, and Running for President* (1994), examines the 1992 campaign from both Republican and Democratic perspectives; Bill Clinton, *Between Hope and History* (1996), is the President's own analysis of his and the nation's past and future; Colin Campbell and Bert A. Rockman, eds., *The Clinton Presidency: First Appraisals* (1996), is a good scholarly analysis and has a useful bibliography; Jeffrey H. Birnbaum, *Madhouse: The Private Turmoil of Working for the President* (1996), is an insider's view; James B. Stewart, *Bloodsport: The President and His Adversaries* (1996), is an excellent reporter's analysis of scandals that plagued the Clintons; Elizabeth Drew, *Showdown* (1996), is important and detailed on the Clinton-Gingrich clash after the 1994 elections; Newt Gingrich, et al., *Contract with America* (1994), is the famous Republican agenda and handbook for the supposed revolution; Robert E. Denton, Jr., and Rachel L. Halloway, *The Clinton Presidency: Images, Issues, and Communication Strategies* (1996), has useful essays, especially on Hillary Rodham Clinton and the health care fight; Bob Woodward, *The Agenda: Inside the Clinton White House* (1994), is especially helpful on the confusion and economic policies of the first two years; see also Dan Balz and Ronald Brownstein, *Storming the Gates*, on the 1994 Republican revival (1996). For the militias, see Kenneth S. Stern, *A Force Upon the Plain* (1996); Michael Novick, *White Lies, White Power: The Fight Against White Supremacy and Reactionary Violence* (1996); and for the regional context, Richard Lowitt, ed., *Politics in the Postwar American West* (1995), especially useful on Indians, environment, and militias.

A helpful overall look at the nation's economic and social health, or the lack thereof, in the 1990s is Urie Bronfenbrenner, et al., *The State of Americans* (1996). On multinational corporations, different views can be found in Thomas H. Lee and Proctor P. Reid, eds., *National Interests in an Age of Global Technology* (1991); and Richard J. Barnett's provocative, detailed analysis in *Global Dreams: Imperial Corporations and the New World Order* (1994).

For the new immigration, see especially David M. Reimers, *Still the Golden Door: The Third World Comes to America*, 2nd ed. (1992). Also of interest are Ronald Takaki, *Strangers from a Different Shore: A History of Asian Americans* (1989) and *A Different Mirror: A History of Multicultural America* (1993); and David C. Gutierrez, *Walls and Mirrors: Mexican Americans, Mexican Immigrants, and the Politics of Ethnicity* (1995). For arguments about the impact of the new immigration, see Michael Lind, *The Next American Nation: The New Nationalism and the Fourth American Revolution* (1992); and Peter D. Salins, *Assimilation American Style* (1997).

On post-cold war foreign policy, debate is vigorous in influential accounts: Ronald Steel, *Temptations of a Superpower* (1995); Samuel Huntington, *The Clash of Civilizations and the Remaking of World Order* (1996); and Francis Fukuyama, *The End of History and the Last Man* (1992). Specific topics are analyzed in Francis Fukuyama, *U.S.-Japan Security Relationships after the Cold War* (1993); Thomas A. Metzgar and Ramon H. Myers, eds., *Greater China and U.S. Foreign Policy* (1996); Michael Mandelbaum, ed., *The Strategic Quadrangle* (1993), on Asia and the major powers; James P. Lilley and Wendell L. Willkie, II, *Beyond MFN* (1994), on trade conflict with China; Martin L. Lasater, *The Changing of the Guard* (1995), discussing Clinton and the vexing Taiwan issues; Alex Dupuy, *Haiti in the New World Order* (1997); Ernest M. Preeg, *The Haitain Delemma* (1996); George H. Grayson, *The North American Free Trade Agreement* (1995); Jerry Rosenberg, ed., *Encyclopedia of the North American Free Trade Agreement* (1995); and H. Richard Friman, *NarcoDiplomacy: Exporting the U.S. War on Drugs* (1996).

For basketball's ups and downs, note especially Allen Guttmann, *Games and Empires* (1994); Susan Cahn, *Coming on Strong* (1994), helpful on women's sports; Douglas A. Noverr and Lawrence E. Ziewacz, *The Games They Played* (1984), good on chronology of all major U.S. sports; Jackie Krentzman, "The Force Behind the Nike Empire," *Stanford*, January–February 1997, pp. 65–70; and Jim Naughton, *Taking to the Air* (1992), the best biography of Michael Jordan, with good sections on merchandising.

# INDEX